SOCIOLOGY IN FOCUS

AQA AS Level Second Edition

Edited by
Michael Haralambos and Peter Langley

Written by
Michael Haralambos, John Richardson,
Paul Taylor and Alan Yeo

Dedication
To our mothers from Michael and Peter

Acknowledgements

Editor (2nd edition)	Kate Baxter
Cover and page design	Caroline Waring-Collins (Waring-Collins Ltd)
Graphic origination	John A. Collins (Waring-Collins Ltd)
Graphics	Tim Button (Waring-Collins Ltd)
Author index and typing	Ingrid Hamer
Reader	Mike Kidson, Wendy Hope

Picture credits

The publisher would like to thank the following for their kind permission to reproduce their photographs:

(Key: b-bottom; c-centre; l-left; r-right; t-top)

Advertising Archives: 80, 82bl, 84, 183tc, 183tr; **Alamy Images:** Martin Beddall 123tr; Brownstock Inc 87b; Chris Gibson 78b; Sally and Richard Greenhill 62tr, 107l; David Hoffman Photo Library 127l; imagebroker 121r; Photofusion Picture Library 62tl; Purestock 77tr; Scottish Viewpoint 147l; The Print Collector 79; vario images GmbH & Co.KG 77tl; **Andrew Allen:** 123tl, 142, 183tl; **AP Wide World Photos:** Dave Caulkin 48b; Pat Crowe II 103tr; Mike Derer 62br; Ricardo Mazalan 112l; Otto Ballon Mierny 44b; Doug Mills 87t; Douglas C Pizac 101; Suzanne Plunkett 176; Aija Rahi 75tr; Alexander Zemlianichenko 6bl; **Art Directors and TRIP photo Library:** Itzhak Genut 19; **Bridgeman Art Library Ltd:** Glasgow University Library, Scotland 113r; Private Collection 113l; **British Library Images Online:** 75b, 75tl, 76t; **John Collins:** 61, 115, 131; **Corbis:** Robbie Jack 46tl; Alessia Pierdomenico/Reuters 21 (supermodel); Ben Radford 21 (sports star); Loretta Rae 124; Reuters 123b; Ramin Talaie 147r; Tomas Van Houtryve 111; **Mary Evans Picture Library:** 125; Illustrated London News 69; **Eye Ubiquitous / Hutchison:** 65l; **Getty Images:** AFP 35, 56br; Hulton Archive 37b, 67b, 82r, 153tc, 153tr, 161r; Matt King 30l; Bill Pugliano 30r; Mario Tama 134; Time & Life Pictures 22tl, 154r; Bruno Vincent 24r; WireImage 86b; **Glenbow Archive:** 112r; **Ronald Grant Archive:** 129b; **Sally and Richard Greenhill:** 62bl, 77b; **Halewood International:** 183b; **Kate Haralambos:** 106; **Hoffman Photo Library:** 103b; **Imperial War Museum:** 121l, 153tl; **Kobal Collection Ltd:** Fox Searchlight 43; **Ladybird Books:** Ladybird Key Words Reading Scheme 94r; **Jeff Morgan:** 46b; **The Museum of English Rural Life, The University of Reading, UK:** 78t; **Mystique Productions Sdn. Bhd:** 158; **North News & Pictures:** 44t; **PA Photos:** Tammie Arroyo/UK Press 21 (film star); Andy Butterton 21 (pop star); DPA 22tr; **Penguin Group USA:** Knock Yourself Up, Louise Sloan 98; **Photofusion Picture Library:** Martin Bond 4; Robert Brook 173, 185l; Jacky Chapman 14b, 36, 156; Paul Doyle 29b, 160; Don Gray 31br; Julia Martin 193; Joanne O''Brien 185r; Louis Quail 191; Paula Solloway 198; David Tothill 186; Ulrike Preuss 12r; Janine Wiedel 127r, 128; **Reuters:** Reinhard Krause 153b; **Rex Features:** 31l, 31tr, 56bl; Adrian Brooks 25r; Paul Brown 22b; Alexander Caminada 48tr, 107r; John Downing 46tr; FM 146; Ipyx Ltd 57; Steve Lyne 162; Alisdair Macdonald 25l; Alisdair Macdonald/ 27; Philip Moore 56t; Camilla Morandi 33; Pietro Pesce 9tr; PKImage 29tr; John Shelley 40; SINOPIX 9br; George Sweeney 24l; Ray Tang 59, 215; The Travel Library 58; Dale Wittner 161l; Richard Young 86t; **TopFoto:** 157; Bill Bachmann/The Image Works 38l; Bill Lai/The Image Works 67t; The British Library/HIP 29tl; Alan Carey / The Image Works 103tl; Bob Daemmrich / The Image Works 14t; Fritz Hoffmann/The Image Works 9tl; Syracuse Newspapers/The Image Works 194; UPP 207; **www.shutterstock.com:** Chris Mole 6br; **www.statistics.gov.uk:** Crown Copyright material is reproduced with the permission of the Controller Office of Public Sector Information(OPSI) 120.

Picture Research by: Louise Edgeworth

Every effort has been made to trace the copyright holders and we apologise in advance for any unintentional omissions. We would be pleased to insert the appropriate acknowledgement in any subsequent edition of this publication.

Cartoons
Unless otherwise credited, the cartoons in this book have been specially drawn by BRICK www.brickbats.co.uk

Cover picture
Hundertwasser
RANGITOTO-TARANAKI-RAKINO, 1973
© J. Harel, Vienna

Contents

Chapter 1   **Culture and Identity** **4**

Unit 1   What is culture? 4

Unit 2   Socialisation 11

Unit 3   Self, identity and difference 18

Unit 4   Age and identity 23

Unit 5   Disability and identity 26

Unit 6   Ethnic identities 28

Unit 7   National and global identities 34

Unit 8   Gender identities 39

Unit 9   Class identities 45

Unit 10   Leisure, consumption and identity 54

Chapter 2   **Families and households** **61**

Unit 1   Defining the family 61

Unit 2   The family and social structure .66

Unit 3   The family and social change 74

Unit 4   Changing family relationships 85

Unit 5   Family diversity 93

Unit 6   Gender, power and domestic labour 105

Unit 7   Childhood and children 112

Unit 8   Demographic trends 116

Chapter 3   **Sociological methods** **120**

Unit 1   Types of data 121

Unit 2   The research process 122

Unit 3   Experiments 128

Unit 4   Social surveys 131

Unit 5   Questionnaires 134

Unit 6   Interviews 139

Unit 7   Observation 142

Unit 8   Secondary sources 147

Unit 9   Types of research 155

Chapter 4   **Education and methods** **160**

Unit 1   The role of the education system 160

Unit 2   Social class and educational attainment 171

Unit 3   Gender and educational attainment 181

Unit 4   Ethnicity and educational attainment 186

Unit 5   Relationships and processes within schools 193

Unit 6   Social policy and education 205

References **217**

Text acknowledgements **223**

Author index **224**

Subject index **226**

1 Culture and identity

Introduction

Is there anybody else exactly like you? You'll probably answer 'no'. We like to think of ourselves as individuals and to see ourselves as unique.

Sociology does not deny this individuality. It does not claim that everybody is the same. However, it does argue that many of us have certain things in common. For example, members of a particular society usually share the same language. In this respect, we are not unique.

Most people live in social groups – in families, communities and nations – rather than as isolated individuals. As the poet John Donne said, 'No man is an island' (nowadays he would say that goes for women too). In other words, we are constantly coming into contact with other people. We are affected by them, we develop bonds with them. Indeed, we only become fully 'human' by participating in society.

Sociology has sometimes been described as the study of people in social groups. In this chapter we shall explore the fascinating story of how individuals are not isolated 'islands' but active members of society. We shall see how we learn certain values and ways of behaving, and how our membership of social groups gives meaning to our lives and shapes our identities.

Unique individuals with many things in common

Sociologists do not always agree on how and why things happen. But they help us to see more clearly how we are both 'individuals' and members of 'society'. And they help us see the connections between the two.

chaptersummary

▷ **Unit 1** identifies the main components of culture.

▷ **Unit 2** looks at socialisation – how people learn the culture of their society.

▷ **Unit 3** turns to the social origins of self and identity.

▷ **Unit 4** discusses age and identity.

▷ **Unit 5** looks at disability and identity.

▷ **Unit 6** describes the changing nature of ethnic cultures.

▷ **Unit 7** explores national and global identities.

▷ **Unit 8** charts the shifting patterns of gender identities.

▷ **Unit 9** considers the importance of class identities.

▷ **Unit 10** examines the relationships between leisure, consumption and identity.

Unit 1 What is culture?

keyissues

1 Are humans ruled by instincts?

2 How does culture shape human behaviour?

3 What are the main components of culture?

1.1 Becoming human

Instincts vs culture

Why do human beings behave the way they do? One view is that it is a matter of *instincts* – biological predispositions that tell us 'instinctively' what we should do. Instincts are

something we are born with rather than something we learn. A great deal of animal behaviour seems to be ruled by instincts. For example, birds seem to follow fairly fixed patterns of behaviour as if they were a set part of their 'nature'.

Nowadays, a popular explanation for human behaviour is to look for the answer in our genes. People vary in their genetic make-up and this might explain why they behave differently. Some scientists claim there is a gene for crime, one for alcoholism, even a 'gay' gene. Some have offered genetic explanations for why men are unable to find butter in the fridge, or why women can't read maps!

Sociologists accept that humans have natural *reflexes* –

activity1 genes or culture?

Item A Nappies and planes

There is no gene or brain pattern which makes men incapable of ironing, shopping, changing nappies or expressing their emotions. And there is none which stops women running governments or multinational corporations, flying fighter planes, abusing children or committing murder. It is culture which explains why women do more of some things and men do more of other things.

Source: MacInnes, 1998

Item B A woman's place

THIS IS YOUR CAPTAIN JENNY ROBINSON SPEAKING...

questions

1 What view does Item A take on the genes versus culture debate?
2 Look at Item B.
   a) Why are the passengers reacting like this?
   b) Is there any justification for their reaction?

for example, we automatically flinch when someone strikes us. They also accept that we have certain biological *needs* that must be met – for example, the need for food and drink. But sociologists believe that human behaviour is too complex and diverse to be explained in simple biological or genetic terms. Rather, they see our actions as the result of our social and cultural environments. We *learn* to think and act in certain ways. And it is our *culture* which teaches us how we should think and act.

Feral children

People become fully human only when they are socialised into the culture of a society – when they learn the way of life of that society. It is culture which allows them to develop their human potential. We can see this in the case of so-called feral children – children raised in the wilds or in prolonged isolation from human company. Some reported cases are pure fantasy but the few authentic cases show that when these children are discovered and enter human society they encounter serious problems. They often seem stupid, unresponsive and animal-like. Deprived of the stimulation of human company, stripped of the opportunity to acquire human language early in life, these children are sometimes barely recognisable as human.

Cultural diversity

If human behaviour really is dictated by our genes or

instincts, we would expect to find people behaving in much the same way all over the world. But what is regarded as normal behaviour varies from one culture to another. If we lived in Victorian Britain or in modern China, we would follow different customs, have different lifestyles. So human behaviour is flexible and diverse. It varies according to the culture we live in. Even the way we display our bodies in public changes over time and from place to place.

The social body Norbert Elias (1978) provides a detailed account of changing cultural attitudes towards the body. In sixteenth century Europe there was little sense of shame or delicacy about bodily matters. People would happily wipe snot on their sleeve or blow their nose on the tablecloth. They usually ate with their hands, and belching, farting, scratching, and even urinating or defecating in public were commonplace. But Elias describes how in the succeeding centuries people gradually became more sensitive to the 'shame' and 'disgust' of bodily functions as they developed 'good manners' and disciplined their bodies to act in a 'civilised' way.

Becoming human – conclusion

The long-running debate over whether human behaviour is largely the result of 'nature' (genes, biology) or 'nurture' (culture, environment) shows no sign of coming to an end. Nature and nurture always interact in complex ways. Even if we have a biological inclination to behave in certain

activity2 from monkey boy to choir boy

Walking through a Ugandan forest, a woman spotted a group of monkeys. To her astonishment, she realised that one member of the group was a small boy. Local villagers 'rescued' this 'monkey boy' and identified him as John Ssabunnya who had been abandoned as a two-year-old.

John, aged 14

For the past three years, John had lived with a troupe of colobus monkeys. He had learned to communicate with them – with chatters, shrieks, facial expressions and body language. He shared their diet of fruit, nuts and berries, he became skilled at climbing trees and, like those who adopted him, he walked on all-fours. He was terrified of his 'rescuers' and fought to remain with his family of monkeys.

John was washed and clothed – much to his disgust – and taken to an orphanage. He gradually learned to behave like a human being. Slowly but surely, he began to sing, laugh, talk, play, dress and walk like children of his age.

Today, John is a member of the Pearl of Africa Choir which has successfully toured the United Kingdom.

Source: *Daily Mail*, 23.9.1999

question

How does the case of John Ssabunnya illustrate the importance of learned behaviour for human beings?

activity3 the body

Afghanistan

Brighton

question

What do these photographs suggest about culture and attitudes towards the body?

ways, this will be channelled by society – the aggressive individual could become a violent criminal or a successful boxer, depending on social circumstances.

Whatever our underlying nature, it is clear that culture has a huge effect on our behaviour. We saw this in the case of feral children. Also, human behaviour is enormously diverse, showing wide variations over time and between societies. Norbert Elias demonstrated how even our intimate body habits are a product of society.

Sociologists suggest that if we want to explain social behaviour, then most of the answers can be found at the social and cultural level.

1.2 Looking at culture

Shared meanings and values

Sociologists usually define culture as the shared meanings, values and norms of a society or group.

Meanings Stuart Hall (1997) describes some of the key features of cultural meanings. First, it is largely thanks to *language* that humans are able to create meanings and make sense of the world. It is through language and other symbols, for example visual images, that people express their emotions and thoughts and communicate with one another. Second, culture is about *shared* meanings. People produce meanings together and so over time each social group builds up shared understandings of the world. Third,

humans are constantly creating new meanings and revising old ones – so culture can be seen as a process or activity.

Values are things we regard as important, the most significant standards or principles in our lives. Love is an obvious example. Other examples are religious convictions and political loyalties. In everyday life, most people believe in the values of honesty, consideration towards others, justice and fairness – although we are not so good at living up to these values!

Norms are social expectations or rules about how people should or should not behave – for example, you should hold the door open for others, you should not grab the last biscuit. There are different rules for different situations – you can let your hair down at an end-of-term party, but the same behaviour would be frowned upon during normal class time. Norms also vary in their degree of seriousness. Committing murder will result in severe legal punishment but bad table manners might only provoke irritation in others.

activity4 *meanings, values, norms*

Item A Meanings

Item B Values

The Cheyenne lived on the Great Plains of North America. This account describes their traditional culture.

The Cheyenne believe that wealth, in the form of horses and weapons, is not to be hoarded by the owner. Instead it is to be given away. Generosity is highly regarded and people who accumulate wealth and keep it for themselves are looked down upon. A person who gives does not expect an equal amount in return. The greatest gift they can receive is prestige and respect for their generous action.

Bravery on the battlefield is one of the main ways a man can achieve high standing. Killing an enemy, however, does not rank as highly as a number of other deeds. Touching or striking an enemy with the hand or a weapon, rescuing a wounded comrade or charging the enemy alone while the rest of the war party looks on are amongst the highest acts of bravery.

Source: Hoebel, 1960

Cheyenne photographed in 1889

Item C · Norms

Culture defines appropriate distances between people when they hold a conversation. In *The Silent Language*, Edward Hall observed that these distances are different in North and South America. This can cause problems when North meets South. In Hall's words, 'The result is that when they move close, we withdraw and back away. As a consequence, they think we are distant or cold, withdrawn and unfriendly. We, on the other hand, are constantly accusing them of breathing down our necks, crowding us and spraying our faces.'

Source: Hall, 1973

questions

1 What meanings does the symbol in Item A communicate?

2 a) Identify the values of the Cheyenne described in Item B.

 b) How do they indicate that values vary from culture to culture?

3 Norms are important. Discuss briefly with reference to Item C.

Roles are the parts we play in society. For example, in today's society, most of us play the roles of son or daughter, father or mother, student or worker. Culture provides guidelines on how these roles should be played. And just as culture varies from society to society, so do the cultural guidelines for role-playing.

Whole way of life

Anthropologists specialise in studying whole societies, especially small-scale, less technologically developed societies. Perhaps, as a result of this, they tend to adopt a sweeping definition of culture. Clyde Kluckhohn (1951) described culture as the distinctive 'way of life' of a group of people. This way of life includes their typical patterns of behaviour – their common lifestyles, the skills and techniques they use to make a living, and all their routines, customs and rituals.

Subculture

The functionalist perspective in sociology sees society as a giant system that 'works' because its various parts support one another. Each part of society has a function – it makes a contribution to other parts and to society as a whole. In this view, the culture of a society is seen as providing a sort of social 'glue' which creates bonds between people. An over-arching culture provides shared values and moral consensus – an agreement about what's right and wrong. These are regarded as essential for ensuring cohesion and harmony in society. Members of society tend to learn the same culture – the same meanings, values and norms.

However, as societies grow larger and more complex, it becomes increasingly difficult to talk about one culture which everybody shares equally. Rather, people select particular norms, values and lifestyles from the wide range on offer. For example, in Britain today there are groups who share many aspects of mainstream culture, but who also have certain beliefs, attitudes and ways of behaving of their own. In other words, they have their own *subcultures*.

High and low culture

High culture refers to artistic and intellectual work which is seen to be of the highest quality. It covers 'great works of art' such as the paintings of van Gogh, the compositions of classical musicians such as Mozart, and highly regarded literature such as the writings of Shakespeare. High culture is seen to be created by a talented few and is thought to be enjoyed mainly by people with refined and sophisticated tastes.

High culture is sometimes contrasted with *low culture* which, as its name suggests, is seen as inferior, of lower quality, as less worthy. Thus the high culture of classical music is contrasted with the low culture of pop music and the high culture of a Shakespearian play is contrasted with the low culture of *Eastenders*. Where high culture is seen to be enjoyed by the 'refined and sophisticated few', low culture is enjoyed by the 'ordinary and unsophisticated' majority.

Clearly the idea of high and low culture is based on a value judgement – one is judged to be superior to the other. Sociologists usually try to avoid value judgements.

Popular culture

Popular culture refers to the cultural pursuits of, and cultural products used by, large numbers of the population. Examples of popular culture include football, pop music, websites such as Facebook and YouTube, television, movies, bestselling novels, DVDs and CDs, newspapers and magazines. It also includes popular fashions and lifestyles.

The term popular culture does not usually carry the same value judgements as high and low culture. As used by sociologists, it simply refers to the cultural products and pursuits which have widespread appeal.

Mass culture

Mass culture is culture which is produced for and marketed to the mass of the population. It is mass produced for mass consumption. It is seen as 'dumbed down', trivial, bland, superficial and undemanding. Examples of mass culture include Hollywood movies, reality TV, newspapers like the *Sun* and the *Star*, and celebrity magazines like *OK* and *Now*.

The consumers of mass culture are seen to be passive. They 'sit there' and consume what they're given. They buy what the ads tell them to buy, participate in the pursuits provided for them, and 'live' the fantasies created for their entertainment. As such, the masses are easily manipulated and open to exploitation. They 'buy in' to mass culture with little thought or critical awareness. They uncritically consume soap operas, celebrity gossip and the latest fashions. This lack of critical judgement prevents them from questioning the society they live in and from discussing the major issues of the day.

Marxism This view of mass culture has certain similarities to the ideas of Marxist sociologists – sociologists who have developed the ideas of Karl Marx (1818-1883). They argue that there are two main classes in capitalist society – the ruling class who own private industry and the subject class made up of workers who sell their labour in return for wages. Workers produce wealth in the form of goods and services, but a large part of this wealth is taken from them in the form of profits by the capitalist ruling class. In this way, the ruling class exploit the subject class – they gain at the expense of the workers.

The workers are unaware of their exploitation. They see the world in terms of *ruling class ideology* – a false picture of reality which supports the position of the ruling class. The mass media is largely responsible for broadcasting this ideology. It presents the capitalist system as normal, reasonable and perfectly acceptable.

And the 'mindless' entertainment it provides dulls any critical awareness, produces feelings of well-being, and disguises the reality of an oppressive society.

Global culture

Global culture refers to those aspects of culture which are worldwide. Many sociologists argue that there is a steadily growing global culture. They point to global music styles – for example, MTV Asia's top 10 singles chart for January 2008 with artists such as Britney Spears, Rihanna, KT Tunstall and Kelly Clarkson is similar to many other charts across the world. Many sports such as soccer, motor racing and boxing have an increasingly global audience and sportspeople such as David Beckham enjoy worldwide fame. Brands such as Nike and Gucci, drinks such as Coca-Cola, and fast-food restaurants such as McDonald's are increasingly global. And cultural icons such as Princess Diana and Nelson Mandela are no longer limited to particular nations.

This growth in global culture is seen as part of the development of *globalisation* – the increasing connections between various parts of the world. Many companies, for example BP, Ford and Sony operate on a global basis and trade is increasingly worldwide. The internet has provided a means of global communication. Globalisation and a global culture go hand-in-hand.

key terms

Instincts Genetically-based directives for behaviour.

Culture The learned, shared behaviour of members of a society. Culture includes meanings, values and norms.

Meanings Things which give sense and significance to people's experiences.

Values Beliefs about what is important, what is worth having, what is right and wrong.

Norms Social expectations or rules about how people should behave. Guides to behaviour.

Roles The parts people play in society.

Subculture Certain meanings, values and norms which are distinctive to a particular group within society.

High culture Artistic and intellectual work seen to be of the highest quality and enjoyed mainly by a sophisticated minority.

Low culture Cultural products judged as lower quality and enjoyed mainly by the unsophisticated majority.

Popular culture The cultural pursuits of and the cultural products used by large numbers of the population.

Mass culture Cultural products produced for the mass of the population which, some argue, are used to manipulate them and disguise their exploitation.

Ruling class ideology A false picture of society which supports the position of the ruling class.

Global culture Those aspects of culture which are worldwide.

Looking at culture – conclusion

Culture is essential to the operation of human society. Without shared meanings, people would be unable to communicate. Without shared values, they would be pulling in different directions. And without norms directing behaviour, there would be no order in society.

From a sociological viewpoint, human behaviour is primarily organised and directed by culture. We are not ruled by instinct, governed by our genes, or directed by biological needs and impulses. If we were, then human behaviour would be much the same in different times and in different societies. It isn't, as can be seen from the wide variation between cultures in different time periods and places.

activity5 global culture

Item A   *Movies*

Buying pirated videos and DVDs in Shanghai, China. Titles include 'Gone With The Wind' and Disney's 'Sleeping Beauty'

Vietnamese edition of '8 Mile' and Russian edition of 'Lord of the Rings'

Item B   *50 Cent in Venice*

American rapper 50 Cent performing in Venice

Item C   *Chinese hip-hop fans*

Chinese hip-hop fans in Beijing

question

What evidence do Items A, B and C provide for a global culture?

summary

1. Although animals sometimes learn new ways of behaving, they are largely controlled by more or less fixed biological instincts.

2. Human behaviour is too complex and too diverse to be explained solely by biologically-based instincts, needs or drives.

3. From a sociological view, human behaviour is largely directed by culture. Culture is learned rather than biologically based.

4. The example of feral children shows the importance of culture in making us fully human. Culture provides us with language, values and a sense of our human identity.

5. Culture varies from society to society.

6. Culture provides meanings, values, norms and roles to guide our behaviour.

7. Sociologists try to avoid making judgements about cultures.

8. As societies become larger and more complex, there are growing numbers of groups with their own subcultures.

9. The idea of high and low culture is based on a value judgement. The term popular culture does not usually carry a value judgement.

10. The idea of mass culture often pictures the majority as easily manipulated and uncritically accepting their position in society.

11. Many sociologists argue there is a steadily growing global culture which they see as part of the process of globalisation.

Unit 2 Socialisation

keyissues

1 What is socialisation?

2 How do people learn social roles?

3 Who are the main agents of socialisation?

2.1 The learning game

In this unit we turn to the question of how individuals adopt cultural values and roles. The answer is that we *learn* culture through a process of *socialisation*. Since culture is not an innate thing, something we are born with, it has to be passed down from one generation to another. So we have to be taught the norms and values of our society or group. Over time we *internalise* many of these – they become part of our personal set of norms and values.

But socialisation is not a simple one-sided process of instruction in which we passively accept what we are told. We are not empty vessels into which culture is poured. Each of us actively participates in our own cultural learning, trying to make sense of society's values and beliefs, accepting some of them but rejecting others.

Types of socialisation

Primary socialisation The early years of life are important in the learning process. This is the stage of *primary socialisation*, when we are normally in intimate and prolonged contact with parents. Our parents are *significant others* – they have a great influence on us and we care about their judgements of us. Significant others play a key part in teaching us basic values and norms.

Secondary socialisation This refers to the socialisation we receive later in life, from a wide range of people and agencies. They include peer groups, teachers, media and casual acquaintances. Sometimes they play a supportive role, adding to the primary socialisation of earlier years. But teachers also introduce us to new and more complex knowledge and skills. And friends sometimes introduce us to values and lifestyles which wouldn't win the approval of our parents!

Re-socialisation We usually have to learn new ways when our roles change. This may be a gradual process – for example, growing into adulthood. At other times it can be dramatic and abrupt. For example, army recruits experience the shock of basic training, when they have to abandon their civilian identity and submit to strict discipline.

Anticipatory socialisation In many cases we have already 'rehearsed' roles before we take them on. We imagine ourselves in them, we read about them, we learn something about them beforehand. For example, the young person who enters medical school already knows a bit about the life of a doctor from personal experience as a patient and from watching television shows such as *ER* or *Casualty*.

2.2 Agents of socialisation

The *agents of socialisation* are the people or groups who play a part in our socialisation. Sometimes they play an important role without us realising it. Sometimes we overestimate the influence they have on us. For some views on this, see Table 1.

Parents

The majority of children still grow up in a family headed by both their natural parents. But over the last thirty years there has been an increase in the numbers of lone-parent

Table 1 Survey of young people aged 11-21

'From whom do you think you have learned the most about sex and growing up?'

Parents	7%
Teachers	22%
The internet	7%
Friends	27%
Brothers and sisters	4%
Newspapers and magazines	12%
TV and radio	13%
Church/clergy	0%
Don't know	9%

Source: *The Observer*, 21.07.2002

acceptable – asking politely – and unacceptable – rudely interrupting. As they get older they use their parents as *role models*. Girls may play with dolls 'just like mummy'. Later in life the roles might be reversed – young people sometimes have to teach their parents about things like mobile phones and computers!

For their part, parents try to instil social norms by setting an example and teaching their children how to behave. They use *sanctions* (rewards and punishments) to guide and control the learning process. If children follow the 'proper' norms, their parents will reward them with smiles, loving attention, praise and treats. But if they misbehave they are likely to be punished by frowns, reprimands, the denial of treats, and maybe even a smack.

This system of rewards and punishments does not guarantee that children will always behave 'correctly' – sometimes they will test the boundaries of acceptable behaviour, and sometimes they will show open defiance. But over a period of time they get a pretty good idea of the social norms held by their parents!

Diversity The socialisation process may vary according to the particular family structure. For example, an 'absent father' may find it difficult to act as a role model for his children, while a step-father may not feel entitled to control his step-children in the same way as their biological father could.

and step-families. So family life has become more diverse. But whatever the particular family set-up, parental figures remain the main agents of primary socialisation. In their first years of life children spend most of their time with their parents and are highly dependent on them. A sense of security during early childhood life is often seen as crucial for developing a stable personality and for effective learning of norms and values.

Learning from parents One way in which young children learn about social norms is by imitating their parents. They may copy the way adults talk, or their table manners for example. By a process of trial and error, they learn what is

activity6 *learning the drill*

US army recruits during basic training

Getting married

question

What types of socialisation apply to the people in these photographs? (More than one type may apply.)

The experience of growing up within a family also varies according to its social and cultural values. For example, a devout Muslim family will ensure that religion plays a strong part in the child's upbringing.

Class and parenting Diane Reay (1998) made a detailed study of 33 mothers in London. All of these women put great effort into 'practical maintenance' of children – feeding, clothing and so on – as well as emotional work – reassuring and encouraging their children. All of them tried to support their children's schooling. However, Reay identified major class differences. The middle-class mothers had time and energy to spend reading to their children and were confident when talking to teachers. The working-class mothers, by contrast, had more of a struggle to make ends meet and so had less time and energy. They also had fewer cultural resources such as verbal confidence and knowledge of how the education system operates. This meant they were less effective in compensating for poor schooling and in persuading teachers to act on their complaints.

Paranoid parents? Frank Furedi (2001) describes a change in the role of parents in recent years. Traditionally, 'good' parents tried to care for and stimulate their children. Nowadays, they often see their main task as protecting their children from danger (accidents, paedophiles, bullies). Furedi believes parents have become paranoid. He thinks

activity7 parents and socialisation

Item A We have ways …

Item B Keeping in touch

Professor Kevin Warwick and Danielle Duval, with the chip that will be placed in her arm

The parents of an 11 year-old girl are having her fitted with a microchip so that her movements can be traced if she is abducted. The miniature chip implanted in her arm will send a signal via a mobile phone network to a computer which will be able to pinpoint her location on an electronic map.

Some children's charities have claimed that these parents are over-reacting as the chances of a child being abducted are small.

Source: *The Guardian*, 3.9.2002

questions

1 What ways do parents have of 'making their children conform'?

2 In what ways does Item B support Furedi's views?

the risks of harm to children have been exaggerated and the new focus on protection is unhealthy. Children are chauffeured and shepherded from place to place by anxious parents. All sorts of risks – adventure trips with schools, even messing around in school playgrounds – are increasingly closed off to them. This may prevent children from developing a healthy sense of adventure.

Education

Modern Western societies are too complex for young people simply to 'pick up' their culture as they go along. They are required to undergo a long period of formal education. In school they are formally taught the culture of their country – its history, language and religions. They also learn technical knowledge such as maths and science that often has practical applications in daily life.

The hidden curriculum School pupils also learn from the unofficial *hidden curriculum* – the background values and expectations that run through the school system. For example, they learn the importance of hard work and success through the exam system. When they take part in sports they learn the value of competition and teamwork. They learn the importance of conforming to rules when they get punished for being late, misbehaving, or not handing in work on time.

School is also a setting where children's social horizons are widened. They may mix with people from different social classes, ethnic groups and cultural backgrounds. They also become more aware of the different identities of people from various ethnic, gender and social class groups.

The importance of schools It is difficult to judge whether schools are becoming more or less important as agents of socialisation. On the one hand, educational qualifications are now seen as essential for getting good jobs. This means that pupils are working harder than ever, with increasing numbers staying on after the minimum leaving age. On the other hand, schools often complain that they have to fight a battle over values. Some pupils may not share the values expressed by the school. Also, teachers often feel they have to compete against the attractions of mass media and youth culture for the attention of pupils.

Schooling the boys An example of the tough uphill task some schools face is provided by Christine Skelton's (2001) study of a primary school in the North East. This school was set in an economically deprived area with a reputation for crime. The teachers regarded many of the local parents as 'inadequate' and so they felt the school had the important task of socialising children properly. When young boys came to school they brought with them the attitudes they picked up from the local 'lads' and 'hard men' – aggression, physical toughness, dominance and hierarchy.

The school attempted to maintain social control by relying on firm measures. It created a sort of fortress (locked gates, fences, security cameras) as a defence against violence and theft. Also, the teachers (both male and female) adopted 'masculine' styles – firm eye

activity8 learning

Pledging allegiance to their country

Playtime in a London primary school

question

What do you think these pupils are learning from the activities shown in the photographs?

activity9 peer groups – the good and the bad

Item A Talking

'I can talk to my friends about things I can't really talk to my parents about, because well – they seem to understand me more, and my parents don't really listen to me, and my friends do, because they've been in the same situation as me'.

Source: Young girl, quoted in Tizard & Phoenix, 1993

Item B 'Behaving badly'

Britain has the worst behaved teenagers in Europe. They are more likely to take drugs, have sex at an early age, indulge in binge drinking and get involved in fights. The collapse of family life is partly to blame. With no guiding hand from the family, youngsters are more likely to fall victim to peer group pressure. Just 64% of teenagers eat with their parents, compared with 89% in France and 93% in Italy. British children spend half their spare time watching television, playing computer games and using the internet.

Source: *Sunday Times*, 29.7.2007

questions

1 What do Items A and B reveal about peer groups?
2 Why do you think *Friends* is so popular with young people?

Item C Friends

FRIENDS

series 8 episodes 1-4

INCLUDES NEVER-BEFORE-SEEN FOOTAGE

DVD

12

---

contact, intimidatory body language – to gain 'respect', show who was 'boss' and instil some 'fear' in the troublesome pupils. Skelton points to the irony that the school's control strategies were in many ways a reflection of the 'tough' values that were prized in the local community!

Peer group

A *peer group* is a friendship group formed by people of roughly the same age and social position. They meet each other as equals rather than being supervised by adults. In the early years of life, children like to play with one another for fun and amusement. But play is also a valuable learning experience. In play situations they learn about social norms (eg, treating others properly) and they develop social skills (eg, negotiating over toys). They can also experiment with social roles (eg, playing shop assistants and customers).

When children become teenagers, they spend increasing amounts of time away from their families and in the company of their friends. Parents often worry that peer group pressures will encourage their children to steal, take drugs, or have sex. Young people themselves often worry about their popularity within the peer group. Nevertheless, these groups perform valuable functions for their members.

Within them, young people begin to develop independence from their parents. This prepares them for taking on adult roles themselves.

Peer power Adler and Adler (1998) studied a group of white middle-class children in the United States. They found that the peer group was enormously important in the lives of these pre-adolescent children. Being popular and having friends made children feel good about themselves, but being socially isolated had the reverse effect. Adler and Adler describe how friendship groups shift and change as children move in and out. Over time a hierarchy develops, both between groups (the leading cliques have higher prestige) and within groups (some members have greater power and influence than others). Friendship cliques exercise their power by accepting some children and excluding others. Within each group, friends are expected to be loyal to the peer values, but 'weaker' members are often bullied and manipulated by the rest.

Mass media

Mass media consume an enormous amount of our time – just think of all those teenagers locked away for hours on end in their bedroom with their own music centre, TV, game console and computer. We seem in constant danger of being overwhelmed by the sheer volume of print (newspapers, magazines, books) and electronic messages (TV, radio, the Internet). So it seems only reasonable to assume that the media have some effect on our attitudes, values and behaviour.

Admittedly, media seldom have a direct *hypodermic effect* – they do not inject their content into us and make us immediately accept what they tell us. But they help to create the cultural climate within which we live. They give us a sense of what values and behaviour are acceptable in the modern world. They provide us with role models – they hold up certain sports stars or showbiz celebrities for us to admire and copy.

Magazines and gender stereotypes The view of the world we get from the media is often highly stereotyped. For example, magazines such as *Cosmopolitan* seem to project an image of women as obsessed with sex and fashion. Likewise, men's magazines such as *Maxim* have been criticised for celebrating a crude 'lad culture' of lager louts, football and 'babes'. However, some people say these magazines are just escapist fun, and most people have little difficulty in separating media stereotypes from the 'real' world.

Bollywood Mass media can play an important role in socialisation. Marie Gillespie (1993) demonstrates this in her study of Sikhs in Southall. She shows how the videos produced by the Indian film industry (known as 'Bollywood') are enormously popular in this community. Whole families watch them together. Gillespie found that these videos have important socialising functions – they create links between Asian communities throughout the world, they socialise younger children into Asian cultures and languages and they help to reinforce a sense of Asian identity. But Gillespie adds that Sikhs are not just a passive audience for these films. Family members respond to them in different ways: older people watch them for nostalgic reasons while younger people are more critical – they sometimes mock the films and complain that they portray India as a backward country.

Religion

Although religions deal with spiritual matters, they also have an influence on social attitudes and behaviour. The major world religions – Christianity, Judaism, Islam, Hinduism, Buddhism – have had a deep impact on the societies in which they are dominant. This influence operates at a number of levels.

First, each religion offers a set of moral values. Over time these become part of the culture of a society. People are exposed to these values even if they do not personally attend a place of worship. Second, the rituals and ceremonies of religion have traditionally been seen as a force for social unity. Collective acts of worship such as marriages, baptisms and funerals bring people together and remind them of their common bonds and shared values. Third, religions provide a moral code (eg, the Ten Commandments) which guides our earthly behaviour. We

can see this when people undergo a religious conversion – it usually means far-reaching changes in their behaviour and lifestyles.

Secularisation? The long-term decline in church attendance in Britain suggests the country is becoming more secular – non-religious. Does this mean that the influence of religion is on the decline? Not necessarily. A decline in churchgoing does not automatically mean that people have abandoned religious ideas and beliefs. Over 70% of the population still say they believe in God, while a minority are turning to New Age beliefs and practices such as the use of crystals, Tarot cards, astrology and feng shui. Religion also plays a significant role among many of Britain's minority ethnic communities.

Muslim girls Charlotte Butler's study (1995) of a group of teenage Muslim girls in the East Midlands shows how religious beliefs can be adapted to fit changing circumstances. These young women, born in Britain, were moving away from the traditions of their parents. They remained firmly committed to their Muslim identity but they were modifying it in certain ways. Their experience of living in Britain had led them to regard certain Pakistani and Bangladeshi customs as irrelevant to their lives. Consequently, they were rejecting customs such as arranged marriages which were not regarded as essential features of Islam.

So these young women were developing more independent lifestyles to fit more easily into the British way of life, while at the same time maintaining their commitment to Islam.

Work

When we enter the workforce we have to be introduced to the skills, norms and values attached to the job. *Occupational socialisation* is a form of secondary socialisation as it occurs later in life, when we already have considerable cultural knowledge and skills.

It may well involve different forms of learning.

Anticipatory socialisation We may have learned a bit about the job beforehand, possibly by talking to people about it or taking a course in preparation.

Re-socialisation When we start work we have to learn new ways of behaving, such as submitting to workplace discipline (things like regular work hours and obeying the boss). This also applies when we move jobs because organisations vary in their styles and traditions.

Agents of workplace socialisation include bosses, colleagues, even customers. Some of these agents socialise us in formal ways, while others socialise us in a more informal fashion.

Formal socialisation The management of a firm takes formal responsibility for socialising employees. For example, they may provide training courses to develop the necessary work skills. In addition, they usually lay down norms about appearance, attitudes and behaviour. Some

activity 10 McJobs

Item A *May I help you?*

Young people often get their first experience of work in 'McJobs' – unskilled, low paid, part-time jobs in fast-food restaurants. They are trained to perform simple tasks in a predictable manner, doing each action in exactly the same way. They have little scope for using their initiative.

Workers are even restricted in what they can *say* on the job. Every interaction with customers is tightly scripted – 'May I help you?', 'Would you like a dessert to go with your meal?', 'Have a nice day!' They are given scripts for any situations that may arise. Workers are no longer trusted to say the right thing.

Source: Ritzer, 2002

Item B *Have a nice day*

questions

1 What are the key features of socialisation into McJobs?
2 Why might these skills be less useful in other kinds of jobs?

---

workplaces impose strict dress codes (eg, collar and tie for men). Behaviour may be controlled by official codes of conduct (eg, rules against private telephone calls and emails). Many firms also try to win the loyalty and motivation of their staff by encouraging them to identify with the company – some Japanese firms even have their own company song!

Informal socialisation This is the socialisation provided by peer groups at work. They introduce us to the informal culture of the workplace. They have their own rituals, such as playing jokes on newcomers (eg, sending them to the stores to fetch a tin of 'tartan paint'). They also have their own norms, many of which may not be approved by management. For example, they may ignore the official rules and do things their own way. Or they may try to slow down the pace of work – any colleague who works too hard may be bullied or mocked.

Canteen culture Canteen culture is the term given to describe the informal culture of police officers as they hang around the station or spend their off-duty hours together. Waddington's research (1999) shows how canteen culture can help socialise police officers. They learn from listening to other officers telling their 'war stories' – how they overcame tricky situations – and pick up practical advice such as 'you can't always play it by the book'.

Waddington argues that this canteen chat actually helps police officers deal with their stressful job. It boosts their occupational self-esteem by giving them a 'heroic' identity (they are out there on the front-line bravely facing 'trouble'). It reinforces their sense of 'mission' (they are doing a valuable job by fighting crime). It also celebrates certain values that are useful in police work (such as a 'macho' emphasis on physical strength and courage).

key terms

Primary socialisation Intimate and influential socialisation (usually from parents) in the early years of life.
Secondary socialisation Socialisation that comes later in life, from various sources.
Agents of socialisation The individuals, groups and institutions which play a part in the socialisation process.
Sanctions Rewards and punishments.
Role models People we use to give us ideas about how to play particular social roles.
Peer group A friendship group formed by people in the same social situation.
Secularisation The view that religion is declining in importance in society.
Occupational socialisation A form of secondary socialisation by which people learn the skills, norms and values of the workplace.

Socialisation – conclusion

Socialisation is an essential element in any society. There are a variety of agents who perform socialisation tasks, but experts disagree on which ones exercise the most influence. Traditionally it was thought that parents, and perhaps the church, had the greatest effect. In modern society the school, peer group and mass media seem to have growing influence.

There is also disagreement about whether these agents have a sufficiently 'responsible' attitude to their socialisation tasks. For example, parents are sometimes accused of simply putting their kids in front of the TV rather than talking to them. Peer groups offer us friendship but they also introduce us to dangerous temptations. Mass media inform us about the world, but sometimes they distort that world.

summary

1. Socialisation is a key feature of any society – it transmits the cultural heritage from one generation to the next. It is the way in which people learn social norms, roles and values.

2. Socialisation is not a one-way street in which people passively accept society's norms and values. They participate in internalising, modifying or rejecting these norms and values.

3. There are different forms of socialisation. Primary socialisation is often thought of as the most important and influential. But secondary socialisation is increasingly significant in fast-changing modern societies.

4. Socialisation is performed by different agents – parents, school, peer group, mass media, religion and work. These agents come into play at different stages of our life, and they have different effects.

Unit 3 Self, identity and difference

keyissues

1 What is identity?

2 How are social identities formed?

3 What is distinctive about postmodern and late modern society?

3.1 Defining identity

Identity refers to the way we see ourselves in relation to other people – what makes us similar to some people and different from others. Identity operates at different levels.

The inner self At one level identity refers to the inner self, that 'little voice' inside our heads. Susan Blackmore (1999) describes this as the 'real you', the bit of yourself that feels those deep emotions like falling in love or feeling sad. It is the bit of you that thinks, dreams and has memories. It is something which seems to persist throughout your life, giving it some kind of continuity.

Personal identity This kind of identity is public and visible – it can be recorded in things like birth certificates, passports, medical files and career records. Each of us is unique on account of our special combination of personal details – our date and place of birth, name, personal biography, family background and by our history of personal relationships and life experiences.

Social identity Social identities are based on our membership of, or identification with, particular social groups. Sometimes these identities are given to us at birth – we are born male or female or with a white or black skin for example. But some social identities involve a greater degree of choice. We may actively choose to identify with some groups such as New Age Travellers or surfers.

We become more sharply aware of our group identities when we can contrast them with groups who are not like us. Social identities are often framed in terms of contrasts – eg, young/old.

This contrast is illustrated by Cecil's (1993) study of Protestants and Catholics in 'Glengow', a small town in Northern Ireland. In Glengow a person's religion was regarded as the most significant way of separating 'us' from 'them'. Both sides relied heavily on stereotypes. Protestants saw themselves as hard-working, thrifty, independent, clean and tidy, but they accused Catholics of being lazy, dominated by priests, untidy and untrustworthy. Catholics saw themselves as easy-going, friendly, generous, intelligent and educated, but saw Protestants as dour, bigoted, mean and lacking in refinement.

3.2 Constructing identities

All identities, even our 'inner' ones, are social to some extent. We would have little sense of identity unless we had a language to reflect on it. And we would have little sense of group differences and similarities if we did not participate in social life. For sociologists, our identity is not something we are born with, but something that is formed by interaction with others in social settings.

Symbolic interactionism and identity

One of the best ways to understand the social character of identity is to look at the ideas of *symbolic interactionism.* This approach to identity was pioneered by George Herbert Mead (1863-1931).

The self Mead argued that a basic feature of human beings is our possession of a sense of self or identity. At an early age we slowly become aware that there are people who are 'not me', in other words that each of us has a separate existence. As we grow up we also begin to form an impression of our own personal qualities and characteristics. Language enables us to reflect on ourselves ('what sort of a person am I?') and to hold little internal 'conversations' (eg, we get angry with ourselves).

Social interaction Interactionists argue that our identity has social origins – it emerges in the course of social interaction. We depend on other people for vital clues about who we are. Charles Cooley coined the term *looking glass self* to convey the idea that we 'see' ourselves reflected in the attitudes and behaviour of other people towards us. For example, we may be uncertain about our new haircut until we see the responses of people around us. Of course, we do not always accept what others think of us, but their opinions are hard to ignore!

Sometimes we take the initiative rather than waiting for others to form an opinion of us. Goffman (1969) calls this the *presentation of self,* a process where we deliberately arrange our appearance (clothes, hairstyle etc) and adopt certain mannerisms in order to make a public statement about ourselves.

The changing self Interactionists challenge the idea that each of us has a fixed, stable self. Identity can change with the passage of time. The 'me' I am now is different in certain ways from the 'me' I was ten years ago. An identity may change slowly, or it may be transformed by a dramatic life event such as bereavement, mutilation, redundancy or being labelled a criminal, which forces a re-examination of one's self.

Social identities – conclusion

Some might argue that we are 'blank sheets' and society simply writes its message on us. For example, if other people look down on us, we develop low self-esteem. If they like us, we think of ourselves as popular. A more realistic approach is that we do not always accept the opinions of others – we interpret them and judge their value according to that interpretation.

The interactionist model certainly alerts us to the social character of identity – it is not something fixed at birth. Our identity can develop and change as we interact with others.

*activity*11 *changes*

Item A No longer me

The following passage was written by a journalist who had horrific operations on his tongue which altered his facial appearance and left him with severe difficulties in speech and eating.

'I found myself having depressing thoughts about who this made me. Would the people I love have loved me if this is how I was when they first met me? Would my friends have become my friends if when we first met I'd been a wounded, honking mute, unable to respond to the simplest questions without dribbling? I also knew the answer was almost certainly no. It had to be. I was not now the person my friends befriended, my wife married. The fact remained: I was not me any more. My friends seemed willing to do almost anything for me but they were responding to who I was before the operation rather than who I had become after it.'

Source: Diamond, 1998

Item B Bar mitzvah

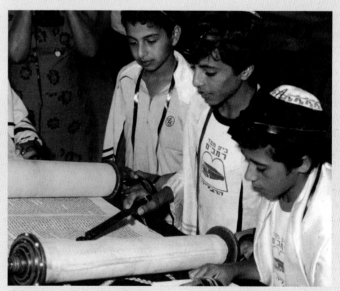

A bar mitzvah is a Jewish ceremony marking the transition of 13 year-old boys to adulthood. The picture shows three boys in a bar mitzvah ceremony.

questions

1 How would symbolic interactionists explain the experience of the journalist in Item A?
2 In what ways are the identities of the boys in Item B likely to change?

3.3 Identity in postmodern society and late modern society

A number of sociologists argue that societies like the UK have moved from the *modern* era to the *postmodern* era during the last quarter of the 20th century. Other sociologists see this change as less dramatic, arguing that we have entered *late modernity*, an extension of the modern era. However, both groups agree that the changes they identify have important effects on identity.

Postmodern culture and identity

Postmodern culture is seen to have the following features.

Images and styles The mass media increasingly bombard us with images, logos and brands. Websites, TV and magazines pump out ads for constantly changing fashions – D&G, Giorgio Armani, Gucci, Yves Saint Laurent, Paco Rabanne, Kenzo, DKNY and Longchamp are just a few of the brands in ads in the January 2008 issues of *Grazia* magazine. They provide a range of images and styles which we can choose from to reflect our chosen identities.

Diversity of lifestyles The dominant mainstream culture is being steadily replaced by a wide variety of 'taste groups' and an increasing diversity of lifestyles. People choose from the lifestyles on offer, selecting those which allow them to express and act out their identities.

Choice Identities in postmodern society are increasingly chosen rather than being imposed by birth or tradition. As Hobsbawn (1996) notes, most identities are now like 'shirts' that we choose to wear rather than the 'skin' we are born with.

Postmodern culture has manipulated the number of identities available. People can choose to combine a variety of identities. For example, one person can combine the identities of a forceful business executive *and* a caring mother *and* a Sikh *and* a British patriot *and* an enthusiastic hang-glider.

Rapid social change Society in the postmodern era changes rapidly. For example, new forms of electronic communication are constantly appearing, from iPhones to new types of interaction on social networking websites. Identities are more fluid and shifting, reflecting the rapid changes in society. The self is no longer fixed as people increasingly try out a wide range of loosely-held identities. The self is there to be invented and re-invented.

Postmodernist sociologists also suggest that identities are becoming more unstable and fragile. Older identities have been seriously undermined by rapid social change. But the new identities which are replacing them are fragile and precarious – they do not always provide a firm sense of 'roots'.

Evaluation Critics have argued that postmodernists have overstated their case. For example, are people as free as the postmodernists claim to choose their identities? Critics argue that there are many factors which limit people's choices and prevent them from choosing and acting out certain identities. For example, being born black or white, rich or poor, male or female still have important influences on people's identities and lifestyles. Being poor, for instance, can prevent people from adopting expensive lifestyles and buying the products which express those lifestyles.

Late modernity and identity

Sociologists who argue that society has entered the phase of late modernity accept some of the claims made by postmodernists. This can be seen from the following features of late modernity which they identify.

Choice and individualisation According to the German sociologist Ulrick Beck, a process of *individualisation* is occurring. This process reduces the control of traditional roles and social structures over people's behaviour (Beck and Beck-Gernsheim, 2001). As a result, people have greater freedom to select and construct their own identities and design their own lifestyles. For example, they have greater freedom to choose and design their relationships – to marry, to cohabit, to divorce, to live in a heterosexual or a gay or lesbian relationship and so on. People are less likely to be forced to conform to traditional marital, family and gender roles.

Social reflexivity This term is used by the British sociologist Anthony Giddens (1991, 2001). In earlier phases of modernity, people were more likely to follow traditional norms and to take those norms for granted. Now they are more likely to be *reflexive* – to reflect on what they are doing, to assess and question their behaviour, to examine what was previously taken for granted. As a result, people are more likely to reflect on their identity, on who they are. This leads many people to turn their identity into a project to be worked on.

Identity politics *Identity politics* is the term used to describe conflicts and struggles over identity. In society today it seems that more and more groups are defining themselves in terms of their identity or 'difference'. Bauman (2001) suggests that the collapse of traditional communities has led people to search desperately for other sources of meaning and security. Many hope to find this meaning in some form of collective identity.

These identity groups often feel they are treated as second class citizens and deprived of their human rights. Examples include ethnic minorities, people with disabilities (eg, wheelchair-users) and groups based on sexual preferences (eg, gays, lesbians, bisexuals, transsexuals). Powerful groups sometimes discriminate against them and treat them as inferior. For example, society may be seen as sexist (men oppressing women)

*activity*12 *Changing identities*

Item A *Identity Kits*

Item B *Images and styles*

Item C *Identity cards*

Will it ever come to this? The Government is planning to sell Identity Scratch Cards. Scratch off the special square and you may win a year's worth of free identity. The winner gets to chose a dream identity, for example, a pop star or a major sports personality.

Source: Iannucci, 1995

question

What do Items A, B and C suggest about identity in postmodern and late society?

activity13 identity politics

Item A Bikers for Jesus

Attending a Bikers for Jesus rally.

Item B Goths

Attending a gothic festival in Leipzig, Germany.

Item C Europride

Europride lesbian and gay pride march, London.

questions

1 What identities are being projected in these photos?

2 Explain why these photos represent identity politics.

or racist (Whites discriminating against ethnic minorities).

Identity politics is new in the sense that it is not just about winning a fair share of wealth and resources for the group concerned. It is also about claiming the 'right to be different'. Identity groups want 'recognition' from the rest of society that they have equal worth, in spite of their cultural differences from others. The struggle is about winning respect, promoting tolerance and challenging negative stereotypes

key terms

Postmodern era A new era seen to follow the modern era.

Late modernity A new phase seen to be an extension of the modern era.

Individualisation A reduction in the control of traditional roles and social structures over people's behaviour.

Social reflexivity People reflecting on what they are doing, and assessing and questioning their behaviour.

Identity politics The conflicts and struggles over group identities in society.

summary

1. Identity can refer to the inner self, personal identity or social identity.

2. All identities are social in the sense that they depend on language and social experience. It is impossible to imagine a society where people have no sense of who they are or what makes them different from others.

3. Social identities express our similarities with others in the same social group. But they also create a divide between 'us' and 'them'.

4. Interactionists claim that the self has social origins – it emerges in the course of social interaction. Our identities may change as we move from group to group, or as a result of important changes in our lives.

5. Sometimes we have social identities imposed on us, at other times we have freedom to choose the groups with whom we identify. The 'presentation of self' is a device we use to create our own identity.

6. Postmodern culture is said to have the following features.
   * An emphasis on image and style
   * Diversity of lifestyles
   * Identities increasingly chosen
   * An increase in the number and importance of identities
   * Rapid social change
   * Identities more fluid and fragile

7. Critics of postmodernist views argue that there are factors which prevent many people from choosing and acting out certain identities.

8. Features of late modernity include individualisation, social reflexivity and a focus on the construction of identity.

9. Identity politics is not just about winning a fair share of resources, it is also about claiming the 'right to be different', winning respect and promoting a favourable image of the group.

Unit 4 Age and identity

key issues

1 How do cultural identities vary according to age?

2 What is happening to youth cultures in postmodern society?

3 Is ageism a problem for older people?

Age and identity

Our lives sometimes seem to be mapped out in terms of different ages which are linked to certain identities and lifestyles. For example, we expect people to be restless and moody in their teens, mature and confident in their forties, but 'slow' and set in their ways in their sixties.

These differences are often explained in terms of the 'biological clock' ageing is seen as a biological process which brings about inevitable changes in outlook and behaviour. But age is also *socially* constructed – it is shaped by culture and society. For example, people in pre-industrial societies were often divided into separate age groups with distinct rights and characteristics. However, in society today there is a more flexible attitude to age – people often try to resist age-related expectations.

4.1 Youth in search of identity

Confused youth Young people in modern industrial societies are frequently described as confused about their identities. There is a lack of public *rites of passage* (rituals, ceremonies) to announce that they have successfully reached adulthood. Neither fully children nor fully adults, they often seem to be experimenting with many different roles and styles in an attempt to find their 'true' selves.

The functionalist perspective in sociology suggests that *youth culture* helps to ease the passage towards stable identities and personalities. Youth culture – the shared tastes, activities and styles of young people – offers young people the collective support of a peer group while they try to 'find themselves'. In the course of trying out different experiences and lifestyles, they gradually mature and 'grow up'.

On the other hand, some sociologists argue that young people are no more confused than adults about their identities. And youth culture may be enjoyed purely for the pleasures it offers, rather than because it offers a solution to any identity crisis.

Rebellious youth Another popular image of young people is that of unruly rebels. Pearson (1983) suggests there is a long history of seeing young people as 'trouble'. Social commentators down the years have expressed similar fears and concerns about youthful troublemakers, viewing them in terms of social breakdown and moral decline.

This image of youth was reinforced over the past fifty years by the emergence of exotic youth subcultures – such as teddy boys, mods and rockers, skinheads, punks and goths. Some sociologists (eg, Jefferson, 1975) offered a 'conflict' explanation of these subcultures. The subcultures were seen as a protest against exploitation and injustice in a class-divided society. One of the striking things about this resistance was that it was largely *symbolic*. It was mainly through their subcultural *styles* that these youths expressed their protest – it was 'resistance through rituals'. By creating new subcultures with their own meanings, rituals and identities, working-class youth refused to accept other people's low opinion of them.

This theory perhaps exaggerates the rebellious streak in young people. A simpler explanation for these subcultures is that they were *fun*. Also, the exotic subcultures which alarmed observers were hardly representative of the mass of ordinary, largely 'conformist' youth.

Postmodern youth Postmodern sociologists draw attention to the increasing diversity of youth identities. They claim that the old-style youth subcultures – stable groups with clear boundaries between them – are fading away. Instead, young people now follow lifestyles based on their *individual* tastes. We now have a 'supermarket of style' (Polhemus, 1997), where young people are faced with an abundance of choices.

Postmodernists admit there are still certain *neo-tribes* with recognisable subcultural styles (eg, goths). Young people often seek out those who share their tastes and enthusiasms. But these groupings tend to be short-lived and superficial. Few young people are totally committed – they are more likely to adopt a casual pick'n'mix approach to style. They play with different looks and styles, sampling and mixing them in all sorts of unexpected and imaginative ways (eg, gay skinheads, bikers for Jesus).

activity14 youth today

Item A Feral gangs

A top policeman painted a horrifying picture yesterday of gangs of 'feral youths'. He said drunken and abusive yobs intimidated entire neighbourhoods, forcing law-abiding families to live in fear. 'It is part of life for these people. These people are feral (wild) by nature, having little control over their behaviour and having little responsibility for their actions and having little parental control over the way they live their lives. I have spoken to parents who are unconcerned that their 14-year-old child has been arrested for a serious assault or robbery.'

Source: *Daily Mail*, 18.5.2005

Item B Typical young people

A nationally representative survey reveals what 13-18 year-olds are really like today.

* They want to enjoy life.
* They have a strong set of values (very family-oriented).
* Their role models are parents and teachers rather than 'celebrities'.
* They have a strong social conscience.
* They are ambitious and hard-working.
* They are much more confident, respectful and caring than adults imagine.

Source: Scout Association, 2007

Item C Pictures of youth

Attacking a police landrover in Northern Ireland.

Item D Cosmetic surgery

A survey has found that three quarters of girls aged between 12 and 14 say they would like cosmetic surgery (plastic surgery, breast implants, operations to remove excess fat etc.). It would make them feel happier about the way they look and stop teasing by friends.

Source: *Daily Mail*, 11.11.2000

Calling for measures to help young people break the cycle of violence.

question

What 'identity' of youths is suggested by each of these items?

4.2 Older identities

The population of Britain is ageing – there are more old people now and they form a larger proportion of the population. Between 1971 and 2005 the numbers of people aged 65 and over rose from 7.4 million (13% of the total population) to 9.6 million (16%). (*Social Trends*, 2007)

This is a welcome sign that people are living longer. At the same time, many people seem to fear old age. They view it as a time when they will decline *physically* (less energy, poorer health), *psychologically* (fading powers of concentration) and *socially* (social participation may drop off).

It is difficult to deny that biological ageing takes its toll – for example, a large majority of disabled adults in Britain are aged 60 and over. Nevertheless, sociologists challenge the notion that ageing has fixed social effects. They argue that old age is something which is socially constructed and varies between groups and over time. The experience of old age is not the same for everyone.

Ageism The problem for many older people is not so much biological age as the discriminatory attitudes of others. They can become victims of *ageism* – insensitive attitudes and assumptions which treat them as if they were less important or less capable than everyone else. Employers may be reluctant to hire them, on the assumption that they are somehow 'past it'. Young people may call them offensive names such as 'senile', 'crumbly', 'wrinklie' and 'geriatric'. Ageism stigmatises older people – it attaches negative labels to them.

In Western societies some older people are now starting to fight against ageism. Grey Power groups are campaigning for better pensions and a better public image. Older people are using their spending and voting power to persuade politicians, retailers and organisations to treat them with dignity and respect.

The cult of youth Society teaches us to celebrate youth. We admire youthful strength and beauty. There is a huge market of products and treatments to help us stay young – such as cosmetic surgery (eg, face lifts, Botox), vitamins and lotions (eg, anti-ageing creams) and fitness regimes (eg, yoga, Pilates).

Old age, by contrast, is often pictured as something to be pitied or feared rather than envied. The mass media circulate images of elderly people as physically unattractive, sexually inactive and chronically ill. No wonder middle-aged people often search anxiously for the dreaded signs of ageing – tell-tale wrinkles, thinning hair, sagging muscles.

activity15 being old and young

Fauja Singh, aged 93, running in the London marathon.

Members of The Zimmers rock band whose record 'My Generation' reached the Top 40. The lead singer Alf Carretta (wearing glasses) is 90 years old.

question

What do these items suggest about how the people in the pictures see old age?

On the other hand, Berger (1971) questions the assumption that 'being young' is a matter of biological age. For Berger, youthfulness is a set of personal qualities – being impulsive, spontaneous, energetic, playful and passionate. These qualities can be found in people of all ages. Not all young people are youthful by any means, and not all youthful people are young!

The mask of old age Featherstone and Hepworth (1989) note that many older people are forced to wear the 'mask of old age' – they are expected to act in terms of ageist stereotypes. For example, even middle-aged grandparents may be under pressure to act the role of an 'elderly' Granny or Granpa. Yet older people sometimes feel just the same way they always did – they still feel young at heart.

Featherstone and Hepworth suggest that increasing numbers of older people are refusing to conform to the stereotypes. They express their identities in lively and imaginative ways – such as exotic foreign holidays, wind-surfing, and salsa dancing. Many of these adventurous attitudes have been pioneered by the 'baby boomer' generation (those raised in the 1960s). This generation is extending the length of what used to be regarded as 'middle age'. And they are carrying their vigorous and active pursuits into the later years of life.

Two nations Older people are individuals, and so their lifestyles and identities vary according to the particular choices they make. But these choices are also shaped by social characteristics such as social class. Britain's pensioners are split into 'two nations'. The retired middle class generally have substantial pensions and savings which enable them to enjoy a comfortable standard of living. But not everyone is lucky enough to grow old gracefully. For many working-class people, old age spells poverty – as many as half of all pensioners live in poverty or on its margins.

key terms

Rites of passage Rituals which mark the movement from one social status or position to another.
Youth culture The subcultures – tastes, activities and lifestyles – of particular groups of young people.
Neo-tribes Loose groupings around shared styles and tastes, with flexible and often fleeting membership.
Stigmatise Attaching negative labels to a group.
Ageism Viewing and/or treating people in a negative way simply because of their age.
Cult of youth 'Worshipping' youthfulness.

summary

1. According to functionalists, youth culture helps young people to establish stable identities and make the transition to adulthood.

2. Some sociologists see working-class youth subcultures as a form of resistance against the inequalities of society. This protest takes the form of style rather than direct action.

3. Postmodernists argue that distinct youth subcultures have splintered and weakened. Young people now move freely between individually-chosen styles.

4. The ageing process involves certain changes in people's lives. But many of the negative effects are a result of social attitudes rather than biological processes.

5. Ageism and the cult of youth mean that older people tend to be stigmatised. However, there are signs that they are adopting more positive and flexible identities and rejecting negative stereotypes.

6. Social class affects the experience of ageing. For many working-class people, old age means poverty.

Unit 5 Disability and identity

keyissues

1. What is disability?
2. What are the aims of the disability rights movement?
3. How do people with disabilities combat stigma?

Our bodies have a physical existence which cannot be ignored. This is especially true for people with disabilities. Disabilities arise from various sources – some are the result of genetic disorders, some are caused by illness or serious accident, and others emerge from the degenerative processes of ageing.

Estimates of the numbers of disabled people in Britain range from six million to twelve million. It all depends on how strictly we define disability. Many conditions are a matter of degree, varying from mild to severe. For example, the Royal Institute for the Deaf estimates that around nine million people in Britain have some degree of hearing loss, from slightly hard of hearing to profoundly deaf (Atkinson, 2006). Similarly, the term 'blindness' covers a wide range of visual impairment.

The 2007 British Social Attitudes Survey revealed that the general public defines disability narrowly. Most of the sample agreed that it includes wheelchair users, but they were less likely to describe arthritis or heart disease as a disability. More worryingly, the survey revealed a great deal of prejudice towards groups such as mentally ill people or those with HIV (O'Hara, 2007).

5.1 Disability rights

Disability is often regarded as a personal misfortune that happens to unlucky people. It is seen mainly as a medical problem. This view has been challenged by the disability rights movement which puts the emphasis on civil rights. The movement makes a fundamental distinction between *impairment* and *disability*.

Impairment This refers to the limitations the physical or mental condition places upon a person's ability to function effectively. For example, people with severe arthritis may find it difficult to wash or dress themselves.

Disability This refers to the restrictions society places on impaired people. Society is seen as dis-abling them through its prejudices – for example, employers may reject job-seekers with a history of mental illness. It also restricts their full social participation by putting barriers in their way – for example, wheelchair users may find it difficult to get access to shops or offices.

So there has been a move towards understanding disability in terms of 'structural oppression'. It is not just a matter of impairment (although that is still a painful reality for many people) but also a battle for social and political rights. Some progress has been made, and the Disability Discrimination Act (1995) now aims to protect people with disabilities from discrimination.

Identity politics

The disability rights movement is also trying to build a more positive identity for disabled people. Disabled people sometimes internalise the negative stereotypes directed at them, resulting in low self-esteem and spoiled identities. But some groups have been set up to promote a prouder image. For example, there are more than 300 deaf social clubs across Britain. One deaf DJ organises raves that fill large venues with thousands of deaf partygoers from all over the world (Atkinson, 2006).

5.2 Spoiled identities

Goffman (1968) describes how people deal with imperfections of the body such as amputated limbs, unsightly scars, ugly facial blemishes and physical disabilities. These imperfections create a gap between the *virtual social identity* (what the person's bodily characteristics should be) and the *actual social identity* (what they really are). This gap can be deeply discrediting – the person's identity becomes *spoiled*.

activity16 *Images of disability*

Item A *'I hoped our baby would be deaf'*

When Polly Garfield and her partner – both deaf – found that their baby was profoundly deaf it was a cause for joy rather than sadness. 'Being deaf is about being part of a cultural minority. We're proud of the language we use and the community we live in. We're delighted that this is something our daughter can share as she grows up.'

For the couple, deafness is not something that needs to be fixed, but an expression of a cultural identity. 'If only people knew about the deaf community, our rich culture and history, our parties and the closeness and pride that we feel in our shared identity. Our language is so colourful, so alive. That's our sound, that's our music.'

Source: Atkinson, 2006.

Item C *Kissing gates*

The law requires public services to make reasonable adjustments to allow disabled access. Some local authorities feel this means that kissing gates and stiles should be removed from the countryside, as they are almost impossible to use if you are in a wheelchair.

This has dismayed farmers, who argue that they provide a cheap and practical solution for access through fields. But the UK Disabled People's Council says it fully supports the move – disabled people have as much right to go into the countryside as non-disabled people.

Source: Levy, 2007

Item B

Arriving at the House of Commons by hearse to protest against the lack of access for many disabled people to trains and stations.

questions

1 How can Items A and B be seen as an example of identity politics?

2 In what way is Item C an example of disability rights?

Goffman insists that it is not the bodily characteristic in itself that is the problem. Rather, it is the stigma which is created when people attach discrediting labels to others. This presents a problem of *stigma management* for those who are given these labels. Goffman identifies two main situations which arise.

Discredited In this situation people are *discredited* in the sense that their imperfection is already visible or widely known. This may create *interaction uneasiness* when others react in an embarrassed or clumsy fashion (eg, people sometimes speak too loudly to a blind person).

The main strategy for discredited individuals is one of *tension management*. They develop social skills to put people at their ease (eg, joking about their stigma to show that it is okay to talk about it). They may try to correct the imperfection (eg, by means of surgery) or resort to *compensation* (eg, the amputee may take up dangerous sports). Others may simply avoid strangers and associate mainly with people who are more understanding.

Discreditable In this situation the person's imperfection is not immediately obvious to others. Examples include HIV, colostomy bags and epilepsy. Here the main strategy is one of *information control* where the individual tries to manage the flow of information so that stigma is avoided. They may try to 'pass' the imperfection as something else (eg, passing off early stages of Alzheimer's as simple absent-mindedness). Or conceal it (eg, wearing a special bra to conceal a mastectomy). Or 'cover' it by passing it off as something less damaging (eg, infertile people may pretend they just don't want children).

However, Goffman points out that those who attempt to conceal their condition risk exposure from people who 'know' about them. There is a constant danger that their secret will be revealed. So some may simply decide that voluntary disclosure of their condition is the best solution.

key terms

Impairment A physical or mental condition which limits a person's capacity to function effectively.

Disability Disadvantage which results from society's failure to allow people with impairments to participate fully in social life.

Spoiled identity A discredited identity resulting from negative labels attached by others.

summary

1. Physical and mental impairments make it harder for people to function effectively. Prejudice and discrimination against people with impairments add to their difficulties.

2. The disability rights movement is creating a more positive view of disabled people and fighting against discrimination

3. Disabled people who are discredited often use tension management techniques. Those who are discreditable often use information management techniques.

Unit 6 Ethnic identities

keyissues

1 What is an ethnic group?

2 What are the main ethnic identities in Britain?

3 In what ways are ethnic identities changing?

6.1 Ethnic groups and identities

In the 1950s and 1960s many thousands of people migrated from New Commonwealth countries such as Jamaica, India, Pakistan and Kenya to Britain. They brought with them the traditional customs, values, religions, diets and languages of their homelands. These cultural features set them apart from one another and from the mainstream cultures of Britain. In other words, they formed distinctive *ethnic groups* – groups with their own cultures based on a sense of shared origin.

Table 2 shows the range of ethnic groups in Britain in 2001.

Table 2 **The UK population by ethnic group**

	% of total population	% of minority ethnic population
White	92.1	n/a
Mixed	1.2	14.6
Asian or Asian British		
Indian	1.8	22.7
Pakistani	1.3	16.1
Bangladeshi	0.5	6.1
Other Asian	0.4	5.3
Black or Black British		
Black Caribbean	1.0	12.2
Black African	0.8	10.5
Black Other	0.2	2.1
Chinese	0.4	5.3
Other	0.4	5.0
All minority ethnic population	*7.9*	*100*

Source: National Statistics Online (based on April 2001 Census data)

Ethnic identities

The members of an ethnic group may have varying degrees of commitment to the group's values and identities. Nevertheless, a shared cultural tradition does tend to create common identities.

African-Caribbean identities

The identities of African-Caribbean people in Britain are shaped by many things including their age and social class. They may follow lifestyles which are not much different from those of White people. However, a black skin colour is significant in a country like Britain where *racism* has not yet been eradicated. Black people may see themselves as the victims or survivors of racism.

African-Caribbean culture and customs have some impact on identities. For example, the use of African-Caribbean ways of speaking or dialects (patois) reinforces their sense of having a distinctive cultural identity.

Black expressive cultures The richness of African-Caribbean culture is celebrated every year in the Notting Hill Carnival. Paul Gilroy (1987) also notes the dazzling contributions Black people have made to mainstream popular culture in Britain – in dance, music and dress (Black youth are often seen as the cutting edge of street fashion). Gilroy believes there is no single Black culture or Black identity but he argues that there are certain common themes that run through all Black cultures. One of these is awareness of the historical experience of slavery, a bitter experience that still has an effect on the outlook of Black people.

activity 17 Black culture

Item A Slavery in Trinidad

Item B Say it loud

James Brown lying in state at the Apollo Theatre, Harlem, New York.

The funeral of James Brown, the 'Godfather of Soul', has been held in Harlem, New York. Thousands turned out to pay tribute to the singer and showman whose music inspired hip hop, funk, disco and rap. But Brown was also a Black icon who coined the phrase 'Say it Loud – I'm Black and I'm Proud'. This was regarded as a powerful 'wake-up call' for Black pride and black consciousness.

Source: *The Guardian*, 29.12.2006

Item C Notting Hill Carnival

questions

1 How might awareness of the history of slavery influence the identity and ethnic awareness of Black Britons?

2 How can Items B and C be seen as examples of Black identity and culture?

activity 18 Muslim women in Britain

Item A Burkinis

Schools have been told they should allow Muslim girls taking swimming lessons to cover themselves from head to toe in special outfits called burkinis. An increasing number of pupils are insisting that conventional swimming costumes are 'immodest'.

Source: *The Mail on Sunday*, 24.6.2007

Burkini designer (in black) and Muslim lifeguard wearing burkinis in Sydney, Australia.

Item B Meet the Islamic Barbie

There is a new must-have toy on the Muslim child's wish list – the Razanne doll. The doll, whose name translates as 'shyness and modesty' is demurely dressed and has an air of humility. Her creators see her as more acceptable than the skimpily dressed Barbie doll. She comes in a range of guises, including 'Dr Razanne' and 'Teacher Razanne' – to show that Muslim women, too, can have careers.

As the mother of one girl puts it, 'What is good about the doll is that it's Razanne's character that counts, not whether she's a perfect 10 in her day-glo summer bikini'.

There are no plans to have a male version – it wouldn't fit with Razanne to have a boyfriend.

Source: *The Guardian*, 30.9.2004

question

How do these items illustrate that Muslim identities in Britain include aspects of the old and the new?

The art of being Black Clare Alexander (1996) made a close study of a group of Black youths in London. She concluded that there are many different ways of being Black. Constructing a Black identity is an 'art' that needs a great deal of work and effort. The youths she studied felt there were 'symbolic markers' of being Black. They felt there is something about certain styles of dress, music, even walking and talking, that make them instantly recognisable as 'Black'.

In a later work, Alexander (2002) notes that the 'cool' styles of Black youth have enjoyed enormous popularity in Britain. Black youth are widely seen as the cutting edge of street-oriented youth culture. They often lead the way in fashion and music (eg, hip hop, rap).

Asian identities

The term Asian masks some important differences. Most of Britain's Asians have origins in Pakistan, Bangladesh and India. The first two are predominantly Muslim but India contains Sikh and Muslim minorities as well as the Hindu majority. Within these main groups there are further sub-divisions.

Britain's Muslim population is split between the Sunni and Shiah traditions and it is further broken down into various sects and territorial and language groups. However, their shared faith and identity as one nation (*ummah*) creates some bonds between these Muslim communities.

Asian lifestyles Each religion has its own place of worship (the Hindu temple, the Muslim mosque, the Sikh gurdwara). Also, each religious group tends to follow its own calendar of fasts (eg, the Muslim *Ramadan*) and feasts (eg, the Hindu *Diwali*). Religion affects dress codes (the Muslim veil, the Sikh turban), diet (Hindus avoid beef, Muslims avoid pork) and moral attitudes (divorce is more acceptable to Muslims than other Asian religious groups).

But there are similarities in the cultural practices of Britain's Asian populations. One example is the custom of arranged marriages where parents play a large part in choosing partners for their children. Another is the stress laid on the extended family (the wider kin group beyond the mother, father and children). Family honour is extremely important and the kin group is always anxious to protect its reputation. This is one of the reasons why the behaviour of young women is closely monitored by relatives.

Until quite recently, many people were unaware of an Asian youth culture in Britain. But that is changing. Bennett

(2001) describes the rising popularity of bhangra (a blend of Indian folk music with Western pop) among Asians in Britain. Another popular form is ragga (a blend of bhangra with rap and reggae). According to Bennett, these 'cross-over' developments have played a major part in the formation of new Asian youth identities.

White identities

It is a mistake to think that ethnicity is something found only among minority groups. Every group has a culture and so even the White majority can be called an ethnic group. Of course, there are many different ways of being White, so it does not mean the same thing to everyone.

Invisible culture? Young Whites sometimes feel they inhabit an invisible culture. This was certainly true of the group studied by Roger Hewitt (1996) in a deprived working-class area of London. They felt a deep sense of unfairness because every culture seemed to be celebrated except their own. They were constantly frustrated whenever they tried to adopt symbols and emblems of White or English cultural identity. For example, the Union flag and the flag of St

George were regarded with suspicion because of their association with far-right racist groups. Hewitt argues that ways must be found of allowing White people to be proud of their own cultural traditions. But this should not be done in a racist manner that excludes people from ethnic minorities from claiming an English identity too.

Ethnic groups and identities – conclusion

Britain is a multicultural society. It contains a number of distinctive ethnic groups, each with their own identity, values and customs. People in Asian or African-Caribbean minority groups often have a keen awareness of their cultural traditions. Of course, some people born into these groups will drift away from them, while others will remain deeply committed to their particular ethnic lifestyles. Some will regard themselves as British but British with a difference – Black British or British Asian.

Identity is not based solely on ethnicity, however. For example, a Black person is not just Black but also a particular gender, age, social class – all of these will have an effect on that person's identity.

activity19 *White England*

Item A *Celebration*

England has much to celebrate: Shakespeare, Dickens, parliamentary democracy, architecture, political philosophers, a philanthropic tradition, the welfare state, scientific developments, the sixties cultural revolution, football, brilliant humourists and much more. Why is it wrong for White English children to take pride in these achievements?

Source: Y. Alibhai-Brown, 1997

Henley Regatta

Item B *Images of White England*

Royal Ascot

Hunting

question

Using these items, suggest why some people might be reluctant to adopt a White English identity.

6.2 Changing ethnic identities

Some experts confidently predicted that ethnic minorities would slowly become *assimilated* – they would gradually abandon their ethnic cultures and adopt the culture of mainstream Britain. It was expected that this trend would affect mainly the second and third generations (those born in Britain). This has happened to some extent – the life of a Sikh is not the same in Britain as it is in the Punjab. Many male Sikhs no longer wear a turban. Yet it is equally clear that minority cultures have not vanished. This suggests that Britain might become a truly *multicultural* society in which different ethnic traditions co-exist peacefully and share certain customs.

Black generations

Modood et al. (1994) interviewed a sample of African-Caribbean people living in Birmingham in order to chart changes in their culture over time. The researchers did not discover one single Black identity, but they detected the general and continuing influence of Caribbean cultural traditions. At the same time, there were some differences between the generations. Religious faith (mainly Christian, and especially Pentecostal) still played an important role for the first generation but it had declined among their children. Patois was not used so much by the first generation but it had enjoyed a resurgence among some of the second generation who saw it as a powerful way of asserting their cultural identity. The main identity among the Caribbeans in the survey was Black – although the first generation sometimes described themselves as West Indian, and their children sometimes called themselves Afro-Caribbean. Young Blacks sometimes put on a defiant display of their ethnic identities as a way of expressing their resistance to racism.

Asians between two cultures

Second or third generation Asians, born or raised in this country, are sometimes portrayed as torn between two cultures – the ethnic traditions of their parents, and British mainstream culture. Sometimes compromises are struck. For example, parents may consult their children over arranged marriages and this helps to prevent conflicts. Others may find that their attempts to balance the two cultures are frustrated by racism in the wider society. They may feel they are never going to be accepted by White society and so they may turn back to their ethnic minority traditions.

Cultural navigation Roger Ballard (1994) believes the supposed conflict between Asian teenagers and their parents has been exaggerated. Ballard recognises that there are some major differences between Asian and mainstream cultures but he found that young Asians manage to navigate between them with relative ease. They simply switch codes – in their parents' home they fit in to Asian cultural expectations, but outside the home they blend into mainstream lifestyles. Of course, being teenagers, sometimes there is friction with their parents. But for the most part young Asians handle the two cultures with few problems.

Living apart together Mirza et al. (2007) conducted a large survey among Muslims living in Britain. They found that the majority of Muslims are well integrated into British society – they live 'together' with non-Muslims. Most of them want to live under British law rather than Islamic (Sharia) law. Generally they prefer mixed state schools rather than faith schools. Many of them feel British and have strong relationships with non-Muslims. Also, many declare that religion plays little part in their lives – many indulge in secular habits such as drinking and pre-marital sexual relationships.

On the other hand, they also live 'apart' to some extent, and this applies especially to young Muslims. Those aged 16-24 were more likely than their parents to say religion was the most important thing in their lives, and more likely to support Sharia law and Islamic schools. Among young Muslims, 74% supported the wearing of veils, compared with only 28% of their parents' generation. Mirza et al. point out the irony – although young Muslims are integrated into British society and have grown up in its culture, they are more conscious than their parents of their difference and separateness.

Hybrid identities

It is difficult to map where one culture ends and another begins. Ethnic cultures change over time and they borrow from one another. So their boundaries are always shifting. One possibility is that people combine different ethnic styles in novel ways. When they do this they create *hybrid* (mixed) lifestyles and identities.

Youth Les Back (1996) found that new hybrid identities were emerging among young people (Whites, Asians, Blacks) in two council estates in South London. These young people are in a transitional stage where they have a great deal of freedom and opportunity to construct new identities. Their cultures are not fixed traditions which they slavishly follow. Rather, they try out new cultural 'masks', experiment with new roles, and play with different styles, meanings and symbols in all sorts of unexpected ways. Back found a great deal of inter-racial friendship and interaction and a great deal of cultural borrowing from other groups (eg, 'cool' language and interest in reggae, soul, hip hop, rap and house). The new identities which were being forged brought Black and White people closer together and helped to blur the divisive lines of race.

Changing ethnic identities – conclusion

When members of ethnic minorities start changing their habits and values, it is not always easy to decide what this means. It may be a step towards assimilation – becoming

activity20 hybrid identities

Item A Joined up cultures

Panjabi MC. His music is a fusion of bhangra and hip hop.

question

In what way do these items represent 'hybrid' identities?

Item B I am me

Salima Dhalla: I don't know how to start to describe myself. I feel identity-less but very unique. On paper I'm 'Asian' but in my head I'm a cocky little person with lots of hopes and ambitions.

My parents are East African, their parents are Indian, I was born in Wales. I went to a White middle-class girls' private school and I have brown skin, short Western hair, Western clothes, Eastern name, Western friends. So I guess I'm in an identity wasteland. Now I will only agree to being *me*.

Source: Kassam, 1997

Item C Blinglish

Surveys have revealed that an increasing number of White youths now talk with a Jamaican patois or hybrid language – 'Blinglish' (a term which suggests the marriage of English to Black street culture's love of displays of wealth, known as 'bling'). The days when popular culture was controlled by White artists have faded. Black youth have a huge influence on mainstream culture.

One of the main reasons White youth follow Black culture is an absence of any credible alternative subculture.

Source: Doward, 2004

part of mainstream culture and society. On the other hand, it may just be a normal development of that ethnic culture (cultures are always changing, however slowly).

The only thing that is clear at the moment is that there is a mixture of continuity and change. There is continuity in the sense that ethnic traditions still mean something to second and third generation members of minority groups. But there are also signs of change. One example is arranged marriages – now subject to much greater consultation with young people.

It is young people who are at the forefront of these changes. And it is among this group that new hybrid forms are most likely to emerge.

key terms

Assimilation The process by which ethnic minorities adopt the mainstream culture and become part of mainstream society.
Black A term sometimes applied to people of African-Caribbean descent, and more generally to people seen to be of 'Black' African origin.
Ethnic group A group with a shared culture based on a sense of common origin.
Hybrid identities Identities which draw on two or more ethnic traditions.
Multicultural society The co-existence of two or more distinctive ethnic groups within one society.
Racism Negative attitudes and discriminatory behaviour towards people of other racial or ethnic groups.

summary

1. Minority ethnic groups in Britain were initially formed through migration from the New Commonwealth. But growing numbers (second and third generation) have been born in Britain.

2. Minority ethnic groups share many values and lifestyles with the White majority. There is a great deal of overlap. But they also have their own distinctive traditions.

3. Not everyone within an ethnic group expresses that ethnicity in exactly the same way. Besides, their identity is based not only on their ethnicity but also on other factors such as gender, age and social class.

4. Ethnic minority cultures and identities are slowly changing. This may represent a normal development of the culture rather than a step towards assimilation. Nevertheless, the divisions between cultures seem to be getting more blurred.

5. Some young people seem to be skilled at navigation between two cultures. But others find it a strain and prefer to give priority to one culture. Yet another possibility is the development of hybrid forms that mix cultural traditions in novel ways.

Unit 7 National and global identities

keyissues

1 What are nation states?

2 How are national identities formed?

3 What forms does nationalism take?

4 How is globalisation affecting national identity?

7.1 Creating nations

Nation states

The world is divided into a number of countries such as Britain, France, Nigeria and Mexico. Most of these countries can also be referred to as *nation states*. A state is an independent self-governing geographical area. The term nation state suggests that the people living within the state are a single 'nation', united by a common identity and a common culture.

However, this is not always the case. A single state might contain a number of nations (eg, the British state governs the nations of Wales, Scotland and England). On the other hand, a single nation might be scattered across different states (eg, Kurds in Iran, Iraq and Turkey). Nevertheless, states usually attempt to create an overall sense of national identity in order to secure the loyalty of their populations.

Many people assume that nation states have existed throughout history. However, Michael Mann (1986) shows that it was only in the seventeenth and eighteenth centuries that maps started to represent the world in terms of separate territories with clearly marked borders. Before then, maps of medieval Europe had only fuzzy and shifting frontiers and it was not always easy to identify a single power in control of a clear-cut territory.

National identity

People become aware of their national identity in lots of ways. Stuart Hall (1992) points out that every nation has a collection of stories about its shared experiences, sorrows, triumphs and disasters. These stories are told in the nation's proud boasts (its democratic traditions, traditions of independence and freedom), its collective memories (the World Wars, 1966 World Cup victory) and its favourite images (England's 'green and pleasant land', cream teas). People draw on these stories in order to construct their sense of national identity.

People are constantly reminded of their national identity by symbols and rituals. Symbols include flags, coins, anthems, uniforms, monuments and ceremonies. The national flag is a powerful symbol of the identity of a nation – it separates those who belong (the 'nation') from outsiders ('foreigners'). Public rituals like Remembrance Day and royal ceremonies are occasions when people are invited to reflect on their shared history and collective identity.

Nevertheless, it is difficult to describe a particular national identity with any confidence. People may disagree on what qualifies someone for membership of the nation (see Table 3). They also disagree on the nation's chief features. Besides, a national identity will alter as the nation itself changes over time.

Table 3 What is the basis of national identity?

Born in country	79
Have citizenship	86
Lived most of life there	76
Able to speak language	88
Religion	34
Respect political institutions and laws	87
Feels British	78

(% of sample saying 'very' or 'fairly' important)

Source: McCrone & Surridge, 1998

Britishness

Identity and belonging became major issues in Britain in the early part of this century. One reason for this was the terrorist threat and the July 2005 bombings in London. There were added fears that the security threat within Britain may have led to a rise in Islamophobia - hostility towards Muslims. The British government responded to these tensions by reviewing its multicultural policies

Sleepwalking into segregation? In a speech in 2005, Trevor Phillips, head of the Commission for Racial Equality, warned that Britain was in danger of 'sleepwalking into segregation'. He feared that Britain's various ethnic groups were drifting further apart – for example, young people from ethnic minorities were less integrated than their parents. A similar view was expressed by Ted Cantle (2005) who described Asians and Whites as leading 'parallel lives' – separate existences. Cantle saw this as a major cause of the violence which broke out in some towns in the north of England in 2001.

Community cohesion Policies are being developed in an attempt to create a more cohesive British identity. This does not mean that ethnic minority groups are expected to abandon all their cultural traditions. But the state is trying to create some over-arching loyalties and shared identities – a social 'glue' to bind Britain's diverse groups together (a 'community of communities'). For example, it has introduced 'citizenship education' in schools, and 'citizenship tests' for those applying to become British citizens.

activity21 flying the flag

Item B Ing-land

Nash Patel flies the St George's Cross flag in his shop and refers proudly to the England football team as 'we'. Yet he is not the stereotypical English football fan. His background is Asian, and England is his adopted country, not his homeland. He refers to the team as 'Ing-land', not the more belligerent terrace chant of 'Ing-er-land'. For Patel, the St George's Cross is now his flag and an expression of pride. He explains 'It's my way of saying thank you to England for making me and my family welcome, giving us an education and letting us make a new life here. I'm a British-Asian now'.

Yet elsewhere a battle is going on for 'ownership' of the flag. Is it a positive statement of identity? Or a reflection of an English nationalism stuck somewhere in the bad old days of racism and violence?

Source: *The Observer*, 28.05.2006

Item B Celebrating

Christine Ohuruogu celebrates with the English flag after winning the women's 400 metres title at the Commonwealth Games in 2006.

question

What do these items suggest about community cohesion?

This attempt to build a sense of pride in Britishness is highly controversial. How do we define Britishness? By its customs (eating fish and chips, watching football)? By its social institutions (Parliament, monarchy, the rule of law)? By a set of values (tolerance, democracy, freedom of speech)? Or is it a matter of full citizenship (eg human rights, equality of men and women)? However we define it, some critics argue that it is not something which can be imposed on people – the sense of belonging needs to grow naturally over time.

National cultures

Each nation tends to be associated with a distinctive culture. The Japanese, for example, have a reputation for politeness and group conformity. But descriptions of national cultures are often based on crude stereotypes which seize on a few characteristics and then exaggerate them. They not only ignore the cultural similarities *between* countries, they also conceal the cultural variations which nearly always exist *within* every country.

For example, Bowie (1993) notes that outsiders generally view Wales in terms of broad stereotypes – the Eisteddfod, Welsh hats and shawls, rugby, male voice choirs. To the outsider, Wales may appear to have a firm sense of identity and a uniform culture. But in actual fact there are major cultural divisions between Welsh and non-Welsh speakers, between north and south, and between industrial and rural

activity22 Englishness

Unspoken rules

Englishness consists of a set of values, outlooks and unspoken rules (when these are broken, it provokes comment).

- Incompetence and lack of ease in social encounters.
- The high value we attach to humour (we joke about everything).
- Desire for order (queuing etc).
- Over-politeness and courtesy (we're always saying sorry!)
- A down-to-earth and matter-of-fact attitude.
- We enjoy moaning and grumbling (this creates social bonding).
- Our class-consciousness.
- A sense of fair play.
- A sense of modesty and self-mockery (we dislike boasting).

Source: Fox, 2005

question

To what extent do you think this list successfully defines Englishness?

areas. Most so-called nations are actually cultural 'hybrids' that contain a mixture of ethnic and cultural groups.

Traditional images National cultures change over time. For example, the traditional image of Scotland is one of Rabbie Burns, whisky, the kilt and bagpipes. But a more up-to-date version might include oil rigs, the new Scottish Parliament, 'silicon glens' (hi-tech computer industries), and Billy Connolly. So the past is not always a reliable guide to the present. Nevertheless, the traditional images and symbols often remain real and meaningful to many people.

Creating nations – conclusion

Most nation states actually contain a mix of cultural groups. This is true of Britain, with the Celtic nations (Scotland, Wales) claiming a different identity from the English one.

Describing a national culture or national identity is a difficult task – there are so many things to choose from, and people will have differing views on the best 'markers'. Besides, national cultures change over time and so the declared identity will be a blend of the past and the present.

Politicians agree that Britain is a multicultural society but they also wish to integrate Britain's ethnic minorities within an over-arching 'British' identity. However, there is little agreement on what defines 'Britishness'.

7.2 Nationalism

Nationalism is a political doctrine that claims the right of every nation to have its own historical homeland and an independent state to run its own affairs. In today's world, nationalism has gained a rather nasty reputation. It can be a divisive force which pitches nations against each other, leading to conflict and violence. One example is the long and violent struggle over land between Israeli Jews and Palestinians. But nationalism can also take less dramatic 'everyday' forms.

Everyday nationalism Nationalism penetrates into the everyday life and outlook of people in societies such as Britain. Billig (1995) calls this *banal nationalism*. It is a set of taken-for-granted assumptions (eg, that nations should be independent, that loyalty to the nation is a good thing). People are constantly reminded of their national identity in lots of subtle ways. Billig lists as examples such things as weather reports (focusing on the nation's weather) and sports coverage (the nation competing against other nations). We are gently reminded of our national identity even by minor details such as the Union flag fluttering in the forecourt of a petrol station. Politicians constantly talk about 'us', 'the nation' in their speeches.

Nationalism and Britain

Over the last decade or so, nationalist parties have enjoyed increasing popularity in Scotland and Wales. This resurgence of nationalist feelings has led to some devolution of powers (a Parliament in Scotland, an Assembly in Wales). Some commentators fear this is a step towards the eventual break-up of Britain. However, others have welcomed the opportunity this presents for a fuller expression of purely English nationalism. For example, the flag of St George is now rivalling the Union flag in popularity at international football matches.

Another possible threat to British national identity comes from membership of the European Union. Some politicians are glad that Britain is shaking off its island mentality and reaching out to other parts of Europe. But others are fearful that Britain will lose its sense of national identity as well as its powers to make its own political and economic decisions.

Nationalist attitudes

A survey by Dowds and Young (1996) revealed interesting variations in nationalist sentiments. The majority of their sample (English, Scots, Welsh) had a fairly well-developed attachment to a British identity. These people declared their patriotic pride in Britain's cultural heritage and national institutions and they expressed confidence in the future of the nation. But a smaller number of people seemed relatively unmoved by the symbols of nation and these were classified as having 'low' nationalist sentiments.

The survey also identified a further division between two kinds of orientation – *inclusive nationalism* and *exclusive nationalism*.

Inclusive nationalism People in this category had no wish to draw tight boundaries around membership of the British nation. They show a generous willingness to include certain 'marginal' groups (eg, immigrants, ethnic minorities) as part of the national community and grant them full civic rights.

Exclusive nationalism In contrast, people in this group place stronger emphasis on maintaining tight national boundaries by excluding immigrants and ethnic minorities. They displayed a rather mean-minded hatred of 'foreigners' and an intense dislike for European 'interference' in British political and economic affairs. Dowds and Young's findings suggest this is a minority view.

Nationalism – conclusion

It is difficult to escape pressures to adopt nationalist sentiments. As Billig points out, they constantly intrude into our everyday lives. In many ways this is legitimate and innocent. After all, every state is entitled to expect the loyalty of its citizens. Also, it is easy to understand why many of us develop a sense of patriotism and an affection for our country and fellow citizens.

More intense forms of nationalism – the 'exclusive' kind – are another matter. They can involve an irrational hatred of external 'foreigners' and an intense resentment of ethnic minorities living in Britain. But the research by Dowds and Young suggests only a small proportion of people take this view.

activity23 views of nationalism

Item A Fanfare for Britain

We are blessed that we are an island. In the past the sea has protected us from rabid dogs, foreign dictatorship and our Continental neighbours, who are very different from us. We have a long and mature tradition of freedom and democracy.

Sadly, the Channel no longer protects us from Brussels' bureaucrats. The European Union is trying to merge us into a Continental culture. Even our heritage of country sports is being threatened. Also, our gentle nationalism has been threatened by large waves of immigrants who resist absorption and try to superimpose their cultures and laws upon us.

But nationality is deeply rooted in ties of blood, family, language and religion. It is time we learned to be an island again.

Source: N. Tebbit, 1990

Christchurch Infants School

questions

1 State why the view expressed in Item A is an example of exclusive nationalism.
2 Explain why Item B seems to display a spirit of inclusive nationalism.

In recent years, nationalist sentiments have been re-awakened by two major developments – devolution within Britain itself (the so-called 'break-up' of Britain) and moves towards a more integrated European Union. Some commentators claim that one result of this is the strengthening of English identity. Nevertheless, in surveys many people still claim a British identity.

7.3 Globalisation

National identity may be under threat from *globalisation*. Globalisation is the term used to describe the process whereby nations are coming closer together culturally and economically. Interaction between nations becomes more frequent and intense as goods, capital, people, knowledge, culture, fashions and beliefs flow across territorial boundaries.

The process of globalisation has speeded up in recent decades with the spread of markets and the growth of global communications networks. The nation states of the world seem to be losing their independence as they become locked into global networks (eg, the world trading system) and over-arching political units (eg, the European Union).

National cultures Globalisation is a complex process and its impact can vary. Most nations have a long history of cultural exchange, and this has not yet wiped out national differences.

In some cases there may be a trend to cultural uniformity. Much of this is due to the United States which has popularised such things as Coca Cola, baseball hats, trainers and jeans. Global influences also spread from the East – examples include Indian food, Chinese martial arts and Buddhist spiritualism.

In other cases, hybrid forms may emerge from the mixing of cultures. This is called *glocalisation* – the process by which 'local' and 'global' cultures interact to produce new forms. For example, Giulianotti and Robertson (2006) describe the ways in which Scots who emigrate to North America hold on to many 'local' Scottish traditions and identities. At the same time, their new 'global' situation means they have to adapt these local customs to suit their new context. For instance, Celtic and Rangers supporters become much more friendly towards each other!

Sometimes there is a resistance to global influences – a French farmer won fame by bulldozing a branch of McDonald's in protest at the introduction of 'fast food' chains into French society. But resistance is not always successful – Paris EuroDisney was built in spite of fierce protests about the 'Hollywoodisation' of French life.

Globalisation – conclusion

If some globalisation theorists are correct, a spreading global culture (with a heavy United States influence) may replace national cultures. Instead of national identities, people may become 'citizens of the world'.

activity24 a small world

Item A McDonald's

The world's largest McDonald's - Beijing, China

Jakarta, Indonesia

question

In what ways do Items A and B reflect the influence of globalisation?

Item B The American dream

My children dress like Americans, talk like Americans, behave like Americans. In their imaginations, their dreams and their souls, America is where they think they are. This is strange, because all three of my children were born in England and have lived here all their lives. Yet they dress like Harlem Blacks, with baseball caps worn backward, baggy jeans and hooded tops. They ghetto-blast rap music, breakdance, moonwalk. They watch American TV shows end-to-end and are fluent in American slang.

When we go to the local cinema, everybody in the audience seems to wear US gear and queue for popcorn, Coke, hamburgers and 26 flavours of ice cream. Afterwards we have a Big Mac with french fries.

Source: Hill, 1995

However, globalisation theorists have been accused of exaggeration. Nation states are still important, even if they are increasingly locked into larger units such as the European Union. Most people still have a sense of national identity, even if there is greater movement between countries. Eating Chinese food is not the same thing as being Chinese.

Most experts recognise that globalisation is a complex process and it does not lead inevitably to a single world culture or identity. Differences in national cultures and identities are still clearly visible in the present-day world. But globalisation theorists are right to point out that many of these differences have been shrinking.

key terms

Nation A population assumed to have a shared identity and culture based on their common descent and historical homeland.
Nation state A territory run by a sovereign government and based mainly (but not solely) on a single nation.
Nationalism A movement or doctrine which stresses the rights to freedom and territory of a nation.
State Public institutions with legal powers over a given territory and a monopoly of the legitimate use of force.
Globalisation The process by which the various countries and cultures of the world become more closely intertwined.
Glocalisation The process by which local and global cultures interact to produce new forms.

summary

1. Nation states have become an established part of the world order. Some of these so-called nation states are actually 'hybrids' and contain a mix of cultural groups within the frontiers of the state.

2. National cultures have some broad distinguishing characteristics. But they usually have a number of internal divisions (they contain different subcultures). They also have many similarities with other national cultures (eg, nations frequently exchange customs, food and dress fashions with one another). Moreover, they change over time (there are differences between the 'traditional' culture and the present-day culture).

3. National identities are created through 'official' channels (eg, flags, ceremonies) and unofficial channels (eg, stories people tell about their nation).

4. 'Britishness' can be defined in many different ways. However, it is clear that politicians are keen to integrate Britain's diverse communities within an overall British identity.

5. Nationalism as a political doctrine attempts to achieve sovereignty for the nation. In Britain, this has led to some devolution for Wales and Scotland.

6. In an everyday sense, nationalism expresses itself in attachment to the nation and its citizens. For many people this takes the form of inclusive nationalism but for a smaller number it leads to exclusive nationalism.

7. Globalisation theorists claim we are moving towards a more interconnected world. National cultures are not sealed off to the same extent, and ideas, values and lifestyles freely flow across frontiers.

8. Globalisation has implications for national identities. The distinctiveness of these identities is becoming eroded under the impact of global exchanges.

Unit 8 Gender identities

key issues

1 What is the difference between sex and gender?

2 How are gender identities formed?

3 Are gender identities changing?

8.1 Sex and gender

As soon as a baby is born the first question we ask is whether it is a boy or a girl. We do this because we see males and females as having different 'natures' and so we assume they will have different identities and destinies. However, sociologists challenge these commonsense assumptions. They claim that many of the differences between men and women are not natural but created by society. We can see this more clearly if we make a distinction between sex and gender.

Sex This refers to the physical and biological differences between males and females. They have different genes, hormones, genitals and secondary sexual characteristics (breasts, hairiness of body and so on). Because sex is a matter of biology, it is usually regarded as something that is more or less fixed.

Gender This refers to the cultural expectations attached to a person's sex. In modern Britain, for example, women are seen as sensitive and caring and therefore more suited to the supposedly feminine tasks of childcare. Many of these gender assumptions are highly exaggerated and stereotypical – see Table 4. But they do have an influence on our expectations and perceptions.

Sexuality Sexual behaviour offers clear examples of different cultural expectations of males and females. It is commonly assumed that males and females have different sexual personalities (women more interested in love, men more interested in sex). Also, men and women are given different sexual 'scripts' to act out – the man does the chasing, the woman is the passive sex-object. There is also a sexual double-standard – sexual promiscuity can enhance a man's reputation but it may earn a woman an undesirable reputation as a 'slag' (Lees, 1986).

Table 4 **Gender stereotypes**	
Feminine	**Masculine**
affectionate	undemonstrative
tender	aggressive
childlike	ambitious
soft spoken	assertive
shy	confident
cooperative	competitive
gentle	dominant

Source: Archer & Lloyd, 1985

Biology or society?

Where do gender differences come from? Are they the result of biological differences – the biological determinist view? Or are they created by society – the social constructionist view?

Biological determinism This approach believes gender is based on nature. The genetic differences between males and females create natural differences in their attitudes and abilities and this explains why they end up in different social roles. For example, Steven Goldberg (1977) argues that males have an inbuilt 'dominance tendency' and this is why they tend to occupy the top roles in society.

Social constructionism This approach argues that gender is based on 'nurture' – socialisation and social environment. Each society creates its own set of gender expectations and steers men and women in the chosen directions. Gender differences cannot be genetically programmed since there are wide variations in masculine and feminine behaviour between societies and over time.

Margaret Mead (1935) showed the cultural flexibility of gender in her famous study of three New Guinea tribes (New Guinea is a set of islands in the Pacific Ocean). Among the Arapesh both sexes were gentle and submissive ('feminine'). Among the Mundugamor both sexes were aggressive, rough and competitive ('masculine'). And among the Tchambuli the gender roles seemed the reverse of Western stereotypes (women made the sexual advances, and men enjoyed a good gossip!).

Mead perhaps over-stated her case – no other study has produced such startling results – but she certainly showed that gender differences are at least to some extent a matter of cultural *choice*.

Sex and gender – conclusion

Reasons for the differences between men and women are a matter of dispute. It is not easy to specify the relative importance of biology and society in accounting for differences in the behaviour of men and women.

Nevertheless, the distinction between sex and gender helps us to see that biological differences do not have a direct effect on social roles. Societies have a wide degree of freedom to choose gender characteristics and gender roles. Variations from society to society show that these differences are, at least to some degree, a matter of socialisation.

8.2 Gender socialisation

Agents of socialisation

Males and females learn their gender identities and roles from a variety of agents of socialisation.

Parents Children are steered towards gender roles and identities by their parents. Parents use different terms of endearment for boys and girls ('my brave soldier', 'my little princess'). They dress boys and girls differently (blue for boys, pink for girls). They *channel* their children's energies in particular directions by giving them different toys – guns for boys, dolls for girls. They *manipulate* their children by encouraging different types of activity – boys can be boisterous but girls should be sweet (Oakley, 1972). Young

activity25 gender, biology and culture

Item A The Tchambuli

The women go around with shaven heads, unadorned, determinedly busy about their affairs. Adult males in Tchambuli society are skittish (highly strung and fickle), wary of each other, interested in art, in the theatre, in a thousand petty bits of insult and gossip. The men wear lovely ornaments, they do the shopping, they carve and paint and dance. Men whose hair is long enough wear curls, and the others make false curls out of rattan rings.

Source: Mead, 1962

Item B Looking good

Men from New Guinea in traditional dress

question

What do these items tell us about the nature/nurture debate?

children also observe gender differences inside the home (mother tends to do most of the housework and cooking).

School Studies suggest that by the time children start school they have already picked up gender stereotypes from home, peer groups and mass media. Even at this early age, they may be keenly aware of gender differences between boys and girls. Sometimes they protest when they see other children behaving out of 'character' – they will laugh at a boy who plays with dolls, or get angry when girls play with 'boys' toys'.

Some of these attitudes may be reinforced by their experiences in school. Certainly this is the view of Christine Skelton (2002), based on her study of Benwood Primary School. She describes the various ways in which gender stereotypes were created and maintained in Benwood.

At school assembly it was the men teachers who would be called upon by the headteacher to move equipment or lead the singing. Teachers who could not recall a boy's name would refer to 'you' or 'that boy', or if it was a girl, 'darling' or 'sweetheart'. Posters and artwork on the walls of the school showed boys being active and naughty but girls being passive and good. Also, teachers read stories that encouraged boys to be 'masculine' heroes. In the school football team, boys were taught how to be 'manly' and how to use an 'acceptable' level of physical violence.

Masculinity and femininity

Hegemonic masculinity Boys tend to be socialised into a style of masculinity which stresses toughness, competition, hierarchy and aggression. This style is called *hegemonic* (dominant) because it crowds out other masculine styles such as artistic and gay masculine identities (Connell, 1995). Young men are put under great pressure to present themselves as hard, strong and independent. So they soon learn to conceal any 'girly' signs of gentleness, kindness and vulnerability.

Swots Emma Renold (2001) demonstrated the power of hegemonic masculinity in her study of boys in their final year of primary school. She argues that some boys construct alternative masculinities – gentle, academic, artistic and non-sporting. But boys who are studious or academic find out very quickly that this conflicts with the hegemonic form of masculinity. They risk being teased and ridiculed for being swots, geeks, nerds and squares rather than 'real' boys. So, although they continue to study hard, they learn to adopt strategies to avoid being seen as feminine. For example, they play down their academic success, they join in the teasing and bullying of other studious boys, and they sometimes behave badly in order to disguise their positive attitude towards study. They also ridicule girls who are seen as too academic, and boys with poor sporting skills.

activity26 girls and boys

Item A   Dating advice

The following advice was provided in the *Tatler* magazine:

> **It is important to remember that girls and boys are not remotely alike. So here are some dating do's and don'ts to guide you:**
>
> ***For girls:***
> Never pretend to know anything about football, even if you do. Balls are strictly boys' territory.
>
> Boys are shy little creatures. Laughing at their jokes is sure to bring them out of their shells. Laughing at their dancing will not.
>
> Remember that girls cannot drink as much as boys. So don't try to keep up with them (it's part of their game plan).
>
> ***For boys:***
> Learn to listen to girls. They're invariably much brighter than boys.
>
> The words 'I love you' are taken very seriously by girls. Avoid bandying them about.
>
> Very few girls are funny. They probably know this, so huge guffaws every time she opens her mouth will only annoy her.

Item B   The football match

question

How do the items illustrate the process of gender socialisation?

Looking right One of the ways a girl expresses her feminine identity is through her appearance. The importance of appearance is described by Sue Lees (1993) in her study of female teenagers in London schools. These girls put great stress on looking right. Lees argues that this is not a natural feminine thing, neither is it a sign of vanity. Rather, it is something girls are forced into in order to show they are 'good' girls rather than 'slags'. The girls she spoke to feared that if they dressed in too 'loose' or 'sexy' a fashion their reputations would be destroyed. So they learn to dress and move in an 'appropriate' way.

According to Lees, a girl is taught that her appearance is crucial to her identity. She learns that her body must be controlled and disciplined. Girls must act modestly, sit with their legs firmly together rather than spread out, and avoid eye contact with any man they meet in the street. They are taught that they should not take up too much space or talk too much.

Feminism The basic assumption shared by feminists is that the gender divisions in society operate to the disadvantage of women. The process of gender socialisation usually encourages traditional gender roles which reinforce and justify male dominance.

But if gender differences are socially constructed then they can be changed. Feminists have shown that many of the so-called natural differences between men and women are simply not true. Women are perfectly capable of building a successful career, and men are perfectly capable of housework – if they try. Therefore feminists have helped transform many of our assumptions about gender. For example, young women nowadays are no longer socialised into thinking that their future consists solely of marriage and children.

Gender socialisation – conclusion

Some experts say that gender differences are so natural that they are bound to emerge in any society. That may or may not be the case. But we can see clearly that most societies help them on their way – they encourage gender differences. They do this through the process of socialisation.

Boys and girls are participants in this learning process and they take an active part in constructing their particular

activity27 real women

Item A Snow White

I WISH SHE'D JUST GO BACK TO THE HOUSEWORK...

Item B Changing attitudes

Percentages disagreeing with the statement: 'A husband's job is to earn the money; a wife's job is to look after the home and the children'.

	1984	1994
Men	34	57
Women	41	61
Employed women	59	77

Adapted from British Social Attitudes surveys

question

What do the items tell us about changes in attitudes to gender?

identities. But they have to do this against a background where certain forms of masculinity and femininity are dominant and others are subordinate. Hegemonic masculinity makes it difficult for boys to forge alternative masculine identities.

Feminists believe that men have greater power and arrange society in a way that suits them. But feminists have challenged this male power in recent decades.

8.3 Changing identities

Gender roles and identities change over time. For example, in the past a woman's place was thought to be firmly in the home. But nowadays more and more women are building careers. This inevitably has an effect on how they see themselves and how they are seen by others. It also reminds us that gender identities can overlap, with men and women adopting similar attitudes and lifestyles. Nowadays, for example, young women are sometimes accused of behaving just as 'badly' as young men.

Behaving badly

One sign that the gender divide may be slowly disappearing is the similarity in the behaviour of 'lads' and 'ladettes'.

Lads Masculinity is something which varies over time. In the 1980s, for example, some claimed that 'New Men' were appearing in Britain. The New Man was a non-sexist, non-aggressive male who was sensitive and considerate, sharing and caring. But in the 1990s this sensitive type was upstaged by the rising popularity of yobbish 'lads'. It became fashionable once again for young men to have a good time through sex, lager, football and loutish behaviour. Some journalists dubbed this new style 'lad culture'. It was celebrated in television programmes such as *Men Behaving Badly* and in men's magazines such as *Loaded*. Its heroes (role models) were football stars or rock stars who behaved in outrageous ways.

Ladettes Today, there is a female counterpart to the lad – the 'ladette'. Following in the wake of the lads, the ladette seems equally willing to booze, swear and indulge her sexual appetites. As ladette culture has spread, new female role models have appeared in the media and they attract a huge following. They are admired for their sassy, don't-give-a-damn attitude and their readiness to compete on equal terms with the lads. Their cultural values are celebrated in magazines like *Cosmopolitan*. Judging by the similar values of lads and ladettes, the gender gap seems to be closing.

However, the extent to which lads and ladettes represent an accurate picture of young people today is open to question. Many see these terms as being used by the media to attract interest rather than accurate descriptions of social change.

Fashion victims

Another area where gender differences seem to be converging is fashion. Traditionally, concern with fashion and personal appearance was seen as the province of women. 'Real' men, by contrast, were careless about how they looked or simply followed convention. However, this is changing.

New masculinities David Abbott (2000) provides a useful overview of men's growing interest in fashion and grooming. Drawing on the work of writers like Frank Mort and Sean Nixon, he describes big shifts in the fashion styles of young men over recent decades. It seems they are taking a keener interest in their clothes, hair and personal appearance. They are growing more confident about expressing themselves through the way they dress and groom (eg, use of aftershave, male perfumes, hair gel, even make-up). Nowadays, they are learning to get pleasure from what was traditionally seen as a feminine preoccupation with personal image. Their identities increasingly revolve around their dress sense, their body image and the right look.

Crisis of masculinity

Not all men are motivated by fashion and style. Heavy manual work such as mining or shipbuilding provided some working-class men with a strong sense of male pride. Now these sorts of jobs are disappearing. New jobs tend to be based around computers and telecommunications and are often taken by women. In education, they see girls' achievement outpacing boys at every age. Mac an Ghaill (1994) describes the insecurity faced by these men as a 'crisis of masculinity'. Their traditional masculine identity is no longer relevant yet they are not comfortable with alternative male identities. Men may respond to this 'crisis' in a number of ways including becoming depressed, fatalistic (giving up), turning to crime, or by adopting new identities.

'The Full Monty': redundant steelworkers practising for their new career as strippers – an unusual way of responding to the crisis of masculinity!

Freedom's children

Helen Wilkinson (1997) refers to research she conducted on a national sample of 18-34 year-olds. This research suggests that the values of this young generation ('freedom's children') are markedly different from those of their parents. There has been a huge shift in values between the generations. Young people nowadays tend to be much more confident and assertive. Although they have to make many difficult decisions, they take it for granted that they can control their own lives and choose their own lifestyles.

Wilkinson was particularly struck by the rising power and confidence of women. They are more willing to take risks, live life 'on the edge', and seek pleasure and fun. Many of them reject the notion of separate spheres for men and women. They have discarded the stereotypes of 'male breadwinners' and 'female homemakers'. Most of them have grown up assuming that sexual equality is their birthright.

Wilkinson believes there has been a growing convergence – coming together – of the values of young men and women. Men's values are becoming more 'feminine' and women's are becoming more 'masculine'. According to her findings, young people are moving away from the old gender stereotypes and roles. Instead, they want to flirt with both their masculine and feminine sides. They value their freedom to choose and their right to express their own individuality.

Changing gender identities – conclusion

Gender differences are becoming blurred as gender identities and lifestyles slowly converge. Many of the differences have been eroded by the impact of feminism, social change and equal opportunities legislation.

There are signs that some gender stereotypes are declining in today's British society. For example, teachers are encouraging young women to plan for a career, not just for marriage and having children.

There is greater flexibility in gender behaviour and both men and women are experimenting with a wider range of gender roles.

However, there is still a long way to go as many gender stereotypes are proving very resistant to change.

key terms

Hegemonic masculinity The dominant style of masculinity which stresses toughness, competition, hierarchy and aggression.
Gender A set of cultural expectations about how males and females should behave.
Sex A classification of males and females according to their biological characteristics.
Sexuality The emotions, desires, attitudes and direction of our sex drive.

*activity*28 *gender games*

Norman on Tuesdays   *Norma on Wednesdays*

Item A *Line dancing*

Norman Horton enjoyed his new hobby of line dancing so much that he decided to go twice a week – once as a man and once as a woman. Mr Horton, aged 58, would set off on Tuesday nights in open-neck shirt, trousers and stetson. But on Wednesdays he transformed himself into Norma, with a frilly blouse, short skirt, gold tights and high heels. A former paratrooper and military policeman, he has been cross-dressing since the age of 12. 'My wife doesn't mind me cross-dressing as long as I don't do it too often and keep it under control.'

Source: *The Guardian*, 17.4.1998

Item B *Bodybuilders*

The top three in the women's bodybuilding world championship, 2002

question

What do the items tell us about changing gender identities?

summary

1. In every society, men and women are expected to behave differently from each other. Biological determinists say this is inevitable because of the biological differences between the sexes. They say men and women have different aptitudes and abilities and so they are suited for different social roles.

2. Social constructionists point out that gender expectations differ from society to society. It is hardly likely, then, that these expectations are rooted in biological differences. Rather, they are the result of socialisation. Societies have considerable choice in deciding which cultural roles they will allocate to men and women.

3. Gender socialisation operates at many levels in society. Parents and schools socialise young children into gender roles, and mass media often reinforce these distinctions.

4. Feminists believe that men benefit from the widespread view that certain tasks (like child-rearing or housework) are naturally the responsibility of women.

5. There are signs that old gender identities are breaking down. They have not vanished altogether but there is some evidence of convergence in male and female identities. At the same time, there is a new flexibility and freedom in the way people express their gender identities.

Unit 9 *Class identities*

keyissues

1 What is social class?

2 How do classes differ in their identities and culture?

3 How is class identity changing?

9.1 Living in a class society

Social class

Income and wealth are unequally distributed across the population of Britain – see Tables 5 and 6. Some groups enjoy high incomes and considerable wealth while others are condemned to poverty. Moreover, this is not a totally random lottery. Your chances of 'winning' or 'losing' depend to a large extent on your social class – your position in the social and economic structure.

Occupation Most sociologists find it convenient to use occupation as a measure of a person's social class. So a *social class* can be viewed as a cluster of occupations

which share a similar economic position. Over the years sociologists have used a variety of occupational classifications to identify social classes. The latest version is the Office of National Statistics (ONS) Social Class Scheme – see Table 7.

Table 6 *Marketable wealth, United Kingdom, 2003*

(stocks and shares, land, homes, savings, possessions etc)

Top 1% of population own 21% of total wealth

Top 5% of population own 72% of total wealth

Top 50% of population own 93% of total wealth

Source: *Social Trends*, 2007, Office for National Statistics

---

Table 7 *Office of National Statistics (ONS) Social Class Scheme*

Class 1	Higher managerial and professional (eg, company directors, lawyers, doctors)
Class 2	Lower managerial/professional (eg, junior managers, social workers, nurses, police sergeants)
Class 3	Intermediate (eg, clerical workers, secretaries, computer operators)
Class 4	Small employers and self-employed (eg, taxi drivers, window cleaners, shopkeepers)
Class 5	Supervisors, craft and related (eg, printers, plumbers, train drivers)
Class 6	Semi-routine (eg, shop assistants, hairdressers, cooks)
Class 7	Routine (eg, waiters, cleaners, labourers)
Class 8	Never worked/long-term unemployed

Source: Office for National Statistics, 2007

Table 5 *Average weekly pay, Great Britain, 2002*

Highest paid	
Treasurers and financial managers	£ 1,234
Medical practitioners	£ 1,159
Solicitors	£ 899
Lowest paid	
Waiters, waitresses	£ 211
Petrol pump attendants	£ 211
Check-out operators	£ 205

Source: Adapted from the *New Earnings Survey*, 2002, Office for National Statistics

activity29 classes apart

Item A Class acts

Opera singer

Greyhound racing at Wimbledon Stadium

Item B Class divisions

A bitter struggle has broken out in Gloucestershire where home owners on a private estate are objecting to an unemployed family of ten moving into a housing association property. Some residents argue they would lower the tone of the neighbourhood. They have signed a petition demanding that the local authority erect a wall to divide the private properties from the rest.

Mrs Monks flicked cigarette ash on the carpet as she said, 'It's bloody snobbery. Those people signing petitions think they're better than us because we ain't working and can't afford to buy a house.'

Mrs Smith, a home-owner, says her objection to the Monks is not personal, just business (it will affect the value of her house). 'Yes, it sounds snooty', she says, 'but I challenge anyone in our position to say they would feel differently.' She added, 'The Monks and us are different types of people. I know some people will think I'm a stuck-up cow, but I've paid for the right to live the way I want to live.'

Source: The Guardian, 22.9.1995

Tina Smith

The Monk family

Item C Chav hunt

A YouTube video shows students at Glenalmond College (an expensive public school) on horseback chasing youths clad in tracksuits and trainers and Burberry caps. Victims are picked off by a shotgun as they run across a field, one of the 'dead' chavs is prodded by a smug-looking aristocrat. In another scene, a cap-wearing chav is hauled from a river like he is a salmon while his hunter pretends to thrash him with a rod. Although the video was probably intended as humour and irony, critics said it came across as brash, crass and arrogant.

Source: Independent Television News, 14.8.2007

question

What do Items A, B and C suggest about class identities and differences?

Class cultures and identities

The narrow view of class is that it is solely a matter of occupation, income and wealth. But class is much wider than money and possessions. When we think of social class we also think of social and cultural features. We see each social class as having its own special identity, its own set of values, its own lifestyles and habits.

Class cultures The French sociologist Pierre Bourdieu (1984) suggests that social classes have their own cultural values, tastes and preferences. This expresses itself in things like their choice of food, music, newspapers and leisure pursuits. Social classes even develop their own ways of walking, talking and eating. They have different attitudes towards the body. For example, working-class people tend to be more tolerant of 'middle-age spread' (putting on weight as they get older) but middle-class professionals are more likely to join fitness programmes in order to keep their bodies trim.

Class identities From an early age we are socialised into the lifestyles and values of the class of our parents. The upbringing of a child in a wealthy detached house in a desirable suburb of London will be very different from that of the child of an unemployed single parent in the council flat half a mile away.

We learn to identify with members of our own social class ('us') and become aware of the differences that separate us from other social classes ('them'). In other words, we become *class conscious*.

9.2 The upper class

The upper class is not listed separately in the ONS scheme. This is partly because it is relatively small – less than 1% of the population according to Kenneth Roberts (2001). But it is also because it is defined by its enormous wealth rather than by the occupations of its members. Britain's upper class enjoys tremendous privileges of wealth and prestige.

The upper class consists of a number of interlocking groups.

- **Landowning aristocrats** These are the 'old' titled families and large landowners. The Duke of Northumberland, for example, owns about 120,000 acres of land as well as a Thames-side mansion and a medieval castle.
- **Entrepreneurs** Nowadays the 'idle rich' are a rare breed. Many of the upper class have gained their wealth from owning or running businesses. Some, such as Richard Branson, are 'self-made' rather than having inherited their wealth.
- **Jet set** The upper class includes a number of people who have made their money in the fields of sport and entertainment. It includes pop stars such as Mick Jagger and Elton John who have knighthoods and mix with aristocracy and royalty.

Upper-class culture and identity

The upper classes share a strong sense of identity. This is because the upper class is 'closed' – its members tend to be the children of upper-class parents. Social closure in the upper class is the result of a shared culture that creates a web of links and contacts. These connections make it difficult for non-members to penetrate the upper class.

The key elements of upper-class culture involve education, family ties and social and leisure activities. According to John Scott (1982), the upper class 'is characterised by a high degree of social cohesion, the main supports of this cohesion being its system of kinship and educational experience'.

Education The children of upper-class families are usually educated in top public schools such as Eton and Harrow and many go on to the most prestigious universities – Oxford and Cambridge. Throughout their education, valuable social contacts are made with each other and with other young people likely to end up in positions of power and influence. These contacts can prove to be extremely helpful later in life – the 'old boy network'. Public schools also socialise their pupils into high levels of self-confidence and an acute sense of their social superiority.

Family, marriage and kinship The exclusive lifestyle and experiences of the upper class mean that its young members tend to socialise with other members of the same class. The result is a tendency for the upper class to intermarry. As time goes on, more and more kinship connections develop between upper-class families.

Social and leisure activities During their socialisation, young members of the upper class are introduced to the exclusive social events that provide a distinctive upper-class lifestyle. Often these are based on old aristocratic traditions and provide a sense of 'real class'. They also provide a circuit where further connections and contacts can be made.

These events include hunting, shooting, Wimbledon (tennis), the Henley Regatta (rowing), Cowes week (sailing), Royal Ascot (horse racing), Glyndebourne (opera) and the Chelsea Flower Show. Together, they provide a clear picture of a distinctive upper-class lifestyle (Roberts, 2001).

However, by no means all of the upper class live a life of glamorous leisure. Chris Rojek (2000) used statistics and biographical data to study the lives of three of the richest men in the world, Bill Gates (owner of Microsoft), Warren Buffett (investor in stocks and shares) and Richard Branson (owner of Virgin). He found that their lives were centred around their work. They worked long hours and, if they did attend exclusive social occasions, used them mainly to make and develop business connections.

Upper-class values

The values of the entrepreneurial upper class centre on their work. Rojek argues that, at least for the seriously wealthy individuals he studied, work is valued as a source of pleasure, fun and excitement.

However, the values of the old aristocratic upper class are based more on the importance of tradition, authority and breeding.

Tradition The old upper class are conservative in their values and politics. They wish to preserve the historical traditions and customs of British society.

Authority A belief in social hierarchy. They think society works best when it is organised into different levels or ranks. People should show proper respect to those in positions of authority.

Breeding and background A 'good' background is seen as a guarantee that someone will have the appropriate attitudes, manners and values.

activity30 upper-class lifestyles

Item A The social circuit

Strawberries and champagne at Royal Ascot

A grouse shoot in Scotland

Item B Richard Branson

Richard Branson in a hot-air balloon over Marrakech

Richard Branson is said to need eight hours sleep but works for the rest of the time. He is well-known for dressing casually and has no expensive tastes in food or drink. He enjoys the excitement of potentially rewarding but risky ventures, as in air and rail transport. He owns a Caribbean island and homes in Oxfordshire and London. Branson is best known for his world record attempts at water-borne trans-Atlantic crossing and long-distance hot-air ballooning. These are extremely expensive and therefore exclusive leisure activities. For Branson, they are brief interruptions in his normal way of life.

Source: Roberts, 2001

questions

1 How is attendance at the sort of events shown in Item A connected to social closure?

2 Compare the lifestyle and values of Richard Branson (Item B) with those of more traditional members of the upper class.

9.3 The middle classes

The term middle classes refers mainly to ONS classes 1 and 2. Sometimes the term is used in a broader way to include all non-manual workers including routine (semi-skilled) white collar workers such as secretaries and office workers. This wider definition would include ONS classes 3 and 4 although the ONS scheme now describes these classes as an 'intermediate' group (presumably somewhere between middle class and working class).

It is very difficult to make general statements about the culture and identity of the middle classes. There are two reasons for this.

The middle class come from diverse backgrounds There has been a spectacular growth in the middle classes – from 30% of the population in 1951 to an estimated 60% by the year 2000. The 'old' middle classes (the established professions and self-employed business people) have been joined by the expanding ranks of public sector professionals (social workers, teachers, civil servants). There has also been a growth in the number of people in office work, sales and personal services.

Many members of today's middle classes have come from working-class backgrounds and many are women. The middle classes – unlike the upper class – are thus very open to 'outsiders' who merely have to achieve reasonably well at school to join their swelling ranks. This means that the social backgrounds of the middle classes are very mixed. They may have little in common with each other, so a shared culture and identity may not be immediately visible.

The middle class includes a wide range of jobs There are large differences in the pay and status of the middle classes. A part-time office worker in a small engineering business has little in common with a top solicitor. A solicitor may earn up to five or six times as much. Yet, if a broad definition of social class is used, both can be placed in the middle classes as both are non-manual occupations.

The diversity of the middle classes means that people in these groups may have little in common, thus making it less likely they will develop a shared culture or identity.

Middle-class culture and lifestyles

Most sociologists have avoided general statements about middle-class culture for the reasons given above. Roberts (2001) is an example, 'The present-day middle classes are distinguished by the fact that there are so many lifestyle variations among them, some related to age, gender, ethnicity and education'.

However, he does argue that the middle classes are characterised by a more active and diverse range of leisure activities than the working class. 'They take more holidays, play more sports, make more visits to theatres and the countryside, and eat out more frequently' (Roberts, 2001).

Fragmentation of middle-class lifestyles Most sociologists suggest that the middle class is broken up or 'fragmented' into different lifestyle groups.

Mike Savage et al. (1992) noted that the middle class is traditionally regarded as respectable and deeply conformist. Yet nowadays, they are often the pioneers of new cultural styles. Savage et al. used survey data to identify three distinctive (but overlapping) middle-class lifestyles.

Postmodern This lifestyle is adopted mainly by artists, advertising executives and 'yuppies'. It combines rather contradictory and diverse interests. They like opera and skiing as well as stock car racing and 'street culture'. They have extravagant, self-indulgent tastes (champagne, expensive restaurants, drug use), but they also follow health and fitness cults (dieting, rigorous exercise).

Ascetic This lifestyle is found mainly among those employed in education, health and welfare. Typically they have high cultural capital – they are confident, well-read and articulate – but modest economic capital – money, wealth, property. They are ascetic in their tastes (their consumption of alcohol is low). Their leisure pursuits tend to be intellectual (classical music) and individualistic (hill walking).

Managerial Managers and government officials tend to be the least distinctive group as far as cultural tastes are concerned. They follow more conventional middle-class activities such as golf or fishing. They are also keen on the countryside and on heritage (they visit National Trust houses and museums).

Middle-class values

Again, these vary according to particular groupings in the middle classes.

Professionals The higher level of this group is made up of doctors, lawyers, architects, accountants and business executives. Nearly all have been to university and place a high value on education, training and independence. Most of the sons of higher professionals end up in similar jobs, suggesting that parents have been successful in passing on the values of hard work and educational achievement (McDonough, 1997).

Teachers, social workers and local government officers are among those who fit into the lower levels of the professions. Those that work in the public sector (employed by local or central government) have shown themselves willing to join with others in collective action (joining trade unions and taking strike action) to defend the welfare state or pursue a pay claim – actions typically associated with the working class.

Roberts (2001) identifies three main values (what he calls 'preoccupations') associated with the professional middle classes.

1 **Service** The middle classes expect a 'service' relationship with their employer. They value trust and responsibility in their work and want to be able to exercise discretion when and where they see fit.

2 **Career** They value the opportunity to gain promotion or to advance a career by changing job. There is a linked concern for the education of their children. The middle classes expect their children to succeed at school and are willing to take any steps necessary to make this happen (private tutors, changing schools, private education).

3 **Meritocracy** This is a belief that positions should be achieved by ability and effort. They are against any form of discrimination and believe that qualifications are very important.

Routine white-collar workers This group are involved in office work but have little freedom and responsibility. The work may involve sitting in front of a computer screen or using a phone all day. Many women work in these jobs and much of the work is part time. Nearly all of it is poorly paid. Some sociologists have gone so far as to suggest these workers should be in the working class and the ONS scale describes them as 'intermediate' (between the middle and working classes).

However, there is little sign that this group hold typical working-class values. Many are not in unions and they do not hold an 'us and them' view of their relationship with their bosses. They see work as a way of improving their quality of life, allowing them to take foreign holidays and buy more consumer goods (McDonough, 1997).

Self-employed and small business owners The middle classes also include entrepreneurs – employers with small and medium sized businesses, and the self-employed. Roberts argues that this group has a distinctive set of values. They are individualistic and proud of it. They believe that people should be independent and stand on their own feet rather than rely on the welfare state. They also place great faith in hard work and discipline – they firmly believe that success in life is a result of effort and application rather than luck.

9.4   The working class

The working class is composed of manual workers (ONS classes 5, 6 and 7). In 1951 this accounted for about 70% of the working population but over the years it has shrunk to under half. Like the middle class, the working class contains a range of occupations which differ in pay, status and power.

Traditional working class

This was the dominant working class type from around the end of the nineteenth century until the 1950s or 1960s. Its culture and values have been lovingly described by writers such as Hoggart (1957) and Young and Willmott (1957). These are some of its key features.

Male breadwinners Men were regarded as the main breadwinners in the family. Many of them worked in heavy and dangerous industries such as mining, steel, shipbuilding and the docks. This bred a form of 'rugged

masculinity' where physical strength and courage were highly valued. Bonds between men were strong and they frequently socialised outside work.

Home The home was often crowded and noisy but it held a special place in people's affections. The burden of housework, cooking and childcare usually fell to women. Many women were full-time housewives, unless poverty forced them to take on part-time jobs.

Family The traditional working class felt marriage was for life and so they disapproved of divorce. The members of the extended family often lived close to one another and there was a lot of visiting, especially among the women.

Community The traditional working class formed close-knit communities where they had large circles of friends and acquaintances. They valued these community bonds. They met one another frequently on the street, in shops and in the local pub, and they took a keen interest in local gossip and affairs.

Class consciousness The traditional working class had a strong class identity. Their identity was sharpened by the experience of working together to improve wages and working conditions. They made a distinction between 'us' (the working class) and 'them' (bosses, the middle class, anyone in authority). They sided with trade unions and the Labour Party.

The 'new' working class

A shift away from 'smokestacks' (large factories employing lots of manual workers) towards 'high-tech' units (employing skilled technicians rather than assembly line workers) has meant that the traditional working class has declined. Sociologists have mapped the resulting changes in working-class culture over the years.

Privatism The working class now live a more private, home-centred life. The old ties of community have been weakened. People increasingly base their life around the home and family activities.

Changing gender roles Britain is hardly a 'unisex' society but the differences in gender roles are now less pronounced among the working class. The old breadwinner/home-minder distinction has largely broken down. Women are much more likely to have jobs and men are much more likely to accept at least some responsibility for housework and childcare tasks.

Materialism Britain's working class has benefited from the general rise in living standards over the past fifty or so years. They are more likely to own homes and cars, spend a lot on consumer goods and enjoy foreign holidays. For many it is no longer a matter of just 'getting by' – they save, plan and invest, just like the middle class.

Social mobility The changing occupational structure of Britain has created greater opportunities for upward mobility into the middle class. So today's working class are less likely to resign themselves or their children to their humble station in life – there is more emphasis on 'getting on' and 'getting

activity31 spot the difference

question

Use the cartoons to spot the differences between the 'traditional' and 'new' working class.

ahead'. Social horizons have widened and they are more ambitious. One effect of this 'ladder of opportunity' may be to weaken class consciousness and class solidarity.

Leisure In the past working-class identity was based around work – the men in the factories or mines, the women in the home. Nowadays, they are more likely to define themselves by their hobbies and recreational activities. Leisure has become a central life interest.

9.5 The underclass

The underclass (ONS class 8) is located at the very bottom of the class pyramid. Its members are so poor and disadvantaged that they are 'under' the normal class structure. They suffer poverty, unemployment, bad housing, ill health and poor educational opportunities. Some sociologists see them as more or less permanently trapped at the bottom. They say children are socialised into this way of life and so the values and lifestyles of the underclass are passed on from one generation to the next (Murray, 1994).

Underclass values Some social scientists claim the underclass are poor or unemployed because of their values and morals – they are often seen as lazy, workshy scroungers. Charles Murray, an American writer, calls them the 'new rabble'. He claims they prefer to live off crime or welfare benefits rather than work. He also accuses them of irresponsible attitudes to parenthood – young women carelessly get pregnant and young men become 'absent fathers' and poor role models for their children. Children who grow up in a household where no-one works are likely to settle into the same lifestyle.

Blaming the victim Many sociologists accuse Murray of unfairly 'blaming the victim'. They say the underclass are not to blame for their social disadvantage. Rather, they have been 'socially excluded' by more powerful groups in society. These powerful groups have adopted policies that create poverty and unemployment. As a result, the underclass has been cut off from the prosperity and opportunities enjoyed by the general population.

The critics of Murray also challenge the idea that the values of the underclass are really so different from the rest of society. They say that most members of the underclass share the same mainstream social values as everyone else (Dean and Taylor-Gooby 1992).

Cause or effect? Even if the underclass has different values, it is not clear what this means. It is possible that their values are the cause of their problems (eg, laziness may lead to unemployment). But it is equally possible that their values are the effect of their disadvantage – if they are constantly denied employment opportunities then they may become apathetic and demoralised. Peter Saunders (1990) indicates how this might happen: 'Inactivity breeds apathy. Empty hours are filled with sleep, and days go by in a dull haze of television programmes and signing on. Sooner or later the unemployed become unemployable.'

Living in a class society – conclusion

Class is a *complex* matter. There is no simple link between class and values. For example, we have seen how certain values (eg, hard work, education) are shared by most social classes. We have also seen how there are different values and lifestyles within each class.

Class is also a *contested* matter – sociologists disagree about it. For example, some sociologists think that routine

activity32 the underclass?

Item A The 'new rabble'

- Low skilled and poorly educated
- Single parent families are the norm
- Depend on welfare benefits and 'moonlighting'
- High levels of crime, child abuse and drug abuse
- Unwilling to get a job
- Children have truancy and discipline problems

Source: Murray, 1994

Item B Murray's view of the underclass

Item C A single parent

Judith Gardam, age 28, single mother who lives on state benefits.

I'm sure if the Government sat down and spoke to me and had a cup of tea with me they'd get to like me. I have learnt about life. I know how to love, I have got compassion, I have feelings for people. But do they have feelings for anybody but themselves? I want something better for the kids and I am attending college part time. But at the moment I feel I am lower than lower class.

Source: Cockburn, 1993

questions

1 Argue the case that the behaviour in Item B is:
   a) caused by the culture and values described in Item A,
   b) creates the culture and values described in Item A.

2 Use Item C to argue that the poorest do not have separate values from the rest of society.

white-collar workers belong to the middle class while others think they are part of the working class. Some believe a distinct underclass exists while others argue that this group is simply the lowest level of the working class.

Also, class culture and values *change* over time. For example, the values of the 'traditional' working class are not the same as those of the 'new' working class.

9.6 A classless society?

A number of sociologists now reject the idea that class is still the dominant force in shaping people's identities. They claim that what matters in contemporary society is no longer class and occupation. Identities are increasingly based on *lifestyle* and *consumption* (Saunders, 1990).

Lifestyles According to Pakulski and Waters (1996), lifestyles are becoming a central organising feature of people's lives and a major source of social and personal identity. These lifestyles are less and less likely to be based on social class.

At one time people tended to follow traditional class-based leisure pursuits. The middle class may have enjoyed golf while the working class were more likely to spend their evening greyhound racing. Nowadays, lifestyles and identities are much more diverse and flexible. They are based on individual choice rather than class background. For example, we might find it difficult to guess the class background of hang-gliders, ballroom dancers or football supporters.

Consumption Another threat to class identities comes from the rise of consumer culture. People may once have built their identities around work and production but nowadays their lives are more likely to be centred on their leisure and the things they spend their money on – their consumption. So identities may no longer be based on how people *earn* their money – a matter of occupation and class – but on how they *spend it* – a matter of consumer lifestyles (Clarke & Saunders, 1991).

Consumer goods are important not so much for themselves as for what they say about the tastes and style of the consumers. People are usually aware that they are making a statement about themselves through their consumption habits. They signal their lifestyles by what they choose to wear, eat, drink, listen to or collect. These consumption choices express and establish their identity.

Answering back

Is it really true that class has become so insignificant? A number of sociologists insist that class is still an important factor in contemporary society. For example, there are still striking inequalities between classes in many areas of life – see Table 8. And these inequalities do not appear to be declining.

Table 8 Class inequalities

Life expectancy People in the top two classes live five years (men) or three years (women) longer than those in the bottom two classes.

Health Among professionals, 17% (men) and 25% (women) report a long-standing illness. Among unskilled workers, the figures are 48% (men) and 45% (women).

Unemployment Unemployment rates are about four times higher among unskilled workers than among professional groups.

Victims of crime In 1995, 4% of affluent (well-off) suburban families were burgled, compared with 10% of families living in council and low-income estates.

Suicide In 1993 in England and Wales, suicide for men was four times greater in the bottom class than in the top class.

Source: Acheson, 1998

Class identity Is it really true that class identities have declined? A survey by Gordon Marshall et al. (1989) found that about 60% of the sample thought of themselves as belonging to a particular social class, and over 90% could place themselves in a class if prompted. These figures suggest that class identities manage to survive in spite of competition from lifestyle and consumer identities. Indeed, Marshall et al. argue that class is the most common and powerful source of social identity. Other identities may have grown in importance but they have not displaced class identities from their central position.

This view is supported by Fiona Devine (1997). After reviewing a wide range of research, she concludes that class is still the most common and significant social identity in Britain. Class identities remain much stronger than identities based on things like shopping tastes or leisure pursuits.

Researching class identity

A survey by Mike Savage et al. (2001) presents a rather more complicated picture. They suggest that class is still an important influence on people's lives and living standards. At the same time, class identities seem to have weakened.

Class out there Savage et al. investigated the class identities of 178 people in the Manchester area. They found that very few of their sample believed Britain was a classless society. Most of them were quite comfortable talking about class 'out there' in society – they were familiar with class terminology and they recognised the social and political importance of class. Also, they talked freely about their own life histories in class terms (eg, some of them described how they had moved from a working-class background into the middle class).

Personal identity However, Savage et al. found that most of the people they interviewed were rather hesitant about identifying *themselves* as members of any class. Most saw themselves as 'outside' classes. They preferred to describe themselves as 'ordinary' or as 'individuals' rather than see themselves as products of some class background. They felt their own individuality was under threat if they were 'labelled' in class terms.

Savage et al. conclude that class identities are generally weak. Most people recognise the relevance of class in the wider society but are not keen to express their own personal identities in class terms. So the typical attitude towards class identity is one of ambivalence – mixed feelings.

A classless society? – conclusion

The recent emphasis on consumption and lifestyles is a response to changes in society. The old class divisions seem to be breaking down and it is not so easy to predict someone's lifestyle purely on the basis of their social class. Lifestyles appear to involve more choice than in the past.

Some sociologists say we should not be deceived by the appearance of diversity and choice in modern society. Many of the differences in lifestyles are rather superficial. When it comes to the important things – life chances, opportunities, power – class is still the most important factor governing our lives. The lone parent on the bleak housing estate has limited freedom to experiment with different lifestyles.

Nevertheless, a distinction has to be drawn between class influences and class identities. Our position in the class structure certainly has an impact on our opportunities and living conditions. But this does not necessarily mean that we are always conscious of class, or that it is our central identity. Savage et al. show that people often have mixed feelings and are hesitant about defining themselves in class terms.

key terms

Social class A group which occupies a particular social and economic position in society.

Class consciousness Awareness of being in a particular social class.

Lifestyle A distinctive set of tastes, attitudes and behaviour.

Underclass The poorest and most under-privileged section of society.

summary

1. Sociologists allocate people to social classes according to their economic position in society. Occupation is usually selected as the most convenient indicator of class.

2. Class seems to affect many other aspects of our lives. Not just the job we do and the money we earn, but also our attitudes, lifestyles and values. You can predict quite a lot about a person's values, behaviour and identity from their social class.

3. Society can be broken down into four major classes: upper, middle, working and underclass. There are some overlaps between these classes in their values, lifestyles and identities. But there are also some broad class differences.

4. The upper class is made up of those who possess great wealth. Members of the upper class share a strong sense of identity based on public school education and family connections.

5. The middle class is made up of people in non-manual jobs. It is difficult to generalise about middle-class culture and identity as the people and jobs making up the expanding middle class are so diverse. Professionals value education highly and take part in a wide range of leisure activities. The self-employed value independence and hard work.

6. The working class consists of those in manual jobs. Traditional working-class culture emphasised class consciousness, community and the extended family. 'New' working-class culture focuses on leisure and the home.

7. Some sociologists believe that an underclass exists consisting of the unemployed and those dependent on welfare benefits. This group has developed its own norms and values. Others dispute this view and see the underclass as sharing similar values to the rest of society.

8. Some sociologists argue that lifestyles and consumption are now more important than class as sources of identity.

9. It would be foolish to think that class has faded into insignificance. People's lives are still greatly affected by their class position. But class identities do seem to be weaker now than in the past.

Unit 10 Leisure, consumption and identity

keyissues

1 What are the main patterns of leisure?

2 Does leisure play a significant role in identity formation?

3 How meaningful are virtual identities?

4 What role does consumption play in identity formation?

5 What are the main explanations of consumer lifestyles?

10.1 Leisure

Leisure can be defined in terms of time – as the time left over after work, or as the time left over after work and free from all non-work obligations (eg, sleeping, shopping, cooking). Alternatively, it may be seen in terms of particular activities and attitudes – the enjoyable things people choose to do with their free hours.

Historical changes

Pre-industrial Britain In pre-industrial Britain there were special occasions for feasts, fairs and fun. However, in daily life there was seldom a clear dividing line between work and leisure. Work was part of everyday life, and most people just stopped for rest or recreation according to the rhythms of the working day and changing seasons.

The industrial revolution Leisure patterns were transformed by urbanisation and industrialisation. For most people, the nineteenth century demanded long hours of toil, under strict supervision, in factories, mines and workshops. As a result, work and leisure became sharply separated.

Walvin (1978) describes how the Victorians cracked down on the 'sinful recreations' of earlier times – such as cock-fighting, violent sports, and heavy gambling and drinking. Employers and the state encouraged 'wholesome recreation' such as mass sports (eg, football, rugby and athletics) which were organised in leagues and closely regulated. The expansion of parks, museums and libraries offered further opportunities for healthy exercise and cultural improvement.

Mass leisure The twentieth century ushered in an age of mass leisure and a wider range of cultural and leisure activities. This was partly due to a long-term reduction in working hours and the appearance of a more leisurely 'weekend'. Another factor was increased spending power which put leisure activities within the reach of ordinary people. Improved transport (eg, railways) created better opportunities for outings such as trips to the seaside.

The newly-emerging leisure industries spotted the chance to make a profit from these developments. Sports such as football became more commercialised (eg, by charging for admission). Also, the 'communications revolution' – the spread of magazines and newspapers, followed by radio, cinema, television and the internet – resulted in massive shifts in cultural pastimes, entertainments and lifestyles (Walvin, 1978).

Patterns of leisure

People in Britain follow a wide range of leisure pursuits. This includes tourism and holidays - there were 43 million holiday trips abroad in 2004. But a great deal of leisure time is spent in the home. For example, it is estimated that the average household views television for about 26 hours per week. Nine out of ten adults watch it every day, and one in ten watches it for over 7 hours a day (*Social Trends*, 2006).

Every year about three quarters of adults take part in a sport, game or physical activity of some sort. The most popular exercise is walking (46%), followed by swimming (35%), keep fit/yoga/dance (22%) and cycling (19%).

As for cultural pursuits, millions of people in Britain visit libraries, the theatre, museums and craft exhibitions every year. Over twelve million people attended plays in London's West End in 2005, and four and a half million visited the British Museum (*Social Trends*, 2007).

Group differences Leisure is not equally distributed across the British population. For some professional groups, hours at work may actually have increased – so they are work-rich but time-poor. In contrast, some groups may be time-rich but lack the money or good health to fully enjoy their leisure.

Alan Warde (2006) uses survey evidence to identify some group differences in sport. Predictably, participation in sport is higher among younger people. Better educated people also have higher participation rates, partly because they feel they have a duty to look after their body. But the particular choice of sport is not strongly class-based (with a few exceptions, such as middle-class preference for golf and squash).

Gender patterns Gender makes a difference to leisure styles. Women tend to carry major responsibilities for housework and childcare, and so they have less time and energy for leisure. Also, their leisure activities may be restricted because of fears for their safety outside the home, especially at night. Sometimes they are faced with a limited range of leisure provisions, or they may find that leisure centres are dominated by males.

There is a problem of 'image' when it comes to sport. A report in 2007 by the Women's Sport and Fitness Foundation found that young women were discouraged from taking exercise because of cultural pressures. Sport is often seen as 'unfeminine', and many young women stop after they leave school. Among 16-24 year-olds, women are half as active in sports as men, and this is especially true for low income and minority ethnic women. Women who remain active tend to choose certain activities – they are over-represented in swimming, keep-fit, walking, horse riding and gymnastics.

Work and leisure It is not always easy to identify clear links between work and leisure. But Stanley Parker (1976) suggests three main types of relationship.

In the *extension* or *spillover* pattern, the experience of work carries over into leisure. People who are stimulated by their work (eg, middle-class professionals) may adopt a lively and energetic attitude to leisure. On the other hand, those who find work uninspiring may adopt lazy or apathetic leisure habits.

In the *opposition* pattern, people deliberately create a contrast between their work and leisure. Those who find work frustrating or exhausting may escape from it by seeking 'explosive compensation' in their leisure (eg, deep-sea fishermen indulging in heavy drinking sessions when ashore).

In the *neutrality* pattern there is no strong link between work and leisure. People divide their lives into separate compartments and they cultivate leisure pursuits as they see fit.

Leisure as a central life interest

The ancient Greeks thought humans express themselves most fully in leisure – it allows them to develop their mind, body and spirit to the highest level. People today may not have such lofty ambitions, but there is growing evidence that leisure is a major source of identity and meaning. Some sociologists believe leisure is replacing work as a 'central life interest' – the sphere of life where we seek fulfilment and a sense of purpose.

Is leisure really capable of providing people with satisfying identities? Kenneth Roberts (1978) presents three sociological models – class, mass and pluralist – which take different views on this issue.

Class domination This is the Marxist model (see page 9). It argues that self-fulfilment is not really possible in a capitalist society. The ruling class exploit workers not only in the workplace but also in their leisure. They derive economic profits from leisure – they brainwash people into buying the latest products or crazes (eg, 'home cinema', Pilates classes). The ruling class also benefit politically – entertainment and leisure are mindless time-fillers which distract people's attention from the way they are being exploited and manipulated.

Mass society This model argues that people today lead rather empty and superficial lives. Unlike the class domination model, it does not see this as a ruling class conspiracy. Rather, it is a result of the poor quality of popular culture. The leisure and entertainment industries try to appeal to the largest (mass) audience and so their standards are low and unchallenging. The mass audiences are seduced into the role of passive consumers in front of an endless stream of trivia (see page 9).

Pluralist model This approach disagrees with the previous two models – it argues that leisure offers rich opportunities for creating lifestyles and identities. For example, popular culture is popular precisely because of its attractive features. Society today is diverse (pluralistic) and people have greater choice and freedom. Some enthusiasts dedicate themselves to their chosen hobbies and recreations – this is 'connoisseur leisure' (Roberts, 1995). Others may be quite content to dabble in a series of 'casual' leisure pursuits.

Postmodern model The pluralist model is similar to some postmodernist accounts of leisure. For example, Taylor and Cohen (1992) suggest that people in postmodern society increasingly seek choice, novelty and diversity. In society today there are 'identity sites' which give them the freedom to create new meanings and identities in a playful way. These identity sites include 'activity enclaves' (hobbies, sex), 'new landscapes' (holidays, adventure) and 'mindscapes' (internal voyages via drugs or therapy).

Leisure – conclusion

Leisure patterns vary across social groups. Nevertheless, leisure fills an important part in people's lives, and for some it is a major source of meaning and identity.

Sociologists take different views on the significance of leisure. Some see it as yet another example of capitalist exploitation. Some condemn it on the grounds of its passive or trivial features. But others defend it as an arena where people can stretch themselves, find genuine pleasure, and establish new and meaningful identities.

activity33 a bit of fun?

Item A A Global sport

Oil-rich sheikhs from the Gulf States are pumping billions of dollars into racing, football, cricket, tennis, rugby, motor sport, athletics and even ocean racing. They host lavish tournaments (eg, Dubai Desert Classic golf tournament, the Bahrein Motorsport grand prix). For Dubai's ruler, sport forms part of a multi-million dollar charm offensive. Through sport, he reasons, he can improve the region's image, drive tourism and reduce its economic dependency on oil and natural gas.

But it comes at a price. A huge army of workers from India, Pakistan, Bangladesh and Sri Lanka have toiled for long shifts and low wages in Dubai, most living in squalid conditions.

Source: *The Observer*, 11.11.2007

Jockey Frankie Dettori presented with a trophy for winning the Dubai World Cup, the world's richest horse race.

Item B Reality TV

Brian celebrates winning Big Brother with Davina McCall.

Item C Exotic holidays

Western tourists mob a tribal elder in Papua New Guinea.

questions

1 How would the class domination Marxist model explain Item A?

2 How would a) mass society and b) pluralist models explain Item B?

3 How would the postmodern model explain Item C?

10.2 Virtual worlds

One of the fastest growing leisure areas is the use of 'new media' – advanced digital media such as mobile phones, electronic games and the internet. These media are increasingly portable and inter-connected (eg, phone, camera, email and internet can be combined in one gadget). Boyle (2007) suggests that what makes the new media different is their greater accessibility and the expanded choice they offer their users.

The internet is often seen as dominated by young males. An Ofcom report in 2007 confirmed that 16-24 year-olds generally spend more time online and send more text messages. But it also describes the emergence of 'silver surfers' – pensioners who sometimes spend far more time online than younger people. The report also notes the *feminisation* of the internet – among 25-34 year-olds, women spend more leisure time online than men.

Virtual communities These are social relationships which are created in cyberspace. The new media have established social networking sites such as MySpace, Facebook and Bebo. These popular websites are used for entertainment and for friendships. Some users of Facebook even send 'virtual flowers' to their friends.

Are these virtual communities really capable of creating deep and lasting social relationships? A survey by Curtice and Norris (2007) suggests it is unlikely that the internet changes social lives dramatically. Rather, people integrate internet use according to their pre-existing attitudes and social skills. For example, some of the keenest users of internet sites are sociable people who already have lots of friends they meet face to face.

Virtual identities People have new opportunities to express their personal and collective identities online. There are websites and chat rooms devoted to all sorts of tastes and lifestyles – fan clubs, support groups, special interests and so on.

The anonymity of the web allows people to invent new identities – they can give themselves a different name, gender or biography. They can create *avatars* – virtual replicas of themselves – in fantasy worlds. For example, *Second Life* is a popular online world with 3.5 million inhabitants where you can design your own avatar. You can choose the appearance, characteristics and behaviour of this avatar as it moves around an imaginary world. In this world you can even buy a house, shop, travel, marry and so on.

Virtual worlds – conclusion Technology has created fresh opportunities for establishing online communities and identities. The boundary between virtual and real worlds is becoming more blurred.

activity34 life on the net

Item A Cybersex

A man in New York has become the first to sue for divorce on the grounds that his wife committed adultery in cyberspace. He discovered her trail of email messages on his computer screen. His wife never met the PC lover with whom she flirted electronically for months.

Source: *The Guardian*, 3.2.1996

Item B The portfolio personality

The internet will transform our sense of self. You can be anyone on the internet. You can develop an infinite number of personalities in discussion groups and chat rooms. You can change sex, age, tastes, opinions, values, even beliefs – endlessly. This process – the development, discovery and expression of your identity – has become the purpose and meaning of life, your life project. We are only beginning to understand how flexible and diverse our selves can be – the portfolio personality.

Source: *The Guardian*, 15.1.1999

Item C Second Life

A beach scene from Second Life. You can buy a great body for a few dollars or pick up an average one for nothing. A couple who married in Second Life went on to marry in real life.

question

Show how these items suggest that the distinction between 'real' and 'virtual' worlds is becoming blurred?

10.3 Consumption

Some sociologists believe consumer lifestyles are an important source of identity in a leisure-based society. They argue that people no longer build their identities around work and production – how they *earn* their money. Rather, they are more likely to base their identities on their lifestyles and consumption patterns – the things they *spend* their money on.

Consumer society Consumption is an essential feature of every society. People need to consume food and drink in order to survive. In pre-industrial societies, people grew their own food, made their own clothes, or bartered goods with others. In capitalist society, however, consumption revolves around *commodities* – goods or services which are sold in the marketplace.

Living standards have risen dramatically, and consumption is no longer solely about physical survival. People can afford to buy consumer goods which are not strictly necessary – for example, dishwashers, new furniture, the latest fashions. The emergence of the department store in the mid-nineteenth century marked a shift in consumer attitudes. Shopping was no longer just about buying the bare essentials of life. The stores encouraged shoppers to browse at their leisure among the wide range of goods on display. It also helped to create the image of shopping as something done mainly by women.

Consumer culture Consumer goods are important not just for their practical use. Consumption is also a *cultural* act – it has symbolic meaning. It tells us things about the tastes and style of the consumers. People are usually aware that they are making a statement about themselves through their consumption habits – what they choose to wear, eat, drink, listen to or collect. These consumption choices express and establish their identities.

Lifestyles Graham Day (2006) points out that there is more to lifestyle than the mere act of consuming. The term also suggests a 'design for living', a characteristic way of acting in the world. To follow a particular lifestyle is to take up a pattern of activity and consumption which indicates the sort of person you are – your identity.

Theories of consumer culture

Mike Featherstone (1991) identifies three broad accounts of consumer culture. These can be called the radical, sociological and postmodern models.

Radical model This is similar to the Marxist class domination model. It sees the expansion of consumer culture as driven by capitalism's search for profits. Clever marketing and advertising create consumer desires – people believe their lives will be happier if they buy the latest goods and services. But this happiness is likely to be

activity35 consumer rites

Item A **Distinctions**

The newly appointed chairman of the Royal Opera was asked by press reporters what sort of person he wished to attract to opera. He replied, 'I don't want to sit next to somebody in a tee shirt, a pair of shorts and a smelly pair of trainers. I'm a relaxed individual but I am passionate about standards of behaviour'.

Source: *The Guardian*, 16.1.1998

Item B **The spirit of shopping**

Shopping has become the new religion.

- We have 'cathedrals of shopping' (shopping malls).
- Shoppers follow rituals – scrutinising the goods, selecting items, queuing and paying.
- Shoppers are offered paradise on earth in the form of desirable goods.
- Shopping is the opium of the masses – its addictive quality reconciles people to capitalism.

But there are differences between shopping and true religion – no Ten Commandments and no nourishment for the soul.

Source: Bartholomew, 1998

The Trafford Centre, Manchester, the UK's biggest shopping shopping mall.

Item C *What to wear*

From 'Trinny and Susannah Undress'. They have given fashion advice to the men in the John Lewis Department Store window.

Item D *Expressing the individual*

People imagine they are expressing their creativity and individuality in their choice of home furnishing. But their ideas probably came from magazines and television, and many people have made the same choices.

Source: Inglis, 2005

questions

1 Explain why Item A is an example of a status distinction.

2 Why is Item B so critical of shopping?

3 What do Items C and D tell us about creativity and individuality in consumer culture?

---

fleeting and shallow, since capitalism is based on exploitation which damages social relationships.

In spite of its failure to deliver real happiness, capitalism seduces and manipulates people with material goods. This has an ideological effect – people are more likely to accept and support the capitalist system. So consumption masks the ruthless and exploitative nature of capitalism. People who buy fashionable jeans in the West are often unaware that these have been manufactured in Third World countries where sweatshop workers are paid pitifully low wages.

Sociological model This model views consumption as a way of creating social distinctions. For example, Bourdieu (1984) argues that social classes develop distinctive lifestyles as a way of establishing their cultural identity and superiority. One way of doing this is by *conspicuous consumption*. Thorstein Veblen (1899) described how wealthy leisure elites make a public show of their supposedly refined tastes and interests. For example, the

ability to speak a classical language (Latin or Greek), or having a good 'nose' for fine wines, sends the message that they are superior people.

Status symbols are used to signal a group's status and social position. For example, wealthy footballers are associated with flash cars, Rolex watches and 'trophy' wives and girlfriends ('WAGS'). These symbols play a part in the 'presentation of self', where people project an identity which they hope others will admire.

Postmodern model Postmodern sociologists argue that lifestyles are no longer determined by social class or occupation. Rather, they are shaped by individual consumer choices – what we choose to wear, eat and drink, where we shop, the goods we buy, our leisure pursuits and interests. Individuals self-consciously arrange these things into a recognisable lifestyle. Unlike the 1950s era of conformity (mass consumption), the postmodern era places value on diversity.

The postmodern model is more likely than the other models to celebrate the pleasures, desires and anticipation which are generated by consumption. It views these as genuine pleasures rather than 'false' desires invented by capitalists. The construction of identity is seen as an active and creative process.

Consumption – conclusion

A great deal of consumer behaviour is still largely a matter of routine shopping for basic needs. Nevertheless, consumption is increasingly a form of cultural expression.

Perhaps only a killjoy would deny that consumption brings genuine pleasures But consumerism can create anxiety and discontent – materialism can breed envy and frustration. Powerful groups sometimes manipulate consumer tastes and engage in exploitative practices.

It is not really clear whether consumer identities are more important than identities based on work. And work still has an influence on consumption – spending power varies across the social classes and this can shape identities and lifestyles.

Nor is it clear to what extent the construction of identity is an individual and a creative process. Lifestyle magazines and TV programmes are constantly telling us what to be and how to live.

key terms

Leisure The time left over from work, or time left over from work and from all non-work obligations, or the enjoyable things that people decide to do in their free time.
Consumption The purchase, use and/or enjoyment of goods and services.
Consumer culture A set of attitudes which encourages and finds meaning and pleasure in consumption.
Conspicuous consumption The public consumption of goods and services in order to gain prestige.
Status symbols Things which are used to signal a group's social standing and to gain prestige.

summary

1. Leisure patterns have changed over the centuries. People today have more leisure time and a wider range of leisure activities. It is possible that leisure has become a central life interest for many people – they find meaning and identity in leisure rather than work.

2. Many leisure activities are shared by most of the population – television viewing is the best example. But social groups have different rates of participation in particular leisure pursuits. Women tend to engage in a narrower range of physical exercise activities.

3. Class domination theorists believe that powerful groups control leisure for material gain (it creates profits) and political gain (it distracts attention from the basic injustices of the capitalist system). They believe that true fulfilment is impossible in a society based on exploitation.

4. Mass society theorists condemn the poor quality of mass culture and mass leisure. Rather than stimulating or enriching people, leisure activities lull them into a state of apathy and passivity.

5. The pluralist model argues that leisure offers choice and provides opportunities for creating different lifestyles.

6. New electronic media allow people to extend or invent identities in virtual worlds. However, they do not always transform people's lives or establish deep and lasting identities. Rather, they are superimposed on people's existing lifestyles and relationships.

7. Consumption has symbolic meaning, and consumer lifestyles are used to express identities. Some sociologists argue that consumer lifestyles are now more important than class as sources of identity.

8. Lifestyles are much more diverse nowadays as people pursue their individual interests. Postmodern theorists argue that lifestyles are freely chosen rather than dictated by class positions.

9. Radical theorists question whether a consumer culture is capable of making people happy. Effective advertising depends on making people discontented and envious..

10. Consumption styles and status symbols can be used to create social distinctions between groups.

2 Families and households

Introduction

Picture the family. Does the image on the right come to mind – mum, dad and the kids? This is the usual picture presented by advertisers. But, for more and more of us, it no longer reflects the reality of family life.

Families are changing. Married women who devote their lives to childcare and housework are a dwindling minority. Marriage itself is declining in popularity. More and more couples are living together without getting married. And more and more marriages are ending in separation and divorce. Families have become increasingly diverse.

What do sociologists make of all this? Some believe that the family is in crisis, and that this threatens the well-being of society as a whole. Others welcome change. They see the diversity of family life as an opportunity for choice. No longer does the old-fashioned idea of the family restrict women to the home, keep unhappy marriages going, and maintain destructive family relationships.

This chapter looks at these different views. It investigates changes in family life and examines the causes and effects of these changes.

chaptersummary

▷ **Unit 1** looks at the problem of defining the family and shows how families vary from society to society.

▷ **Unit 2** outlines the main sociological theories of the family and considers government policy towards the family.

▷ **Unit 3** examines the relationship between family life and industrialisation.

▷ **Unit 4** outlines and explains changing patterns of marriage, cohabitation, childbearing, divorce and separation.

▷ **Unit 5** looks at family diversity, focusing on lone-parent families, reconstituted families and gay and lesbian families.

▷ **Unit 6** examines changes in the division of domestic labour and the distribution of power in the family and asks to what extent they are linked to gender.

▷ **Unit 7** focuses on children and asks how ideas of childhood have changed.

▷ **Unit 8** looks at changes in birth rates, death rates and family size in the UK since 1900.

Unit 1 Defining the family

keyissues

1 How has the family been defined?
2 What are the problems with definitions of the family?

1.1 What is the family?

In 1949, the American anthropologist George Peter Murdock provided the following definition of the family.

'The family is a social group characterised by common residence, economic cooperation and reproduction. It includes adults of both sexes, at least two of whom maintain a socially approved sexual relationship, and one or more children, own or adopted, of the sexually cohabiting adults.'

Spelling out this definition:

- Families live together – they share the same *household*.
- They work together and pool their resources – to some extent they share domestic tasks and income.
- They reproduce – they have children.
- They include an adult male and female who have a sexual relationship which is approved by the wider society – for example, they have a marital relationship.
- This heterosexual couple have at least one child – either their biological offspring or an adopted child.

The nuclear family

George Peter Murdock based his definition of the family on a sample of 250 societies ranging from hunting and gathering bands, to small-scale farming societies to large-scale industrial societies. Although he found a variety of family forms within this sample, Murdock claimed that each contained a basic nucleus consisting of a husband and wife and one or more children, own or adopted. This is the *nuclear family*. Murdock believed that the nuclear family is 'a universal social grouping' – in other words, it is found in all societies.

activity1 defining the family

Item A Lone-parent family

A single mother and her children

Item B Extended family

An extended family

Item C Nuclear family

A heterosexual married couple and their children

Item D Gay family

A gay couple and their adopted childen

questions

1 Which of these 'families' fit/s Murdock's definition? Explain your answer.
2 Do you think those that do not fit should be regarded as families? Give reasons for your answer.

Extended families

Murdock saw the other family forms in his sample as extensions of the nuclear family. These *extended families* contain *kin* – relatives based on 'blood' or marriage – in addition to the nuclear family. The nuclear family can be extended in various ways.

Polygamy Marriage in the West is *monogamous* – it involves one wife and one husband. In many societies, marriage is *polygamous* – a person is permitted additional wives or husbands. Men may have more than one wife – a system known as *polygyny*. Or, in a small number of societies, women may have more than one husband – a form of marriage known as *polyandry.*

Other forms of extension Apart from additional marital

activity2 polygamy

Item A **Polygyny**

Adama is a wealthy man. He lives in a village called Sobtenga in Burkina Faso, a country in northwest Africa. Ten years ago he had two wives.

Zenabou, his first wife, thought polygyny was a good idea. It provided her with a 'sister' to share the burdens of domestic work and childcare. Now she is not so sure. Adama has taken two more wives, the youngest of whom, Bintu, is only 16. He is besotted with Bintu and she clearly enjoys the attention. Despite grumbling, his other wives accept the situation, for marriage is seen primarily as an economic affair. Adama's 12 oxen are proof that he can provide security for his wives and children.

Polygyny is much more common than polyandry. It is found in many small-scale traditional societies, particularly in Africa. As the example of Adama suggests, polygyny is a privilege of the wealthy. Not every man can afford two or more wives and in any case there aren't enough women for this. Census figures from 1911 for the Pondo of South Africa show that only 10% of men had two wives and only 2% had more than two.

Source: Mair, 1971 and Brazier, 1995

Adama's wives – Zenabou, Bintu, Meryan and Barkissou

Item B **Polyandry**

The Nyinba people of Nepal practice fraternal polyandry – two or more brothers are married to one wife. They inherited this custom from their Tibetan ancestors who migrated to Nepal centuries ago. They also inherited a love for trading and herding which, together with cultivating the meagre soil, make up the traditional Nyinba economy. Polyandry suits this economy. 'With one or two husbands always on herding or trading trips, one husband will always be at home to care for the wife,' explained Maila Dai, a trader from the village of Bargaau. 'We think polyandry is just like insurance for the wife. If one husband is no good or leaves his wife, there's always another brother.'

Polyandry among the Nyinba of Nepal. The 12 year old girl on the right is engaged to five brothers, three of whom are pictured here.

Polyandry has been explained as a way of preventing land from being divided up into less profitable units when a family of sons inherits from the previous generation. It also concentrates the wealth of each household by maintaining a large population of working adult males under one roof.

To the Nyinbas, its advantages are obvious. 'All our brothers work together,' explained Dawa Takpa, 'so we can be wealthy people. If we all go our own way, how can we survive? We have to study, do agricultural work, take care of animals and trade, so we have to work together.' 'For me,' said Tsering Zangmo, who at 21 is the wife of three brothers (the youngest of whom is seven), 'polyandry is fine. If I had only one husband, I would be very poor.'

When asked about jealousy between her husbands, Tsering Zangmo replied, 'But they are brothers. They are never jealous.' However when pressed she giggled and blushed, admitting, 'Well, they only have a very little jealousy. If you like one husband very much, you have to be secret so the others don't know. We make love in the middle of the night, lying naked in sheepskins. We'd never do it just before going to sleep or just before waking up as the others might hear us.'

Source: Dunham, 1992

questions

1 How can polygamous families be seen as extensions of the nuclear family?

2 Judging from Items A and B, what are the advantages and disadvantages of polygyny and polyandry?

partners, families can be extended in a variety of ways. For example, a three-generation extended family may include grandparents within the family unit. Similarly, uncles and aunts (brothers and sisters of the married couple) may form part of the family unit.

1.2 Diversity in family systems

Many sociologists and anthropologists have seen the nuclear family, either in its basic or extended form, as universal, normal and natural. Others have rejected this view. For example, Felicity Edholm (1982), in an article entitled 'The unnatural family', argues that there is nothing normal and natural about the nuclear family. She claims that family and kinship relationships are *socially constructed*. They are based on culture rather than biology. The links between husband and wife, parent and child, are constructed very differently in different societies. In Edholm's words, 'Relatives are not born but made'. Here are some examples Edholm gives to support her argument. They are taken from traditional cultures and may not apply today.

Parent-child relations – genes Ideas about the biological relationship between parents and children vary from society to society. For example, the Lakker of Burma see no blood relationship between mother and child – the mother is simply a container in which the child grows. As a result, sexual relationships between children of the same mother are permitted – because they are seen as non-kin, such relationships are not seen as incest.

Parent-child relations – adoption Most sociologists consider the tie between mother and child as basic and inevitable. However, in some societies, many children do not live with their biological parents. For example, in Tahiti, in the Pacific Ocean, young women often have one or two children before they are considered ready to settle down into a stable relationship with a man. They usually give these children for adoption to their parents or other close relatives. Children see their adoptive mother and father as 'real' parents and their relationship with them as far closer than with their natural parents.

Marriage and residence Some sociologists argue that 'marriage' varies so much from society to society that it makes little sense to use the same word for these very different relationships. For example, the basic social group amongst the Nayar of Northern India is made up of men and women descended through the female line from a common ancestor. Brothers and sisters, women and children live together – children are members of their

A Tahitian family

mother's group, not their father's. Nayar girls 'marry' a man before puberty and later take as many lovers as they like. Her 'husband' may or may not be one of these lovers. Children are raised in their mother's social group. 'Husbands' and fathers do not share the same residence as their 'wives' and have little to do with their children.

According to Edholm, examples such as these show that the family is socially constructed. Rather than seeing the family as a natural unit created by biological necessities, it makes more sense to see it as a social unit shaped by cultural norms. And as culture varies from society to society, so do families. In view of this diversity, Edholm rejects the claim that the nuclear family is universal.

Family diversity today

Edholm's research focused on family diversity in non-Western societies. There is evidence that family diversity is steadily increasing in modern Western societies. In Britain, 26% of families with dependent children were headed by lone parents in 2000 (*Social Trends*, 2002). This was partly due to divorce, partly to never-married mothers, and, to a much smaller extent, to the death of one partner.

Reconstituted families – families in which one or both of the adult couple bring children from a previous relationship – are steadily increasing. There has also been a rapid growth in *cohabitation* – unmarried couples living together, often in a long-term relationship. And, in recent years, a small but growing number of lesbian and gay families have appeared.

This diversity in today's Western societies will be examined in later units.

1.3 Defining the family revisited

Where does this diversity of so-called families leave us? Is it possible to come up with a definition which covers this diversity? David Cheal (1999) summarises some of the responses to this problem.

We don't know Faced with the diversity of family forms, some sociologists frankly admit that no one really knows what a family is. This is not a useful state of affairs. For example, how can different family forms be compared if a 'family' cannot be identified?

Extensions and reductions Following Murdock, some sociologists have seen all families as extensions or reductions of one basic and elementary form – the nuclear family. So, extended families are extensions, lone-parent families are reductions. Not everybody agrees that the variety of family forms can be seen as extensions or reductions of the nuclear family. For example, if a woman decides to produce a child by *in vitro* fertilisation and rear the child herself, can this be seen as a 'reduction' of the nuclear family?

Abandon the idea One solution is to stop using the term family and replace it with a concept such as *primary relationships* (Scanzoni et al., 1989). Primary relationships are close, long-lasting and special ties between people. There is no problem placing the wide diversity of 'families' under this heading. But, it does away with the whole idea of family – an idea which is vitally important to individuals, to the 'family group', and to the wider society.

Ask people From this point of view, families are what people say they are. If families are socially constructed,

activity3 family diversity

Item A The Ashanti

The Ashanti of West Africa are a matrilineal society (descent is traced through the mother's line). While a child's father is important, he has no legal authority over his children. This rests with the wife's family, particularly her brother. It is from the mother's brother that children inherit, though the father is responsible for feeding, clothing and educating them. Many Ashanti men cannot afford to set up a household of their own when they first marry. Since men never live with their wife's brothers, and children are the property of the wife's family, couples often live apart. Only about a third of married women actually live with their husbands.

Source: Fortes, 1950

An Ashanti puberty ritual at which a girl becomes a woman. She belongs to her mother's family.

Women and children in the Trobriand Islands

Item B The Trobriand Islanders

Some matrilineal cultures, such as the Trobriand Islanders, think that the father's role in the conception of a child is minimal. He simply 'opens the door' or, at most, shapes the growing embryo through intercourse.

Source: Beattie, 1964

question

The family is a social construction shaped by cultural norms and beliefs. Discuss with reference to Items A and B.

then sociologists should discover how people in society construct, define and give meaning to families. This approach may lead to a bewildering diversity of families. But, if this is the social reality within which people live, then this may well be the reality which sociologists should investigate.

key terms

Household A group of people who share a common residence.

Nuclear family A family consisting of an adult male and female with one or more children, own or adopted.

Extended family A family containing relatives in addition to the nuclear family. An extension of the nuclear family.

Kin Relatives based on marriage or genes.

Monogamy A system of marriage involving two adults, one of each sex.

Polygamy A system of marriage involving two or more wives, or two or more husbands.

Polygyny A system of marriage involving two or more wives.

Polyandry A system of marriage involving two or more husbands.

Reconstituted family A family in which one or both partners bring children from a previous relationship.

Cohabitation Living together as a partnership without marriage.

Primary relationships Close, long-lasting and special ties between people.

summary

1. According to Murdock, the nuclear family is the basic form of family. He sees all other family forms as extensions of the nuclear family.

2. Murdock claims that the nuclear family is a universal social grouping – that it is found in all societies.

3. Edholm argues that the family is a social construction based on culture rather than biology. She rejects the view that the nuclear family is universal.

4. Cross-cultural evidence indicates that family forms vary considerably. Recent evidence from Western societies indicates increasing family diversity.

5. Sociologists have responded to the problem of defining the family in the following ways.
   - By admitting that they don't really know what the family is
   - By seeing all family forms as extensions or reductions of the nuclear family
   - By rejecting the concept of family and replacing it with the concept of primary relationships
   - By accepting the definitions of the family used by members of society – the family is what people say it is.

Unit 2 The family and social structure

key issues

1. What are the main sociological theories of the family?
2. How have government policies affected the family?

2.1 Functionalist theories of the family

Functionalist theories see society as made up of various parts, each of which contributes to the maintenance and well-being of the system as a whole.

Some functionalist theories are based on the idea that societies need *consensus* – agreement about norms and values – in order to survive. As a result, they are also known as *consensus theories*.

Functionalists often assume that if a social institution such as the family exists, then it must have a *function* or purpose – it must do something useful. As a result, the family is usually seen to perform functions which benefit both its members and society as a whole.

George Peter Murdock

According to Murdock (1949), the family is a universal institution with universal functions. In other words, it is found in all societies and it performs the same functions everywhere. These functions are vital for the well-being of society. They are:

Sexual In most societies, there are rules limiting or forbidding sexual relationships outside marriage. This helps to stabilise the social system. Without such rules, conflict may result.

Economic In many societies, the family is a unit of production – for example, a 'farming family' producing food. In the West today, the family acts as a unit of consumption – buying goods and services for the family group. These economic functions make an important contribution to the wider society.

Reproduction The family is the main unit for the reproduction of children. Without reproduction, society would cease to exist.

Educational The family is largely responsible for *primary socialisation*, the first and most important part of the socialisation process. Without socialisation, there would be no culture. And without a shared culture, there would be no consensus about society's norms and values.

Murdock believes that the nuclear family, either alone, or in its extended form, performs these 'vital functions'. He cannot imagine a substitute. In his words, 'No society has succeeded in finding an adequate substitute for the nuclear family, to which it might transfer these functions. It is highly doubtful whether any society will ever succeed in such an attempt.'

Talcott Parsons

The American sociologist Talcott Parsons focuses on the nuclear family in modern industrial society. He argues that the family has become increasingly specialised. Functions for which families were responsible in pre-industrial societies, for example, looking after the elderly or educating children, have been taken over in industrial societies by specialised institutions such as social services and schools (Parsons & Bales, 1955).

However, Parsons claims that the family retains two 'basic and irreducible' functions. These are:

1 the *primary socialisation* of children
2 the *stabilisation of adult personalities*.

Primary socialisation This is the first and most important part of the socialisation process. Parsons argues that every individual must learn the shared norms and values of society. Without this there would be no consensus, and without consensus, social life would not be possible.

For the socialisation process to be really effective, shared norms and values must be 'internalised as part of the personality structure'. Children's personalities are moulded in terms of society's culture to the point where it becomes a part of them.

The stabilisation of adult personalities This is the second essential function of the family. Unstable personalities can threaten the stability and smooth-running of society. According to Parsons, families help to stabilise adult

activity4 functionalism and the family

Item A Family shopping

Item B The 'warm bath theory'

Item C 'The bottle'

The drunken husband – a 19th century view of domestic violence

questions

1 Functionalists often argue that the family's economic function as a unit of production has been replaced by its function as a unit of consumption. Explain with some reference to Item A.

2 Look at Items B and C.

   a) Parsons' theory is sometimes known as the 'warm bath theory'. Why?

   b) Critically evaluate this theory. Refer to Item C in your answer.

personalities in two ways. First, marital partners provide each other with emotional support. Second, as parents, they are able to indulge the 'childish' side of their personalities – for example, by playing with their children.

Family life provides adults with release from the strains and stresses of everyday life. It provides them with emotional security and support. This helps to stabilise their personality and, in turn, the wider society.

Conclusion Although the functions of the family have become fewer and more specialised, Parsons believes they are no less important. He cannot imagine an institution other than the family performing these 'basic and irreducible' functions.

Criticisms of funtionalism

The following criticisms have been made of functionalist views of the family.

- Functionalists assume that on balance families perform useful and often essential functions both for their members and for society as a whole. Married couples are pictured as living in harmony, as good in bed, and as effective socialisers of the next generation. Critics argue that this does not reflect the realities of family life.
- As a result of this picture of happy families, functionalists tend to ignore the 'dark side' of family life – conflict between husband and wife, male dominance, child abuse, and so on. They give insufficient attention to the *dysfunctions* of the family – the harmful effects it may have on the wider society.
- Functionalists tend to ignore the diversity of family life in industrial society. For example, there is little reference to lone-parent families, cohabiting families and reconstituted families. Nor do they pay much attention to variations in family life based on class, ethnicity, religion and locality.
- Parsons' view of the family has been criticised as sexist since he sees the wife/mother as having the main responsibility for providing warmth and emotional support, and for de-stressing her hardworking husband.

key terms

Functionalism A theory which sees society as made up of various parts, each of which tends to contribute to the maintenance and well-being of society as a whole.
Consensus theories Functionalist theories based on the idea that societies need consensus or agreement about norms and values.
Function The contribution a part of society makes to the well-being of society as a whole.
Dysfunction The harmful effects that a part of society has on society as a whole.
Primary socialisation The first and most important part of the socialisation process whereby young people learn the norms and values of society.

2.2 New Right perspectives

Like functionalists, New Right thinkers see the family as a cornerstone of society. They also see a 'normal' family as the nuclear family unit. For example, John Redwood, a Conservative MP, stated in 1993 that 'the natural state should be the two-adult family caring for their children'. And for him, the two adults are a male and a female.

In recent years there has been growing concern about the state of the family. It is 'in decline', 'under threat', 'fragmenting', 'breaking down'. This view of the family was put forward by New Right thinkers from the 1980s onwards.

Evidence They point to the following evidence to support their claims. There has been an increase in:

- Lone-parent families
- Fatherless families
- Divorce rates
- Cohabitation
- Gay and lesbian couples.

As a result of these changes, the two-parent nuclear family headed by a married couple consisting of an adult male and female is steadily decreasing as a proportion of all families.

Causes The following have been seen as causing these changes.

- A breakdown of 'traditional family values'.
- Over-generous welfare benefits to single mothers which allow fathers to opt out of their responsibilities for raising and providing for their children.
- The influence of feminism which has devalued marriage, domesticity and childrearing, and encouraged women to seek fulfilment outside the home.
- Increased sexual permissiveness.
- Greater tolerance of gay and lesbian relationships as alternatives to heterosexual marriage.

Consequences According to the New Right, these changes have serious consequences. The 'fragmented family' is no longer performing its functions effectively. In particular, it is failing to provide adequate socialisation. This can result in children and young people underachieving at school and behaving in anti-social ways ranging from rudeness to crime.

Over-generous welfare benefits can lead to welfare dependency. Lone mothers become dependent on state benefits and, in effect, are 'married to the state'.

Solutions For the New Right, there are two main solutions to these problems. First, a return to traditional family values – life-long marriage and a recognition of the duties and responsibilities of parenthood. Second, a change in government policy – redirecting welfare benefits and social service provision to support and maintain two-parent families and penalising those who fail to live up to this ideal.

Sociology and the New Right New Right thinkers have tended to be journalists and politicians rather than sociologists. However, a few sociologists have developed similar arguments. For example, Norman Dennis and George Erdos make the following points in *Families Without Fathers* (2000).

Increasing numbers of children are born outside marriage and raised by single mothers. This places the children at a disadvantage. On average, they have poorer health and lower educational attainment than children from two-parent families.

Dennis and Erdos's main concern is the effect on boys. They grow up without the expectation that adulthood involves responsibilities for a wife and children. This can result in irresponsible, immature, anti-social young men.

According to Dennis and Erdos, families without fathers are not an adequate alternative to the standard nuclear family. Families are not just changing, they are 'deteriorating'.

*activity*5 *New Right perspectives*

Item A **Fatherless families**

According to the American sociologist Charles Murray, increasing numbers of 'young, healthy, low-income males choose not to take jobs'. Many turn to crime (particularly violent street crime) and regular drug abuse.

Many of these boys have grown up in a family without a father and male wage earner. As a result, they lack the male role models of mainstream society. Within a female-headed family dependent on welfare benefits, the disciplines and responsibilities of mainstream society tend to break down. Murray believes that work must become the 'centre of life' for young men. They must learn the disciplines of work and respect for work. And they must learn to become 'real fathers', accepting the responsibilities of parenthood.

Murray believes that the socialisation and role models required to develop these attitudes are often lacking in female-headed, low-income families. He claims that, 'Over the last two decades, larger and larger numbers of British children have not been socialised to norms of self-control, consideration for others, and the concept that actions have consequences'. In Murray's view, when it comes to effective socialisation, 'No alternative family structure comes close to the merits of two parents, formally married'.

Source: Murray, 1990, 2001

Item B **Welfare dependency**

Item C **A typical Victorian image**

'The abandoned mother'

questions

1 Read Item A. Why does Murray see the nuclear family as superior to other family structures?

2 What points is the cartoon in Item B making?

3 How does Item C question the idea that welfare dependency has led to the breakdown of the family?

Criticisms of New Right views

Blaming the victims Critics argue that the New Right tends to 'blame the victims' for problems that are not of their own making. Many of these problems may result from low wages, inadequate state benefits, lack of jobs and other factors beyond the control of lone parents.

Value judgements The New Right sees the nuclear family consisting of husband, wife and children as the ideal. Other family arrangements are considered inferior. Critics argue that this reflects the values of the New Right rather than a balanced judgement of the worth of family diversity in today's society. Who is to say that families without fathers are necessarily inferior? Why should everybody be forced into the nuclear family mould?

An idealised view of the past New Right thinkers may be harking back to a golden age of the family which never existed. Even in Victorian times – supposedly *the* era of traditional family values – lone parenthood, cohabitation and sexual relationships outside marriage were by no means uncommon.

2.3 Marxist theories

Marxists reject the view that society is based on value consensus and operates for the benefit of all. Instead, they see a basic conflict of interest between a small powerful ruling class and the mass of the population, the subject class. The family is seen as one of a number of institutions which serves to maintain the position of the ruling class.

Modern industrial societies have a capitalist economic system. Capitalism is based on the private ownership of economic institutions, for example, banks and factories.

In capitalist economies, investors finance the production of goods and services with the aim of producing profits. These investors form a ruling class. The subject class – the workers – produce goods and services and are paid wages for their labour. The ruling class are seen to exploit the subject class – they gain at the workers' expense since their profits come from the workers' labour.

Marxists argue that the economy largely shapes the rest of society. Thus, a capitalist economic system will produce a certain type of society. Institutions such as the family, the education system and the political system are shaped by the requirements of capitalism and serve to support and maintain it.

Inheritance and private property In *The Origin of the Family, Private Property and the State*, first published in 1884, Friedrich Engels argued that the modern nuclear family developed in capitalist society. Private property is at the heart of capitalism and it was largely owned by men. Before 1882 in Britain, married women could not own property – it passed to their husband on marriage.

A key concern of the capitalist was to ensure that his property passed directly to his legitimate heirs – those he had fathered. According to Engels, the monogamous nuclear family provided the answer. It gave men greater control over women – until the late 19th century wives were seen as chattels, as their husband's property. With only one husband and one wife, doubts about the paternity of children are unlikely. And with only one wife, there are no disputes about which wife's children should inherit. Within the nuclear family, a man could be fairly sure that he had legitimate children with a clear right to inherit his wealth.

activity6 the next generation

question

Give a Marxist interpretation of the role of the family illustrated in this cartoon.

Maintaining capitalism In some respects, Marxist views of the family are similar to those of functionalists. For example, both see the family as a unit which reproduces and socialises children. In other respects, their views are very different.

Marxists see the family as a means for:

- Reproducing 'labour power' – reproducing future generations of workers
- Consuming the products of capitalism
- Providing emotional support for workers, so helping them to cope with the harsh realities of capitalism
- Socialising children to accept the inequalities of capitalist society.

From a Marxist viewpoint, the family helps to maintain an unjust and exploitative system.

Criticisms of Marxism

Marxist views of the family follow logically from Marxist theory. If, for example, the family provides emotional support for workers, then this helps them to accept the injustices of the capitalist system. This makes sense if capitalism is seen as essentially unjust. However, many sociologists reject this view of capitalism and, as a result, Marxist views of the family.

Sociologists generally agree that the economic system has some influence on the family. However, most would disagree with the view that the family is shaped by the needs of that system.

> ## key terms
>
> **Marxism** A theory which sees a basic conflict of interest between those who own the economic institutions and those who are employed by them.
> **Capitalism** A system of production in which the economic institutions, eg banks and factories, are privately owned.

2.4 Feminist theories

Feminists start from the view that most societies are based on patriarchy or male domination. *Radical feminists* see patriarchy as built into the structure of society. *Marxist feminists* see it as resulting from class inequalities in capitalist society. Both see the family as one of the main sites in which women are oppressed by men.

Domestic labour Within the family most of the unpaid work – housework and childcare – is done by women. This applies even when women are working full time outside the home. Women make the main contribution to family life, men receive the main benefits (Delphy & Leonard, 1992).

Marxist feminists argue that the wife's unpaid domestic labour is invaluable to capitalism. She produces and rears future workers at no cost to the capitalist. And she keeps an adult worker – her husband – in good running order by feeding and caring for him (Benston, 1972).

Emotional labour The inequalities of domestic labour also apply to 'emotional labour'. Radical feminists claim that it's wives rather than husbands who provide emotional support for their partners. Wives are more likely to listen, to agree, to sympathise, to understand, to excuse and to flatter (Delphy & Leonard, 1992).

Marxist feminists take a similar view, seeing the emotional support provided by wives as soaking up the frustrations produced by working for capitalism.

Economic dependency Married women are often economically dependent on their husbands. In most couples, it is the wife who gives up work to care for the children. Mothers often return to part-time rather than full-time employment in order to meet their childcare and domestic responsibilities.

Male domination Feminists see the family as male dominated. As noted above, wives are usually economically dependent. Men often control key areas of decision-making such as moving house and important financial decisions. And they sometimes use force to maintain control. Domestic violence is widespread and the majority of those on the receiving end are women. Around 570,000 cases are reported each year in the UK and probably a far larger number go unreported (Hopkins, 2000).

Criticisms of feminism

Ignores positive aspects of family life Critics argue that feminists are preoccupied with the negative side of family life. They ignore the possibility that many women enjoy running a home and raising children.

Ignores trend to gender equality There is evidence of a trend towards greater equality between partners (see Section 6.2). Critics argue that rather than celebrating this trend, feminists remain focused on the remaining inequalities.

> ## key terms
>
> **Feminism** A view which challenges the power of men over women.
> **Patriarchy** A social system based on male domination.
> **Radical feminists** Feminists who see patriarchy as the main form of inequality in society.
> **Marxist feminists** Feminists who see patriarchy as resulting from class inequalities.
> **Domestic labour** Unpaid work such as housework and childcare, within the home and family.

activity7 housewives

Magazine cover from 1955

Magazine cover from 2003

question

How might a feminist analyse these magazine covers?

2.5 Social policy and the family

In recent years, governments have been increasingly concerned about families. And government policies have reflected this concern.

These policies are influenced by values. Should government policies be shaped by 'traditional family values' which see the nuclear family as the ideal? Or, should they recognise the increasing diversity of family life and support *all* family types?

The New Right

The New Right comes down firmly on the side of the nuclear family (see Section 2.2). It's the best kind of family and should be encouraged. The rest are second-best and should be discouraged. How does this translate into social policy?

Encouraging nuclear families Governments should 'explicitly *favour* married parenthood over all other choices for raising children' (Saunders, 2000). Taxes and welfare benefits should be directed to this end. The marriage contract should be strengthened and married couples should have special legal rights and safeguards.

Discouraging family diversity According to the New Right, over-generous welfare benefits have supported the rapid increase in lone-parent families. These benefits should be reduced so lone-parenthood becomes a less attractive option. Cohabitation should be discouraged by denying unmarried couples the legal rights and privileges given to married couples. And divorce should be made more difficult to discourage marital break-up (Morgan, 1999; Saunders, 2000).

Supporting all families

Critics of the New Right argue that governments should not

attempt to impose one type of family and force everybody into the same mould. Instead, they should recognise that families are diverse and the trend is towards increasing diversity. Government policy should therefore support *all* families (Bernardes, 1997).

It is not the job of government to force couples to stay together by making divorce more difficult. Nor should rights and privileges be denied to those who cohabit simply because they aren't married. Governments should not make judgements about which form of family is best and base policy on such judgements. They should accept the decisions people have made about *their* form of family life and develop policies to support all families.

Family policy in the UK

Conservative policy This section looks at family policy from 1990. The Conservative Party under John Major was in government from 1990 to 1997. It showed a clear preference for the married, two-parent nuclear family. Lone parents were denounced in what one writer described as 'an orgy of lone-parent bashing' (Lister, 1996). John Major himself heralded the virtues of 'traditional family values' in his Back to Basics campaign. However, this campaign was quietly brushed under the carpet, not least because many Cabinet members were divorced – hardly a reflection of traditional family values.

Talk rather than action characterised the Major years. There were only two significant pieces of legislation directed at the family. In 1991, The Child Support Act was passed which led to the formation of the Child Support Agency. The main aim was to force absent fathers to pay maintenance for their children in the hope of reducing welfare payments to lone mothers. Although the government claimed this would help lone mothers, any money received from the fathers was deducted from the mothers' benefits.

The Family Law Act of 1996 introduced a one year waiting period before a couple could divorce. The intention of the act was to support the institution of marriage. Couples were encouraged to take every possible step to save their marriage. However, the act was never implemented as judges saw it as unworkable.

Labour policy The tone of Labour's words on family policy was milder than those of the Conservatives. There was an attempt to steer a middle course between supporting both marriage and the nuclear family and providing help for other forms of family. There was no 'back to basics' but no 'anything goes' either. Labour has been careful not to condemn alternatives to the nuclear family (Lewis, 2001).

This can be seen from *Supporting Families* (1998) – a discussion document which suggested ways of providing 'better services and support for parents'. The emphasis is on *all* families. The government doesn't want to 'interfere' in family life, to 'pressure people' into a preferred family form, or to 'force' married couples to stay together. It accepts that many lone parents and unmarried couples

raise children successfully. But, at the end of the day, 'marriage is still the surest foundation for raising children'.

This is what Labour said. What have they done?

Labour's family policy has formed part of its welfare policy. Summed up in Tony Blair's statement, 'Work for those that can, security for those that can't', this policy seeks to move those who can work from welfare into work and to improve benefits for those who can't.

Labour's New Deal schemes are designed to help people find paid employment. One of these schemes is aimed at lone parents, most of whom are lone mothers. Since April 2001, all lone parents are required to attend an annual interview about job opportunities. The Working Families Tax Credit tops up the wages of parents moving from benefits to low paid jobs.

Various childcare schemes have been introduced. For example, the Sure Start programme provides health and support services for low-income families with young children.

One of Labour's stated aims is to take all children out of poverty. Various benefits have been increased with this in mind. For example, Child Benefit has been increased by 26% in real terms from 1997 to 2001 (Page, 2002). According to the Children's Secretary Ed Balls, Labour has 'lifted 600,000 children out of poverty'. However, the number of children living in poor families rose for the first time in six years in 2005-06 by 200,000 to 3.8 million (*Guardian*, 30.10.2007).

Labour's policies focus on money and work – children need money, parents have a responsibility to work (Lewis, 2001).

Recent developments Political parties are increasingly recognising the realities of family life – that family diversity is here to stay. Politicians are realising that the clock can't be turned back, that they have a responsibility to support all families. Alternative family forms are no longer condemned.

This can be seen clearly from David Willetts' speech at the Conservative (Tory) Party Conference in October 2002. He announced, 'Let me make it absolutely clear: the Tory war on lone parents is over'. He admitted that families come in all shapes and sizes, and that the state had a duty to support them all. Talking about lone parents, he said, 'We'll support them and value them and, above all, we'll back them'. Yet, despite this, Willetts' claimed that the evidence was 'overwhelming' that it was better for children to be brought up by two parents in a stable marriage.

The Conservative leader David Cameron echoes these views. His argument runs as follows.

- 'Families matter because almost every social problem comes down to family stability.'
- Children need a stable family background.
- The evidence shows that a 'married family' is more likely than other forms to provide this stability. For example, married couples are less likely to break up than cohabiting couples.

- It therefore makes sense for the state to support the 'married family'.
- One option is to support marriage by using the tax and benefit system to give favourable treatment to married couples.

Although he recognises that governments should support all types of family, David Cameron clearly favours the 'married family' (www.conservatives.com). It is noticeable that the proposed tax allowances for married couples with children do not extend to cohabiting couples with children.

The Conservatives have tended to focus on marriage seeing it as the best social context for raising children. Labour have tended to focus on children, whatever the social context in which they are raised. They have been reluctant to single out marriage for support, arguing that it would discriminate against lone parents and cohabiting couples. Gordon Brown made the following statement at the 2007 Labour Party Conference.

'I say to the children of two parent families, one parent families, foster parent families; to the widow bringing up children: I stand for a Britain that supports as first class citizens not just some children and some families but supports all children and all families.'

summary

1. Functionalists argue that the family is a universal institution. It performs functions which are essential for the maintenance and well-being of society.

2. Parsons argues that the family performs two 'basic and irreducible' functions in modern industrial society – primary socialisation and the stabilisation of adult personalities.

3. The New Right sees the nuclear family as the ideal family form. They believe the nuclear family is under threat. Alternative family forms, particularly lone mother families, fail to provide adequate socialisation.

4. Marxists argue that the modern family has been shaped to fit the needs of capitalism. It helps to maintain an economic system based on exploitation.

5. Feminists see the family as patriarchal – it is dominated by men and serves the needs of men.

6. According to the New Right, government policy should favour marriage and the nuclear family.

7. Others argue that governments should recognise family diversity and support all family forms.

8. The main political parties now agree that family diversity is a reality and that governments have a duty to support all types of family. However, Conservatives tend to see the 'married family' as the best social arrangement for raising children. Labour tend to focus on supporting children, whatever types of family they are raised in.

Unit 3 The family and social change

key issues

1 What is the relationship of the family to industrialisation and urbanisation?

2 Has there been a trend towards nuclear families?

3.1 The family in pre-industrial society

Farming families

Before the industrial revolution, most people lived on the land. Family members worked together to produce goods and services – the family unit was a *production unit*. Activity 8 Item A shows people working together in Medieval England. The people working together are probably from the same family.

In many developing countries today, the farming family continues as a production unit. This can be seen from Activity 8 Item B which describes a farming family in Manupur, a village in India.

Cottage industry

Before the industrial revolution, many goods were produced by craftsmen and women in their homes and in small workshops. This type of production is sometimes known as *cottage industry* as goods were often produced in cottages. As with farming, the family was the main unit of production in cottage industry. Activity 9 provides a description of families producing cloth in Halifax in West Yorkshire.

Kinship-based societies

Many small-scale, non-Western societies are organised on the basis of kinship. People's roles and the institutions of society are largely based on kinship relationships – relationships of 'blood' and marriage. Families are embedded in a wider network of kin, they are closely linked to people they are related to. Societies like this are sometimes known as *kinship-based societies.*

For example, many African societies were traditionally organised on the basis of *lineages* – groups descended from a common ancestor. Lineages often owned land and formed

activity8 farming families (1)

Item A Farming in Medieval England

Harvesting

Milking sheep to make cheese and butter

Item B Farming families in India

Husband and wife picking crocuses to make saffron in Kashmir, India

The day begins early for a farmer in Manupur, around four in the morning. He must first feed the animals (oxen, cows, buffalo) and give them water.

The oxen are tied to the cart at around five o'clock in the morning and the men are ready to go to the fields and work. Meals are brought to the field by the son, or, if necessary, by the daughter. The distance between the house and the farm is sometimes over a mile, and it would be a waste of precious time to go home.

During sowing and harvest times, work may go on as late as 10:00pm. Once home, the animals must be tended. If the farmer has a young son, grass has already been cut; if not, he must employ someone to do it. It remains for him to prepare the fodder, and to feed, wash, and clean the animals.

The farmer's wife has an even greater burden of work. She must prepare the meals (breakfast, lunch, and dinner) and tea (early morning, mid-afternoon, and late night). Meals are made for the husband and the children and, if there are few children, for the labourers who have to be hired. The buffalo must be milked twice a day, morning and evening. The milk is used to make lassi, a yoghurt drink for warm mornings, and to make butter late in the evening. Dishes must be washed after every meal.

Source: Monthly Review Press, 1972

questions

1 How might the people in each of the pictures in Item A be related?

2 Why is a family essential for the farmer in Item B?

---

political units – important decisions which affected all members of the lineage were made by a council of elders.

The importance of marriage in kinship-based societies can be seen from the following quotation and the example in Activity 10. The French anthropologist, Claude Lévi-Strauss (1956), recalls meeting a pathetic looking man during his research among the Bororo of central Brazil. The man was 'about thirty years old: unclean, ill-fed, sad, and lonesome. When asked if the man was seriously ill, the answer came as a shock: What was wrong with him? – nothing at all, he was just a bachelor, and true enough, in a society where labour is systematically shared between man and woman and where only the married status

permits the man to benefit from the fruits of woman's work, including delousing, body painting, and hair-plucking as well as vegetable food and cooked food (since the Bororo woman tills the soil and makes pots), a bachelor is really only half a human being.'

Pre-industrial families

The evidence suggests that families in pre-industrial societies were often extended beyond the basic nuclear family. The example of producing textiles in Activity 9 suggests that the family was extended to include three generations – note the old woman in the picture.

activity9 cottage industry

Around 1720, Daniel Defoe (author of *Robinson Crusoe*) journeyed to Halifax in West Yorkshire. This is what he saw.

'People made cloth in practically every house in Halifax. They keep a cow or two and sow corn to feed their chickens. The houses were full of lusty fellows, some at the dye-vat; some at the loom, others dressing the cloths; the women and children carding, or spinning; all employed from the youngest to the oldest. The finished cloth was taken to the market to be sold.'

Source: "A Tour through the Whole Island of Great Britain" (1724–1727) by Daniel Defoe

Spinning in a cottage in the early 1700s

question

What evidence does this activity provide which suggests that the family is a unit of production?

There is evidence that the family was *multifunctional* – that it performed a number of functions. For example, as a production unit it had an economic function, as part of a wider kinship group it sometimes performed political functions, and by socialising children and providing them with job training, it had an important educational function.

A person's status or position in society was often ascribed – fixed at birth – by their family membership. Daughters tended to take on the status of their mothers, sons the status of their fathers.

3.2 Industrialisation, urbanisation and families

The industrial revolution began in Britain around 1750. It brought a number of important changes in society.

- A large part of the workforce moved from agriculture and small cottage industries to industrial work, producing manufactured goods in factories.
- Manufacturing industry was mechanised – machinery was used to mass produce goods. Small home-based

activity10 the economics of marriage

In many pre-industrial societies, marriage is essential for economic reasons. In traditional Inuit (Eskimo) society, men build igloos and hunt. Women gather edible plants and catch fish. Their skill in sewing animal skins into clothes is indispensable in the Arctic climate. Sewing is a skill that men are never taught, and many of the skills of hunting are kept secret from women.

Source: from Douglas, 1964

question

Why is marriage in traditional Inuit society essential for both husband and wife?

Inuit women beating fish skin to make into 'fish leather'

activity11 *loss of functions*

Item A **Factory production**

Item B **National Health Service**

Item C **Home for the elderly**

question

How can these pictures be used to argue that many of the functions of the family have been reduced or lost in modern industrial society?

family businesses could not compete with this.

- Towns and cities grew in size and the majority of the population was concentrated in large urban areas rather than small villages. This process is known as *urbanisation*.

This section examines the impact of these changes on the family.

Talcott Parsons – the isolated nuclear family

The American functionalist sociologist, Talcott Parsons (1951) argued that industrialisation has led to the *isolated nuclear family*. He sees this as the typical family form in modern industrial society. Compared to pre-industrial times, the nuclear family – the married couple and their children – are isolated from the wider kinship network. Although there are usually relationships with relatives

outside the nuclear family, these are now a matter of choice rather than necessity or obligation and duty.

Loss of functions According to Parsons, the main reason for this isolation is a loss of functions performed by the family. For example, the typical modern family is no longer a production unit – its adult members are now individual wage earners. In addition, local and national government has taken over, or reduced the importance of, many of the functions of the family. Schools, hospitals, welfare benefits and the police force have reduced the need for a wide network of kin (see Activity 11).

Achieved status In modern industrial society, status is achieved rather than ascribed. In other words, a person's position in society is achieved on the basis of merit – ability and effort – rather than ascribed on the basis of family membership. Children are unlikely to follow their parents' occupations. Job training is performed by the educational system and the employer rather than the family.

Geographical mobility In modern industrial society, extended family networks may be *dysfunctional* – they may be harmful to society. A modern industrial economy requires a geographically mobile workforce – workers who are able to move to places where their skills are in demand. Large extended families tend to be tied down by obligations and duties to their relatives. They are bulky and unwieldy units compared to the small, streamlined isolated nuclear family.

Summary Parsons argues that the isolated nuclear family is ideally suited to modern industrial society. Although it is slimmed down, it can still perform its essential functions – the socialisation of children and the stabilisation of adult personalities (see pages 67-68).

activity12 farming families (2)

Item A Families in rural Ireland

The following description is taken from a study of farming families in Ireland in the 1930s.

An elaborate system of cooperation had grown up between farmers and their relatives. Men often lent one another tools and machinery. Women clubbed together to make up a tub or firkin of butter or lend a girl when a family was shorthanded for the work of dairying.

Help from extended family members is especially important at harvest time when grass is mowed and collected. One farmer was helped by the sons of three others, his second cousins, and in due course he mowed their meadows. Another was helped by the son of his cousin and his nephew. He took his mowing machine to do the fields of their fathers. There were, however, five cases of farmers who although obviously shorthanded had no help. Two of these were bachelors who could not return the help, and two 'strangers' who would not be expected to.

Source: Frankenberg, 1966

Item B Haymaking

Haymaking in Berkshire in 1906

Baling hay on a modern farm

questions

1 a) What evidence of extended families is provided by Item A?

   b) How can this evidence be used to question Laslett's conclusions?

2 Judging from Item B, why are farmers today less likely to rely on extended family members?

Peter Laslett – the family in pre-industrial England

Historical research has questioned the view that most people in pre-industrial societies lived in extended families. The historian Peter Laslett (1965, 1977) examined parish records which record the names of people living together in households – 'under the same roof'. He found that only about 10% of households in England from 1564 to 1821 included kin beyond the nuclear family. The figure for Great Britain in 1981 was similar – around 9% – but by 2001 it had dropped to under 5% (*Social Trends*, 2002).

Laslett claims that his research shows that nuclear families were the norm in pre-industrial England. He found a similar pattern in parts of Western Europe. His research was based on *households*, but people do not have to live under the same roof to form extended families. It is not possible from Laslett's data to discover how much cooperation occurred between kin who lived in different households. Extended families may have been important even though relatives lived in neighbouring households. This can be seen from Activity 12.

Michael Anderson – the working-class extended family

Historical research by Michael Anderson (1971) suggests that the early stages of industrialisation may have encouraged the development of extended families. Anderson took a 10% sample of households from Preston in Lancashire, using data from the 1851 census. He found that 23% of households contained kin beyond the nuclear family. Most of these households were working class. This was a time of widespread poverty, high birth rates and high death rates. Without a welfare state, people tended to rely on a wide network of kin for care and support. Anderson's study suggests that the working-class extended family operated as a mutual aid organisation, providing support in times of hardship and crisis.

The mid-19th century was a period of rapid urbanisation as people moved from rural areas to work in factories – for example, in the cotton mills of Preston. Overcrowding was common due to a shortage of housing and a desire to save on rent. As a result, people often moved in with their relatives.

activity13 mutual support

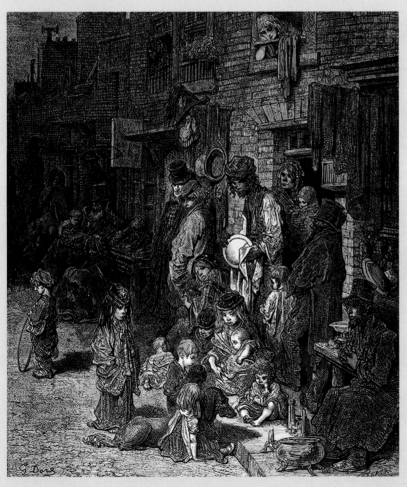

Gustav Doré's engraving of Wentworth Street, Whitechapel, London in the 1870s

question

Suggest ways in which members of the working-class extended family might help each other during the 19th century.

3.3 Industrialisation, women and families

Ann Oakley (1974) argues that industrialisation had the following effects on women and family life.

During the early years of industrialisation (1750-1841) the factory steadily replaced the family as the unit of production. Women were employed in factories where they often continued their traditional work in textiles. However, a series of factory acts, beginning in 1819, gradually restricted child labour. Someone now had to care for and supervise children, a role which fell to women. The restriction of women to the home had begun.

Women were seen by many men as a threat to their employment. As early as 1841, committees of male workers called for 'the gradual withdrawal of all female labour from the factory'. In 1842, the Mines Act banned the employment of women as miners. Women were excluded from trade unions, men made contracts with their employers to prevent them from hiring women and laws were passed restricting female employment in a number of industries. Tied down by dependent children and increasingly barred from the workplace the restriction of women to the home continued.

Slowly but surely women were being locked into the mother-housewife role and confined to the home. In 1851, one in four married women were employed, by 1911, this figure was reduced to one in ten. From 1914 to 1950 the employment of married women grew slowly but the mother-housewife role remained their primary responsibility. Even by 1970, when about half of all married women were employed, most saw their occupational role as secondary to their duties as a wife and mother and their responsibility for the home.

Oakley concludes that industrialisation had the following effects on the role of women. First, the 'separation of men from the daily routines of domestic life'. Second, the 'economic dependence of women and children on men'. Third, the 'isolation of housework and childcare from other work'. The result is that the mother-housewife role became 'the primary role for all women'.

Recent evidence indicates that the position of married women is changing. By 2000, 75% of married or cohabiting women of working age (16-59) in the UK were economically active (ie, either in work or seeking work). There has been a steady decline in full-time mothers and housewives. In 1991, 17% of women of working age gave their occupation as 'looking after family/home'. By 2001, this had declined to 13% (*Social Trends*, 2002).

*activity*14 *the mother–housewife role*

question

How does this magazine cover from 1957 reflect Oakley's picture of the mother-housewife role in the 1950s?

3.4 Families in the 20th century

There is evidence that the working-class extended family continued well into the 20th century. Research indicates it was alive and well in the 1950s in a Liverpool dock area (Kerr, 1958), in a Yorkshire mining town (Dennis, Henriques & Slaughter, 1956) and in the East End of London (Young & Willmott, 1957).

Bethnal Green In their study of Bethnal Green in the East End of London, Michael Young and Peter Willmott define an extended family as 'a combination of families who to some large degree form one domestic unit'. The extended family does not have to share the same household – ie, live under the same roof – as long as its members are in regular contact and share services such as caring for children and elderly relatives. Activity 16 is based on Young and Willmott's research in Bethnal Green.

Greenleigh In the second part of their research, Young and Willmott studied families from Bethnal Green who had been rehoused in Greenleigh, a new council estate in Essex. Young and Willmott describe their family life as *privatised* – it had become home-centred and based on the nuclear family. Living 30 miles from Bethnal Green, wives lost regular contact with their mothers and became more dependent on husbands for companionship and support. Husbands were cut off from social contacts in Bethnal Green, for example, visiting the pub with workmates, and became more involved in domestic activities. Gardening, watching television and other home-centred leisure activities largely replaced the extended family.

Young and Willmott's findings are reflected in later studies such as John Goldthorpe and David Lockwood's (1969) research into affluent (highly paid) manual workers in Luton in the 1960s. Many had moved to Luton in search of better paid jobs. They led privatised, home-centred lives – the home and nuclear family were the focus of their leisure activities.

Stages of family life

Many sociologists have argued that there is a long-term trend towards the nuclear family. Michael Young and Peter Willmott take a similar view. In a study entitled *The Symmetrical Family* (1973), they bring together their earlier research, historical evidence, and data from a survey they conducted in London in the early 1970s. They argue that the family in Britain has developed through three stages.

Stage 1 The pre-industrial family The family at this stage is a production unit – family members work together in agriculture and cottage industries.

Stage 2 The early industrial family The industrial revolution disrupted the unity of the family as its economic function was taken over by large-scale industry. Men were

activity15 *Bethnal Green*

Item A *Mother and daughter*

The link between mother and daughter in Bethnal Green is often strong. The following example shows how much their lives are sometimes woven together. Mrs Wilkins is in and out of her mother's all day. She shops with her in the morning and goes round there for a cup of tea in the afternoon. 'Then any time during the day, if I want a bit of salt or something like that, I go round to Mum to get it and have a bit of a chat while I'm there. If the children have anything wrong with them, I usually go round to my Mum and have a little chat. If she thinks it's serious enough I'll take him to the doctor.' Her mother looked after Marilyn, the oldest child, for nearly three years. 'She's always had her when I worked; I worked from when she was just a little baby until I was past six months with Billy. Oh, she's all for our Mum. She's got her own mates over there and still plays there all the time. Mum looks after my girl pretty good. When she comes in, I say, "Have you had your tea?", and she says as often as not, "I've had it at Nan's".'

Source: Young & Willmott, 1957

Item B *Contact with kin*

Contacts of married men and women with parents

	Fathers		Mothers	
	Number with father alive	Percentage who saw father in previous 24 hours	Number with mother alive	Percentage who saw mother in previous 24 hours
Men	116	30%	163	31%
Women	100	48%	155	55%

Source: Young & Willmott, 1957

questions

1 In view of Young and Willmott's definition, does Mrs Wilkins in Item A belong to an extended family? Give reasons for your answer.

2 Mr Sykes who lives near his mother-in-law in Bethnal Green said, 'This is the kind of family where sisters never want to leave their mother's side'. How does Item B suggest that this kind of family is widespread?

increasingly drawn out of the home into industrial employment. The family was 'torn apart' – long working hours meant that men had little time to spend with their wives and children. Poverty was widespread. Kinship networks were extended, mainly by women, to provide mutual support. Extended families continued well into the 20th century in low-income, working-class areas such as Bethnal Green.

Stage 3 The symmetrical family This type of family first developed in the middle class. By the 1970s, it had spread to the working class. It has three main characteristics.

- It is nuclear.
- It is home-centred and privatised – family life is focused on the home. Husband and wife look to each other for companionship. Leisure is home-based – for example, watching TV. The family is self-contained – there is little contact with the wider kinship network.

- It is *symmetrical* – the roles of husband and wife are increasingly similar. Although wives are still mainly responsible for childcare, husbands play a greater part in domestic life.

Stratified diffusion Young and Willmott argue that the development of the stage 3 family has occurred through a process of *stratified diffusion*, whereby new ideas of family life were started by the higher social classes and gradually filtered down to the lower classes. As the working class has come to enjoy shorter working hours, more comfortable homes and a higher standard of living, family life has become increasingly privatised and nuclear. There is less need for the traditional mutual aid network of the extended family. There is more opportunity to devote time and money to home and children.

Stage 4 Young and Willmott suggest a possible fourth stage in family life. They argue that if stratified diffusion

activity16 *three stages of family life*

Item A Early 20th century

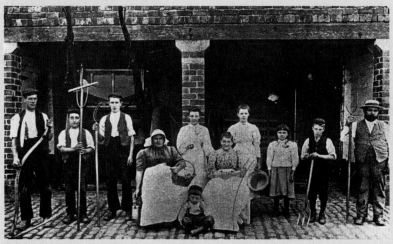

A Lancashire farming family

Item B 1954

Chatting over the garden fence

Item C 1970s

It's the little things that make it home OXO

A shot from an Oxo commercial

question

Match each picture to one of Young and Willmott's three stages of family life. Explain your choices.

continues, then the upper classes will be setting the trends for family life in the future. Their survey included a sample of managing directors' families. It indicates a trend away from the symmetrical family towards a more asymmetrical form. Husbands were highly involved in their work and domestic responsibilities were left mainly to their wives. Couples spent less time in joint activities than the typical privatised family.

Criticisms of Young and Willmott

1 Their theory suggests an historical 'march of progress' in which family life gets better and better. They have been criticised for failing to address the negative aspects of changes in the modern family.

2 Many sociologists are unhappy about the concept of stratified diffusion, implying as it does that the working class automatically follow norms established by the middle class. Goldthorpe and Lockwood's Luton study, while showing privatised lifestyles among affluent manual workers, showed that they still retained a distinctive working-class outlook on life.

3 Feminists have attacked Young and Willmott's concept of the symmetrical family. For example, they claim that women are still mainly responsible for household tasks such as cooking and cleaning (McMahon, 1999).

4 The extended family may be more important than Young and Willmott's picture of the largely independent nuclear family suggests.

The modified extended family

The picture presented so far is a steady march of progress blossoming into the privatised, self-sufficient, self-centred nuclear family. Kin beyond the nuclear family appear to play a minor role. A number of sociologists argue that this process has been exaggerated. Important services are often exchanged between nuclear family members and extended kin, though the ties that bind them are not as strong as those in the traditional extended family.

The term *modified extended family* is sometimes used to describe such family groupings. Members come together for important family events and provide support in times of need. Improved communications, such as email, telephones, cars and air travel, mean that contact over long distances is easier than before.

The following studies suggest that sociologists have tended to underestimate the importance of kinship beyond the nuclear family.

North London in the 1980s Peter Willmott (1986) studied married couples with young children in a North London suburb. Two-thirds saw relatives at least once a week, nearly two-thirds were helped by mothers or mothers-in-laws when a child was ill, and nearly three-quarters were helped with babysitting – again mainly by mothers or mothers-in-law. Four-fifths looked to relatives, mainly parents or parents-in-law, when they needed to borrow money.

Luton in the 1980s In 1986-1987, Fiona Devine (1992) studied Vauxhall car workers and their families in Luton. In part, this was a restudy of Goldthorpe and Lockwood's 1960s' research which pictured the working-class family as privatised and self-contained. Devine's research suggests that the degree of privatisation has been exaggerated. Most couples had regular contact with kin – especially parents and, to a lesser extent, brothers and sisters. Many had been helped by kin to find jobs and housing when moving to the area.

Manchester in the 1990s Research in the 1990s largely confirms the findings of earlier studies. A study of Greater Manchester by Janet Finch and Jennifer Mason (1993) found that over 90% of their sample had given or received financial help from relatives, and almost 60% had shared a household with an adult relative (apart from parents) at some time in their lives. In addition, many reported giving and receiving practical assistance, emotional support, and help with children. While emphasising that family relationships are based on a sense of obligation, Finch and Mason also found that help was negotiated and not necessarily given automatically.

Declining contact, 1986-1995 The above studies indicate the continuing importance of kin beyond the nuclear family. However, there is evidence of a decline in contact with kin. The British Social Attitudes (BSA) Survey is based on a representative sample of adults aged 18 and over. The 1986 and 1995 Surveys looked at frequency of contact with kin. They indicate a significant decline. The figures suggest that people are less likely to visit or be visited by anybody at all – relatives or friends. The data showing this is presented in Activity 17.

Why has contact declined? The average journey time between relatives has increased only very slightly since 1986. There is no evidence that friends have replaced relatives. The most likely explanation appears to be the increasing proportion of women working outside the home. The most marked fall in contact has been among women in full-time employment – for example, a drop of nearly 20% seeing their mother at least once a week (McGlone et al., 1999).

Social change and the family – conclusion

Functions of the family There is no simple, straightforward relationship between industrialisation and the functions of the family, the structure of family relationships and the content of family roles. Sociologists generally agree that industrialisation ended the family's role as a unit of production. However, some argue that this has been replaced by an equally important economic function – the family as a *unit of consumption*. Goods and services are increasingly bought and consumed in the name of the family – houses, family cars, home improvements, family holidays and so on. Rising living standards resulting from industrialisation have enabled the family to become a unit of consumption.

Has the family lost many of its functions? Some

activity17 declining contact

questions

1 a) Briefly summarise the data in Item A.

   b) How does it indicate that friends have not taken over from family?

2 What does Item B suggest is the reason for reduced contact with relatives?

3 Items A and B refer to face-to-face contact with relatives. This may exaggerate the extent of the decline of contact. Why? Refer to Item C in your answer.

sociologists argue that the functions of the family have not been reduced or lost. Instead, they have been supplemented and supported. For example, Ronald Fletcher (1966) claims that traditional functions such as the care and education of children have been supported rather than removed by state schools, hospitals and welfare provision.

Structure of the family Does industrialisation lead to the development of isolated nuclear families? Not necessarily, as Anderson's study of Preston in 1851 indicates. However, many sociologists believe there is a trend in this direction. Although extended family networks continued well into the 20th century, available evidence suggests that they have largely disappeared in their traditional form.

However, the picture of the privatised, self-contained nuclear family has probably been exaggerated. Contact between kin beyond the nuclear family is widespread – sufficient to use the term modified extended family to describe many families. However, there is evidence that contact declined fairly significantly towards the end of the 20th century.

Family roles Have family roles changed as a result of industrialisation? To some extent yes, though not simply in one direction. For example, women were an important part of the labour force during the early years of industrialisation, most had turned to the home by the beginning of the 20th century, then most had returned to paid employment by the start of the 21st century.

Family diversity This unit has looked at some of the changes in family life since industrialisation. However, it has not examined some of the more recent changes mentioned in Unit 2 – the growth in lone-parent families, reconstituted families and cohabitation, the rise in the divorce rate, and the increase in gay and lesbian families. These changes will now be examined.

key terms

Symmetrical family A nuclear family in which the roles of husband and wife are increasingly similar. It is home-centred, privatised and self-contained.

Stratified diffusion The spread of ideas and behaviour through the class system from top to bottom.

Modified extended family A weaker version of the traditional extended family. Members don't usually share the same household. However, contact is regular and important services are often exchanged.

Unit of consumption A group of people who consume goods and services as a unit.

summary

1 Families in pre-industrial society performed a range of functions. These included economic, educational and welfare functions.

2 Pre-industrial families were often extended – they formed part of a wider kinship network. This wider network was needed to effectively perform the family's functions.

3 Talcott Parsons saw the isolated nuclear family as the typical family structure in industrial society. He argued that family members no longer needed to rely on large kinship networks because many of the family's functions had been taken over by specialised agencies.

4 According to Parsons, an industrial economy requires a geographically mobile labour force. The small, streamlined nuclear family meets this requirement.

5 Peter Laslett's research shows that only 10% of pre-industrial households in England contained kin beyond the nuclear family. However, family members do not have to live under the same roof to form extended families.

6 Michael Anderson's research on Preston households in 1851 suggests that the early years of industrialisation may have encouraged the formation of extended families in the working class. Such families may have operated as mutual aid organisations before the days of the welfare state.

7 During the early years of industrialisation, married women often worked in factories. They were gradually excluded from the labour force and restricted to the home. The mother-housewife role became their primary role. Today, the majority of women have returned to the labour force.

8 Defined by Young and Willmott as 'a combination of families who to some large degree form one domestic unit', extended families continued well into the 20th century in many working-class areas.

9 Young and Willmott claim that the family in Britain has developed through three stages: 1) the pre-industrial family 2) the early industrial family 3) the symmetrical family.

10 Studies from the 1950s to the early 1970s claimed that the typical family structure was nuclear. Families were pictured as privatised, home-centred and self-contained.

11 Studies from the 1980s and 1990s suggested that this picture of privatisation and self-containment was exaggerated. Kin beyond the nuclear family still played an important role. Many families could be described as modified extended families.

12 However, evidence from the British Social Attitudes Survey indicates that contact with kin beyond the nuclear family declined towards the close of the 20th century.

Unit 4 *Changing family relationships*

keyissues

1 How have patterns of marriage, cohabitation, childbearing, separation and divorce changed?

2 What explanations have been given for these changes?

4.1 Marriage

Apart from a few ups and downs, the number of marriages per year in the UK increased steadily from 1838 (when they were first recorded) until the early 1970s. Since then there has been a significant decline, from 480,000 marriages in 1972 to 283,700 in 2005 (unless mentioned, the figures in this unit are taken from *Social Trends* and National Statistics online).

These figures refer both to *first marriages*, in which neither partner has been married before, and to *remarriages* in which one or both partners have been married before.

First Marriage The number of first marriages in England and Wales peaked in 1940 at 426,100 (91% of all marriages) then fell to 146,120 in 2005 (60% of all marriages).

Remarriage Remarriages increased from 57,000 in 1961 (14% of all marriages) to 98,580 in 2005 (40% of all marriages). Most remarriages involve divorced persons rather than widows and widowers. The largest increase occurred between 1971 and 1972 following the introduction of the Divorce Reform Act of 1969, and then levelled off.

Age at marriage Over the past 40 years, people have tended to marry later. In 1971, the average age for first marriages in England and Wales was 25 for men and 23 for women. By 2005, it was 32 for men and 29 for women. The increase in cohabitation – living together as a couple – partly accounts for this. Many couples know see cohabitation as a prelude to marriage.

Civil partnerships The Civil Partnership Act came into effect in the UK in December 2005. The Act grants same-sex couples identical rights and responsibilities as opposite-sex married couples. There were 18,059 civil partnerships formed in the UK between December 2005 and the end of December 2006.

key terms

First marriage A marriage in which neither partner has been married before.
Remarriage A marriage in which one or both partners have been married before.

activity18 patterns of marriage

Item A *Marriages and divorces*

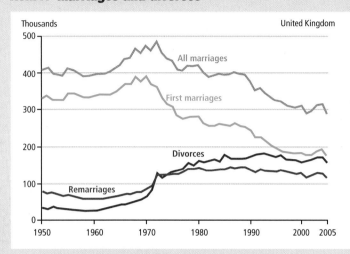

Source: *Social Trends*, 2007, Office for National Statistics

Item B *Keep on marrying*

Patsy Kensit with husband number three, Liam Gallagher. The marriage is now over.

Item C *Wary of marriage*

Sue Sharpe studied working-class girls in London schools in the early 1970s. She found their main concerns were 'love, marriage, husbands, children, jobs, and careers, more or less in that order'. A third wanted to be married by 20 and three-quarters by 25.

When she returned to the same schools in the early 1990s, she found the girls' priorities had changed to 'job, career and being able to support themselves'. In her words, 'Young people had witnessed adult relationships breaking up and being reconstituted all around them. Girls in particular were far more wary of marriage. Now, only 4 per cent wanted to be married by 20, although there was still a feeling of "A wedding day – that sounds good fun".'

Source: Sharpe, 1976 and 1994

Joan Collins with husband number five, Percy Gibson.

questions

1 a) Describe the trends shown in Item A.

   b) What does Item A suggest about the relationship between divorce and remarriage?

2 Why does the term 'serial monogamy' fit Patsy Kensit's and Joan Collins's marital history?

3 How might Item C help to explain
   a) the decline in marriage
   b) the later age of marriage?

Singlehood

Some people never marry. They either choose to remain single or fail to find a suitable marriage partner. There are increasing numbers of 'never-married' people. For example, in England and Wales only 7% of women born between 1946 and 1950 remained unmarried by the age of 32, compared with 28% of those born between 1961 and 1965. There is a similar trend for men.

Many 'never-married' people cohabit – they live with a partner as a couple. There has been a steady increase in cohabitation in recent years as the following section

indicates. There has also been a steady increase in singlehood – living without a partner.

Creative singlehood In the past, being single was seen as a negative status, particularly for women. They had 'failed' to find a marriage partner, their situation was 'unfortunate', they were 'spinsters' and 'old maids' – terms with negative overtones.

Today, views are changing. The term *creative singlehood* is sometimes used to describe a positive view of singlehood whereby people choose to remain single as a lifestyle option.

activity19 singlehood

Item A *Creative singlehood*

Never-married people who live alone tend to see their situation in positive terms. They have chosen to remain single. They emphasise the importance of independence and freedom. As one single woman in her 30s put it, 'It was the freedom of it really, come and go when I like'.

Others emphasise the importance of work. One woman said, 'Until the age of 30 there was always a man in my life, but around the age of 30, it all started to change and work took over. By the age of 35, I had come to the conclusion that I should knock it on the head and concentrate on work'.

Source: Hall et al., 1999

Singles' night in a supermarket

Item B *Single women*

Women are choosing to live alone because they have the capacity to do so. New opportunities in education and employment over the past few decades mean there is now a third way for women between living with and looking after their aged parents, or getting married. Single women tend to have much more developed and intense social networks and are involved in a wide range of social and other activities. Single men, by contrast, tend to be lonely and isolated. The signs are that living alone is good for women but bad for men.

Source: Scase, 2000

Girls' night out

questions

1 How does the term creative singlehood apply to Item A?

2 Why are more women choosing to remain single? Refer to both items in your answer.

4.2 Cohabitation

Definition Cohabitation is living together as a couple without being married. It involves a shared residence in which a couple set up home together. Love is the most common reason people give for cohabiting (McRae, 1999).

Extent and age From 1976 to 1998, the proportion of non-married women under 50 who were cohabiting more than trebled – from 9% to over 27%. Cohabiting couples tend to be young – nearly 40% of non-married women aged 25 to 29 were cohabiting in 1998. The picture is similar for men (Haskey, 2001).

In Britain in 2005, 24% of non-married men and women under 60 were cohabiting, around twice the proportion in 1986 (*Social Trends*, 2007).

Cohabitation and marriage Cohabitation before marriage has now become the norm. Figure 1 shows the proportions of first and second marriages in which the couple lived

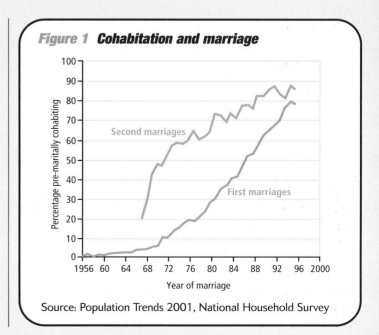

Figure 1 *Cohabitation and marriage*

Source: Population Trends 2001, National Household Survey

together before marriage. For first marriages in the 1950s the figure was less than 2%, by 1996 it was 77%. For second marriages, the figure rose from less than 20% in 1967 to 84% in 1996 (Haskey, 2001).

Reasons for cohabitation The 1998 British Household Panel Survey asked people why they chose to cohabit. These are the reasons they gave.

- For most people, cohabitation is part of the process of getting married – it is a prelude to marriage, *not* an alternative to marriage.
- Over half saw cohabitation as a trial marriage – it provided an opportunity to test the relationship before making it legally binding.
- Around 40% saw cohabitation as an alternative to marriage – they saw advantages to living together rather than marrying.
- Some mentioned the absence of legal ties – this gave them more freedom to end the relationship (*Social Trends*, 2002).

Causes

Over the past 50 years, cohabitation has increased rapidly. What accounts for this increase?

Changing attitudes Attitudes towards sexual relationships and living arrangements outside marriage have changed. Cohabitation is no longer seen as 'living in sin' or described with negative phrases such as 'living over the brush'.

Evidence for change can be seen from the 1996 British Household Panel Survey. Asked whether they thought 'living together outside marriage was always wrong', a third of those aged 60 and over thought it was wrong compared with less than a tenth of those under 30 (*Social Trends*, 2002).

Effective contraception From 1967, reliable contraception was made readily available to unmarried women with the passing of the NHS (Family Planning) Act. For the first time, full sexual relations could be an expression of love for a partner rather than a means of reproduction. Effective contraception made it possible for couples to cohabit with little fear of pregnancy (Allan & Crow, 2001).

Changes in parental control, education and housing There is some evidence that parental control over children has decreased over the past 50 years. The 1960s are often seen as the decade when young people revolted against the authority of their parents and the 'older generation'.

The expansion of higher education means that increasing numbers of young people are leaving home at an earlier age for reasons other than marriage. For example, there were 173,000 female undergraduates in the UK in 1970/71 compared with over 1.4 million in 2004/05. As a result, many young people have more freedom from parental authority at an earlier age, and they are able to live in their own housing. This makes it easier for couples to cohabit. In addition, building societies are now more likely to lend to unmarried couples – at one time they were very unlikely

to lend to those 'living in sin' (Allan & Crow, 2001).

Changes in divorce The divorce rate has increased rapidly over the past 50 years. Couples in which one or both partners are divorced are the most likely to cohabit. Having already achieved independence from their parents, they are less likely to be affected by parental control. Also, if their divorce has not gone through, cohabitation is their only option if they want to live as a couple.

The rise in divorce means that the view of marriage as a 'union for life' has less power. This may lead many people to see cohabitation, without its binding legal ties, as an attractive alternative to marriage. Some people actually give 'fear of divorce' as a reason for cohabiting (McRae, 1999; Allan & Crow, 2001).

4.3 Divorce and separation

This section looks at the breakup of partnerships. It is mainly concerned with divorce.

Trends in divorce

In the UK, as in other Western societies, there has been a dramatic rise in divorce during the 20th century. This can be seen from the actual number of divorces each year and from the increase in the *divorce rate* – the number of divorces per thousand married people.

Table 1 shows both these measures for *decrees absolute* (final divorces) in England and Wales from 1931 to 2006. Both the number and rate of divorce peaked in 1993. Since then, there has been a gradual decline.

Table 1 Divorce: decrees absolute (England and Wales)

Year	Numbers	Rate per 1,000 married population
1931	3,668	0.4
1951	28,265	2.6
1964	34,868	2.9
1969	51,310	4.1
1972	119,025	9.5
1981	145,713	11.9
1991	158,745	13.4
1993	165,018	14.2
1996	157,107	13.9
1998	145,214	12.9
2000	141,135	12.7
2006	132,562	12.2

With reference to various issues of Population Trends, Office for National Statistics

Interpreting divorce statistics

Divorce statistics provide an accurate measure of one type of marital breakdown – the legal termination of marriages. However, marriages can end in other ways.

Separation The married couple end their marriage by separating – living in separate residences. However, they remain legally married. Some couples obtain separation orders granted by magistrates' courts.

Empty-shell marriages The couple live together, remain legally married, but their marriage exists in name only. Love, sex and companionship are things of the past.

As the divorce rate increased, there may have been a decrease in separations and empty-shell marriages. From 1897-1906, around 8,000 separation orders were granted each year compared to 700 divorces. By 1971, only 94 separation orders were granted compared to over 74,000 divorces. There are no figures on informal ('unofficial') separations. Nor are there any figures on the extent of empty-shell marriages. Such marriages were often maintained in order to 'keep up appearances' and avoid the stigma (shame) of divorce. This stigma considerably reduced during the last half of the 20th century.

As the next section indicates, divorce has become easier and cheaper throughout the last century. In view of this, people who previously separated or endured empty-shell marriages are probably more likely to choose divorce.

Cohabitation Marriage is only one form of partnership. As noted earlier, cohabitation is an increasingly popular form of partnership. Available evidence suggests that, in any given period, a significantly higher number of cohabitations are terminated than marriages (Allan & Crow, 2001).

Conclusion Are partnerships becoming more unstable, more likely to break up? In view of the evidence outlined above, it is not possible to answer this question. However, one sociologist, Robert Chester (1984), believes that the increase in divorce rates probably reflects an increase in marital breakdown – though he admits this cannot be proved.

key terms

Divorce The legal termination of a marriage.
Divorce rate The number of divorces per thousand married people.
Separation A married couple who end their relationship and live in separate residences but remain legally married.
Empty-shell marriage The couple share the same residence, remain legally married, but their marriage exists in name only.

Explaining changing divorce rates

Changes in the law Before 1857 a private Act of Parliament was required to obtain a divorce in Britain. This was an expensive and complicated procedure beyond the means of all but the most wealthy. In 1857 the Matrimonial Causes Act set up a new court for divorce. The grounds for divorce included adultery, cruelty and desertion. At least one partner had to be proven guilty of one of these 'matrimonial offences'. Although the costs of obtaining a divorce were now reduced, they were still beyond the reach of most people.

Throughout the first half of the 20th century a series of Acts simplified divorce proceedings, reduced the costs involved and widened the grounds for divorce. The financial burden of divorce was eased for the less well-off by the Legal Aid and Advice Act of 1949 which provided free legal advice and paid solicitors' fees for those who could not afford them.

The Divorce Reform Act of 1969 involved a major change in the grounds for divorce. Before this Act, a 'matrimonial offence' had to be proven, a 'guilty party' had to be found. However, many people who wanted a divorce had not committed adultery, been guilty of cruelty, and so on. The 1969 Act defined the grounds for divorce as 'the irretrievable breakdown of the marriage'. It was no longer necessary to prove guilt but simply to show that the marriage was beyond repair. The Act came into force in January 1971 and was followed by a rapid rise in the divorce rate.

The Matrimonial Family Proceedings Act of 1984 came into effect in 1985. This Act reduced from three years to one the time a couple had to be married before they could petition for a divorce.

Changes in the law have made divorce a lot easier. The grounds for divorce have been widened, the procedure has been simplified and the expense reduced. Changes in the law have provided greater opportunities for divorce. However, this doesn't explain why more and more people are taking advantage of these opportunities.

Changing expectations of love and marriage Since the 1950s, a number of sociologists have argued that changes in people's expectations of love and marriage have resulted in increasingly unstable relationships. Functionalists such as Ronald Fletcher and Talcott Parsons claim that people expect and demand more from marriage. Because of this, they are less likely to put up with an unhappy marriage and more likely to end it with divorce. Ronald Fletcher (1966) argues that a higher divorce rate reflects a higher value placed on marriage. In terms of this argument, the fact that a large proportion of divorcees remarry suggests that they are not rejecting the institution of marriage but simply expecting more from the relationship.

More recently, the British sociologist Anthony Giddens (1992) has seen a trend towards what he calls *confluent love*. This form of love focuses on intimacy, closeness and emotion. It forms the basis of relationships rather than the feelings of duty and obligation reflected in the traditional marriage vows of 'for better or worse, for richer or poorer, 'til death do us part'. Intimate relationships based on confluent love tend to last as long as partners find satisfaction and fulfilment.

activity20 divorce and the law

Divorce rates (England and Wales)	
Year	Rate
1931	0.4
1951	2.6
1964	2.9
1972	9.5
1981	11.9
1991	13.4
2000	12.7
2006	12.2

With reference to various issues of *Population Trends*, Office for National Statistics.

question

How might changes in the law have affected the divorce rate?

The decision to marry is increasingly based on confluent love. When marriage ceases to provide the intimacy demanded by confluent love, individuals are likely to end it. If Giddens is correct, then marriage is an increasingly unstable and fragile institution, and divorce will become more frequent.

Overloading marriage Research from the United States indicates that individuals have become increasingly dependent on their partners for emotional support. From 1985 to 2004, research participants reported they had fewer close relationships with friends, colleagues, neighbours and extended family members. Increasingly isolated, they demanded more and more support from their partners. According to the American historian Stephanie Coontz (2006), this can lead to marital breakup by overloading the relationship.

Individualisation According to the German sociologists Ulrich Beck and Elisabeth Beck-Gernsheim (2001), today's society is characterised by individualisation. The norms which define appropriate behaviour are becoming less powerful. As a result, people are increasingly liberated from the restrictions society places on their behaviour and free to develop as individuals. A high value is placed on self-expression, individual fulfilment and independence. Individualisation can place a strain on marriage, since marriage can restrict freedom and self-expression. High divorce rates can be seen as a result of individualisation.

Changing social values Throughout the 20th century divorce became more socially acceptable. Couples were less likely to stay together in order to 'keep up appearances' and to avoid the stigma and shame formerly associated with divorce.

The rising divorce rate has led to the 'normalisation' of divorce. This, in itself, has made divorce more acceptable as a means of dealing with a failed marriage (Cockett & Tripp, 1994).

The economic position of women Women have often been 'trapped' in unhappy marriages because they cannot support themselves and their children without their husband's income. Unless they can become economically independent, their opportunities to divorce are severely restricted (Kurz, 1995).

Over the past 50 years, married women's chances of economic independence have improved significantly. Increasing numbers of women have entered the labour market, divorce settlements have taken more account of the financial needs of women, and welfare benefits for women with dependent children have improved (Allan & Crow, 2001). Although most women find themselves financially worse off after divorce, they are able to live independently from their former husband.

Women and marriage Feminists have seen rising divorce rates as symptomatic of all that is wrong with traditional patriarchal marriage – male dominance and the unequal division of domestic labour, with women still largely responsible for housework and childcare even when they are employed outside the home (see page 71). It is women rather than men who are increasingly dissatisfied with marriage.

There is some evidence for this view. Divorced men are more likely to remarry than divorced women. According to Diana Gittins (1993), this is because women are more disillusioned with marriage. In the 1940s, around two-thirds of divorce petitions were brought by husbands. By 2000, the situation was reversed with 70% of petitions brought by wives (*Population Trends, 109*, 2002). This may indicate that women are more dissatisfied with marriage than men. Or, it may reflect a greater need to settle financial and housing arrangements, particularly for women with dependent children (Allan & Crow, 2001).

activity21 case studies

Item A Sarah

Sarah, 39, runs a public relations consultancy. During her marriage she was largely responsible for caring for the children – two girls – and running the home – 'all the washing, the cleaning and the cooking' – as well as working full time. She found that, as the children grew older, 'I started to resent what I saw as the inequality in our lives'. Her husband Adam 'could not see what I thought was glaringly obvious'. She felt that she couldn't be herself because 'he used to put me down and was so controlling'.

She decided to divorce Adam. She notes, 'Economic independence played a big part. I knew I could afford to run my own life because I had a successful business, and it made it possible for me to initiate the breakup. I feel so much more myself, being in control of my life. I think it's hard for women to stay married today. We have high expectations, but men and women are still not equal and so many women are resentful about being expected to do it all.'

Source: Appleyard, 2002

Item B Jan

Jan, 43, is a writer. She has four children, three with her former husband and one with her new partner Mike. 'I met Mike four years ago, and happy as we are, I have no desire to marry. I want to be in control of my life – and the majority of women today feel the same.'

'The reason so many are initiating divorce is because we don't have to be dependent on – or controlled by – a man. We want to lead our lives in a way that makes us happy, without being answerable to men. When I was married, I was expected not only to bring money into the house, but to do all the domestic chores as well. The big issue between us was always money. He was earning £30,000 a year, which was a big salary, but I wasn't allowed to buy as much as a magazine without asking him first.'

Source: Appleyard, 2002

Item C Domestic labour

question

To what extent do Items A, B and C support the explanations given for divorce?

key terms

Confluent love A term used by Giddens to describe a form of intimate relationship which is dependent on both partners finding fulfilment and satisfaction in the relationship.

Individualisation A process which increasingly releases people from society's norms and allows them to develop greater independence and self-expression.

Who divorces?

So far, this section has been concerned with the rise in divorce rates. The focus now is on the social distribution of divorce – on the variation in divorce rates between different social groups. This variation is particularly apparent for age and social class groups.

Age In general, the earlier the age of marriage, the more likely it is to end in divorce. For women who were under 20 when they married in the late 1980s, 24% had separated within 5 years compared with 8% who married between the ages of 25 and 29. Reasons suggested for the high divorce rate of young marrieds include:

- The bride is more likely to be pregnant which places a strain on the marriage.

- Money problems – young people are more likely to be low paid or unemployed.

- Lack of experience in choosing a suitable partner.
- Lack of awareness of the demands of marriage.
- More likely to 'grow apart' as their attitudes and beliefs are still developing.

Social class In general, the lower the class position of the husband, the more likely the couple are to divorce. Financial problems appear to be the main cause. Unemployment, reliance on state benefits and low income are all associated with high divorce rates (Kiernan & Mueller, 1999).

Other factors A number of other factors are associated with high divorce rates. They include:

- Experience of parents' divorce – this may cause psychological problems which are carried forward to the child's marriage. Or, it may simply make divorce more acceptable.
- Remarriages are more likely to end in divorce than first marriages. Maybe the problems which caused the first divorce are carried through into the second marriage.
- Differences in class, ethnicity and religion between the couple are associated with higher divorce rates. They will have less in common, they may have different expectations about marriage, and these differences may result in conflict.

The consequences of divorce

Divorce has a variety of consequences – for the couple involved, for their children, their relatives and friends, and for the wider society. This section looks at the effects of divorce on children and on the wider society.

Divorce and children Opinions about the effects of divorce on children abound. Some see it as uniformly harmful and argue that parents should go to great lengths to stay together for the sake of the children. Others argue that if divorce frees children from a bitter and hostile family environment then, on balance, it is beneficial. In these circumstances parents should divorce for the sake of the children.

In a study entitled *Divorce and Separation: The Outcomes for Children*, Rodgers and Pryor (1998) reviewed some 200 studies. They attempted to find out whether claims about the harmful effects of divorce on children were supported by research evidence.

The review confirmed that children of divorced or separated parents have a higher probability of experiencing a range of problems such as poverty, poor housing, behavioural problems (eg, bedwetting and anti-social behaviour), teenage pregnancy and educational under-achievement. Although children of divorced and separated parents have around twice the chance of experiencing these sorts of problems, only a minority actually do so. A key question is why a minority of children appear to suffer from divorce while most do not.

Rodgers and Pryor suggest that it is not divorce alone which causes these problems, but the association of divorce with other factors. These include:

- Financial hardship – which may have an effect on educational achievement.
- Family conflict – which may create behavioural problems for children.
- Parental ability to cope with the changes that divorce brings – if parents cannot cope, then children are less likely to do so.
- Multiple changes in family structure – if divorce is accompanied by other changes, such as moving in with a step-family, children are more likely to experience problems.
- Quality and degree of contact with the parent who has left – children who have regular contact appear to cope better.

According to Rodgers and Pryor, these findings help to explain why some children experience problems with divorce, while the majority, at least in the long term, do not.

A large-scale research project conducted by Mavis Hetherington (2002) in the USA reached similar conclusions. Her findings are based on a longitudinal study over 25 years of 2500 people from childhood in 1400 families. Her evidence includes tens of thousands of hours of videotapes of families at dinner, at play, relaxing and having rows. Hetherington concludes that three out of four children experience little long-term damage from divorce. She admits that 25% have serious emotional or social problems which compares with 10% from families that stay together. In her view, the negative effects on children have been exaggerated and we must accept that 'divorce is a reasonable solution to an unhappy, acrimonious, destructive marital relationship' (Hetherington, 2002).

Divorce and society From a New Right perspective (see pages 68-70) high divorce rates, and the lone-parent families that often result from divorce, are a serious threat to society. Most lone-parent families are headed by women. They lack a father-figure – a male role model who can provide discipline and an example for the future. This can lead to inadequate socialisation, particularly for boys, which can result in anti-social behaviour. Some New Right thinkers see a direct relationship between rising divorce rates and rising crime rates. In Patricia Morgan's (1999) words, 'large numbers of fatherless youths represent a high risk factor for crime'. A return to 'traditional family values' is needed to strengthen marriage, and 'tougher' laws are required because divorce has become 'too easy'. These measures will lower the divorce rate and so reduce the threat to social stability.

In contrast, many feminists strongly object to any barriers to divorce. Compared to the past, the present divorce laws provide freedom and choice, particularly for women. Restrictions on divorce may force them to endure unhappy marriages, and in some cases, physical and sexual abuse of themselves and their children. Liberal divorce laws offer greater independence for women and represent a positive step towards gender equality.

summary

1. There has been a significant decline in first marriages and in the overall total of marriages since the early 1970s. Within this total, there has been an increase in the numbers and proportion of remarriages.

2. There has been an increase in singlehood – living without a partner.

3. There has been a large increase in cohabitation from the 1970s onwards. Cohabitation before marriage is now the norm. While most people see it as a prelude to marriage, some see it as an alternative to marriage.

4. The following reasons have been suggested for the increase in cohabitation.
   - Changing attitudes
   - Availability of reliable contraception
   - Reduction of parental control
   - Expansion of higher education
   - Increased availability of housing for non-married people
   - Increase in divorce rate.

5. Reasons for the rise in divorce include changes in:
   - the law, leading to cheaper and easier divorce
   - rising expectations of love and marriage
   - overloading marriage
   - individualisation
   - attitudes towards divorce
   - the economic position of women and their view of marriage.

6. Divorce is not spread evenly throughout the population – eg there are age and class variations in divorce rates.

7. Most children appear to experience no long-term harm from their parents' divorce.

8. While the New Right sees the rise in divorce as a threat to society, feminists tend to see it as an expression of women's right to choose.

Unit 5   Family diversity

keyissues

1. How diverse are families?
2. What are the main explanations for family diversity?

5.1 Introduction

Family diversity as a theme This unit is entitled *Family diversity*. Read any recent introductory textbook on the sociology of the family and one statement rings out loud and clear – families and households in today's society are more complex and diverse than ever before. Here is a typical statement by Susan McRae in her introduction to *Changing Britain: Families and Households in the 1990s* (McRae,1999). 'Britain today is a much more complex society than in past times, with great diversity in the types of household within which people live: one-person; cohabiting; families with children and families without; stepfamilies; lone parents – whether divorced or never-married; gay and lesbian couples; pensioners.'

Family diversity as a cause for concern Alongside this recognition of family and household diversity is concern. For some, particularly the New Right, increasing diversity means increasing breakdown. A picture is presented of the family in crisis. Alternatives to the 'traditional family' are poor substitutes for the real thing. So, the families formed by cohabiting couples, the reconstituted families created by remarriage, and families headed by lone parents or by gay or lesbian couples are at best, second best. For some, they represent a disintegration of traditional family values, a breakdown of the traditional family.

The ideology of the nuclear family What is this wonderful family compared to which all others fall short? It is the nuclear family of mum, dad and the kids. For some, it was found in its ideal form in the 1950s with mum as a full-time mother and housewife and dad as the breadwinner. The couple are male and female rather than same-sex, they are married rather than cohabiting, and married for the first rather than the second or third time.

This image of the nuclear family is fostered by advertisers. Called the *cereal packet image of the family* by Edmund Leach (1967), it portrays happy, smiling nuclear families consuming family products from Corn Flakes to Oxo.

This picture can be seen as ideological. An ideology is a misleading view, based on value judgements, which obscures reality. Diana Gittins (1993) argues that the idealised picture of the nuclear family acts as a powerful ideology, defining what is normal and desirable and labelling alternative family forms as abnormal and undesirable.

It creates the impression that the nuclear family headed by a married, heterosexual couple is the only family unit that can effectively raise the next generation.

key term

Ideology A misleading view based on value judgements which obscures reality.

activity22 pictures of the family

Item A   A TV ad

Item B   Book covers

iea

Farewell to the Family?

Public Policy and Family Breakdown in Britain and the USA

Patricia Morgan

"Having won its intellectual battle for the market, London's Institute of Economic Affairs has turned its attention to the social underpinnings of a free society"
Martin Wolf, *The Financial Times*

Second Edition: Revised and Updated
Choice in Welfare No. 21

iea

The Fragmenting Family: Does It Matter?

John Haskey
Kathleen Kiernan
Patricia Morgan
Miriam E. David (Editor)

Choice in Welfare No. 44

questions

1   How can ads portraying the nuclear family be seen as ideological?

2   How do the book covers in Item B picture the family today?

5.2   Changing households

This section looks at changes in household composition in Britain over the past 40 years. A *household* consists of people who occupy a dwelling unit, for example a house or a flat. Looking at household composition provides one way of assessing the extent of family diversity. And it gives an indication about what might be happening to the nuclear family.

Table 2 shows the changing proportions of each type of household from 1961 to 2006. During this period the proportion of households made up of a couple with dependent children has declined from 38% to 22%. During this same period, the proportion of lone-parent with dependent children households has risen from 2% to 7%. These figures have sometimes been used to indicate a decline in nuclear families. They have also been used to argue that the nuclear family is no longer the dominant family type.

Table 3 provides a somewhat different picture. It looks at the percentage of people living in each type of household. It shows that in 1961, 52% of people lived in households made up of a couple with dependent children. By 2006, this figure had dropped to 37%. Even so, this is still a lot of people living in nuclear family households.

Figures for one year are just a snapshot of one part of a family's life cycle. Many households contain people who have been, or will be, members of nuclear family households – for example, couples with no children and people living alone. And the majority of British children still live in couple-headed households – 76% in 2006,

Table 2   Households: by type of household and family

Great Britain   *Percentages*

	1961	1971	1981	1991	2001	2006
One Person						
Under state pension age	4	6	8	11	14	14
Over state pension age	7	12	14	16	15	14
Two or more unrelated adults	5	4	5	3	3	3
One family households						
Couple						
No children	26	27	26	28	29	28
1-2 dependent children	30	26	25	20	19	18
3 or more dependent children	8	9	6	5	4	4
Non-dependent children only	10	8	8	8	6	7
Lone parent						
Dependent children	2	3	5	6	7	7
Non-dependent children only	4	4	4	4	3	3
Multi-family households	3	1	1	1	1	1
All households (=100%) (millions)	16.3	18.6	20.2	22.4	24.1	24.2

Source: *Social Trends*, 2002, 2007, Office for National Statistics

| Table 3 **People in households: by type of household and family in which they live** |

Great Britain *Percentages*

	1961	1971	1981	1991	2001	2006
One person	4	6	8	11	12	12
One family households						
Couple						
No children	18	19	20	23	24	25
Dependent children	52	52	47	41	39	37
Non-dependent children only	12	10	10	11	9	8
Lone parent	3	4	6	10	12	12
Other households	12	9	9	4	5	5
Total population (millions)	51.4	54.4	54.8	56.2	57.2	57.1

Source: *Social Trends*, 2002, 2007, Office for National Statistics

compared to 92% in 1972 (*Social Trends*, 2007). This suggests that living in a nuclear family is a phase that most people, as children and adults, go through in the course of their life (O'Brien, 2000).

Family diversity assessed

The extent of family diversity should not be exaggerated. Most people, as children and adults, live parts of their lives in nuclear families. Even so, the trend is towards family diversity as the figures in Tables 2 and 3 indicate. There has been a significant decline in:

- the proportion of households made up of a couple with dependent children
- the proportion of people in such households and
- the proportion of dependent children living in couple families.

This decrease in nuclear families has been matched by an increase in lone-parent families. This indicates an increase in family diversity.

The terms nuclear family and couple family conceal further diversity. The couple may be:

- married for the first time
- remarried
- cohabiting
- opposite sex
- same sex.

Over the past 30 years there has been a significant increase in remarriage, cohabitation and same-sex couples. Again, this can be seen as indicating an increase in family diversity.

The rest of this unit looks at specific examples of family diversity, focusing on lone-parent families, reconstituted families, and gay and lesbian families.

5.3 Lone-parent families

Definition

The official definition of a lone-parent family goes as follows. A mother or father living without a partner, with their dependent child or children. The child must be never-married and aged either under 16 or 16 to under 19 and undertaking full-time education. Partner in this definition refers to either a marriage or cohabitation partner (Haskey, 2002).

The above definition is not as straightforward as it seems. What about a father who does not live with the mother and child but is in regular contact, takes part in 'family' decisions and provides for the family in various ways – from income support to helping the child with homework? Is he still a member of the family?

A number of separated and divorced couples attempt to share the responsibility for raising their children. This is known as *co-parenting* or *joint parenting*. It is difficult to see such arrangements as simply lone-parent families (Neale & Smart, 1997).

Faced with this kind of problem, some sociologists have argued that the term *lone-parent household* is more precise. It simply states that the 'absent parent' is not part of the household – ie, does not live under the same roof (Crow & Hardy, 1992).

Types of lone parents

Lone parents are a diverse group. This can be seen from the ways they became lone parents. The various routes into lone parenthood are summarised below.

- The ending of a marriage either by separation or divorce (separated and divorced lone parents)
- The ending of cohabitation where the partners separate (single lone parents)
- Birth to a never-married, non-cohabiting woman (single lone parents)
- Death of a partner – for example, a husband dies leaving his wife with dependent children (widowed lone parents).

Despite these diverse routes into lone parenthood, most lone-parent families have one thing in common, they are headed by women – over 90% in 2006.

Trends in lone-parenthood

In Britain, since the early 1970s, lone-parent families, as a proportion of all families with dependent children, have steadily increased – from 7% in 1972 to 24% in 2005 (*Social Trends*, 2007).

During the 1960s, divorce overtook death as the main source of lone-parent families. From then until the mid-1980s, a large part of the increase was due to marital breakup – the separation or divorce of a married couple. After 1986, the number of single lone mothers grew at a faster rate. This group is made up of 1) never-married cohabiting women whose partnership ended after their child was born and 2) never-married women who were not cohabiting when their child was born. Each group accounts for around half of single lone mothers.

Table 4 illustrates these trends. It shows various types of lone parent families as a percentage of all families with dependent children.

The above statistics are snapshots at particular points in time. Families move in and out of lone parenthood. It is estimated that the average length of time spent as a lone parent is a little over 5 years (Allan & Crow, 2001). The routes in and out of lone parenthood are summarised in Activity 23.

Explaining the trends

Why has lone parenthood increased so rapidly over the past 35 years?

Divorce As Table 4 shows, a large part of the increase from 1971 to 1991 was due to marital breakup. The divorce rate rose rapidly after the Divorce Reform Act came into force in 1971. Reasons for the rise in divorce are outlined on pages 89-92.

Table 4   Lone-parent families

Great Britain   *Percentages*

	1971	1981	1991	2001	2005
Lone mothers					
Single	1	2	6	9	11
Widowed	2	2	1	1	1
Divorced	2	4	6	6	8
Separated	2	2	4	4	4
All lone mothers	7	11	18	20	24
Lone fathers	1	2	1	2	2
All lone parents	8	13	19	22	26

Source: *General Household Survey*, 2005, Office for National Statistics

---

key terms

Cereal packet image of the family Stereotypical view of the family common in advertising. The family is presented as nuclear with a traditional division of labour.

Lone-parent family A parent without a partner living with their dependent children.

Dependent children Children either under 16 or 16-19 and undertaking full-time education.

Co-parenting/joint parenting Parents who continue to share responsibility for raising their children after they have separated or divorced.

---

activity23 moving in and out of lone parenthood

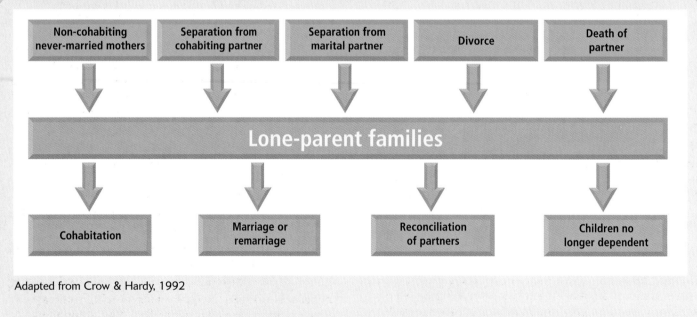

Adapted from Crow & Hardy, 1992

question

Lone parenthood is not a permanent status. Explain with reference to the above diagram.

Cohabitation breakup Over the same period, the number of marriages was steadily declining and the number of couples cohabiting increasing. Reasons for the increase in cohabitation are outlined on page 88.

Since 1986, the number of single lone mothers has grown at a faster rate than any other category of lone parent. By 2005, they accounted for over 45% of all lone mothers in Britain. Roughly half became lone mothers as a result of a breakup of their cohabitation. Cohabiting couples with children are twice as likely to end their relationship than married couples with children (Haskey, 2001).

Non-cohabiting never-married mothers This group form the other half of single lone mothers. Their children were born outside marriage and cohabitation. Their numbers have increased rapidly since the mid-1980s.

Choice Very few women give lone parenthood as their first option. In other words, the vast majority would prefer to raise their children with a partner. For example, in one study only one out of 44 lone mothers had deliberately decided to become a lone mother from the outset (Berthoud et al., 1999).

However, this does not rule out choice. Many women choose to end a marriage or cohabitation. They see this decision as a solution to a problem. It ends a relationship which is unhappy, which may be violent and abusive, and destructive for themselves and their children (Bernardes, 1997). In this sense, they are choosing to become a lone parent.

Similarly, many non-cohabiting never-married mothers choose lone parenthood from the options available to them. These options are:

- An abortion
- Give the baby up for adoption
- In some cases, the opportunity to cohabit with or marry the father.

Many women decide against these options and choose lone parenthood. To some extent, this choice reflects changing attitudes.

Finally, a growing number of women are actively choosing to become single mothers. They take steps to become pregnant with the intention of raisng the child themselves. In 1988, 28,000 women in England and Wales did not register the father's name on their child's birth certificate. This number rose to nearly 50,000 in 2006. Many of these women will have actively chosen to become single mothers (Hill, 2007).

Changing attitudes As outlined in the previous unit, there is greater tolerance of births outside marriage (see page 98). The stigma attached to children of unmarried mothers has reduced considerably. The term 'bastard' is rarely heard, and the less offensive 'illegitimate', which implies improper or immoral, is passing out of common usage.

There is far less pressure for single mothers to get married. The term 'shotgun wedding', frequently used in the 1950s and 60s, is not often heard today.

Lone-parent families are becoming increasingly acceptable. They are less likely to be described with negative phrases such as 'broken families' and 'incomplete families'.

Changing attitudes towards lone parenthood reflect a growing acceptance of the diversity of family life. This makes lone parenthood a more likely choice.

However, it is important not to exaggerate changing attitudes. As the following quotation shows, lone parents and their children are often still seen as second-class families. 'I think single parents have a lot to prove because we're constantly being told that we're not a correct family; that we can't look after our children the same as a two-parent family' (quoted in Beresford et al., 1999).

Economic independence Lone parenthood is only possible if individuals are able to support themselves and their children. However, for the majority, economic independence from a partner means barely making ends meet.

Most lone-mother families live in poverty – defined as living below 50% of average income after housing costs have been met. Often, the low pay levels of many 'women's jobs' plus the costs of childcare mean that lone mothers are better off on state benefit than in paid employment. However, there is some evidence that government New Deal schemes are helping some lone parents and their children out of poverty (see page 73).

Views of lone parenthood

The parents' views As noted earlier, becoming a lone parent was not usually the lone mother's or father's first choice option. The vast majority would rather raise their children with a partner in a happy relationship. Failing this, most choose to become lone parents. Many decide to separate from their partners, believing that it is better to become a lone parent rather than endure an unhappy and destructive relationship. Many decide to keep their child and raise it themselves, seeing this as preferable to abortion, to adoption, or to cohabiting with or marrying the child's other parent.

And, although being a lone parent is far from easy, many see benefits. In the words of one lone mother, 'I'm a bloody sight better off than many women who are married and have to run around after the husband as well as the kids' (Sharpe, 1984).

New Right views These views are outlined on pages 68-70. To recap, lone-parent families fail to provide adequate socialisation. In lone-mother families, there is no father present to discipline the children and provide a male role model. This can lead to underachievement at school, and anti-social behaviour ranging from rudeness to crime. Boys grow up with little awareness of the traditional responsibilities and duties of a father. Lone mothers become dependent on state benefits. Their children lack examples of the disciplines and responsibilities of paid employment.

As noted earlier, if the children of lone parents do have more problems, this may have little to do with lone parenthood as such. It may well result from the poverty that most lone parents experience (Allan & Crow, 2001).

Feminist views Lone parenthood usually means lone mothers. From a feminist viewpoint, this indicates that women have the freedom to choose. Rather than seeing the lone-parent family as a malfunctioning unit, some see it as an alternative family form in which women are free from male domination. And there is evidence that many single mothers welcome this independence and the opportunity it provides to take control of their own lives (Graham, 1987).

activity24 lone parents

Item A Household income

Families with dependent children
Great Britain: 2005

Family type		£0.00–£100.00	£100.01–£200.00	£200.01–£300.00	£300.01–£400.00	£400.01–£500.00	£500.01–£700.00	£700.01–and over
		Gross weekly household income						
Married couple	%	4	4	5	6	9	19	53
Cohabiting couple	%	5	6	6	12	10	27	35
Lone parent	%	11	30	19	13	10	11	6

Source: General Household Survey, 2005, Office for National Statistics

"Thoroughly engaging and informative."
—CYNTHIA NIXON

No Man? No Problem!

knock yourself up

A Tell-All Guide to Becoming a Single Mom

Louise Sloan

Item B DIY guide to single motherhood

This guide to becoming a single mother was published in the USA in 2007. It was met with praise and criticism. Cynthia Nixon, who plays Miranda in the TV series *Sex and the City*, praised the book as 'a thoroughly engaging and informative book about the decision to become a single mother'. Others were not so kind. The author, Louise Sloan, has been called 'the epitome of selfishness' and 'a woman screeching about the human rights of her own child, whom she is deliberately handicapping by condemning him to a fatherless life'.

Source: Hill, 2007

Item C Justifying single motherhood

Louise Sloan, author of *Knock Yourself Up* states that 'Independent women today are not prepared to sit dolefully on a shelf as their fertility runs out. Nor are they willing to settle for Mr You'll Have To Do or "accidentally" get pregnant by a lover reluctant to commit'.

Source: Hill, 2007

questions

1 What does item A indicate about the economic situation of many lone parents?

2 Look at Items B and C. Argue the case for and against choosing to become a single mother.

5.4 Reconstituted families

Many lone parents find new partners and form new families. These *reconstituted families* or *stepfamilies* are defined as a married or cohabiting couple with dependent children, at least one of whom is not the biological offspring of both partners (Haskey, 1994).

Compared to lone-parent families, there has been little research, public debate or government policy directed towards reconstituted families. This may be because such families tend to present themselves as 'normal' family groupings. And it may be because they are sometimes seen as a 'solution' to the so-called 'problem' of lone parenthood (Allan & Crow, 2001).

There has been a rapid increase in the number of reconstituted families. In 1998–99, they accounted for around 6% of all families with dependent children in Britain. By 2005, the figure rose to 10% (*General Household Survey*, 2005).

Diversity and reconstituted families

Reconstituted families are a diverse group. Parentline Plus, formerly the National Stepfamily Association, has identified 72 different ways in which stepfamilies can be formed. For example, some are formed by first marriage, some by remarriage, some by cohabitation. And once formed, this diversity continues. For example, some children may have

Table 5 Stepfamilies

Type of stepfamily	Great Britain: 2005
	%
Couple with child(ren) from the woman's previous marriage/cohabitation	86
Couple with child(ren) from the man's previous marriage/cohabitation	11
Couple with child(ren) from both partners' previous marriage/cohabitation	3

Source: *General Household Survey*, 2005, Office for National Statistics

close and regular relationships with their absent biological parent, other children may hardly see them.

Children are likely to stay with their mother after the break-up of a partnership. This can be seen from Table 5 – 86% of stepfamilies contain at least one child from the female partner's previous relationship.

Tensions within reconstituted families

Reconstituted families tend to present themselves as 'normal', 'ordinary' families. And, if estimates are correct, they may well become 'the norm'. Many reject labels such

*activity*25 *the 'new extended families'*

questions

Reconstituted families have been described as the new extended families.

a) What does this mean?

b) What advantages does it suggest?

as stepfamilies, step-parents and stepchildren. Despite this desire to present themselves simply as a family, reconstituted families experience particular problems.

Families are social groups with boundaries. These boundaries include some people (these are my family members) and exclude others (these are not). Clear boundaries give families a definite sense of identity and unity. Sometimes the boundaries of reconstituted families are not clearly drawn. They may become fuzzy when partners from the couple's previous relationships become involved in the new family, especially if the children maintain a close relationship with the non-residential 'natural' parent. This may weaken the boundaries of the reconstituted family and threaten its unity (Allan & Crow, 2001).

Being a step-parent can be a difficult and delicate relationship. There are no clearly stated norms defining this role. For example, to what degree should a step-parent be involved in disciplining the child? Things are made more difficult if the child resents sharing their biological parent with a new partner and, in some cases, with other children. The role of the stepfather is often shifting and uncertain – a sort of uncle, father, big brother, friend or companion depending on the time and place (Bedell, 2002).

The additional strains of reconstituted families may help to explain their high level of breakup. A quarter of stepfamilies break up during their first year. And half of all remarriages which form a stepfamily end in divorce. But, as Peter Eldrid of Parentline Plus warns, 'It's important not to assume that every difficulty you face is to do with being a stepfamily. All families have upheavals' (quoted in Bedell, 2002). And, as reconstituted families become increasingly common, norms will probably develop to clarify the roles of those involved, so reducing the tension that lack of clarity brings.

New opportunities

Research has tended to focus on the problems of reconstituted families. There is another side to the coin. For the adults, they offer the chance of a successful partnership after an earlier one has failed. And, if the parents are happy and committed to making the new family work, then the children are likely to be happy too (Bedell, 2002).

Reconstituted families can provide new and rewarding relationships for all concerned. The family expands overnight with step-brothers and sisters, step-cousins, step-parents and uncles, and step-grandparents. An expanded family network can lead to arguments, jealousy and conflict. But, it can also lead to a wider support network and enriched relationships.

5.5 Gay and lesbian families

Until recently, there was little research on gay and lesbian families. This began to change in the 1990s.

Families of choice Judging from a series of in-depth interviews conducted in the mid-1990s, many gays and lesbians are developing new ways of understanding the idea of family (Weeks et al., 1999a). Many believe they are *choosing* their own family members and creating their own families.

These *families of choice* are based on partnerships, close friends and members of their family of origin. This network provides mutual support, loving relationships and a sense of identity. It feels like a family. As one interviewee put it, 'I think the friendships I have are family' (Weeks et al., 1999b).

Same-sex partnerships In recent years, increasing numbers of gays and lesbians have formed households based on same-sex partnerships. And many are demanding the same rights as heterosexual partnerships – for example, the right to marry and adopt children. This does not mean they wish to copy heterosexual relationships, they simply want the same rights as everybody else.

In practice, same-sex partnerships tend to be more democratic than heterosexual partnerships. Many gay and lesbian couples strive for a relationship based on negotiation and equality (Weeks et al., 1999a).

Same-sex parents A growing number of lesbians are choosing to have children and to raise them with a female partner. Many use artificial insemination with sperm donated by friends or anonymous donors. In the traditional sense of the word, they are choosing to have a 'family'.

Gay men have more limited options. Either they must find a surrogate mother to bear their children, or else adopt. In the UK, the adoption route was closed until 2002 when an Act of Parliament made it legal for gays and lesbians to adopt children.

Children Concerns about children's gender identity and sexual orientation have been the main focus of research on gay and lesbian parenting. Most studies show that children raised by gay and lesbian parents are no different from those raised by heterosexuals (Fitzgerald, 1999). The evidence suggests that what matters is the parent-child relationship rather than the sexual orientation of the parents.

key term

Family of choice A family whose members have been chosen, rather than given by birth and marriage.

5.6 Families and cultural diversity

This section looks at the effects of social class and ethnicity on family life.

Social class and family diversity

Many sociologists argue that social class has an important influence on family life. They make the following points.

Income inequality In general, the lower a person's class position, the lower their income. Income inequality leads to variations in living standards, housing quality and lifestyles. For example, low-income families are more likely

activity26 families of choice

Item A A 'legal' family

Noah and Mackenlie pose with their parents, Hazel, left and Donna, right. Hazel is the biological parent of Noah, and Donna is the biological parent of Mackenlie. The two lesbians cross-adopted each other's child to legally form their family.

Item C A neighbour's response

'We (a lesbian couple) live together in a stable unit with a child. It sometimes feels like a marriage. But I only have to walk out into the street to know that it's not. There's one neighbour next door that just won't speak to us. She spoke to us before we had the baby, and now she won't speak to us.'

Source: Journal of Social Policy 1999, 28:689–709, Cambridge University Press

Item B Our family

Amanda and her partner Ruth decided to have children – they each had a son. The father is a close friend. He is now seen as part of the family. Amanda writes:

'Our children love having two mummies. They know they are different. They are proud of being special. At this young age, mummies are still hot property, and to have two is twice as nice. They see their dad regularly, and ring him when they want. And having three parents, they get all the extra grandparents, aunties, uncles, and cousins too. All our families have been fantastic. Some of them had their doubts when we first told them that we were having children, but since our boys first came into the world they have been cherished by an extended family that goes beyond a basic biology.

I'm excited about our future. I know things will not always be easy. I know that as our children get older, and learn about sexuality and the pressures of conformity, they will have many questions. They may face prejudice themselves. I hate that thought, but I know that as a family we have the strength to help them deal with it.'

Source: *The Independent*, 4.2.2002

question

There's no particular problem with gay or lesbian families – apart from some heterosexuals! Discuss.

---

to live in overcrowded and substandard housing, and less likely to own a car or afford a family holiday.

Life chances These refer to a person's chances of obtaining things defined as desirable – eg, good health – and avoiding things defined as undesirable – eg, unemployment. Often, there is a fairly close relationship between social class and life chances. For example, the higher the class position of a child's parents, the more likely the child is to attain high educational qualifications and a well paid, high status job.

Family breakup As noted earlier, the lower the class position of a married couple, the more likely they are to divorce. High divorce rates are related to poverty – to low income and reliance on state benefits (Kiernan & Mueller, 1999).

Ethnicity and family diversity

To some degree, ethnic groups have their own subcultures – norms and values which differ from those of mainstream culture. And to some degree, these subcultures influence family life. This section takes a brief look at ethnic minority groups and family diversity in the UK.

Diversity within ethnic groups There is a danger in talking about 'typical ethnic families'. Often there is as much family diversity within minority ethnic groups as there is within White society.

And there is a danger of ignoring cultural variation *within* ethnic groups. For example, within the South Asian community there are variations in religion – Sikhs, Muslims and Hindus – in countries of origin – India, Pakistan and Bangladesh – and in regions within those countries – for example, Goa and Bengal.

Finally, there is a danger of exaggerating differences between minority ethnic and White families and of creating stereotypes in the process – for example, Asians live in extended families and their marriages are arranged.

Asian families Most Asian households are based on nuclear families. However, around 20% are extended families, a higher proportion than other groups. Although there is a trend towards nuclear families, wider kinship ties remain strong (Westwood & Bhachu, 1988).

Asians are more likely to marry and to marry earlier than their White counterparts. Cohabitation and divorce are rare (Berthoud & Beishon, 1997). Marriages are sometimes arranged, but there is little research on this subject. There is some evidence which suggests that the couple have more say in arranged marriages as Western ideas about love and romance become more influential (Allan & Crow, 2001).

African-Caribbean families In 2001, nearly 48% of African-Caribbean families with dependent children were lone-parent families compared to around 22% for Britain as a whole (*Social Trends*, 2007). African Caribbeans have the lowest marriage rate, the highest proportion of single (never-married) lone mothers, and the highest divorce rate (Berthoud et al., 1999).

Statistics such as these have led some researchers to talk about the 'problem' of the 'African-Caribbean family'. However, this ignores the strength of wider kinship networks – in particular, the support provided for lone mothers by female relatives. This support can cross national boundaries with family members in the UK and West Indies providing support for each other (Goulborne, 1999).

Multicultural families Recent statistics suggest an increase in the number of partnerships between people from different ethnic groups. Elisabeth Beck-Gernsheim (2002) uses the term *multicultural families* for families in which the partners come from different ethnic backgrounds. She recognises that such couples may face prejudice from their ethnic groups of origin, and conflict because they bring differing expectations of family life to the relationship. However, she is cautiously optimistic about the promise of multicultural families. They may help to break down barriers between ethnic groups. And they reflect a growing opportunity for individual choice – people are now choosing partners who fulfil their personal needs rather than being directed by the concerns of their parents or the norms of their ethnic group.

key terms

Life chances A person's chances of obtaining things defined as desirable and avoiding things defined as undesirable.
Multicultural families Families in which the partners are from different ethnic groups.

5.7 Family diversity and society

This section examines family diversity in the context of the wider society. It looks at views which see increasing family diversity as a reflection of broader changes in society as a whole.

Giddens and late modernity

According to the British sociologist Anthony Giddens, we live in an era known as *late modernity*. This era is characterised by choice and change. Opportunities to choose an identity and select a lifestyle are increasingly available. In the pre-modern era, tradition defined who people were and what they should do. Today, people have far more freedom to try on different identities and to try out different lifestyles (Giddens, 1991; 1992).

Where does the family fit into late modernity? If Giddens is correct, family diversity is a reflection of the opportunities and priorities of late modernity. People have greater freedom to construct their own domestic arrangements. They are not bound by existing family forms and family roles. There are more choices available and more opportunities to experiment, create and change.

Within limits, people can tailor their partnerships and their families to meet their individual needs and to reflect their own identities. They can choose to cohabit or to marry, to end one partnership and to begin another. The emphasis is on building and constructing family units, on creating and defining family relationships. People build reconstituted families. They enter uncharted territory constructing gay and lesbian families with no clear patterns to work from. They choose to become lone parents rather than accept an unsatisfactory relationship.

According to Giddens (1992), relationships in late modernity are increasingly based on *confluent love* – deep emotional intimacy in which partners reveal their needs and concerns to each other. Commitment to the relationship lasts as long as the individual receives sufficient satisfaction and pleasure from it. Failure to experience this is justification, in itself, for ending the relationship. If Giddens is correct, this helps to explain the fragility of partnerships in late modernity, as seen in the high rates of separation and divorce.

Evaluation Giddens's views of late modernity help to explain the trend towards family diversity. However, he may have exaggerated people's freedom to choose. Take lone-parent families. In one sense they are *not* based on choice – at least not first choice. Many single (never-married) mothers did *not* choose to become pregnant. However, they did choose to have the baby and raise it themselves (Allen & Dowling, 1999). Similarly, divorced lone mothers did not set out to become lone parents. This was a second-best choice after the failure of their marriage.

Even so, there is evidence to support Giddens' claim of increased choice in late modernity. People can choose between marriage and cohabitation, they can choose to remain married or to divorce, they can choose to become a lone parent or to maintain a partnership, they can choose to become a single mother, they can choose to remain a lone parent or to form a reconstituted family. There is far greater freedom to make these choices than there was 50 years ago.

Postmodernity

Some sociologists believe that the modern age has ended and that we now live in the *postmodern* era. They describe this era as a time of change, of flux, of fluidity and uncertainty. Gone is the consensus or agreement about norms and values which characterised most of the modern age.

The American sociologist Judith Stacey (1996) sees family diversity as a reflection of postmodern society. There is no one family form to which everyone aspires. There are no generally agreed norms and values directing family life. In her words, 'Like postmodern culture, contemporary family arrangements are diverse, fluid and unresolved'.

Stacey welcomes this diversity, seeing it as an opportunity for people to develop family forms which suit their particular needs and situations. She looks forward to

activity27 class, ethnicity and family diversity

Item A *Class differences*

Outside the family home

Outside the family home

Item B *A multicultural couple*

This couple have a business specialising in wedding accessories for multicultural couples

questions

1 With reference to Item A, suggest how class differences might affect family life.
2 Look at Item B.
   a) What problems might this couple experience?
   b) How can an increase in multicultural families be seen as a positive development?

activity28 choice and creativity

Item A   Lesbian families

'With no script to follow, we are making up our own story and hoping that we'll live happily ever after.'

Amanda Boulter referring to her lesbian partner and their two boys. Quoted in *The Independent*, 4.2.2002.

'I don't necessarily think we should be wanting to mimic everything, kind of anything that heterosexual couples or heterosexual relationships have. I don't see that we need to be mimicking them. I think it's about having choice and about being able to be creative and decide what we want for ourselves.'

Source: Journal & Social Policy 1999, 28:689–709, Cambridge University Press

questions

1   How does Item A reflect Giddens' picture of late modernity?

2   Look at Item B. To what extent are reconstituted families based on choice?

Item B   Reconstituted families

---

the possibility of more equal and democratic relationships which she sees in many gay and lesbian families.

Evaluation Stacey's research was conducted in Silicon Valley in California, home to many of the world's most advanced electronics companies. This is hardly typical of American society in general. She also studied research findings on gay and lesbian families. Again, these groups are hardly typical. Despite this, Stacey may well have identified those at the forefront of a trend which is spreading to the wider society.

key terms

Late modernity The term used by Giddens to describe the contemporary period, which is characterised by choice and change.

Postmodernity The era after modernity which is characterised by fluidity, uncertainty and a lack of consensus.

Confluent love Deep emotional intimacy which individuals expect from their partnerships.

summary

1.   Many sociologists see families and households in today's society as more diverse than ever before.

2.   In Britain, nuclear family households have declined as a proportion of all households. The proportion of people living in these households has also declined. Despite this, living in a nuclear family is a phase that most people go through.

3.   There is diversity within nuclear families – eg, the couple may be married or cohabiting.

4.   In Britain since the early 1970s, lone-parent families have increased from 8% to 26% of all families with dependent children.

5.   Lone parents are a diverse group – eg, some were previously married, some cohabiting, some neither.

6.   Although very few women choose lone parenthood as their first option, choices are involved – eg, whether to keep, abort, or give the baby up for adoption.

7.   Lone parenthood has become increasingly acceptable.

8.   There has been a rapid increase in reconstituted families. They are a diverse group – eg, some are formed by

cohabitation, some by first marriage, others by remarriage.

9.   There are particular tensions in reconstituted families, partly because the roles of family members often lack clear definition.

10.   Reconstituted families offer new opportunities – they can lead to a wider support network and enriched relationships.

11.   Gay and lesbian parents are adding further diversity to family life.

12.   Most studies show that children raised by gay and lesbian parents are no different to those raised by heterosexuals.

13.   Social class and ethnic differences add yet further diversity to family life.

14.   According to Anthony Giddens, family diversity results from broader changes in late-modern society. In particular, family diversity reflects the growing freedom to choose identities and select lifestyles.

15.   According to Judith Stacey, family diversity reflects the lack of consensus, the uncertainty and the fluidity of postmodern society.

Unit 6 *Gender, power and domestic labour*

keyissues

1   To what extent is the division of domestic labour linked to gender?

2   To what extent is this division unequal?

3   What does this indicate about the distribution of power?

4   What changes have taken place in these areas?

6.1 Introduction

This unit looks at *domestic labour* – work conducted by people as members of a household. It looks, for example, at housework and childcare and asks who does what.

Most of the research in this area focuses on the contribution of husband and wife to domestic tasks. It asks four main questions.

- First, to what extent is the division of domestic labour based on gender? For example, are certain household tasks done by men and others by women?

- Second, is the division of domestic labour equal – do partners pull their own weight, is the division of labour fair?

- Third, what does this indicate about the distribution of power within the family? Is power shared equally between husband and wife or do men dominate the domestic scene?

- Fourth, what changes have taken place in these areas? For example, is there a move towards a more equal distribution of power?

6.2 Gender and the domestic division of labour

In 1973, Michael Young and Peter Willmott announced the arrival of the *symmetrical family* (see pages 81-82). They claimed that *conjugal roles*, the roles of husband and wife, were becoming increasingly similar. In the home, the couple 'shared their work; they shared their time'. Husbands increasingly helped with domestic chores such as washing up and cleaning. They also helped more with raising children, though this still remained the main responsibility of the wife. Decisions about family life were largely shared. It appeared that the division of labour based on gender was breaking down.

In 1974, Ann Oakley dismissed this view of the sharing caring husband. Young and Willmott had claimed that 72% of husbands 'help in the house'. To be included in this figure, husbands only had to perform one household chore a week. In Oakley's words, this is hardly

convincing evidence of 'male domestication' (Oakley, 1974). Oakley's own research conducted in the early 1970s shows a clear division of labour along gender lines. Based on interviews with 40 women with one or more children under 5, it shows clearly that wives saw housework and childcare as their responsibility and received little help from their husbands.

Since these early studies, there has been considerable research on gender and the division of domestic labour. This research shows that most women:

- still become mothers and housewives

- experience a period of full-time housework, though this is becoming shorter

- return to work part time when their youngest child is at school.

This early period of full-time housework sets the pattern for the future, as the following findings indicate.

- Housework and childcare remain the primary responsibility of women.

- As women enter the labour market in increasing numbers, there is some evidence of men making a greater contribution to domestic tasks.

- However, this increased contribution is not significant. As a result, most working wives have a *dual burden* or a *dual shift* – paid employment and domestic labour (Allan & Crow, 2001).

The findings summarised above are taken from small-scale studies often based on interviews, and large-scale surveys usually based on questionnaires. For example, Fiona Devine's small-scale study of car workers' families in Luton indicated that men's contribution to domestic labour increased when their wives re-entered paid employment. But the man's role is secondary – 'Above all women remain responsible for childcare and housework and their husbands help them' (Devine, 1992).

This picture is reflected in large-scale surveys such as the British Social Attitudes Survey and the British Household Panel Survey. These surveys show a clear gender division of labour in most household tasks. However, they do indicate a slight trend towards sharing tasks.

Evidence from the Time Use Surveys conducted by the government in 2000 and 2005 is shown in Activity 29, Item A, and in Table 6 (Layder et al., 2006). Item A compares the amount of time spent on housework in 2005 by women and men in full-time employment – a total of 151 minutes a day by women and 113 minutes a day by men. Table 6 compares the amount of time spent on housework and childcare by all women and men in 2000 and 2005. It shows a decrease in time spent on housework and an increase in time spent on childcare. It also shows that significant gender differences remain.

Table 6 Time Spent on housework and childcare Great Britain, 2000 and 2005

Activity	2000	2005
	Average minutes per person per day	
Housework		
Men	128	101
Women	215	180
Childcare (of own household members)		
Men	11	15
Women	28	32

Source: The Time Use Survey 2005, Office for National Statistics

Gender and domestic tasks – evaluation

Much of the research into gender divisions of domestic labour is based on *time-use studies*. This research asks who does what and how long does it take them. There are problems with this method.

Time Women tend to underestimate time spent on domestic labour. This often happens when several tasks are performed at the same time. For example, women often combine childcare with tasks such as cleaning and preparing meals. As a result, they underestimate the amount of time spent on childcare (Leonard, 2000).

Men tend to overestimate time spent on domestic labour. For example, in one study, men estimated they spent an average of 11.3 hours a week on childcare. However, their diary entries showed only 1.7 hours a week (Pleck, 1985).

Urgency Time-use studies say little about the urgency of tasks. Women's domestic tasks, such as cooking and

activity29 gender and domestic labour

Item A Gender divisions

Time spent on housework by full-time workers, Great Britain, 2005

Categories (top to bottom): Cooking, washing up; Shopping, appointments; Cleaning, tidying; Repairs and gardening; Washing clothes; Pet care. X-axis: Minutes per day, 0 to 40. Legend: Women, Men.

Source: The Time Use Survey 2005, Office for National Statistics

Item B Household tasks

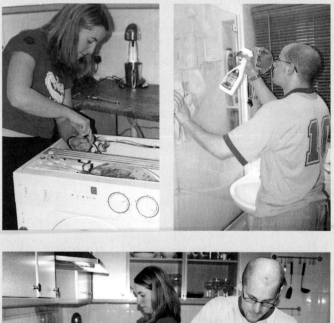

questions

1 Look at Item A. To what extent are tasks allocated on the basis of gender?

2 Look at Item B. Judging from Item A, which of these pictures are untypical?

washing clothes, are more urgent than typical male tasks such as gardening and household maintenance (McMahon, 1999).

Responsibility vs help There is a big difference between being responsible for a task and helping with a task. For example, being responsible for cooking and cleaning is not the same as helping with those tasks. Being responsible requires more thought and effort, it can be more tiring and more stressful (McMahon, 1999). Again, this aspect of gender divisions and domestic tasks is not revealed by time-use studies.

Job satisfaction Time-use studies tell us little about the amount of satisfaction women and men derive from domestic labour. Typical female tasks are often experienced as tedious, boring and monotonous. Typical male tasks are more likely to be experienced as interesting and creative. For example, some men regard DIY and gardening as hobbies rather than chores (Allan, 1985).

key terms

Conjugal roles Marital roles, the roles of husband and wife.
Symmetrical family A family in which the roles of husband and wife are similar.
Dual burden/dual shift The double burden/shift of paid employment and domestic labour.
Time-use studies Studies which examine how people use their time – how long they spend on various activities.

6.3 Gender and the division of emotion work

So far domestic labour has been defined as household tasks such as ironing and cooking, and time spent looking after children. Little has been said about the emotional side of domestic labour. Partnerships and families are kept together as much if not more by *emotion work* than by the more practical household tasks. Emotion work refers to the love, sympathy, understanding, praise, reassurance and attention which are involved in maintaining relationships.

According to many women, it is they rather than their male partners who are responsible for most of the emotion work. In other words, emotion work is gendered. A study conducted by Jean Duncombe and Dennis Marsden (1993, 1995) based on interviews with 40 couples found that most women complained of men's 'emotional distance'. They felt they were the ones who provided reassurance, tenderness and sympathy, while their partners had problems expressing intimate emotions. Men showed little awareness or understanding of their 'shortcomings', seeing their main role as a breadwinner – providing money rather than emotional support.

These findings are reflected in other studies. For example, research into family meals shows that women give priority to their partner's and children's tastes, often at the expense of their own. They do their best to make mealtime a happy family occasion (Charles & Kerr, 1988).

activity30 emotion work

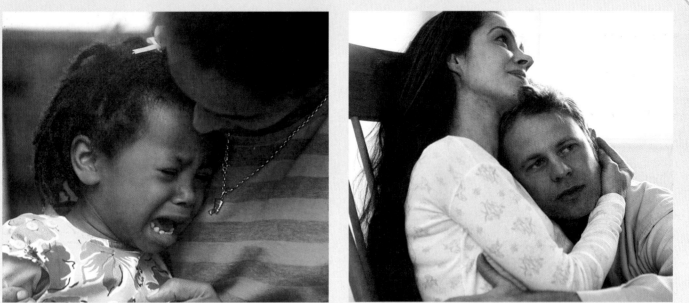

questions

1 How do the pictures illustrate emotion work?
2 Why do you think women are primarily responsible for emotion work in the family?

According to Duncombe and Marsden (1995), many women have to cope with a *triple shift* – 1) paid work 2) housework and childcare and 3) emotion work.

---

key terms

Emotion work The emotional support which members of a social group – in this case the family – provide for each other.
Triple shift The three areas of responsibility which many women have – 1) paid work, 2) housework and childcare, 3) emotion work.

6.4 Family finances

So far, this unit has outlined evidence which indicates that domestic tasks, childcare, and emotion work are divided along gender lines. This section looks at money management within families. It reaches a similar conclusion – access to and control over money are gendered. And this division of labour along gender lines tends to favour men.

Systems of money management Jan Pahl's *Money and Marriage* (1989) identified various systems of money management used by the 102 couples in her study. They ranged from a *housekeeping allowance system* whereby the husbands give their wives a fixed sum of money for housekeeping expenses and control the remaining money, to a *pooling system* where both partners see themselves as equally responsible for and jointly controlling money management. A later study by Carolyn Vogler and Jan Pahl (1994), based on interviews with over 1200 British couples, showed that whatever money management system was used, men tended to come out on top.

Inequalities in money management Vogler and Pahl report the following results. When asked who gets most personal spending money, 58% of couples said it was equally distributed, 12% said the husband, 4% the wife, and the rest disagreed amongst themselves. When asked who suffers cutbacks when money is tight, it was wives who reported most hardship. They were more likely to cut back on their own food and clothing, and shield their children and husband from hard times. And when asked who has the final say in important financial decisions, 70% say both, 23% the husband and 7% the wife.

Trends Vogler and Pahl see a trend towards greater equality in access to and control of family finances. They argue that greater equality depends in part on women's full-time participation in the labour market. There is a large body of research which indicates that the partner with the largest income has the biggest say in family decision-making.

6.5 Domestic labour, power and gender

Are families *patriarchal* or male dominated? Are women exploited by their male partners? Do men get the best deal in the home? Do they get their own way in domestic situations?

Are these questions still relevant today? Aren't partnerships rapidly moving towards equality? Haven't many already reached the stage where the domestic division of labour is equal?

These questions are about *power*. This section looks at various ways of defining and measuring power and applies them to family life.

Decision making

The decision-making model measures power in terms of who makes the decisions. For example, if wives made most of the decisions concerning the home then, in this context, they would have most power. However, this fails to take account of the importance of the decisions. For example, the wife may make more decisions but those decisions are minor and trivial. The really important decisions are made by her husband.

The following study uses the decision-making approach and takes the importance of decisions into account. Stephen Edgell (1980) interviewed 38 middle-class couples. He asked them who made the decisions and how important those decisions were. Wives dominated decision making in three areas – interior decoration, children's clothes, and spending on food and other household items. These decisions were frequent and seen as not very important. Men had the main say when it came to moving house, buying a car and other major financial decisions. These decisions were infrequent and seen as important. Other decisions, such as holidays and children's education were made by both husband and wife (see Item A, Activity 35).

Based on decision making and the importance of the areas of decision, it appears that husbands have more power than their wives.

Evaluation This study is over 20 years old and is based on a small, unrepresentative sample – 38 middle-class couples. It uses the decision-making approach. There are a number of problems with this approach. For example, it ignores agenda-setting – which issues should be placed on the agenda to be decided upon. The person who sets the agenda may use this power to their own advantage.

Non-decisions

The decision-making approach fails to take account of non-decisions. Many actions do not involve conscious decisions – as such, they can be seen as 'non-decisions'. They are based on taken-for-granted assumptions – for example, women should take primary responsibility for childcare. Often there is little or no discussion because those involved are simply following social norms which are largely unquestioned.

In terms of domestic labour, there are a number of non-decisions. The following are traditionally seen as women's work.

- Washing, cleaning, ironing
- Childcare
- Emotion work.

activity31 *gender, power and domestic labour*

Item A **Making decisions**

Decision area	Perceived importance	Frequency	Decision maker
Moving	Very important	Infrequent	Husband
Finance	Very important	Infrequent	Husband
Car	Important	Infrequent	Husband
House	Very important	Infrequent	Husband and wife
Children's education	Very important	Infrequent	Husband and wife
Holidays	Important	Infrequent	Husband and wife
Weekends	Not important	Frequent	Husband and wife
Other leisure activities	Not important	Frequent	Husband and wife
Furniture	Not important	Infrequent	Husband and wife
Interior decorations	Not important	Infrequent	Wife
Food and other domestic spending	Not important	Frequent	Wife
Children's clothes	Not important	Frequent	Wife

Source: Edgell, 1980

Item B **Satisfaction**

Many women appear to be satisfied with the domestic division of labour. They recognise that they do most of the work, but only 14% said they were dissatisfied with their partner's contribution.

Source: Baxter & Western, 1998

Item C **Choice**

In recent years, there has been a string of newspaper articles about successful and powerful career women who gave up highly-paid jobs in order to take care of their children. They include:

- Lisa Gordon, corporate affairs director of Chrysalis Records who earned £336,000 a year.
- Penny Hughes, formerly in charge of Coca-Cola UK, who gave up £250,000 a year.
- Tina Gaudoin, former editor of the glossy women's magazine *Frank*.

Source: Guardian, 02.12.02

Item D **The triple shift**

questions

1　Judging from Item A, who has most power – husbands or wives? Give reasons for your answer.

2　a)　Use Items B, C and D to argue that men have more power than women.

　　b)　Using the same information, criticise this view.

It is often taken for granted that the man's job is more important than his partner's, since she will probably give up paid employment when the couple have children.

Who benefits? Those who gain from non-decisions can be seen as more powerful than those who don't. Take the assumption that men's jobs are more important than their female partner's jobs. This assumption lies behind the following behaviour of newly-wed couples.

- Around 1/3 of men changed jobs at or near their wedding. Typically, this change advanced their careers.

- Over 2/3 of women changed jobs at or near their wedding. Typically, this resulted in lower pay and lower job status (Mansfield & Collard, 1988).

Judging by this study, men gain and women lose from the taken-for-granted assumption that men's jobs should take priority over women's jobs. In terms of the consequences of this non-decision, men have more power than women.

At some time in their lives, most women are full-time mothers and housewives. Who benefits from following these traditional social roles? According to many feminist writers, men are the beneficiaries. First, they gain from avoiding the negative aspects of these roles. Second, they directly benefit from much of their partner's domestic labour.

Full-time domestic labour means that the wife is economically dependent on the male breadwinner. This reduces her power in the household. There is a tendency to see housework as low status, as different from 'real' work (Oakley, 1974). Typical women's jobs – washing, ironing and cleaning – are often experienced as boring, monotonous and unfulfilling. And these are the very jobs which directly benefit their partner, providing him with clean clothes and a clean home. Similarly, women's responsibility for emotion work can be seen as an example of 'he gains, she loses'.

Allocating housework and emotion work to women is often based on a non-decision – it is 'normal' and 'natural' for women to perform such tasks therefore there is no decision to make. In terms of this view of power, men gain at the expense of women therefore men have more power than women.

Evaluation Choosing winners and losers is based on judgements. What's wrong with being a housewife and a mother? Housework might be boring and monotonous but so are many jobs outside the home. Today, many women have the freedom to choose between a career and becoming a full-time mother and housewife. This is hardly a non-decision. And many women who give up paid employment feel they've gained from the decision (see Activity 31).

There is, however, plenty of evidence to support the view that in general men gain and women lose. Take the triple shift – women combining paid work, domestic labour and emotion work. The clear winner here is the man.

Shaping desires

Power can be seen as the ability to shape the wishes and desires of others in order to further one's own interests. In this way, a dominant group can persuade others to accept, or actually desire, their subordinate position. In terms of this argument, men have power over women because many women accept and even desire their traditional roles as mothers and housewives, and accept their subordinate status. For example, women often put their partners and children's preferences first when shopping for food. And they usually put 'the family' first when spending on clothes and entertainment (Charles, 1990).

Women get satisfaction from self-sacrifice. Her loved ones gain pleasure from her actions. This confirms her identity as a good mother and wife (Allan & Crow, 2001). The fact that she wants to serve and sacrifice can be seen as an indication of male power.

Evaluation This view of power is based on the assumption that it is not in women's interests to accept or desire their traditional roles as housewife and mother. Any pleasure they experience from their 'subordination' is 'false pleasure' because it disguises their exploitation and makes it more bearable.

But who is to say that women in the family are exploited and oppressed? As noted earlier, it's a matter of weighing the evidence and making a judgement.

Power and same-sex households

So far, this section has looked at the distribution of power in heterosexual families – families in which the partners are male and female. The focus now moves to power in same-sex families where both partners are either male or female.

Equality as an ideal Most studies of gay and lesbian partnerships are based on interviews. Bearing in mind that people don't always do what they say, this is what the interviews reveal. Same-sex couples emphasise equality and strive to remove power differences from their relationship. They see issues like the division of domestic labour as a matter for discussion and negotiation. They feel that being lesbian or gay offers more opportunities for equality. As one woman put it, 'It's much easier to have equal relations if you're the same sex' (Weeks et al., 1999a).

Women focus on alternatives to the unequal division of domestic labour which they see in heterosexual relationships. Men focus on alternatives to the macho male and the passive female which they see in heterosexual relationships. In both cases the emphasis is on equality (Weeks et al., 1999a).

Lesbian households A study of 37 cohabiting lesbian couples by Gillian Dunne (1997) indicates how far these ideals are translated into reality. Some of the couples have children, and in most cases childcare was shared.

Similarly, time spent on housework tended to be shared equally. However, when one partner was in full-time employment, she did less housework than her partner in part-time work.

Explanations Why are same-sex relationships more equal than heterosexual relationships? Gillian Dunne (1997) suggests the following reasons.

- Gender inequalities in the labour market shape gender inequalities in partnerships. Men generally have jobs with higher status and pay than their partners and this tends to shape their relationships at home.

- Gay and lesbian partnerships are free from the social norms and conventions which surround and direct heterosexual relationships. They are not weighed down by this cultural baggage. As a result, they have more freedom to construct 'families of choice' (see pages 100-101).

key terms

Decision-making approach A method for measuring power in terms of who makes the decisions.
Agenda-setting Deciding which issues will be placed on the agenda to be decided upon.
Non-decisions Issues which never reach the point of decision making.

summary

1. The division of domestic labour is gendered – household tasks are divided along gender lines.

2. Housework and childcare remain the primary responsibility of women.

3. There is evidence of a gradual increase in men's contribution to domestic labour, especially where their partners are in full-time employment.

4. There are problems with time-use studies of domestic labour. For example, women tend to underestimate and men to overestimate time spent on household tasks.

5. Emotion work is mainly performed by women. As a result, many women have a triple shift – 1) paid work, 2) housework and childcare, 3) emotion work.

6. Research into money management within families indicates that control over money is gendered – men tend to have greater control.

7. There is evidence of a trend to greater equality in access to and control of family finances, especially where women are in full-time employment.

8. Research indicates that power is unequally distributed in families, with male partners having the largest share.

9. Decision-making studies indicate that in general husbands have more power than their wives.

10. Non-decisions – issues that do not reach the point of decision-making – tend to favour men. They are likely to gain at the expense of their partners.

11. There is a tendency for many women to accept their subordinate position. From this, it can be argued that men have power over women.

12. Studies of lesbian and gay households suggest that there is a more equal division of domestic labour between partners.

activity32 same-sex relationships

Item A Talking about relationships

'Everything has to be discussed, everything is negotiable.'

'There are no assumptions about how you will relate, what you will do, who does what.'

Source: Journal of Social Policy 1999, 28: 689–709 Cambridge University Press

question

With some reference to Items A and B, suggest why the domestic division of labour in lesbian families may be more equal than in heterosexual families.

Item B Partners and mothers

Lesbian couple sharing childcare

Unit 7 Childhood and children

keyissues

1 How have views of childhood changed?

2 How have children been affected by these changes?

The social construction of childhood

Childhood can be seen as a *social construction*. From this point of view, it is not a natural state or a biological stage. Instead, it is shaped and given meaning by culture and society. As a result, the idea of childhood, the types of behaviour considered appropriate for children, the way children should be treated, and the length of time that childhood should last, are socially constructed.

Cross-cultural evidence Evidence from different cultures provides support for the view that childhood is a social construction. If childhood were simply a 'natural' state, then it would be similar across all cultures. This is not the case.

Anthropological studies show that other cultures treat children in ways which might seem unusual or even unnatural in contemporary Britain. Raymond Firth (1963), in his study of the Pacific island of Tikopia, found that children carried out dangerous tasks such as using sharp

activity33 childhood across cultures

Item A *Child soldier*

Item B *Blackfoot boys*

A member of a local militia in Zaire

The Blackfoot Indians lived on the Plains of Western Canada. Children were taught the skills of horse riding at an early age. One of Long Lance's earliest recollections was falling off a horse. He was picked up by his eldest brother and planted firmly on the horse's back. His brother said, 'Now, you stay there! You are four years old, and if you cannot ride a horse, we will put girls' clothing on you and let you grow up a woman.'

Fathers were responsible for the physical training of the Blackfoot boys. They wanted to harden their bodies and make them brave and strong. Fathers used to whip their sons each morning with fir branches. Far from disliking this treatment, the youngsters proudly displayed the welts produced by whipping. Sometimes they were whipped in public and they competed to see who could stand the most pain.

Source: The autobiography of a Blackfoot Indian Chief, Long Lance 1956

question

How do Items A and B indicate that childhood is socially constructed?

tools and fishing in the open sea. They were allowed to carry out these tasks when they themselves felt ready rather than when adults decided they were competent or safe to do so.

A brief history of childhood

In *Centuries of Childhood* (1962), the French historian Philippe Ariès argued that the concept of childhood did not exist in medieval Europe. He based his argument on contemporary letters, diaries and other documents, plus the way children were depicted in paintings of the time. Ariès claimed that soon after children were weaned, they were regarded as little adults and treated as such. From an early age, they worked alongside adults in the fields or in cottage industries, they dressed like adults and in many ways behaved like adults.

The emergence of modern childhood Ariès sees the modern concept of childhood developing from the separation of children from the world of adults. This process began in the 16th century when the upper classes sent their children to schools to be educated. In the early years of the industrial revolution, child labour was widespread – children and adults worked side by side. Throughout the 19th century, a series of factory acts banned the employment of children in mines and factories. By the end of the 19th century, elementary state education was compulsory in most European countries. Children were now physically separated from adult settings and had a separate legal status.

This process was accompanied by the development of experts specialising in children – child psychologists, paediatricians (doctors who specialise in children), educationalists and parenting experts. According to Ariès, 'Our world is obsessed by the physical, moral and sexual problems of childhood'. Children are seen as different from adults. As a result, they have special needs. Because of this

activity34 *little adults*

Item A *Medieval Europe*

In medieval society the idea of childhood did not exist. This is not to suggest that children were neglected, forsaken or despised. The idea of childhood is not to be confused with affection for children: it corresponds to an awareness of the particular nature of childhood, that particular nature which distinguishes the child from the adult, even the young adult. In medieval society, this awareness was lacking. That is why, as soon as the child could live without the constant solicitude (care) of his mother, his nanny or his cradle-rocker, he belonged to adult society.

Source: Ariès, 1962

Item B *Paintings*

Family saying grace before a meal (1585)

question

What evidence do the paintings in Item B provide to support Ariès' statement in Item A?

Group of doctors (right) and men, women and children (left), 15th century

they require treatment, training and guidance from an army of specially trained adults. This is very different from the Middle Ages when 'the child became the natural companion of the adult'.

Evaluation Ariès has been criticised for overstating his case. In certain respects, children in medieval Europe were seen as different from adults. For example, there were laws prohibiting the marriage of children under 12 (Bukatko & Daehler, 2001). However, many historians agree with the broad outline of Ariès's history of childhood in Western Europe.

> ## key term
>
> *Social construction* Something that is created by society, constructed from social meanings and definitions.

Images of childhood

Wendy Stainton Rogers (2001) looks at the social construction of childhood in 20th century Europe. She identifies two 'images' of childhood – 'the innocent and wholesome child' and 'the wicked and sinful child'. Both images coexist – they exist together. Both have a long history and continue to the present day. They can be seen in a variety of forms – for example, in novels such as Arthur Ransome's *Swallows and Amazons* with its charming and wholesome children and William Golding's *Lord of the Flies* where children descend to their 'natural' savage and barbaric selves.

Each image suggests a particular way of acting towards children. The image of the innocent and wholesome child suggests that children should be protected from everything that is nasty about the adult world, from violence and from the worries and concerns of adults. Childhood should be a happy, joyous and carefree time. By contrast, the idea of an essentially sinful child suggests that children should be restrained, regulated and disciplined.

Both these views of childhood imply that adults should be concerned about children and take responsibility for their upbringing.

The welfare view The first view suggests that children are vulnerable and need protection. This 'welfare view' forms the basis of social policy towards children in the UK today. For example, the Children Act of 1989 states that 'When a court determines any question with respect to the upbringing of a child ... the child's welfare shall be the court's paramount consideration'.

The control view The second view assumes that children are unable to control their anti-social tendencies. As a result, they need regulation and discipline. This 'control view' is reflected in education policy – children must submit to education and the form and content of their education must be strictly controlled from above.

According to Wendy Stainton Rogers, these images of childhood are social constructions. She argues that 'there is

no *natural* distinction that marks off children as a certain category of person'. Seeing children as innocent and wholesome or wicked and sinful or a mixture of both is not right or wrong, it is simply a meaning given to childhood at a particular time and place (Stainton Rogers, 2001).

Childhood in an age of uncertainty

Nick Lee (2001) sees a change in the social construction of childhood towards the end of the 20th century. He claims that for most of the century adults and children were seen as 'fundamentally different kinds of humans'. Adults were stable and complete, children were unstable and incomplete. Adults had become, children were becoming. Adults were self-controlling, children were in need of control.

In the early 21st century, 'growing up' is no longer seen as a journey towards personal completion and stability. This is because adulthood is no longer complete and stable. Adult relationships are increasingly unstable as indicated by high divorce rates. The labour market is changing rapidly and 'jobs for life' are a thing of the past. With new partners and new jobs, adults are in a constant state of becoming. They are living in an 'age of uncertainty'.

Where does this leave children? For much of the 20th century, childhood was defined in relation to adulthood. Adults and children were very different. Children had yet to become full human beings. They were not fully rational, they were not seen as 'persons in their own right', they had to be guided along the path to adulthood by child experts and child trainers such as teachers and social workers.

By the 21st century, adults were becoming more like children. Both were in a continual state of becoming, both were defining and redefining their identities, both were unstable and incomplete.

This growing similarity between adults and children is leading to a new social construction of childhood. Children are seen increasingly as 'beings in their own right'. As such, they have their own concerns, their own interests, and should have their own rights, just like adult members of society. This is reflected in the UN Convention on the Rights of the Child (1989). Article 3 states:

> 'In all actions concerning children, whether undertaken by public or private social welfare institutions, courts of law, administrative authorities or legislative bodies, the best interests of the child shall be a primary consideration.'

Changes in the social construction of childhood result in changes in the way adults treat children. This can be seen from the 1989 Children Act which stated that in court proceedings, 'the child's welfare must be paramount'. In cases of divorce, the court used to decide which parent had custody of the children. Since 1989, the child's view is taken into account – children have a say in decisions about who they will live with. This is a long way from the traditional view that children should be seen and not heard.

The end of childhood?

Will the 21st century see the end of childhood? Will new social constructions end up abolishing the whole idea of childhood?

According to Neil Postman (1983) in *The Disappearance of Childhood*, this process is well underway. Postman argues that childhood is only possible if children can be separated, and therefore protected from, the adult world. In his words, 'Without secrets, of course, there can be no such thing as childhood'. The mass media, and television in particular, have brought the adult world into the lives of children. Secrecy has been wiped out by television. As a result, the boundaries between the worlds of children and adults are breaking down. Postman believes that in the long run, this means the end of childhood.

Dual status Postman has been criticised for overstating his case. Clearly television and the media in general have brought adult priorities and concerns into the lives of children. But childhood is a long way from disappearing. For example, children in late 20th century Western societies have become a major economic force. Their tastes and preferences, not just in toys and games, but also in information and communication technologies such as personal computers and mobile phones, have a major effect on what is produced and purchased (Buckingham, 2000).

According to Nick Lee (2001), childhood has not disappeared, it has become more complex and ambiguous. Children are dependent on their parents, but in another sense they are independent. There is a mass children's market which children influence – they make choices, they decide which products succeed and fail, though at the end of the day, they depend on their parents' purchasing power.

This is one of the ambiguities of childhood in the 21st century. Things are not clear-cut. Children are both dependent and independent.

summary

1. Many sociologists see childhood as a social construction rather than a natural state. Ideas about childhood vary between different societies and different times.

2. According to Philippe Ariès,
   - The concept of childhood did not exist in medieval Europe. Children were seen as little adults.
   - Modern ideas of childhood as a separate state began with the onset of formal education and the gradual withdrawal of children from the workplace.

3. Wendy Stainton Rogers identifies two images of childhood in modern Western society – 'the innocent and wholesome child' and 'the wicked and sinful child'. The first image suggests that children are vulnerable and need protection – the welfare view. The second image suggests children need regulation and discipline – the control view.

4. According to Nick Lee, adulthood has become less stable and more uncertain. In these respects, it has become more like childhood. This similarity has led to a change in the social construction of childhood in the 21st century. Children are increasingly seen as having their own rights and interests.

5. Neil Postman argues that the media is breaking down the boundaries between the worlds of children and adults, leading to the 'disappearance of childhood'.

6. Postman has been criticised for overstating his case. Childhood is a long way from disappearing. For example, children remain a distinct group – they are a major force in the market place. And they remain dependent on their parents.

activity35 ambiguities of childhood

Item A 'Pester-power'

Children can influence what adults buy through 'pester-power'. In the UK, the take-up of satellite and cable television, video, camcorders and home computers is much higher in households with children: 35% of households with children now subscribe to cable or satellite television, for example, as compared with 25% overall; while 90% of households with children have access to a video cassette recorder as compared with 75% overall.

Source: Buckingham, 2000

Item B Young and sophisticated

Aged 11

question

Why is childhood in the 21st century seen as 'ambiguous'? Make some reference to Items A and B in your answer.

Unit 8 Demographic trends

keyissues

1 What are the main demographic trends in the UK since 1900?

2 What explanations have been given for changes in births, deaths and family size?

7.1 Demographic changes

Demography is the study of populations. It includes the measurement of births, deaths and migration which can lead to changes in population size and structure. Demography also involves an examination of the reasons for changes in populations. For example, it attempts to explain why people in the UK are living longer.

This section presents a brief overview of the main demographic trends in the UK since 1900. The material is drawn from various issues of *Social Trends, Annual Abstract of Statistics* and from National Statistics Online.

A growing population

In 1901, the population of the UK was 38.2 million. By mid-2006, it had grown to 60.6 million. The rate of population growth has slowed during these years. Between 1901 and 1911, the growth rate averaged 1% per year. In the 21st century it is around 0.25% per year.

The main factor accounting for population growth has been *natural change* – the difference between births and deaths. Every year since 1901, apart from 1976, there have been more births than deaths. Since the late 1990s, migration into the UK has been an increasingly important factor in population growth. For example, between 2001 and 2005, migration resulted in an average annual increase of 182,000 people compared to an average annual increase of 92,000 people through natural change.

Births/fertility

Births are measured in three main ways.

Actual numbers This refers to the actual number of live births in a population over a given time period. Overall, there has been a decline in the actual number of live births in the UK. In 1901, there were nearly 1.1 million, in 2005 there were nearly 723,000.

Birth rate This measure refers to the number of live births per thousand of the population per year. For example, if the birth rate is 15, then 15 live babies were born for each thousand members of the population in that year. The UK birth rate has fallen steadily from an average of 28.6 in 1900-02 to 12.0 in 2005.

The total fertility rate (TFR) This is the measure most commonly used by demographers. The total fertility rate is the average number of children that a woman would have during her lifetime. It is calculated each year on the available evidence.

Overall the TFR in the UK has declined. It is estimated that the TFR in 1900 was 3.5 children per woman. Official TFR measurements began in 1940. Since then, TFR peaked at 2.95 in 1964 during the 1960s 'baby boom'. It reached a record low of 1.63 in 2001 and rose to 1.84 children per woman in 2006.

Deaths/mortality

Mortality means death. It is measured in two main ways.

Actual numbers This refers to the actual number of deaths in a population over a given time period – usually a year. Despite the large population growth in the UK between 1901 and 2005, the annual number of deaths has remained fairly steady. In 1901 there were 632,000 deaths in the UK, in 2005 there were 582,000.

Death rate The death rate for the population as a whole is the number of deaths per thousand of the population per year. The death rate in the UK has fallen from an average of 18.4 in 1900-02 to 9.4 in 2005. When the population grows steadily and there is little change in the annual number of deaths the death rate will automatically fall.

Infant mortality rate This measure refers to the number of deaths of infants under one year per thousand live births. The infant mortality rate in the UK has fallen dramatically from 142 in 1901 to 5.1 in 2005. Infant mortality accounted for 25% of deaths in 1901 and for less than 1% in 2005.

Life expectancy

Life expectancy is the number of years a person can expect to live based on data from a particular year. Table 7 shows life expectancy at birth in the UK for males and females. For example, the average life expectancy for females born in 1901 was 49 years. By 2003-05, females could expect to live for 81 years.

Table 7 **Life expectancy at birth, UK**

	1901	1951	1991	2003-05
Males	45.5	66.1	73.2	76.6
Females	49.0	70.9	78.8	81.0

Adapted from various issues of *Social Trends* and *Annual Abstract of Statistics*, Office for National Statistics

Ageing population

The UK has an ageing population. This means that the average age of the population is increasing. The proportion of older people is growing and the proportion of younger people is declining. For example, from 1971 to mid-2006, the population over 65 grew by 31% (from 7.4 to 9.7 million) whilst the population under 16 declined by 19% (from 14.2 to 11.5 million). People are living longer and women are having fewer children.

Family size

As the section on births has shown, fertility in the UK has fallen from 1900 to 2006. The total fertility rate (TFR) is used as a rough indicator of family size. It is estimated that the TFR in 1900 was 3.5 children per woman. The TFR in 2006 was 1.84.

Today the most common family size is two children. In England and Wales, 37% of women reaching age 45 in 2006 had a completed family size of two children. The proportion of women having three or more children has fallen from nearly 40% for women born in 1941 to 30% for women born in 1961. Childlessness has increased in recent years. One in ten women born in 1941 were childless compared to nearly one in five women born in 1961.

key terms

Demography The study of populations.
Natural change The difference in the size of a population resulting from the difference between births and deaths.
Birth rate The number of live births per thousand of the population per year.
Total fertility rate (TFR) The average number of children that a woman would have during her lifetime.
Death rate The number of deaths per thousand of the population per year.
Infant mortality rate The number of deaths of infants under one year per thousand live births.
Life expectancy The number of years that a person can expect to live.
Ageing population A population in which the average age is increasing.

7.2 Explaining demographic changes

Mortality

There has been a significant decline in mortality in the UK from around 1830 to the present day. Life expectancy has steadily increased. The death rate has steadily declined and there has been a dramatic fall in infant mortality. Various causes have been suggested for the decline in mortality. They include the following.

Advances in medicine Around 60% of the decline in mortality from 1850 to 1970 was due to a decrease in infectious diseases. How much of this was due to advances in medicine?

The first half of the 20th century saw the introduction of a range of vaccines (from the 1920s onwards) and antibiotics (from the mid-1930s). However, all the major diseases – tuberculosis, measles, scarlet fever, pneumonia and whooping cough – were steadily declining *before* the introduction of effective medical treatment (Hart, 1985). Around two-thirds of the fall in mortality comes from a decline in mortality during the first 15 years of life. The major reduction in infant and child death rates from 1900 to 2006 occurred during the early years of the 20th century, well before widespread immunisation which dates from the 1940s and 50s.

Advances in medicine have made a contribution to the decline in mortality. However, there are probably more important factors accounting for this decline.

Welfare measures

During the later years of the 19th century and the early years of the 20th century, national governments and local authorities began to assume more responsibility for the health and welfare of their citizens. There were marked improvements in the disposal of sewage, the removal of refuse and the purification of water – all of which provided a healthier environment.

In 1902, Bradford started the first school meals service and in 1914 the government made free school meals 'for the needy' compulsory. In 1907, school medical examinations were introduced. The Liberal governments of 1905-1915 directed help towards the poorest groups in society. For example, the 1911 National Insurance Act provided sickness benefit for workers with low incomes.

Measures such as these raised living standards and reduced malnutrition amongst the poorest.

Nutrition and living standards

The first half of the 20th century saw a rapid decline in *absolute poverty* – the inability to obtain adequate food and shelter. A number of researchers argue that adequate nutrition is the most important factor accounting for the decline in mortality, particularly the decline in infant and child mortality. A healthy diet raises levels of resistance to infection and increases the chances of recovery from infection (Livi-Bacci, 2007).

Fertility

Overall, there has been a decline in the birth rate and the total fertility rate in the UK from 1900 onwards. Women are having fewer children and families are becoming smaller. Various reasons have been suggested for this. They include the following.

Economic factors The cost of raising children has steadily risen from 1900 to the present. The minimum school leaving age rose from 14 in 1918, to 15 in 1947 and 16 in 1973. Growing numbers of young people are continuing to further and higher education. As a result, children are becoming increasingly expensive as their economic dependency on parents lasts longer and longer.

activity36 demographic trends in the UK

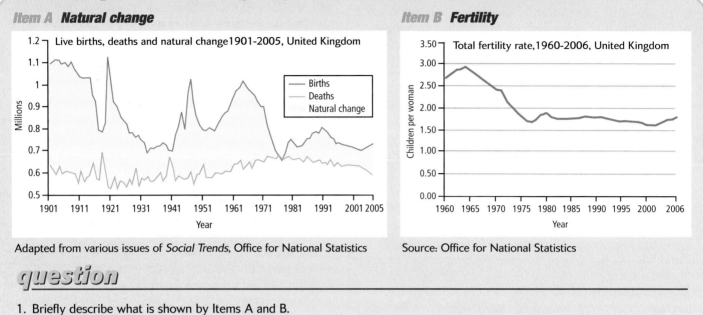

Item A Natural change

Live births, deaths and natural change1901-2005, United Kingdom

Legend: Births / Deaths / Natural change

Adapted from various issues of *Social Trends*, Office for National Statistics

Item B Fertility

Total fertility rate,1960-2006, United Kingdom

Source: Office for National Statistics

question

1. Briefly describe what is shown by Items A and B.

Surveys by building societies and insurance companies illustrate this. For example, research by LV (formerly Liverpool Victoria) estimated that the cost of raising a child and supporting them through university was £180,000 in 2006, a rise of 28% over the past four years. A survey by the Skipton Building Society in 2006 reported that 20% of respondents said they would remain childless because of the cost of a child, while another 20% who already had children said they would not have any more because they could not afford it (Womack, 2006).

Individualisation According to the German sociologists Ulrich Beck and Elisabeth Beck-Gernsheim (1995, 2001), we are now living in the second modernity which began around the mid-1970s. They see this era as characterised by individualisation and risk. Individualisation means that people are increasingly released from the norms, roles and belief systems of the wider society. To a greater extent, they are free to construct their own lives. And they increasingly demand a 'life of their own'.

Children can conflict with this demand – they impose and intrude, they place limits on parents' freedom, they restrict their options and make demands on their time, energy, emotions and finances. As a result, children are often postponed, their numbers are reduced and, in a growing number of cases, people choose not to have them.

Risk Beck and Beck-Gernsheim argue that risk, uncertainty and insecurity characterise societies in the second modernity. For example, relationships are increasingly seen as a source of risk and uncertainty with the high divorce rate and the even higher rate of cohabitation breakup. Having children is an added risk factor. It can put a strain on a couple's relationship. It is a financial risk. And, if mothers take time out of paid employment when their children are young, it increases the risk of not finding a job when they wish to re-enter the labour market. One way to reduce risk is to have fewer children or none at all.

Changing opportunities Researchers often point to expanding educational and occupational opportunities for women as reasons for the decline in fertility. There was a rapid increase in female undergraduates between 1970/71 and 2000/05. And during those same years, the proportion of women in paid employment increased from 56% to 70% (*Social Trends*, 2007) These changes provide alternatives to women's traditional role as mothers and child-raisers. One way of taking advantage of these growing options is to have fewer children or no children.

Changing attitudes Research indicates that women's concerns and priorities are changing. For example, Sue Sharpe's study of working-class girls in London schools in the early 1970s found that their main concerns for the future were 'love, marriage, husbands and children'. When she returned to the same schools in the 1990s, the girls' priorities had changed to 'job, career and being able to support themselves' (Sharpe, 1976 and 1994).

Attitudes to childlessness have changed. The word 'childless' suggests a loss. Now many women who choose not to have children see themselves as 'childfree' – they emphasise liberation from children rather than loss of children. From this point of view, the decision about whether or not to have children is a lifestyle option.

key terms

Childless women Women who, for whatever reason, do not produce children.
Childfree women Women who choose not to have children as a lifestyle option.

summary

1. The population of the UK has grown from 38.2 million in 1901 to 60.6 million in 2006.
2. Most of this growth is due to natural change.
3. Actual numbers of live births, the birth rate and the total fertility rate have all fallen since 1901.
4. The annual number of deaths has remained fairly steady since 1901. However, the death rate has almost halved from 1900 to 2005.
5. There has been a dramatic fall in infant mortality and a steady rise in life expectancy from 1901 to 2005.
6. The UK has an ageing population.
7. There has been a decline in family size and an increase in childlessness.

8. The following reasons have been suggested for the decline in mortality.
   - Advances in medicine
   - Welfare measures from local and national government
   - Improvements in nutrition and living standards.
9. The following reasons have been suggested for the decline in fertility.
   - Economic factors – the growing cost of children
   - Individualisation
   - The growing risk and uncertainty of societies in the second modernity
   - Changing opportunities for women
   - Changes in women's concerns and priorities.

activity37 *mortality and fertility*

Item A School Meals

Green Lane School kitchen, Bradford

School meals, Bradford, 1908

Monday	Lentil and tomato soup. Currant roly-poly pudding.
Tuesday	Meat pudding (stewed beef and boiled suet pudding). Ground rice pudding.
Wednesday	Yorkshire pudding, gravy, peas. Rice and sultanas.
Thursday	Scotch barley broth. Currant pastry or fruit tart.
Friday	Stewed fish, parsley sauce, peas, mashed potatoes. Cornflour blancmange.

(All these meals included bread)

Item B Tuberculosis

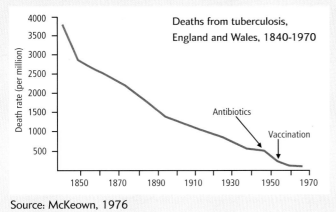

Deaths from tuberculosis, England and Wales, 1840-1970

Source: McKeown, 1976

Item C Generations apart

Grace, aged 71
'Having children wasn't something that even occurred to me to question. In those days, it was automatically accepted that motherhood was just what girls did.'

Source: *The Observer*, 18.03.07

Vicki, aged 17
'I used to be neutral about the idea of being a mother but as I've got older and seen the sacrifices I would have to make, I've become really against the idea. The first word that springs to mind when I think about being a mother is 'trapped'. I feel that if I want to be successful in my career, I don't have any choice except not to become a mother.'
'I'm not alone in this decision. A substantial number of my female friends are quite definite that we never will. I genuinely don't think I'll regret my decision when I'm an old woman. I want to be able to look back at a life of achievements, adventures, success and one packed full of friends.'

Source: *The Observer*, 18.03.07

questions

1 Look at Item A. How might school meals have made a contribution to the decline in the death rate?
2 What does Item B suggest about the contribution made by medical advances to the reduction of deaths from tuberculosis?
3 How might the comments in Item C help to explain the decline in fertility?

3 Sociological methods

Introduction

Are the following statements true or false?

- There has been a steady increase in lone-parent families.
- Low family income reduces a child's chances of success in education.
- More and more women are taking up paid employment.

According to the 2007 edition of *Social Trends*, published by the Office of National Statistics, all the above statements are true.

- In Britain in 1981, 12% of families with dependent children were headed by lone parents. By 2006, this had doubled to 24%.
- In England in 2005/06, 32.6% of pupils receiving free school meals attained five or more grades A* to C at GCSE. The figure for pupils who did not receive free school meals – those from higher income families – was significantly higher at 60.7%.
- Between 1971 and 2006, the employment rate for working-age women in the UK rose from 56% to 70%.

The statements at the beginning of this introduction are not based on opinion or prejudice, guesses or gossip. They are based on research.

Research involves systematically collecting and analysing information. The term *data* is often used for information gathered as part of a research project. This chapter looks at sociological research methods – the methods used by sociologists to collect and analyse data.

national STATISTICS

2007 edition
United Kingdom
No. 37
ISSN 0306-7742

Social Trends

chaptersummary

- ▷ **Unit 1** looks at the kinds of data used in research.
- ▷ **Unit 2** provides an overview of the research process.
- ▷ **Units 3 and 4** look at two types of research – experiments and social surveys.

- ▷ **Units 5, 6 and 7** examine three methods of data collection – questionnaires, interviews and observation.
- ▷ **Unit 8** looks at secondary sources of data.
- ▷ **Unit 9** examines further types of research, including life histories, longitudinal studies and comparative studies.

Unit 1 Types of data

keyissues

1 What types of data do sociologists use?
2 How good is that data?

1.1 Primary and secondary data

One of the first questions sociologists ask when starting a research project is 'What kind of data will I use?' There are two main types of data – *primary data* and *secondary data*. Often researchers use both types.

Primary data refers to information which was not present before the research began. It is generated by the researcher during the actual process of research. It includes data produced by questionnaires, interviews and observations.

Secondary data refers to data which already exists. It includes data from historical records, official statistics, government reports, diaries, autobiographies, novels, newspapers, films and recorded music.

1.2 Quantitative and qualitative data

A second question sociologists ask when starting research is 'What form do I want the data in?' There are two forms of data – *quantitative data* and *qualitative data*. Researchers often use both forms.

Quantitative data This is data in the form of numbers. Examples of quantitative data are given in the introduction to this chapter. Here are some more examples from the year 2000. Twenty-six per cent of 16 to 24 year olds in England and Wales had taken cannabis in the past year.

In Britain, nine per cent of people with managerial/ professional occupations went to the opera in the past year compared to one per cent of people with unskilled manual jobs (*Social Trends*, 2002).

Quantitative data is particularly useful for measuring the strength of relationships between various factors. The above examples would be useful data for measuring relationships between 1) age and illegal drug use and 2) social class and leisure activities.

Qualitative data This refers to all types of data that are not in the form of numbers. It includes:

- Descriptive data from observations, eg a description of behaviour in a pub
- Quotes from interviews, eg a woman discussing her marriage
- Written sources, eg diaries, novels and autobiographies
- Pictures, eg photographs, paintings and posters
- Films and recorded music.

Qualitative data can often provide a richer and more in-depth picture of social life than the numbers provided by quantitative data. Many sociologists combine quantitative and qualitative data in their research.

1.3 Validity and reliability

A third question sociologists often ask when starting research is 'How good will my data be?' Ideally, they want data which is valid and reliable.

Validity Data is valid if it presents a true and accurate description or measurement. For example, official statistics on crime are valid if they provide an accurate measurement of the extent of crime.

Reliability Data is reliable when different researchers using the same methods obtain the same results. For example, if a number of researchers observed the same crowd at the same sporting event and produced the same description of crowd behaviour, then their account would be reliable. The method – in this case observation – produces reliable results.

However, reliable data may not be valid. Say the crowd was at a baseball match in the USA, and the sociologists were English and knew nothing about baseball. They may well fail to understand the crowd's responses to the game. As a result, their description of the crowd's behaviour may be reliable – they all produce the same descriptions – but invalid – their descriptions are inaccurate.

activity1 types of data

Item A **World War 1 recruiting poster from USA**

Item B **A Hamar woman**

Item C **Social class and leisure**

Great Britain   *Percentages*

	Managerial/ professional	Other non-manual	Skilled manual	Semi-skilled manual	Unskilled manual
Sporting events	24	20	18	15	7
Plays	29	17	8	6	5
Opera	9	3	2	1	1
Ballet	7	3	1	1	1
Contemporary dance	4	2	1	1	1
Classical music	17	8	4	2	2
Concerts	19	17	13	9	5
Art galleries/Exhibitions	30	18	8	6	7

Source: *Social Trends*, 2002, Office for National Statistics

questions

1 What types of data are Items A, B and C, quantitative or qualitative? Give reasons for your answer.

2 How might a sociologist studying images of gender use Item A?

3 How might a sociologist use the data in Item C?

4 Ask 10 people what the rings round the neck of the woman in Item B indicate. Are their observations a) valid, b) reliable?

These rings or torques made of iron are engagement presents. They indicate her future husband's wealth and are worn for life.

key terms

Data Information collected as part of a research project.

Primary data New data produced by the researcher during the research process.

Secondary data Data which already exists, which can then be used by the researcher.

Quantitative data Numerical data – data in the form of numbers.

Qualitative data All types of data that are not in the form of numbers.

Validity Data is valid if it presents a true and accurate description or measurement.

Reliability Data is reliable when different researchers using the same methods obtain the same results, ie the same description or measurement.

summary

1. Sociologists often use both primary and secondary data in their research.

2. Quantitative data is useful for measuring the strength of relationships between various factors.

3. Qualitative data can provide a rich and in-depth picture of social life.

4. Ideally, research data should be both valid and reliable.

Unit 2 The research process

keyissues

1 What practical and theoretical considerations influence the research process?

2 What ethical issues are raised by sociological research?

Designing a research project, conducting the research, and analysing the results involve a number of decisions. These include choosing a topic, selecting appropriate research methods, and deciding whether the research is morally right.

2.1 Choosing a topic

Choosing a topic for research is influenced by a range of factors. Some of these will now be briefly examined.

Values of the researcher Researchers are likely to study something they consider to be important. And what they see as important is influenced by their values. For example, a sociologist who believes strongly in equality of opportunity may study the relationship between social class and educational attainment, since there is evidence that class inequality prevents equality of educational opportunity. Similarly, a sociologist who believes in gender equality may study the position of women at work and in the home, comparing their workloads and rewards with those of men.

Values of society The values of researchers often reflect the values of society. Feminists have criticised mainstream (or 'malestream') society as male-dominated and based on male values. They have made similar criticisms about sociology. For example, sociological research has traditionally focused on male concerns and male interests. As a result, female issues have been seen as unimportant and, until fairly recently, as unworthy of research. For example, Ann Oakley (1974) broke new ground when she chose to research housework, a topic then considered by many male sociologists to be of little significance.

Values in society change and with them the priorities and concerns of researchers. Today, gender inequality is seen as a major issue. And in sociology it forms the focus of a large number of research projects.

Funding Choosing a research project is also influenced by a number of practical issues. For example, is it affordable? Most research projects conducted by professional sociologists require outside funding. Research funds are

activity 2 *choosing a research topic*

Vegetable gardening

Women's jobs

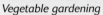
questions

1 Choose one of these topics for research.
2 Explain why you have chosen this topic.

Asian and White rioters in Bradford, 2001

available from various sources – charitable foundations such as the Joseph Rowntree Foundation and the Runnymede Trust, government organisations such as the Economic and Social Research Council (ESRC), and industry. Each funding body has its own priorities. For example, industrial organisations will tend to fund projects dealing with their own particular concerns, such as solutions to stress in the workplace. The choice of research project is often shaped by the priorities of the funding body.

Availability of data It makes little sense to choose a research topic where there is little or no data available and little chance of producing it in the future. For example, there is probably insufficient data to conduct a study of child abuse in Anglo Saxon England. And there is little chance of conducting a systematic study of secret service organisations such as MI5 and MI6.

Theoretical position Choosing a research topic is also influenced by the theoretical position of the sociologist. As noted earlier, feminist sociologists will tend to select topics

which reflect feminist issues – in particular gender inequalities.

Every theoretical position sees certain aspects of society as particularly important. For example, Marxism sees the class system as the foundation of capitalist society. As a result, Marxists tend to focus on topics such as class inequality, class conflict and class identity.

2.2 Choosing research methods

Having selected a topic, the researcher must then choose appropriate methods to collect and analyse data. The choice of methods depends on a number of factors. Some of these factors will be introduced briefly in this section and examined in more detail in later sections.

Practical considerations

Some methods are more suitable than others for conducting particular types of research. Think about the problem of studying a teenage gang whose members sometimes commit illegal acts. They are often hostile to outsiders, particularly those they see as representing authority. Asking gang members for interviews or presenting them with questionnaires is unlikely to produce the required data. However, joining in their activities and gaining their trust can allow the researcher to obtain information by observing their behaviour. This method has been used successfully by a number of sociologists studying gang behaviour.

A researcher can only observe and record the behaviour of a small number of people. What if the research involved making general statements about the relationship between social class and criminal behaviour? Some sociologists have claimed that members of the working class are more likely to commit crime than members of other social classes. It would take a lifetime of observation to assess this claim. For purely practical reasons, some sociologists have turned to official statistics on crime to investigate the relationship between social class and criminal behaviour. (However, there are problems with the use of official statistics as Section 8.1 shows.)

Theoretical considerations

A number of sociologists suggest there are two main research traditions, or approaches to research, within sociology (Halfpenny, 1984). These 'approaches' are often called *interpretivism* and *positivism*. They are based on different views of human behaviour. They sometimes lead to the use of different research methods.

Interpretivism Some sociologists argue that understanding human behaviour involves seeing the world through the eyes of those being studied. People give meaning to their own behaviour and to the behaviour of others, they define situations in certain ways and act accordingly. To understand their behaviour, it is essential to discover and interpret the meanings and definitions which guide their actions.

This view of human activity is sometimes called interpretivism. Sociologists who support this view tend to favour particular research methods. For example, many see *participant observation* – observing the people being studied by joining their activities – as a suitable method for discovering the meanings which guide their actions.

activity3 choosing methods

Item A Casual sex

Laud Humphreys studied casual sex between gay men in public toilets in the USA. His main method of research was observation. He pretended to be a 'voyeur-lookout'. A voyeur doesn't join in but gets pleasure from watching the activities of others. A lookout warns of approaching police.

Source: Humphreys, 1970

Item B Sex for money

Don Kulick used observation to study transsexual prostitutes in Brazil during 1996. He rented a small room in a house with 13 transsexual prostitutes. The prostitutes are referred to as 'travestis'.

'I associated with travestis pretty much continually during those eight months, eating breakfasts of sweetened coffee and buttered rolls with them when they woke up about midday, chatting with them as they sat in doorsteps, plucking whiskers from their chins in the late afternoon sun, crowding onto mattresses with them as they lay pressed together smoking cigar-sized joints and watching late-night action movies on television. Every night, from about 8pm until 1 or 2am, I walked the streets with them at their various points of prostitution.'

Source: Kulick, 1998

question

Why do you think Humphreys and Kulick chose observation as their main research method?

A 'lady boy' transsexual prostitute in Bangkok, Thailand

Interpretivists also tend to favour in-depth, unstructured interviews since this method gives people the opportunity to talk about their behaviour as they see it. Asking them to fill in a questionnaire is unlikely to provide such freedom of expression.

Interpretivist sociology attempts to discover and understand the meanings and definitions that direct social life. It assumes that some research methods are better than others for this purpose.

Positivism By contrast, positivist sociology tends to model itself on the natural sciences such as physics and chemistry. It favours 'hard', quantitative data, rather than the 'soft' qualitative data often used by interpretivist sociology. It is less concerned with the meanings people attach to their behaviour and more with the behaviour itself.

Behaviour can be directly observed and quantified – for example, number of visits to the opera in one year. Meanings cannot be directly observed, they can only be interpreted, for example the meanings that direct people to go to the opera.

Positivist sociology attempts to measure behaviour by translating it into numbers. This makes it possible to use statistical tests to measure the strength of relationships between various factors. This may indicate causal relationships – that one factor causes another.

Some research methods are more likely to produce data in a numerical form. Questionnaires are an example. It is fairly easy to translate the answers to a questionnaire into numbers. And some existing data is available in a numerical form – for example, official statistics.

Positivist sociology attempts to explain human behaviour by discovering cause and effect relationships. It requires data in the form of numbers for this purpose. Some research methods are designed to do this and, as a result, tend to be favoured by positivist sociologists.

Social facts Positivists argue that sociologists should focus on social facts rather than actions which can be explained by the unique experience of individuals. Social facts are aspects of society – for example, the institutions and values of society. Social facts direct individual behaviour but have an existence outside individuals – they are part of the wider society. The following example illustrates this view.

Suicide is usually seen as a very personal act which can only be explained in terms of an individual's experience – for example, he took his own life because his wife left him and he was depressed. However, the suicide rate – the number of suicides as a proportion of the total population – can be seen as a social fact. It can be argued that the suicide rate is determined by factors in the wider society – by social facts external to the individual.

This view is illustrated in Activity 4, Item A which argues that one social fact – the level of social isolation in society – causes another social fact – the suicide rate. Here the explanation is social (found in society) rather than individual (found in individual experience).

Social facts are external to individuals and direct their behaviour. In this sense, they are similar to the forces which are external to and direct the behaviour of matter, which is studied by the natural sciences. According to positivists, this means that the methods and approaches of the natural sciences are often appropriate for the study of social facts.

Dividing sociologists into interpretivists and positivists is a simplistic and rough and ready division. However, it's a useful starting point for understanding different approaches to research. A flavour of this difference can be seen from Activity 4.

2.3 Ethical issues

Ethical considerations can have an important influence on the research process.

Ethics are moral principles – beliefs about what is right and wrong. In terms of research, ethics are the moral principles which guide research. Sociological associations in many countries have a set of ethical guidelines for conducting research. Sociology departments in universities usually have an ethics committee to ensure that research conducted by members of the department is in line with these guidelines.

There is a growing awareness that those who participate in research have rights and that researchers have responsibilities and obligations. For example, should participants be informed about the purpose of the research and what their participation involves? Should researchers make every effort to ensure that participants come to no physical or psychological harm? Is it ever justifiable to deceive participants about the purpose of the research? These are some of the ethical questions researchers should consider.

Informed consent Many researchers argue that those they are studying should be given the opportunity to agree or refuse to participate in the research. This decision should be 'informed' – information must be made available on which to base a decision to participate or not. Researchers should therefore provide information about the aims of the research, what the conduct of the research involves, and the purposes to which the research will be put.

Deception This means that information is withheld from participants and/or they are provided with false information. They may be unaware they are participating in a research study. They may be misled about the purpose of the study and the events that may take place during the research.

Clearly, participants cannot give informed consent if they are deceived. Is deception ever justifiable? Some researchers argue that deception is justified if there is no other way of gathering data. This means using a research method such as *covert (hidden) observation* so that people are unaware they are participating in research. Or, it means misleading participants about aspects of the research. For example, Humphreys (1970) gathered further

activity4 researching suicide

Item A Explaining suicide

In a famous study entitled *Suicide*, first published in 1895, the French sociologist Emile Durkheim examined the suicide rates of different groups in society. He compared the following groups and, using official statistics, found that in each case, the group on the left had a higher suicide rate than the group on the right.

City dwellers : Rural dwellers
Older adults : Younger adults
Unmarried : Married
Married without children : Married with children

Durkheim argued that members of each group on the left are more socially isolated than those on the right. For example, married couples without children have fewer ties to bind them together than married couples with children.

Durkheim believed he had found a causal relationship between two social facts, the level of social isolation and the rate of suicide – the higher the level of social isolation, the greater the likelihood of suicide.

Source: Durkheim, 1970

questions

1 How do Items A and B illustrate positivism and interpretivism?
2 Explain Item C from a) Durkheim's and b) Atkinson's view.

Item B Understanding suicide

From an interpretivist view, suicide is a meaning which people give to certain deaths. The job of the sociologist is to discover why particular deaths are defined as suicides. From observations of inquests and discussions with coroners, the British sociologist J. Maxwell Atkinson believes that coroners have a picture of a typical suicide and a typical suicide victim. Road deaths are rarely seen as suicides whereas deaths by drowning, hanging, gassing and drug overdose are more likely to be interpreted as suicides. The typical suicide victim is often seen as a lonely, friendless, isolated individual with few family ties.

Source: Atkinson, 1978

Item C A typical suicide?

The Maniac Father and The Convict Brother Are Gone – The Poor Girl, Homeless, Friendless, Deserted, Destitute, and Gin Mad, Commits Self Murder.

(From a series of illustrations entitled 'The Drunkard's Children' drawn by George Cruikshank in 1848)

---

information about some of the gay men in his research by calling on their homes and pretending to be conducting a health survey.

Privacy Researchers generally agree that participants' privacy should be respected. The problem here is that most research intrudes into people's lives. It has been argued that if participants consent to take part in research, then they accept this. However, they may be unaware of the extent of the intrusion. With hindsight, they may see it as an invasion of privacy.

Certain research methods, which are generally considered ethical, may result in an invasion of privacy. Take the case of the informal, unstructured interview – it often develops into a friendly chat between researcher and participant. In this relaxed atmosphere, participants may reveal all sorts of personal and private matters which they may later regret.

Confidentiality It is generally agreed that the identity of research participants should be kept secret. According to the British Sociological Association's *Statement of Ethical*

Practice (1996), confidentiality must be honoured 'unless there are clear and overriding reasons to do otherwise'. It has been argued that when people in powerful positions misuse their power, then there may be a case for naming names (Homan, 1991).

Protection from harm There is general agreement that research participants should be protected from harm. This includes any harmful effects of participating in the actual research process and any harmful consequences of the research.

Publication of research findings may harm those who have been studied. For example, a study by Jason Ditton of workers in a bread factory revealed all sorts of fiddles and petty thefts. As Ditton himself recognised, management may well clamp down on such practices after publication of his book (Ditton, 1977).

Ethics and the research process As noted earlier, all researchers have values which define what is right and wrong. To some extent, these ethical values will affect every stage of the research process. If, for example, researchers see poverty, male domination, racial discrimination, or private education as ethically wrong, then they may choose to study these topics in order to reveal the wrongs and discover ways to right them.

key terms

Interpretivism An approach which focuses on the meanings and definitions which guide and direct behaviour.
Positivism An approach which attempts to explain behaviour in terms of cause and effect relationships.
Participant observation A research method where the researcher joins the activities of those they are observing.
Social Facts Aspects of society which are external to individuals and which direct their behaviour.
Covert observation Hidden observation. Participants are unaware that they are being observed as part of a research project.
Ethics Moral principles – beliefs about what is right and wrong.

summary

1. The choice of research topic may be influenced by the
    - values of the researcher
    - values of society
    - type of funding
    - availability of data
    - theoretical position of the researcher.

2. The choice of research methods may be influenced by practical, theoretical and ethical considerations.

3. There are two main approaches to research in sociology – interpretivism and positivism. Each approach tends to favour particular research methods.

4. The research process is influenced by ethical considerations. Most sociologists believe that participation in research should be based on informed consent, that participants should be protected from harm, that their privacy should be respected and their confidentiality assured.

activity5 ethics and research

Item A The National Front

Nigel Fielding conducted a study of the National Front, which many, including Fielding, considered to be a vicious, racist organisation concerned with White supremacy. Part of his research involved attending local meetings of the Front, during which he concealed his real reason for being there. In order to avoid suspicion he contributed to discussions, appearing to be sympathetic to the Front's beliefs.

Source: Fielding, 1981

Item B Missing lessons

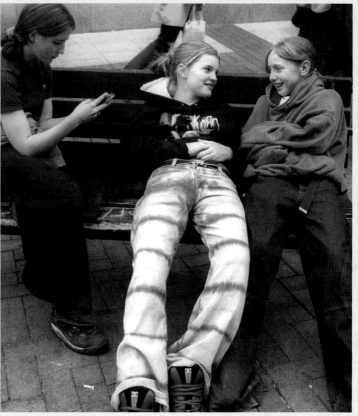

Val Hey studied friendship between girls. Her research was based on observation in two schools. She would sometimes give the girls small gifts and even excuses to miss lessons in exchange for cooperating in her research.

Source: Hey, 1997

Item C *Illegal drug use*

In their study of illegal drug use, Howard Parker and his colleagues found that some of the responses to their questionnaires revealed that individuals were not coping with their drug use. The researchers had to decide whether to offer help and advice or maintain the confidentiality they had promised.

Source: Parker et al., 1998

Smoking cannabis

questions

1 Why do you think Fielding chose to study the National Front?

2 Discuss the ethical issues involved in his research methods.

3 Do you think Hey (Item B) was justified in helping the girls truant from lessons? Explain your answer.

4 How would you have dealt with the problem faced by Parker in Item C? Give reasons for your decision.

(In the end, the researchers decided to treat each case individually.)

Unit 3 *Experiments*

keyissues

1 What are the main types of experiments?

2 Why are experiments rarely used by sociologists?

3.1 Laboratory experiments

For most people the word experiment conjures up a picture of white-coated researchers in a laboratory using scientific equipment to prove or disprove something. This is quite a good starting point for understanding the experimental method.

The main aspects of the experimental method can be illustrated by the following example. This experiment was conducted to test the *hypothesis* or supposition that, 'The speed of a boat depends on the shape of its hull'.

Controlling variables In order to discover the effect of hull shape on speed it is necessary to identify and control all the variables or factors which might affect speed. This is difficult to do outside a laboratory since variables such as wind strength and temperature cannot be controlled. In a laboratory, it is possible to control such variables and keep them constant so that hull shape is the only factor which

varies – from oval, to triangular, to rectangular, etc. In this way it is possible to find out how hull shape affects speed.

Quantifying results The results of experiments are usually quantified – presented in the form of numbers. Thus the speed of a model boat in the laboratory can be measured in centimetres per second using a metre rule and a stopwatch. Using a standard objective system of measurement is important as it reduces reliance on the judgement of the investigator and is therefore more likely to produce reliable data. And, it allows other researchers to *replicate* or repeat experiments and directly compare the results.

Correlation and causation If changes in one variable (eg, the shape of the hull) are matched by changes in another variable (eg, the speed of the boat) then there is a *correlation* between the two variables. But this does not mean that one causes the other. However, being able to control variables in a laboratory does help us to judge whether the correlation is causative rather than coincidental. In the case of the boat, the only apparent change is in hull shape so any change in speed is likely to result from this.

Laboratory experiments and people Laboratory experiments have been very successful in the natural sciences such as physics and chemistry. However, many sociologists have serious doubts about their application to human beings. This is partly because people act in terms of their definitions of situations. They are likely to define laboratories as artificial situations and act accordingly. As a result, their actions may be very different from their behaviour in the 'real' world. An attempt to get round this is the *field experiment,* an experiment which takes place in people's everyday situations.

activity6 laboratory experiments

Item A Imitative aggression

A group of nursery school children watched an adult mistreating a Bobo doll – a large inflatable rubber doll – by punching it, kicking it and hitting it with a mallet. The experimenter, Albert Bandura, then exposed this group and another group who had not watched the violence to the following 'frustrating experience'.

The children were shown a room full of exciting toys and given the impression they could play with them. They were then told they could not play with them. They were then taken, one by one, to a room of unattractive toys which included a Bobo doll and a mallet. As Bandura had predicted, those who had earlier watched the mistreatment of the Bobo doll were more likely to imitate this behaviour and show aggression towards the doll.

Source: Bandura, 1973

Imitating adults – attacking a Bobo doll.

Item B The real world

Can the results of laboratory experiments be applied to the real world? For example, does the Bobo doll experiment suggest a link between violence in films and violence in real life? Unlike people, Bobo dolls are designed to be knocked around, they invite violent behaviour. As such, they are hardly suitable for an investigation into imitative aggression. Critics of experiments argue that the many differences between the laboratory situation and real life undermine any attempts to apply research findings to the claim that films promote aggressive or violent behaviour by imitation.

Source: Williams, 1981

Described as 'sickeningly violent, appallingly funny and arrestingly accomplished', Reservoir Dogs became a cult movie in the mid-1990s (Chronicle of the Cinema, 1995).

questions

1 What hypothesis is being tested in Item A?

2 Do you agree with the views outlined in Item B? Give reasons for your answer.

3.2 Field experiments

Field experiments are conducted in normal social situations such as the classroom, the factory and the street corner. The following example was devised to test the effect of social class on interaction between strangers (Sissons, 1970). An actor stood outside Paddington Station in London and asked people for directions. The actor, place and request were kept the same but the actor's dress varied from a businessman to a labourer. The experiment indicated that people were more helpful to the 'businessman'. It could therefore be argued that people were responding to what they perceived as the actor's social class. However, there are other possibilities. For example, the actor may behave more confidently in his role as businessman and people might respond to his level of confidence rather than level of class.

Lack of control Field experiments are always going to be inexact and 'messy'. It is impossible to identify and control all the variables which might affect the results. For example, it is difficult, if not impossible, to control the social class of the people asked for directions in the above experiment. Most of them may have been middle class. If so, they may have been more helpful to the 'businessman' because he seemed 'more like them'.

The Hawthorne effect Whether in the laboratory or in more normal social contexts, people are often aware they are participating in an experiment. And this in itself is likely to affect their behaviour. This particular *experimental effect* is often known as the *Hawthorne effect* since it was first observed during a study at Hawthorne Works of the Western Electricity Company in Chicago in the late 1920s. The researchers conducted an experiment to discover whether there was a relationship between the workers' productivity and variables such as levels of lighting and heating and the frequency of rest periods. The researchers were puzzled as the results appeared to make little or no sense. For example, productivity increased whether the temperature in the workplace was turned up or down. The only factor which appeared to explain the increase in productivity was the workers' awareness that they were part of an experiment – hence the term Hawthorne effect.

Experimenter bias People act in terms of how they perceive others. They will tend to respond differently if the

experimenter is young or old, male or female, Black or White and so on. People also tend to act in terms of how they think others expect them to act. This might explain the results in the experiment involving the actor dressed as a businessman and a labourer. He might be conveying two different expectations and this may affect the responses to his request for directions. For example, he may expect more help in his role as businessman and unintentionally convey this to the participants. The unintended effect of the experimenter on those being studied is known as *experimenter bias*.

Ethical questions Is it right to experiment on human beings? This depends partly on the nature of the experiment. Nearly everybody would reject the medical experiments performed on inmates against their will in Nazi concentration camps. However, fewer people would object to the actor asking directions outside Paddington Station. Should people be told they are the subject of an experiment? Yes, according to the British Psychological Society, unless it's absolutely necessary to deceive them, and then they must be told immediately afterwards (British Psychological Society, 1998).

summary

1. There are two main types of experiments – laboratory experiments and field experiments.

2. Experiments are often designed to test hypotheses.

3. Experiments are usually intended to measure the strength of relationships between two or more variables.

4. Ideally, laboratory experiments allow the researcher to control all the important variables.

5. Laboratory experiments have been criticised for creating artificial situations. Critics argue that as a result, findings from laboratory experiments may not apply to everyday social situations.

6. Field experiments help to avoid artificiality, but they do not provide the same control of variables.

7. Both laboratory and field experiments have been criticised for experimental effects. As a result, their findings may be low in validity.

activity7 asking directions

Same man...

different response

questions

1 Suggest reasons for the different responses pictured above.

2 Using this example, outline some of the problems with field experiments.

Unit 4 Social surveys

keyissues

1 What is a social survey?

2 What types of sample are used for social surveys?

4.1 What is a social survey?

Survey data The National Readership Survey tells us that in 2000, *The Sun* was the most popular daily newspaper in Britain – read by 20% of adults. The International Passenger Survey tells us that Spain was the most popular overseas holiday destination in 2000 – visited by 28% of UK residents who had a holiday abroad. And the British Gambling Prevalence Survey informs us that the National Lottery Draw was the most popular gambling activity in Britain in 1999, with 65% of people aged 16 and over participating. (All figures from *Social Trends*, 2002.)

Definition The above information comes from *social surveys*. A social survey involves the systematic collection of the same type of data from a fairly large number of people. Social surveys are usually designed to gather information on the same variables – eg, age and cinema attendance – from those participating in the survey. This often means asking everybody the same set of questions.

4.2 Sampling

Nearly all social surveys are based on a *sample* of the population to be investigated. 'Population' is the term given to everybody in the group to be studied. The

population might be adult males, female pensioners, manual workers, 16-19 year old students, parents with dependent children and so on. A sample is a selection of part of the population. Samples are necessary because researchers rarely have the time and money to study everybody in the population. For example, if their research was based on women aged 16 and over in the UK, it would cover over 23 million people.

Most researchers try to select a sample which is *representative* of the population. This means that the sample should have the same characteristics as the population as a whole. Thus, if a researcher is studying the attitudes of British women, the sample should not consist of 1000 nuns, 1000 women over eighty or 1000 divorced women since such groups are hardly representative of British women. With a representative sample, *generalisations* are more likely to be true – findings from the sample are more likely to be applicable to the population as a whole.

Sample design and composition

Sampling unit Who should be included in a sample? In many cases it is fairly easy to define a *sampling unit* – ie, a member of the population to be studied. Dentists, males between 30 and 40 years of age, females who own their own businesses, people with one or more GCE A levels, can be defined without too many problems. However, other groups are not so easy – how would you define a semi-skilled manual worker or a person living in poverty? Who would you include in a population of 'criminals'? Do you limit the population to those convicted of a crime? Or do you include everybody who has ever broken the law, in which case you would include nearly every adult in the UK?

Sampling frame Once the research population has been defined, the sample is selected from a *sampling frame* – a list of members of the population to be studied. In some cases an appropriate sampling frame is readily available, eg the Electoral Register for a study of voting behaviour. In other cases researchers may have to rely on listings, such as the Postcode Address File or telephone directories, which may or may not be suitable for their purposes. And all listings have drawbacks – not everyone is included, they are often out of date, certain groups are likely to be over or under-represented, eg the poor are less likely to appear in telephone directories. Sometimes, those who have data needed for a sampling frame are unwilling to release it. This happened to Howard Newby (1977) when the Ministry of Agriculture refused to supply information for his study of Suffolk farmworkers. Newby had to use the *Yellow Pages* for his first sampling frame. Many farmworkers were absent from this directory and those included were probably unrepresentative of the group.

The design and composition of the sample will partly depend on the type of sample used. Some of the more common types will now be outlined.

Types of sample

Random samples A *random sample* gives every member of the sampling frame an equal chance of being selected. Every name is given a number and then a list of random numbers is used to select the sample. This avoids bias in selection. If researchers choose who to include and who to leave out, they may select a sample which supports their hypothesis.

Systematic samples This form of sampling systematically selects people from the sampling frame by choosing every 5th, 10th, 20th, or whatever, sampling unit. This method was used by Young and Willmott (1957) in their first study of Bethnal Green (see page 51). They selected every 10th name from the borough's electoral register.

Neither random nor systematic samples necessarily produce representative samples. Few sampling frames cover everybody in the research population. For example, on electoral registers certain groups are unrepresented (those not old enough to vote) or under-represented (the unemployed).

Even if the sampling frame covers the entire research population, a representative sample is not guaranteed. Simply because it *is* random, a random sample may select, for example, a disproportionate number of Labour voters from an electoral register. However, the larger the sample the less likely this will be. Systematic sampling can lead to an unrepresentative sample if the sampling frame is organised systematically. For example, a list of married couples in which husband follows wife would lead to an all male sample if every 10th person was selected.

Stratified samples Stratified samples offer a solution to the problem of representativeness. The population is divided into separate *strata* in terms of one of more characteristics, eg age, gender, ethnicity, class. A sample is then drawn which reflects those characteristics. Thus if the aim is to reflect gender divisions in the UK, 51% of the sample will be randomly selected from the female stratum and 49% from the male stratum. In terms of gender, the sample will be representative of the population as a whole.

A stratified sample can only be selected if researchers have sufficient information. In some cases, this is fairly easy to obtain. For example, the distribution of age in the UK population can be obtained from census data and this can then be mirrored in the sampling frame. In other cases, the necessary information is difficult or impossible to obtain. Religion provides an example. How do we get accurate information on the distribution of atheists, agnostics, Catholics, Protestants, Muslims, Hindus and so on in the population as a whole? And even if we can discover this, available sampling frames such as electoral registers may be no use at all since they provide no information about religious belief and practice.

Quota samples A market researcher stands on a street corner looking for likely 'victims'. She has to find twenty women between the ages of 30 and 45 to answer a questionnaire on magazine readership. She fills her quota with the first twenty women passing by who a) fit the required age group and b) agree to answer her questions. The sample selection is not random – it is not randomly selected from a sampling frame. The researcher simply fills her quota from the first available bodies. This method is known as *quota sampling*. It is 'a method of stratified sampling in which the selection within strata is non-random' (Moser & Kalton, 1971).

Quota sampling is often used for opinion polls and market research. It has its advantages – it is simpler, quicker and cheaper than stratified random sampling. However, it is less likely to produce a sample which is representative of the research population. For example, where and when a quota is filled can make significant differences to the sample. Stopping people on the street during weekday working hours would exclude many people in paid employment. And the fact that researchers can choose who they interview can bias the sample still further. Faced with two young men one 'smart' and 'pleasant' looking, the other just the opposite, researchers would probably choose the former. In quota sampling, people in the same strata do not have an equal chance of being selected.

Snowball and volunteer samples Sometimes researchers have great difficulty obtaining people for their samples. First, lists for a sampling frame might not be available. Second, the research population might be so small that normal sampling methods would not supply the numbers needed. Third, members of the research population might not wish to be identified. Think of the problems in locating the following: burglars, heroin users, collectors of ancient Greek coins, gay men, members of a Masonic Lodge. One possibility is to use a network of like-minded or like-situated individuals. This is the basis of *snowball sampling*, so-called because of its similarity to rolling a snowball.

Snowballing works like this. The researcher finds someone who fits the bill. They are asked to find another person who fits and so on. In this way a network of members of the research population is built up and this forms the basis for the sample.

Snowballing has the obvious advantage of creating a sampling frame where other methods may fail. However, it is unlikely to provide a representative sample since it is not random and relies on personal recommendation.

Volunteer samples provide an alternative to snowballing. Advertisements, leaflets, posters, radio or TV broadcasts, newspaper or magazine articles announce the research and request volunteers for the sample. Annette Lawson (1988) wrote a newspaper article about her study of adultery. She used the article to obtain a volunteer sample by asking readers who had experienced adultery to complete a questionnaire. Five hundred and seventy-nine readers responded to her request.

Volunteer sampling has much the same advantages and disadvantages as snowballing. In addition, volunteer samples are *self-selected* which may systematically bias the sample in a particular direction. For example, those who volunteer may have a particular reason for doing so.

4.3 Responding to surveys

Response rates It's one thing creating a representative sample, it's quite another getting everybody in the sample to participate in the survey. The *response rate* – the percentage of the sample that participates – varies widely. For example, Shere Hite's *The Hite Report on the Family* (1994) based on questionnaires in magazines had a mere 3% response rate, whereas everybody Ann Oakley (1974) asked to take part in her research on housework agreed to do so.

There are many reasons for non-response. They include:

1 Failure to make contact because people have moved, are on holiday, in prison, working away from home or simply out when the researcher calls.

2 Contact is made, but the interview cannot be conducted because the person is ill, deaf, experiencing some personal tragedy or can't speak English.

3 The person refuses to participate. Reasons may include no time, no interest, sees no point in the research, is suspicious of, dislikes, or is embarrassed by the researcher.

Problems of non-response Does non-response make the sample unrepresentative? Does it bias the sample and produce systematic error? Often the answer is we don't know since little or nothing is known about those who do not participate. Sometimes information on non-participants does become available. This happened in the surveys attempting to predict the 1992 General Election result. Opinion polls underestimated the Conservative vote by 8.5%. Over half of this underestimate was due to those who refused to participate – they were much more likely to vote Conservative. This produced an unrepresentative sample and in large part accounted for the failure to predict the election result (*Horizon*, BBC TV, 1994).

Evidence such as this suggests that non-response can be a serious problem.

summary

1. Social surveys are designed to provide information about particular populations.

2. They are based on samples which aim to represent the research population as a whole.

3. Whatever type of sample is used, there is no guarantee that it will be representative.

4. A high level of non-response can result in an unrepresentative sample.

key terms

Social surveys Systematic collection of the same type of data from a particular population.

Sample A selection from the research population.

Sampling unit A member of the research population.

Sampling frame A list of members of the research population.

Random sample A sample which gives every member of the sampling frame an equal chance of being selected.

Systematic sample A systematic selection of people from the sampling frame, eg every 10th member.

Stratified sample A sample which attempts to reflect particular characteristics of the research population. The population is divided into strata in terms of age, gender etc, and the sample is randomly drawn from each stratum.

Quota sample A stratified sample in which selection from the strata is not random.

Snowball sample Members of the sample select each other.

Volunteer sample Members of the sample are self-selected, eg they choose to respond to a questionnaire printed in a magazine.

Response rate The percentage of the sample that participates in the research.

activity8 sampling

Item A   A stratified random sample

We wish to study the career plans of university students and have sufficient funds to interview 125. Before selecting the sample, the sampling frame is stratified into departments, eg Physics and Chemistry, and years, eg students in their first year of study. There are 5,000 students in the university and the sample of 125 is one fortieth of this total. The example below shows the numbers of students randomly selected from years 1, 2 and 3 in the Physics department.

Source: Arber, 1993

Stratification by department and year

Department	Year	Number in year	Number in sample
Physics	1	120	3
	2	100	3
	3	100	2
Total		320	8

Item B   A volunteer sample

Shere Hite's (1994) report on family life in three Western societies received a great deal of publicity. Some of its 'findings' were dramatic. More than one in four women 'have no memory of affection by their father'. Four out of ten fathers frighten their sons with their violent tempers. And 31% of girls and young women 'report sexual harassment or abuse by a male family member'.

Hite's findings were based on 3028 completed questionnaires. Her sample was a self-selected volunteer sample. Hite distributed 100,000 questionnaires, mainly in

Will the readership of Penthouse, a men's magazine, provide a representative sample?

magazines such as *Penthouse* in America, *Women Against Fundamentalism* in Britain and *Nouvelles Questions Feminists* in France. Her statistics come from the 3% who responded. She claims that self-selected samples are acceptable as long as the study is large enough.

Source: Kellner, 1994

questions

1   Why do you think the researchers in Item A decided to use a stratified random sample?

2   According to one critic, Hite's 'findings' are rubbish (Kellner, 1994). Discuss this claim with reference to a) her sampling procedure and b) the response rate.

Unit 5 Questionnaires

keyissues

1   What are questionnaires?

2   What are their advantages and disadvantages?

5.1 What are questionnaires?

Questionnaires are lists of questions. They are the main method for gathering data in social surveys. They are sometimes handed to or posted to the respondent – the person answering the questions – and he or she is asked to fill them in. This is known as a *self-completion questionnaire*. They are sometimes read out by an interviewer who records the answers. This is known as an *interview questionnaire* or a *structured interview*.

Comparable data In theory questionnaires produce data

which can be directly compared. Everybody is answering exactly the same questions and are therefore responding to the same thing. Any differences in the answers will therefore reflect real differences between the respondents.

This is fine in theory. However, it's easier said than done. As we shall see, the same questions worded in exactly the same way can mean different things to different people. And in the case of the structured interview there is the problem of *interviewer bias* – the effect an interviewer may have on respondents' answers. Imagine how the age, gender and personality of an interviewer might affect your answers on a sensitive subject such as sexual behaviour.

Quantifiable data Questionnaires are usually designed to generate data which can be easily quantified – put into numbers. Here is an example from *British Social Attitudes: the 17th Report* (Source: UK Data Archive, 2000). It shows the percentage of respondents who chose each option. Constructing questions in this way makes it easy to quantify the results.

A frank scene in a film shows a man and woman having sex. How would you feel about this being shown on one of the regular television channels?

	% agreeing
Should not be allowed to be shown at all	23
Only after midnight	18
Only after 10pm	35
Only after 9pm	18
Only after 8pm	3
Allowed to be shown at any time	2

Numerical data lends itself to statistical techniques. It makes it possible to discover whether or not there is a correlation – a statistical link – between two or more variables.

Operationalising concepts Questionnaires are designed to measure things. And to do this, those 'things' must be *operationalised*, ie put in a form which allows them to be measured. How, for example, do you measure the strength of religious belief? The example below is from the 1998

Belief in God, Britain, 1998 (%)

I don't believe in God.	10
I don't know whether there is a God and I don't believe there is any way to find out.	15
I don't believe in a personal God but I do believe in a Higher Power of some kind.	14
I find myself believing in God some of the time but not at others.	14
While I have doubts, I feel that I do believe in God.	23
I know God really exists and I have no doubts about it.	21
Don't know and no answer.	3

Source: UK Data Archive, 1998

British Social Attitudes Survey. It is an attempt to measure people's belief in God. Respondents were asked to choose the statement which best fits their beliefs.

Operationalising concepts is difficult, especially when sociologists themselves cannot agree on their meaning. For example, how do we operationalise concepts such as poverty and social class? Often concepts are operationalised in different ways in different studies which means the results are difficult, if not impossible, to compare. And the problem of comparability becomes even greater when we attempt to discover what respondents really mean when they answer questions. This problem will be looked at shortly.

Coding answers Answers to questions are *coded*. This means they are classified into various categories. When concepts, such as belief in God, are operationalised, the questionnaire can be pre-coded. The responses to the Belief in God questionnaire are pre-coded into seven categories. The researcher simply has to count the number of people who choose each category. Quantifying the data is easy.

It is more difficult to code a written answer. Consider the following.

Question	Do you believe in God?
Answer	It depends what you mean by God. Do you mean a God that just exists apart from this world? Or, do you mean a God that controls what happens in this world? Sometimes, I think I believe in the first type of God.

This answer is difficult to code. Researchers usually have a list of categories in terms of which written answers are coded. Often, however, written answers don't fit neatly into a particular category. For example, the above answer would not fit neatly into any of the categories in the Belief in God questionnaire.

Written answers are sometimes difficult to code. As a result, they are difficult to quantify.

5.2 Types of questions

Closed questions There are two main types of questions used in questionnaires – closed and open. In *closed questions*, the range of responses is fixed by the researcher. The respondent usually has to select one answer from two or more given alternatives. The questions above on sex on television and belief in God are examples of closed questions. Here is a different example in which the respondent is asked to rank the alternatives provided.

> Which do you feel are the most important factors in choosing a university? Please rank the following in order of importance to you. Number them from 1 = most important, to 7 = least important.
>
> Closeness to a town or city
> Good academic reputation
> Good chance of getting a job after graduation
> Attractive campus
> Good social facilities
> Good accommodation
> Availability of real ale
>
> Source: Newell, 1993

Closed questions are relatively easy, quick and cheap to classify and quantify. They are pre-coded in the sense that the categories are set and the respondent simply has to choose one or rank some. However, the researcher has chosen the available responses and in this respect is imposing his or her choice of alternatives on the respondent. Look at the question above on choosing a university. Can you think of any 'important factors' not given? There is a way round this problem by adding 'other, please specify' which asks the respondent to add, in this case, any other reasons for choosing a university.

Open questions An *open question* asks the respondent to answer a question in their own words. Open questions give the respondent more freedom, but coding the responses can be difficult and time consuming. In many cases it might be difficult to fit responses into a particular category.

Most researchers see closed questions as suitable for simple, factual data such as age, gender and income level. Open questions are usually seen as more suitable for data on attitudes and values where respondents are required to express how they feel. An open question allows them to say things in their own way.

5.3 Types of questionnaires

Self-completion questionnaires

Self-completion questionnaires can be left with respondents either to be picked up later or posted back to the researcher. *Postal questionnaires*, as their name suggests, are mailed to respondents with a request to mail them back to the researcher. Usually most of the questions in self-completion questionnaires are closed and pre-coded.

Self-completion questionnaires have the following advantages and disadvantages.

Advantages

- Inexpensive – no interviewers to pay, cheap to classify results.
- As a result, often possible to survey a large sample.
- Fast and efficient analysis possible with pre-coded closed questions. Answers can be easily quantified and entered straight on to computers.

- Postal questionnaires allow a geographically dispersed sample to be contacted easily and cheaply.
- No interviewer bias – the interviewer does not influence the respondent's answers.

Disadvantages

- A relatively low response rate – often well below 50% for postal questionnaires. This may destroy the representativeness of the sample.
- Respondents may not understand the questions or follow the instructions.
- Answers may be incomplete, illegible or incomprehensible.
- Closed questions may seriously limit what respondents want to say.

Structured interviews

In a structured interview the interviewer reads out the questions and records the responses in writing, on audio-tape or on a portable computer.

Advantages

- Response rate usually much higher than for postal questionnaires.
- Interviewers can explain the purpose of the research, clarify questions and ask for further details. This can result in more information.
- Respondents who cannot read and write can be included in the survey.

Disadvantages

- More expensive – interviewers are usually paid.
- Cost increases if sample spread over a wide area.
- Interviewer bias.

5.4 Questions and answers

Constructing a questionnaire is not easy. The researcher must make sure that questions are clear and unambiguous. Where possible, words and phrases should be simple and straightforward. Leading questions, eg 'Don't you agree that …' should be avoided as they direct the respondent to a particular answer. Questions should be meaningful and relevant – there's not much point in asking people if they've enjoyed their holiday abroad if they've never been out of the country. And, most importantly, the questions must mean the same thing to all respondents. If they mean different things respondents are, for all intents and purposes, answering different questions. And this means that their answers cannot be directly compared.

Researchers sometimes use a *pilot study* to iron out problems with questionnaires. They test the questions on a relatively small number of people who share the characteristics of the main sample. A pilot study can be invaluable for removing ambiguity and misunderstanding. Yet all the preparation in the world cannot completely remove the basic problems of questions and answers.

What do answers mean? Are respondents telling the truth? Yes and no. Are they giving the answers they think the researcher wants? Sometimes. Do all respondents understand the questions? Not always. Do the questions mean the same to all respondents? Probably not. Do respondents' answers reflect their behaviour in everyday life? Maybe. Given all this, what appears to be a precise, reliable and efficient research method – the social survey – may be nothing of the sort.

Creating an impression Everybody plays the game of 'impression management'. They try to manage the impression of themselves which others form. This can shape their responses to a questionnaire and more particularly to a structured interview. Consider the following example.

Survey after survey has shown a high level of church attendance in the USA, far higher than for any comparable Western industrial society. Yet figures produced by the churches tell a somewhat different story. For example, surveys conducted by Gallup suggested that 35% of Episcopalians (a type of Christians) in the USA had been to church in the last 7 days, yet figures from the churches indicated that only 16% actually did so. Why the discrepancy? It appears that many respondents were concerned with giving the 'right' answer to the interviewer – they wished to appear upright, decent and respectable and regular church attendance was, to many, a way of giving this impression (Bruce, 1995).

Examples such as this suggest that researchers must know as much as possible about what questions and answers mean to respondents. Only then can they write appropriate questions and be in a position to interpret the answers.

Words and meanings For a questionnaire to do its job, questions have to have the same meaning for all respondents. The following example from the USA illustrates how easy it is for a question to be interpreted differently. A survey of reading habits produced the unexpected result that working-class respondents read more books than middle-class respondents. This result was largely due to the interpretation placed on the word 'book'. Unlike most middle-class respondents, those from the working-class included magazines in their definition of books.

This illustrates that the more researchers know about those they study, the better the questions they ask and the better their interpretation of the answers.

5.5 Theoretical considerations

Positivism Two research traditions – positivism and interpretivism – were introduced on pages 146-147. As noted, positivists tend to favour 'hard', quantitative data. Positivist sociologists attempt to measure behaviour by translating it into numbers. This makes it possible to use

key terms

Self-completion questionnaire A questionnaire completed by the respondent.
Structured interview/interview questionnaire A questionnaire read out by an interviewer who also records the answers.
Operationalise Translating concepts into a form which can be measured.
Coding Classifying answers into various categories.
Closed questions Questions in which the range of responses is fixed by the researcher.
Open questions Questions which allow the respondent to answer in their own words.
Postal questionnaire A questionnaire mailed to respondents with a request to mail it back after completion.
Pilot study A preliminary study designed to identify any problems with the main study.

statistical tests to measure the strength of relationships between variables. This may indicate causal relationships – that one variable causes another.

It is fairly easy to translate the answers to a questionnaire into numbers. This is particularly so with closed questions. As a result, positivists tend to favour questionnaires as a method of producing data.

Interpretivism By contrast, interpretivists are concerned with the meanings which guide and direct human actions. Many interpretivists would reject questionnaires as a means of discovering meanings. They argue that questionnaires, particularly those with closed questions, fail to give people the freedom to talk about their behaviour as they see it.

summary

1. Questionnaires are the main method for collecting data in social surveys.
2. In theory, questionnaires provide directly comparable data.
3. Closed questions are pre-coded. They produce data which is easy to quantify.
4. Answers to open questions can be difficult to code and quantify.
5. Self-completion questionnaires and structured interviews each have their advantages and disadvantages.
6. It can be difficult to discover what respondents' answers actually mean.

activity9 asking questions

Item A On the toilet

A study based in Bristol asked nearly 2,000 people to fill out a questionnaire on how many times they went to the toilet during the week and the shape, size, consistency and texture of their faeces. They were required to tick whether it was 'like a sausage or snake but with cracks on its surface' or 'fluffy with ragged edges' and so on.

Source: O'Connell Davidson & Layder, 1994

Item B Non-existent videos

The Video Recording Bill was passed by the Conservative government in 1984. Its aim was to place strict controls on 'video nasties'. Survey evidence was used to support the bill. Children were given a list of video titles and asked to indicate which they had seen. Forty per cent claimed to have seen at least one of the video nasties on the list.

Later, Guy Cumberbatch presented children with a list of fictitious titles such as 'I vomit on your cannibal apocalypse'. Sixty-eight per cent claimed to have seen at least one of these non-existent videos.

Source: Harris, 1984

Have you watched this video?

Item C Saying one thing, doing another

In the early 1930s, Richard LaPiere, a social psychologist at Stanford University, travelled 10,000 miles across the USA with a young Chinese-American couple. At the time, there was widespread prejudice against Asians and there were no laws preventing racial discrimination in public accommodation. They visited 250 hotels, restaurants and campsites and only once were they refused service. After the trip, LaPiere sent a letter to all the places they had visited asking, 'Will you accept members of the Chinese race as guests in you establishment?' 92% said 'no', 7% said 'uncertain, depends on the circumstances' and only 1% said 'yes'.

Source: LaPiere, 1934

questions

1 Read Item A. Comment on the accuracy of the data which this questionnaire might produce.

2 What problems do Items B and C raise for interpreting answers to questionnaires?

Unit 6 *Interviews*

keyissues

1 What are the main types of interviews?
2 What are their advantages and disadvantages?

6.1 Types of interviews

Structured interviews As outlined in the previous unit, structured interviews are simply questionnaires which are read out by the interviewer who then records the respondent's answers. The same questions are read out in the same order to all respondents.

Semi-structured interviews Each interview usually has the same set of questions, but in this case the interviewer has the freedom to 'probe'. Respondents can be asked to clarify their answers, to provide examples, and to develop what they've said.

Unstructured interviews By comparison, unstructured interviews are more like an everyday conversation. They are more informal, open-ended, flexible and free-flowing. Questions are unlikely to be pre-set, though researchers usually have certain topics they wish to cover. This gives the interview some structure and direction.

Group interviews The interviews discussed so far involve two people – an interviewer and a respondent or interviewee. Group interviews involve the interviewer and a group of respondents – usually between 8 and 10 people. In some group interviews, the respondents answer questions in turn. In others, known as *focus groups*, participants are encouraged to talk to each other. They are guided rather than led or directed by the interviewer – for example, they are asked to discuss particular questions or topics.

Structured interviews – advantages and disadvantages

Why use different types of interviews? Each type has its strengths and weaknesses. Structured interviews have many of the advantages and disadvantages of questionnaires. They are particularly suitable for simple, straightforward, 'factual' information such as a respondent's age, gender, educational qualifications and occupation.

Structured interviews are seen as more likely to produce comparable data – since all respondents answer the same questions this should allow researchers to directly compare their responses and identify similarities and differences. Quantifiable data is more likely since questions can be structured to provide yes/no answers or choices between given alternatives. And, as structured interviews are more formal than other types, there may be less chance of interviewer bias.

However, structured interviews can place strict limitations on respondents' answers. This is particularly true of closed questions which force respondents to choose between pre-set alternatives. This prevents respondents from answering in their own words and in their own way.

Semi-structured interviews – advantages and disadvantages

This type of interview has many of the advantages of the structured interview. In addition, it allows the interviewer to probe – to jog respondents' memories, and ask them to clarify, spell out and give examples of particular points. This can add depth and detail to answers.

However, this gain is accompanied by a loss of standardisation and comparability (May, 2001). Although the basic questions are pre-set, probes are not, which results in non-standard interviews. This means that each interview is somewhat different. As a result, the data is not strictly comparable since, to some extent, interviewees are responding to different questions.

Group interviews – advantages and disadvantages

Focus groups are becoming increasingly common in sociological research. They have been used to study the effects of long-term imprisonment, victims of crime, conflicts within organisations and changes in working practices among steel workers (May, 2001; Walklate, 2000).

The results of focus group interviews are sometimes different from those of individual interviews. This does not mean that one is 'right' and the other 'wrong'. Interaction within groups affects people's opinions. Since much of our lives is spent in groups, it is important to obtain data from this source (May, 2001).

Some researchers find focus groups provide a rich source of qualitative data. In her study of victims of crime, Sandra Walklate (2000) claims that without the use of focus groups, many of the shades of meaning and subtleties of people's views would be lost.

Unstructured interviews – advantages

Unstructured interviews are often seen to have the following advantages.

Sensitive groups Some groups are less likely than others to provide information for researchers. They might be suspicious of outsiders, hostile towards them, afraid of them or simply uncomfortable in their presence. An unstructured interview can allay these feelings as it provides an opportunity for understanding and trust to develop between interviewer and interviewee. This can be seen from the following example. Postal surveys were used in London to find out why people did not apply for welfare benefits to which they were entitled. The response rate was very low, due partly to fear and suspicion, a reaction often found amongst the frail and the elderly. Research indicated that a one-to-one interview was the most effective way of gaining information, in large part because interviewers were able to put respondents' minds at rest (Fielding, 1993).

Sensitive topics Unstructured interviews are also seen as particularly suitable for sensitive topics. Respondents may be more likely to discuss sensitive and painful experiences if they feel that the interviewer is sympathetic and understanding. Unstructured interviews provide the opportunity for developing this kind of relationship. Joan Smith's (1998) study about the family background of homeless young people produced detailed and in-depth information using unstructured interviews.

Respondent's viewpoint Structured and semi-structured interviews give respondents few opportunities to develop their answers and direct the interview into areas which interest them. The researcher has constructed the questions and, in the case of closed questions, the range of possible answers. In these respects the researcher has decided what's important.

An unstructured interview offers greater opportunity for respondents to take control, to define priorities and to direct the interview into areas which they see as interesting and significant. In this way, they have a greater chance to express their own viewpoints. And this can lead to new and important insights for the researcher.

Validity and depth If respondents feel at ease in an interview situation they will be more likely to open up and say what they really mean. Unstructured interviews can provide this opportunity. They are therefore more likely to produce valid data and to produce richer, more vivid and more colourful data. They also allow interviewers more opportunity to pursue a topic, to probe with further questions, to ask respondents to qualify and develop their answers. Because of this, the resulting data may have more depth.

Meanings and attitudes Many researchers see unstructured interviews as particularly suited to discovering meanings, values, attitudes, opinions and beliefs. People often take these for granted and find it difficult to spell them out. For example, what exactly are people's religious beliefs; what does music really mean to them; what do they really think about the welfare state? Unstructured interviews can explore such areas without the limitations of pre-set questions.

Meanings and opinions are not simple and clear-cut. There are shades of meaning. Opinions are not cut and dried, they are hedged with qualification. A skilled interviewer can encourage and enable people to spell out this complexity. Structured interviews with pre-set questions are unlikely to capture this range of meaning. However, not everybody agrees with this view. The British Social Attitudes Survey uses a very detailed structured interview and a self-completion questionnaire to discover attitudes on a range of issues.

Unstructured interviews – disadvantages

Interviewer bias Interviewer bias is unavoidable. To some extent the interviewer will affect the responses of the interviewee.

Interviewers are people with social characteristics – they have a nationality, ethnicity, gender, social class, age group and so on. They also have particular personalities – they may be shy or outgoing, caring or uncaring, aggressive or unaggressive. These social and psychological characteristics will be perceived in certain ways by interviewees and will have some effect on their responses. In some cases this may systematically bias the results.

A number of American studies have examined the effect of the social characteristics of interviewers and respondents. J. Allan Williams Jr (1971) claims that the greater the status difference between interviewer and respondent, the less likely respondents are to express their true feelings. He found that African-Americans in the 1960s were more likely to say they approved of civil rights demonstrations if the interviewer was Black rather than White.

Social desirability In general, people like to present themselves in a favourable light. This can result in respondents emphasising socially desirable aspects of their behaviour and attitudes in the presence of interviewers. As noted in the previous unit, Episcopalians in the USA tend to exaggerate the frequency of their attendance at church in order to appear upright and respectable (see page 158).

Respondents tend to be open about and even exaggerate aspects of their behaviour which they see as socially desirable, and to conceal or minimise aspects seen as undesirable.

Validity Do respondents tell lies? Is their memory hazy or faulty? Is what they say in interviews different from what they have done or will do? In some cases the answer is yes to all these questions. An instance has been given above in the case of church attendance. Voting intention is a case where people's intentions expressed in interviews and their actions at a later date are sometimes different. And there is evidence that some people tell downright lies, for example when recounting their sexual activity to an interviewer (O'Connell Davidson & Layder, 1994).

Comparability Interviews, particularly those at the unstructured end of the continuum, can develop in all sorts of directions. As a result, data from one interview to the next can vary considerably. This makes comparisons between data from different interviews difficult. It also means that generalisations should be treated with caution.

Coding and quantifying It is difficult to code and quantify much of the qualitative data produced by unstructured interviews.

6.2 The interview process

Books on research methods are full of advice on how to conduct effective interviews and how to avoid pitfalls and problems.

Non-directive interviewing The standard advice is to be *non-directive*, to avoid leading respondents and to allow them to express themselves in their own way. The idea is to minimise interviewer bias. It is important to establish *rapport* – a friendly and understanding relationship – while at the same time appearing sensible and businesslike. Interviewers should not be too familiar, they must maintain a certain distance or respondents will be unduly influenced. Probing is allowed, in order to get respondents to clarify or develop their answers, but it must be used with care as it can easily lead to bias (Fielding, 1993).

Active approaches Non-directive interviewing can result in an artificial situation which makes respondents feel uneasy. Some sociologists have found that non-directive approaches can be frustrating for both parties. Platt (1976) notes that respondents 'would have liked guidance on what I regarded as relevant, but I was anxious not to mould the data to my preconceptions by giving them any. This produced a few tortured interviews in which an unhappy respondent spoke at length on aspects of the research which it was probably clear were not of interest to me.'

There is some evidence that more direct and aggressive interviewing techniques can produce more information. Howard Becker (1971) used this approach with some success in his interviews with Chicago schoolteachers. He found that many of the teachers were prejudiced against working class and ethnic minority pupils, information they would not normally volunteer. However, by adopting an aggressive approach Becker states, 'I coerced many interviewees into being considerably more frank than they had originally intended'.

summary

1. There are four main types of interview – structured, semi-structured, unstructured and group interviews.

2. Structured interviews are seen as more likely to produce comparable data.

3. The probes available with semi-structured interviews can add depth and detail to answers.

4. Unstructured interviews provide an opportunity to develop trust and understanding. This is important with sensitive groups and sensitive topics. It can add validity and depth to respondents' answers.

5. Unstructured interviews are more prone to interviewer bias and social desirability effects, both of which will reduce validity.

6. Focus groups provide an opportunity to obtain people's views in a group situation. They can be a rich source of qualitative data.

7. The standard advice to interviewers is to avoid direction and develop rapport. However, on occasion, more active approaches may produce better results.

activity10 interviewing

Item A Interviewers

Item B Three interviews

Interview 1 An eight-year-old Black boy from Harlem in New York is interviewed by a 'friendly' White interviewer who presents him with a toy jet plane and asks him to describe it. The setting is formal. There are long silences followed by short two or three word answers, which hardly provide an adequate description of the plane.

Interview 2 Another Black boy from Harlem is interviewed. Again the setting is formal but this time the interviewer is Black and raised in Harlem. The boy responds in much the same way as the boy in the first interview.

Interview 3 The boy and the interviewer are the same as in the second interview. This time the interviewer sits on the floor, the boy is provided with a supply of crisps and his best friend is invited along. The change is dramatic. The boy is enthusiastic, talkative, and gives a detailed description of the toy plane.

Source: Labov, 1973

questions

1 You are being interviewed on a) your sexual behaviour and b) your views on race relations. Choose an interviewer for each interview from Item A. Explain your choices.

2 Explain the idea of interviewer bias using your answers to Question 1.

3 Suggest reasons for the similarities and differences between the three interviews in Item B.

Unit 7 | Observation

keyissues

1 What are the main types of observation?
2 What are their advantages and disadvantages?

7.1 Participant observation

How do we really find out about the way of life of a group of people? One way is to join them – to participate in their daily activities and observe what they say and do. This research method is known as *participant observation*.

It was used by John Howard Griffin (1960) a White journalist who dyed his skin black in order to discover what it was like to live as a Black man in the southern states of America in the late 1950s. It was used by the anthropologist Bronislaw Malinowski who spent many years studying the Trobriand Islanders of New Guinea. He observed the most intimate details of their lives as he peered into grass huts gathering data for *Sex and Repression in Savage Society* (1927). And it was used by the sociologist Erving Goffman (1968) when he adopted the role of assistant to the athletics director in order to study the experience of patients in a mental hospital in Washington DC.

Ethnography

Participant observation is one of the main research methods used in *ethnography*. Ethnography is the study of the way of life of a group of people – their culture and the structure of their society. Often researchers attempt to 'walk a mile in their shoes' – to see the world from their perspective, discover their meanings and appreciate their experiences. Many argue that participant observation is the most effective method of doing this.

Participant observation gives researchers the opportunity to observe people in their natural setting as opposed to the more artificial contexts of the laboratory or the interview. It allows researchers to see what people do as opposed to what they say they do.

Participant observation has produced a number of classic ethnographies – Elliot Liebow's (1967) study of Black 'streetcorner' men in Washington DC; William F. Whyte's (1955) account of an Italian-American gang in Boston – and a range of anthropological studies of small scale non-Western societies from the Yanomamo of Amazonia (Chagnon, 1968) to the Mbuti of Zaire (Turnbull, 1961).

Gaining entry

Participant observation cannot work unless the researcher gains entry into the group and some degree of acceptance from its members. This can be difficult. Many groups don't want to be studied, especially those whose activities are seen as deviant or criminal by the wider society. However, as the following examples indicate, it is often possible to enter even closed groups.

For his research into casual sex between men in public toilets – the 'tearoom trade' – Humphreys (1970) acted as a lookout. By performing this useful and accepted role, he gained the trust of those he observed without having to join their sexual activities.

On other occasions, researchers have to participate more directly in order to gain entry. Dick Hobbs (1988) wanted to research the relationship between criminals and detectives in the East End of London. He agreed to coach a local soccer team when he discovered that Simon, a detective, was the father of one of the players. He developed a friendship with Simon who provided him with introductions and vouched for him (said he was OK). Hobbs also drank in *The Pump*, a local pub that was frequented by several detectives. These contacts enabled Hobbs to gain entry into the world of the detectives – he joined their conversations and observed their activities.

Sometimes researchers are forced into even greater participation to gain entry. Festinger (1964) found that the only way to observe a small religious sect was to pretend to be a believer and become a member of the sect.

The above examples are of *covert* research where the identity and purpose of the researcher are kept hidden. *Overt* research, where those being studied are aware of the researcher's role and purpose, has its own problems of access and acceptance. People often reject what they see as nosy, interfering outsiders, unless they are sponsored by a trusted member of the group who grants the researcher entry. This happened in Judith Okely's (1983) study of traveller-gypsies. Entry was a long and difficult process until she gained the friendship and trust of a family who had recently suffered a tragic death. The sympathetic and understanding relationship she developed with members of this family provided entry to the rest of the group.

Conducting research

Looking and listening Participant observation involves looking and listening. The general rule is to 'go with the flow' rather than forcing the pace and influencing people's behaviour. Since the aim is to observe people in their normal setting, the researcher must not disturb that setting. Blending into the background is usually recommended, though this is not always possible. For example, a participant observer in a classroom can stand out like a sore thumb. This can result in an 'artificial' lesson. However, it's surprising how soon he or she becomes invisible and taken for granted. In his study of a secondary school, Walford (1993) found that it took four weeks of observation before any class misbehaved. However, the situation changed rapidly after this time and Walford was soon watching 'mock wrestling' and chairs flying around the classroom!

Asking questions Watching and listening are not always adequate for the researcher's purposes. Sometimes a participant observer must take a more active role in order to obtain information. This usually involves asking questions. In such cases, the dividing line between participant observation and unstructured interviews is blurred. For example, William Whyte (1955) discussed his observations with Doc, the leader of the gang Whyte was studying, to the point where Doc became 'a collaborator in the research'.

The key informant Doc became a *key informant* – a member of the group who has a special relationship with the researcher and provides vital information. As noted earlier, Dick Hobbs developed a friendship with a detective called Simon. In Hobbs' (1988) words, Simon 'emerged as my principal police informant, granting me formal and informal interviews, access to documents, and introductions to individuals and settings that would otherwise be inaccessible'.

Hanging around A good deal of participant observation is informal, unplanned and unstructured – it consists of 'hanging around'. In his study of pilferage from the docks in St Johns, Newfoundland, Mars (1982) wandered round the wharves and sheds chatting to the dockers, and hung round bars drinking with them in the evening.

Recording observations Recording the findings of participant observation can be a problem, especially when the research is covert. Researchers usually write up the day's findings each evening whilst events are still fresh in their mind. In some cases the toilet has proved a useful place to make brief notes, which are written up in a more detailed form later (Festinger, 1964; Ditton, 1977). However, a lot relies on the researcher's memory which is inevitably selective.

In the field Participant observation can be a long process with a year or more being spent 'in the field'. It can require dedication, stamina and courage. Researchers are often cut off from the normal supports of family and friends, sometimes living a double life in an alien setting. And participant observation can be dangerous. For example, Haralambos (1994) was threatened with guns on more than one occasion during his research into African-American music on the south side of Chicago.

Many of the advantages and disadvantages of participant observation have been mentioned already. Some of the more important will now be summarised.

Advantages of participant observation

Validity What people say and what they do are sometimes very different, as indicated earlier in the units on questionnaires and interviews. Participant observation offers the chance to discover what people actually do, the chance to obtain valid data. For example, Haralambos (1994) observed African-Americans who a few hours earlier had said they disliked blues, singing and dancing to blues music and quite obviously enjoying themselves.

Insight Looking back on his observation of a street-corner gang in Boston, William Whyte noted, 'As I sat and listened, I learned the answers to questions that I would not have had the sense to ask if I had been getting my information solely on an interviewing basis'. This comment has been echoed by many participant observers. For example, during her observation of the Moonies, a religious movement, Eileen Barker (1984) handed out leaflets advertising a concert organised by the Moonies at the Royal Albert Hall. She found that trying to convince members of the public to take an interest actually helped to convince her that the concert was a worthwhile activity. Barker's participation provided an insight into the workings of religious sects – by selling the group's beliefs to others they are actually selling those beliefs to themselves.

Other research methods rely to a greater extent on prior knowledge. For example, to ask relevant questions in an interview you must already know something about the group under investigation. Participant observation can provide the kind of insight, fresh information and new directions for research which are less likely to come from other methods.

Insider's view Many supporters of participant observation argue that it offers the best opportunity to discover how people see the world in which they live. Other research

methods are more likely to reflect the priorities of the researcher to the exclusion of those of the researched. For example, the designer of a questionnaire has decided what is relevant and significant and this may bear little relationship to the lives of those being studied.

By watching and listening, a participant observer has the chance to discover the priorities and concerns, the meanings and definitions of people in their everyday situations. There may therefore be less likelihood of distorting people's view of the world.

Practicality Sometimes participant observation may be the only method with any chance of success. Some groups are closed to outsiders – their members reject requests for information. Such groups may include those involved in criminal activity, those whose behaviour is regarded as deviant by the wider society (eg, certain religious sects) and those who are hostile to the wider society (eg, some members of ethnic minority groups). Under these circumstances, joining the group, participating in its members' activities, obtaining their cooperation and even their trust, may be the only way of obtaining information.

Disadvantages of participant observation

Time, money and personal cost As already noted, participant observation can involve personal cost – stress and even danger. And costs in terms of time and money can be considerable – some researchers spend years in the field. However, given the quality of information that participant observation can produce, many would see these costs as reasonable.

Loss of objectivity The personal involvement which participant observation demands can reduce objectivity. An observer can identify so strongly with a group that the behaviour of its members is invariably seen in a positive light. In rare cases, this identification is carried to its extreme – observers 'go native', join the group and never return to their former lives.

Conversely, researchers can view those they observe in a negative light. Something of this can be seen from the Policy Studies Institute study of policing in London. At times researchers had to walk away from situations when they found the behaviour of the police racist and offensive. This does not necessarily result in a biased view, but it does little to encourage objectivity.

Changing behaviour Would you change your behaviour if a participant observer joined your social circle? The answer is yes, even if you weren't aware you were being observed. This is how 'Doc', William Whyte's main informant in the streetcorner gang, saw the effect of participant observation on his own behaviour. In Doc's words, 'You've slowed me up plenty since you've been down here. Now, when I do something, I have to think what Bill Whyte would want to know about it and how I can explain it. Before, I used to do things by instinct' (Whyte, 1955).

Given the importance of observing everyday life in its

normal setting, do comments like this invalidate the findings of participant observation? While recognising the problem, many researchers would say no. After a while most people get used to an observer and carry on more or less as normal. This is how David Hargreaves (1967) saw his effect as a participant observer in a boys' secondary school. 'Initially my presence caused changes in the boys' behaviour though once they became accustomed to me, they behaved normally.'

Replication Participant observation studies are difficult, if not impossible, to replicate – repeat under the same or very similar conditions. There are various reasons for this. Participant observation is often unsystematic – there are no fixed procedures; things happen and the observer tags along.

Participant observation relies heavily on the personal qualities of the researcher. To some degree, these qualities will affect how well they get on with those they observe, what they see and how they interpret it. And this reduces the chance of replication, as the following example suggests. In the late 1920s, Robert Redfield (1930) studied the village of Tepoztlan in Mexico. He found a close-knit society characterised by cooperation and a strong sense of belonging. Seventeen years later, Oscar Lewis (1951) studied the same village. He pictured a society divided by fear, envy and distrust. Maybe the differences were due to changes during the intervening years but, more probably, they reflect differences between the two observers.

Generalisation Sample sizes in participant observation studies are small. The researcher can't be everywhere observing large numbers of people. In view of the small numbers, it is not possible to generalise from the findings of participant observation. However, these findings can be used to refute or support generalisations from larger studies. Or they can produce fresh insights which can then be investigated on a larger scale.

Ethical questions All research involves ethical issues – questions of right and wrong. Participant observation, particularly when it is covert (hidden), brings these issues centre stage. According to the British Sociological Association, sociologists should explain the purpose of their research to those they study. However, these are guidelines rather than hard and fast rules (Hornsby-Smith, 1993).

Many sociologists would justify covert research under particular circumstances. For example, Nigel Fielding (1993) justified his covert observation of the National Front 'on the basis that this racist group was particularly hostile to sociology'. Laud Humphreys (1970) argues that covert participant observation is the only practical way to observe the 'tearoom trade' – casual sexual encounters between gay men in public toilets. He justifies his research because it destroys various harmful myths – for example, straight people are not drawn into gay sex – and it shows that gays

are *not* a threat to society and that extensive police surveillance is therefore unnecessary.

Theoretical considerations

Positivism From a positivist viewpoint, participant observation has its uses. It provides information which can be used to construct relevant and meaningful questions for a questionnaire. And this will produce quantifiable data.

However, as an end in itself, a participant observation study is not particularly useful. It produces little if any quantifiable data. And the numbers observed are small – too small to provide a representative sample which can form a basis for generalisations.

Interpretivism As noted earlier, participant observation gives the researcher an opportunity to capture the 'insider's view' – to see the world from the point of view of those being observed. Interpretivists are concerned with the meanings and definitions which direct action. Often these meanings and definitions are taken for granted. People are not aware of them. Observing their behaviour provides an opportunity for the researcher to interpret these taken-for-granted meanings. As a result, interpretivists tend to favour participant observation as a method for collecting data.

7.2 Non-participant observation

The researcher need not participate to observe people's behaviour. A *non-participant observer* is like a birdwatcher in a hide, observing behaviour without joining in. For example, a researcher may secretly observe children's behaviour in a school playground from an upstairs room in the school. They may use a *behaviour schedule* – a checklist of activities which are noted as and when they occur.

Compared to participant observation, non-participant observation has a number of advantages and disadvantages.

Advantages
- The observer is less likely to influence the group, especially if group members are completely unaware of his or her presence.
- Researchers have more opportunities for using research aids such as behaviour schedules and notebooks.

Disadvantages
- As non-participants, researchers have fewer opportunities for discovering the meanings which direct the actions of those they observe.
- As a result, researchers are more likely to impose their own interpretations and meanings on to behaviour they observe (O'Connell Davidson & Layder, 1994).

key terms

Participant observation The researcher participates in the activities of those he or she is observing.

Ethnography The study of the way of life of a group of people. It often involves an attempt to see the world from their point of view.

Covert research The identity of the researcher and purpose of the research are hidden from those being studied.

Overt research The identity of the researcher and purpose of the research are made clear to those being studied.

Key informant A member of a group being observed who develops a close relationship with the researcher and helps them by answering questions, introducing them to other members, and so on.

Non-participant observation The researcher observes, but does not participate in the activities of those being studied.

Behaviour schedule A checklist of activities which are noted on the schedule when they occur.

summary

1. Many researchers argue that participant observation is the most effective method of seeing the world from the perspective of those being studied.

2. Participant observation involves looking and listening.

3. The advantages of participant observation include:
   - The chance to discover what people actually do
   - The chance to gain new insights
   - The opportunity to take the insider's view
   - Practicality – it may be the only method with a chance of success.

4. The disadvantages of participant observation include:
   - Time, money and personal costs
   - A possible loss of objectivity
   - The possibility of changing the behaviour of those observed
   - Difficulties in replicating research
   - Small samples, therefore not possible to generalise
   - Ethical problems, particularly with covert observation.

5. Non-participant observation is less likely to affect the behaviour of those observed. But, it provides fewer opportunities for discovering the meanings which direct their actions.

activity11 participant observation

Item A Just hang around

The following extract is taken from William Whyte's participant observation study of an Italian-American gang.

Sometimes I wondered whether just hanging on the street corner was an active enough process to be dignified by the term 'research'. Perhaps I should be asking these men questions. However, one has to learn when to question and when not to question as well as what questions to ask.

I learned this lesson one night in the early months when I was with Doc (the gang leader) in Chichi's gambling joint. A man from another part of the city was regaling us with a tale of the organisation of gambling activity. I had been told that he had once been a very big gambling operator, and he talked knowingly about many interesting matters. He did most of the talking, but the others asked questions and threw in comments, so at length I began to feel that I must say something in order to be part of the group. I said: 'I suppose the cops were all paid off?'

Whyte's research was carried out in the Italian-American community of South Boston. Many east coast American cities have large Italian communities. This picture shows 'Little Italy' in New York.

The gambler's jaw dropped. He glared at me. Then he denied vehemently that any policemen had been paid off and immediately switched the conversation to another subject. For the rest of that evening I felt very uncomfortable.

The next day Doc explained the lesson of the previous evening. 'Go easy on that "who", "what", "why", "when", stuff, Bill. You ask those questions, and people will clam up on you. If people accept you, you can just hang around, and you'll learn the answers in the long run without even having to ask the questions.'

Source: Whyte, 1955

Item B **In the classroom**

The following extract is taken from David Hargreaves's study of an all-boys secondary school in England. He sat at the back of the classroom to observe lessons. Later, he talked to some of the boys about the behaviour of the teachers. This is what they said.

'When you're in he tries to act calmly as though he's a little angel and all that.'

'They put on a show for you. They put the good act on, smiles and all that.'

'Like if Mr O's getting mad 'cos someone's ripped a book or something, but if you're in he seems to drop it. If you weren't there, he'd get real mad.'

Source: Hargreaves, 1967

Item C **In the pub**

Dick Hobbs's research involved much heavy drinking in pubs and he experienced some of the dangers of 'going native'. He writes: 'I often had to remind myself that I was not in a pub to enjoy myself but to conduct an enquiry and repeatedly woke up the following morning with an incredible hangover facing the dilemma of whether to bring it up or write it up'.

Source: Hobbs, 1988

Item D **Backstage**

As part of his research, Rubenstein completed police training and rode as an 'armed observer' in patrol cars in Philadelphia – and perhaps that degree of involvement has helped to produce what will surely become a classic. His *City Police* is an insider's view of backstage police behaviour. In microscopic detail, Rubenstein takes us into the policeman's world. The information he collected on violence and corruption could only have been gained by a trained observer who was accepted by the policemen.

Source: *Punch*, 1979

questions

1 Item A points to one of the main problems of participant observation. What is this problem and how is it usually dealt with?

2 What are the advantages and disadvantages of participant observation indicated by Items B, C and D?

Unit 8 *Secondary sources*

keyissues

1 What are the main secondary sources of data?

2 What are the advantages and disadvantages of using these sources?

Primary data So far, this chapter has been mainly concerned with *primary data* – data produced by researchers using methods such as questionnaires, interviews and observation. Primary data is new data that did not exist before the research began.

Secondary data There is a vast range of existing information which is available for sociological research. It includes letters, diaries, novels, autobiographies, legal documents, parish records, official statistics, newspapers, magazines, television and radio programmes, recorded music, films, photographs and paintings. These sources of information are known as *secondary sources* and the data itself as *secondary data*.

This unit looks at a number of secondary sources and assesses the usefulness of secondary data.

8.1 Official statistics

Sources of official statistics

Official statistics are numerical data produced by national and local government bodies. They may be a by-product of the normal workings of a government department. For example, the claimant count measure of unemployment – a measure of unemployment based on the number of people who claim unemployment-related benefit – is a by-product of administering the benefit system. Or official statistics may result from research designed to produce them – for example, the Labour Force Survey collects information on unemployment from a quarterly survey of 60,000 households.

Official statistics cover a wide range of behaviour including births, deaths, marriage and divorce, the distribution of income and wealth, crime and sentencing and work and leisure. The following are among the main sources of official statistics.

1 **Government departments** Departments such as Children, Schools and Families and the Home Office regularly request information from organisations such as local tax offices, social services departments, hospitals, job centres and police stations. This information is then processed and much of it published.

2 **Surveys** The Office for National Statistics is the government agency responsible for compiling and analysing many of the UK's economic, social and population statistics. Surveys are a major source of statistical data. Every ten years the Office for National Statistics carries out the Census of the Population which covers every household in the UK. Each head of household must, by law, complete a questionnaire that deals with family composition, housing, occupation, transport and leisure. Other large scale surveys include the annual General Household Survey based on a detailed questionnaire given to a sample of nearly 12,000 people and the New Earnings Survey based on a 1% sample of employees drawn from Inland Revenue PAYE records.

Using official statistics

Official statistics provide a vast array of quantitative data. However, sociologists cannot accept them at face value – they must use them only with care and caution. It is essential to bear the following points in mind.

How are official statistics constructed? Sociologists must know how official statistics are constructed in order to assess the quality of the data they provide. The example of unemployment statistics shows why.

As noted earlier, there are two main sources of data for unemployment statistics – the benefit system and social surveys. And there are two main definitions of unemployment – the claimant count definition which uses data from the benefit system, and the International Labour Organisation definition which uses data from the Labour Force Survey. Although both measures show broadly the same levels of and trends in unemployment, there are differences.

Sociologists using official statistics on unemployment should be aware of how these statistics have been constructed. This applies to all official statistics, no matter what the topic.

Who decides what statistics are collected and published? Official statistics are government statistics. Elected representatives and government officials decide what information is important and useful and, on this basis, what data to collect and publish. And, maybe more importantly, they decide what *not* to collect and publish.

These decisions may be 'political'. They may reflect the concerns and priorities of government rather than a desire to provide sound and reliable information. For example, Muriel Nissel, the first editor of *Social Trends*, an annual publication of the Office for National Statistics has written, 'From time to time, there has been great pressure on directors of statistics in departments to withhold or modify statistics, particularly in relation to employment and health, and professional integrity has forced some to threaten resignation' (Nissel, 1995).

Are official statistics politically biased? Does the actual construction of statistics reflect government interests? Are they shaped to present the government of the day in a favourable light? The following evidence suggests that in some cases this might happen.

According to the Labour Party, Conservative governments changed the method used to count unemployment over 30 times between 1982 and 1992. And in practically every case, these changes resulted in a drop in the official level of unemployment (Denscombe, 1994). At best, some would argue, this is politically convenient, at worst it is outright fiddling to present the government in a better light.

Do official statistics provide valid measures?

Do official statistics really measure what they claim to measure? For example, do the annual crime statistics produced by the Home Office provide an accurate measurement of crime? Even the Home Office accepts that the answer is no. Similar criticisms can be made for a range of official statistics from unemployment and suicide to the distribution of income and wealth.

The problem of validity was examined with reference to suicide statistics in Activity 4. It is looked at again in terms of crime statistics in Activity 12.

Advantages of official statistics Despite the above warnings, official statistics can be very useful for sociological research. They have the following advantages.

- Published statistics are readily available and cost little or nothing to use.
- Care is taken to select representative samples and sample sizes are often large. Surveys as large as the General Household Survey are usually outside sociologists' research budgets.
- Many government surveys are well planned and organised with detailed questionnaires or interview schedules. As such, they meet the standards of sociological research.
- Surveys are often conducted regularly, for example on a fortnightly, monthly, annual or ten yearly basis. This can allow for comparisons over time and the identification of trends.
- Sometimes official statistics are the only major source of information on a particular topic.

Perspectives on official statistics

A positivist view From this perspective (see pages 146-147), official statistics are a potentially valuable source of quantitative data. They have their faults but, in may cases, they provide measures of behaviour that can be used to investigate possible cause and effect relationships.

An interpretivist view From this perspective (see page 146), official statistics are not 'facts', they do not represent some objective reality 'out there' in the real world. Instead, they are definitions and meanings in terms of which people construct social reality. The job of the sociologist is to discover these meanings and how they are constructed. For example, an interpretivist sociologist would not use suicide statistics to explain why people commit suicide. Instead, they would ask why certain kinds of death are defined as suicide. In this sense, suicide is a meaning (see page 146).

Take crime statistics. The question is not whether they are accurate or inaccurate. A crime is simply a meaning given to an event. And the job of the sociologist is to understand how this meaning is constructed.

A Marxist view From a Marxist viewpoint, official statistics are an aspect of ruling class ideology. Generated by government departments and agencies, official statistics derive from questions asked by, information processed by, and results either suppressed or made public by a state which represents the interests of the capitalist class. As such, they provide information which helps to maintain and justify the power of capital and disguise the reality of exploitation and oppression.

key term

Official statistics Statistics produced by local and national government, government agencies and organisations funded by government.

summary

1. Sociologists using official statistics should be aware of how those statistics have been constructed.

2. Decisions on what statistics to collect and publish may be politically biased.

3. In some cases, official statistics fail to produce valid measures.

4. Official statistics can provide valuable data for sociological research.

5. Positivists see official statistics as a potentially valuable source of quantitative data. Interpretivists see official statistics as meanings in terms of which people construct their social reality. Marxists see official statistics as an aspect of ruling class ideology.

activity12 crime statistics

Item A *Ethnicity and crime*

In 2005, Black Caribbeans and Black Africans made up around 3% of the UK population, but 15% of the prison population.

The police rely on the public to report crimes to them. Evidence indicates that White people are more likely to report Black rather than White suspects. Black males were five times more likely to be stopped by police under stop and search powers. If arrested for the same offence, Blacks were more likely to be charged than their White counterparts. And if found guilty of the same offence, Black people were more likely to be sent to prison.

Research indicates that statistics which link ethnicity and crime result from a series of decisions based on prejudice and discrimination. This is why so many Black people end up in prison.

Source: May, 2001 and Prison Reform Trust, 2006

Stop and search in Brixton, South London

Item B *The social construction of crime statistics*

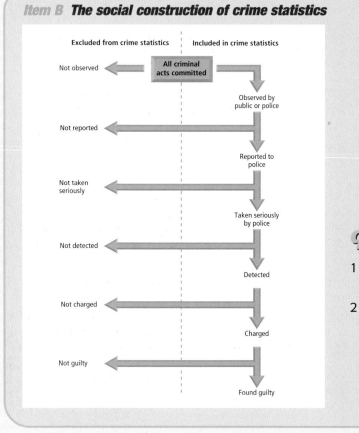

Excluded from crime statistics | Included in crime statistics

All criminal acts committed

Not observed

Observed by public or police

Not reported

Reported to police

Not taken seriously

Taken seriously by police

Not detected

Detected

Not charged

Charged

Not guilty

Found guilty

questions

1 a) What are the statistics in Item A actually measuring?

  b) Do they indicate a link between ethnicity and crime?

2 Look at Item B.

  a) Why does it suggest that crime statistics must be treated with caution?

  b) Item B assumes that there are such things as 'criminal acts' which are either included in or excluded from official statistics. Criticise this view.

8.2 Documents

The term *documents* covers a wide range of written and recorded material. It includes letters, diaries, memoirs, autobiographies, novels, newspapers, advertisements, posters, photographs and radio and television broadcasts.

This section looks at some of the ways sociologists have analysed documents. Ray Pawson (1995) distinguishes three main types of analysis, 1) formal content analysis, 2) thematic analysis and 3) textual analysis.

Formal content analysis

This method attempts to classify and quantify the content of a document in an objective manner. Say you were interested in the portrayal of gender roles in children's fiction published during the last five years. You could take a sample of the books and analyse each in terms of the same pre-set categories. For example, which activities are shared by girls and boys and which are limited to one or the other. The results are then quantified and interpreted. If, for example, preparing food and taking care of younger brothers and sisters is limited to girls, then it could be argued that gender roles remain distinct.

Critics accept that formal content analysis can often effectively measure simple straightforward aspects of content – see the example in Activity 13, Item A. However, they argue that it says little about the meaning of a document, either in terms of its meaning to the audience or the meaning the producer intends to communicate.

Thematic analysis

This approach looks for the motives and ideologies which are seen to underlie documents. For example, a news broadcast may reflect the interests of powerful groups in society. The job of the researcher is to uncover this underlying ideology. The Glasgow University Media Group combined content and thematic analysis in their analysis of TV news broadcasts in the 1970s and 80s. They made a strong case that there is a pro-management, anti-union bias in the reporting of industrial disputes.

However, there are a number of problems with thematic analysis. Who is to say that the sociologist's interpretation of the underlying ideology is correct? And if it is correct, does the existence of such ideology matter? Readers of *The Sun*, for instance, may see through or ignore or be unaware of its right-wing views. This may well explain why a significant minority of *Sun* readers regularly vote Labour.

Textual analysis

Rather than looking for underlying ideologies, this method involves a close examination of the 'text' of a document to see how it encourages a particular reading and creates a particular impression. Ray Pawson (1995) gives the following example from a newspaper headline, GIRL GUIDE, 14, RAPED AT HELLS ANGELS CONVENTION. This is an example of the 'innocent victim'/'wicked perpetrator' pair which creates the impression of two extremes, one good, the other evil. It is one of the many tricks of the trade used to convey particular messages.

As with thematic analysis, the problem with textual analysis is reading things into the text which may have little or nothing to do with the intentions of the producers or the interpretations of the audience.

Audience research

Some researchers argue that the focus of document research should be the audience. From this viewpoint, the audience is not made up of passive consumers who are brainwashed by underlying ideologies or swayed by textual 'tricks of the trade'. Instead, it sees audiences actively negotiating the meaning of messages with the outcome of negotiation ranging from acceptance to indifference to opposition (Pawson, 1995).

The news game But finding out how audiences respond is far from easy. Jenny Kitzinger's use of the 'news game' provides a novel and interesting alternative to the methods examined so far. Small 'audience groups' averaging three people from different social backgrounds were given a set of 13 photographs taken from TV news items and documentaries about AIDS. The groups were asked to select pictures and use them to write a news report on AIDS. Kitzinger (1993) concluded from this exercise that audiences are selective in their interpretation of news. They highlight certain views and modify or oppose others. They are able to 'read between the lines' of news reports, to uncover dominant themes and to construct alternative accounts which draw on their personal experience and political beliefs. This gives some indication of the variety and complexity of audience responses.

The 'news game' was first used by Greg Philo to study audience response to the media and the miners' strike of 1984/85. It represents an important change of direction – from the document, to the document in relation to the audience.

Audience understandings In more recent research, Greg Philo and David Miller (2002) examined BBC and ITN TV news broadcasts of the Israeli/Palestinian conflict. The broadcasts focused on images of violence and the bleak prospects for peace. The researchers' audience sample included 300 young people aged 17-22. The responses of this sample show how TV news affected their knowledge and understanding of the conflict.

News broadcasts made little reference to the history and background of the Israeli/Palestinian conflict. Broadcasts referred to 'occupied territories' but provided no explanation of what they were. Only 9% of the young people sampled knew it was Israelis occupying Palestinian land, 71% had no idea what the term meant, and 11% actually thought it was the Palestinians occupying Israeli land. Broadcasts showed Palestinians burning the American flag and mentioned their distrust of American peace proposals. There was little or no mention of why. For example, there was hardly a reference to the fact that the USA supplied some three billion dollars of aid to Israel

each year, much of it in military hardware. When asked to explain Palestinian distrust of the Americans, 66% of the sample had no idea, 24% thought America 'supported' Israel and only 10% mentioned money and arms (Philo & Miller, 2002).

This study shows the importance of audience research. Sociology is the study of people in society. When researchers examine 'documents' such as TV news, a major concern is how they affect members of society. And this requires researchers to discover the meanings people give to those documents and the understandings they draw from them. To do this they must 'ask the audience'.

Historical documents

For studying the past, historical documents are often the major and sometimes the only source of information. Max Weber's classic study *The Protestant Ethic and the Spirit of Capitalism* could not have been written without a range of historical documents. For example, he illustrates the spirit of capitalism with quotes from two books by Benjamin Franklin, *Necessary Hints to Those that would be Rich* (1736) and *Advice to a Young Tradesman* (1748). Weber builds a strong case for the religious basis of the capitalist work ethic by quoting from the speeches and writings of ministers such as John Calvin (1509-1564).

Geoffrey Pearson's *Hooligan: A History of Respectable Fears* (1983) provides a more recent example of the use of historical documents. Pearson looks back to Victorian England and forward to today to show that 'for generations Britain has been plagued by the same fears and problems'. He looks at 'hooliganism' – street crime and violence – the moral panics it generates and its 'discovery' time and time again as something new, in contrast to the 'good old days'. Pearson builds up a substantial case for this argument with a range of historical documents which include newspapers, magazines such as *Punch* and *The Teacher's World*, contemporary novels and government reports.

Using historical documents Historical documents are often a long way from the objectivity which sociologists strive for. They are usually biased, prejudiced, one-sided and concerned with putting over a particular point of view. However, as long as researchers take them for what they are, historical documents provide a rich and valuable source of data. Thus Lord Ashley's announcement in the

House of Commons in 1843 that, 'the morals of the children are tenfold worse than formerly' (quoted in Pearson, 1983) cannot be seen as a balanced assessment of juvenile morality. However, for Pearson's study of 'respectable fears', it is a very useful piece of data since it exemplifies a fear that has recurred throughout the past two centuries.

Historical documents bring their own problems of interpretation because they are from a different era, a different culture, and those who produced them are often dead. Add to this the fact that interpretation relies heavily on the researcher's viewpoint and background and it is clear that there is plenty of room for disagreement. For example, J. Berger argued that a number of paintings from the 17th and 18th centuries showed how art patrons at the time were very concerned with material possessions. He saw this concern as linked to the rise of capitalism. However, as Berger himself notes, this interpretation was hotly disputed by an art critic (discussed in Macdonald & Tipton, 1993).

Assessing historical documents John Scott (1990) provides four 'quality control criteria' for assessing documents which are particularly applicable to historical documents.

Authenticity The first refers to authenticity. Is the document genuine or a forgery? As the famous 60 volume *Hitler Diaries* which surfaced in 1983 showed, forgeries can fool even top historians. Or, is the document an original or a copy? For example, the writings of Roman historians have been copied and recopied by hand. How true to the originals are the copies?

Credibility Is the author of the document 'sincere' or does he or she distort the evidence in order to mislead the reader? There are plenty of examples of distortion, deceit and outright lies in documents. Former US President Nixon denied all knowledge of the illegal break-in at the Democratic Party's headquarters which became known as the Watergate Affair. This lie appeared in TV and radio broadcasts by Nixon and his officials, and in White House press releases.

Representativeness To what extent is the document representative? For example, is a newspaper article typical of the articles which appear in that particular newspaper? The question of representativeness is particularly important in the case of historical documents as many have been lost or destroyed. Those that remain may be untypical. For example, a study of witchcraft in 17th century New England was based on court records relating to 114 suspects. The researcher believes that these surviving records are only the 'tip of the iceberg', a 'tip' which may well be unrepresentative (discussed in O'Connell Davidson & Layder, 1994).

Meaning What does a document mean? This ranges from

activity13 *analysing documents*

Item A *Content analysis*

Television programmes containing reference to or depiction of disability

Genre	Number of programmes	Percentage of total programmes	Number with disability	Percentage of total with disability
News	221	27	54	42
Current affairs	28	4	0	0
Documentary	155	19	21	16
Magazine	70	9	20	16
Informational	59	7	4	3
Debate	15	2	2	2
Religious	9	1	2	2
Quiz	24	3	3	2
Music/dance	38	5	0	0
Educational	5	0.6	2	2
Game show	44	5	0	0
Chat show	24	3	4	3
Sport	36	4	1	1
Special broadcast	46	6	12	9
Special interest programme	3	0.4	3	2
Other	27	3	0	0
Total	804	99	128	100

Source: Cumberbatch & Negrine, 1992

Item B *Newspaper headlines*

We must help the innocent AIDS victims

EXPRESS GOES INTO ACTION TO PROTECT THE INNOCENT

Now innocents demand millions

CURSE HITS ORDINARY FAMILIES

Agony of innocent mum

FURY OF THE INNOCENTS

Innocent AIDS victim leaves legacy of hope

The AIDS innocents

Trauma of youngsters facing prejudice in the playground

Innocent victims face cash blow

An innocent victim tells of his agony

These headlines refer to men and women infected with the AIDS virus through blood transfusions, and mother to child transmission in the womb.

Source: Kitzinger, 1993

the literal meaning of the text – can the researcher 'literally' understand it, eg can the researcher read a text in Anglo Saxon English – to higher level interpretations of meaning and significance. As the previous section on analysing documents has indicated, questions of meaning will never be settled.

Item C *First World War posters*

Item D *The Israeli/Palestinian conflict*

Palestinian boy with a slingshot hurling stones at a Jewish settlement in the occupied territories

questions

1 a) What does Item A tell us?

   b) What further information might be useful?

2 Analyse the headlines in Item B using thematic and textual analysis.

3 What use might a sociologist studying gender make of the posters in Item C?

4 a) What additional information would you need in order to understand what's going on in Item D?

   b) Do you think most young people in the UK have this information? Explain your answer.

summary

1. There are three main methods for the analysis of documents – formal content analysis, thematic analysis and textual analysis. In each case, the analysis is conducted by the researcher.

2. In recent years, the focus has moved towards audience research. The emphasis here is on how audiences interpret documents.

3. For studying the past, historical documents are often the major and sometimes the only source of information.

4. Historical documents are usually biased and one-sided but this does not necessarily detract from their usefulness.

5. Historical documents can be assessed in terms of their authenticity, credibility, representativeness and meaning.

activity 14 historical documents

Item A The diaries of a cabinet minister

Richard Crossman was an MP and cabinet minister in the Labour government of 1964-1970. His political diaries were published after his death in 1975.

Memory is a terrible improver – even with a diary to check the tendency. And it is this which makes a politician's autobiography so wildly unreliable. But if I could publish a diary of my years as a minister without any editorial improvements, as a true record of how one minister thought and felt, I would have done something towards lighting up the secret places of British politics and enabling any intelligent elector to have a picture of what went on behind the scenes between 1964 and 1970.

Of course the picture which this diary provides is neither objective nor fair – although as a lifelong political scientist I have tried to discipline myself to objectivity. In particular, I have tried to avoid self-deception, especially about my own motives; the tendency to attribute to others my own worst failings; and the temptation to omit what might make me look silly in print. I have been urged by many to remove all the wounding passages about colleagues or officials. I have not done so because it would make the book untrue, and I hope that when some of them find me intolerably unfair, they will recall the follies and illusions I faithfully record about myself. A day-by-day account of a Government at work, as seen by one participant, is bound to be one-sided and immensely partisan. If it isn't, it too would fail to be true to life.

Source: Crossman, 1975

Item B Images of Africans

The crest of Sir William Hawkins, an English sea captain who made a fortune from the slave trade in the 16th century.

A bill of sale

This advert for Pears soap was actually painted on a rock in the Sudan by invading British forces.

questions

1 With some reference to Item A, suggest why diaries might be preferable to autobiographies as a source of information.

2 a) Provide a sociological interpretation of the documents in Item B.

b) Critically assess your interpretation.

Unit 9 *Types of research*

keyissues

1 Why use different types of research?

2 What are their strengths and weaknesses?

This chapter has already looked at three types of research – experiments, social surveys and ethnography. This unit looks at several more.

9.1 Life histories

As their name suggests, *life histories* are accounts of people's lives which they tell to researchers.

Something of the flavour and significance of life histories can be obtained from a brief discussion of *Cheyenne Memories*, the life history of John Stands In Timber (1884-1967) as told to the anthropologist Margot Liberty. He was a member of the last generation who experienced the traditional way of life of the Cheyenne Indians during the 19th century.

The Cheyenne were a non-literate society, so oral accounts are particularly important. Stands In Timber's account of his life and the history and culture of his people is given from the Cheyenne point of view. In Margot Liberty's words, 'John has given us the history of the Cheyennes as they themselves recall and interpret it' (1967). Much of the material is new, that which isn't confirms, complements and amplifies 19th century ethnographic accounts.

Advantages Life histories have illuminated many areas of social life. For example, *The Polish Peasant in Europe and America*, a five volume work first published from 1918 to 1920, included an extensive life history of a Polish peasant which provided many valuable insights into the experience of migration from Poland to the USA (Thomas & Znaniecki, 1958). *The Jack Roller* (Shaw, 1930) is a story, written in his own words and from his own point of view, of a young American 'jack roller', the 1930s equivalent of today's 'mugger'. It is this first-hand account of people's experience of their life as they see it which many researchers regard as the main value of the life history. It can provide insights and information which are not obtainable from any other source, as Stands In Timber's life history shows. It can give a picture of the process and development of social life over time. It can also serve as a basis for confirming or questioning other interpretations and accounts. And it can direct researchers into new areas and encourage them to ask new questions.

Disadvantages However, as the title *Cheyenne Memories* suggests, the life history is heavily dependent on people's memory which is inevitably patchy and selective. To some

extent, it will also reflect their attitudes and opinions. Some would see this as a serious criticism of the life history. For example, Stands In Timber has been criticised by other members of his tribe for being too pro-Crow – the Crow are traditional enemies of the Cheyenne.

A further criticism concerns the researcher. There is a temptation for researchers to lead the respondent as life histories are recounted, particularly when areas of interest to them are touched upon. For example, Margot Liberty (1967) writes, 'My tendency was at first to press him for stories. I soon found it far better to trust his own instinct. Where he did not volunteer material freely he usually had little to say.'

While accepting many of the criticisms of life histories, supporters argue that they are far outweighed by the valuable information that a good life history can provide.

9.2 Case studies

A case study is a study of one particular case or instance of something. It may be a study of a particular school, factory or hospital, or a study of a single individual such as a manual worker, a mother with dependent children, or a retired person. The life history is an example of a case study. Using examples from the previous section, it is the study of one Cheyenne Indian or one Polish peasant.

Case studies have a number of advantages.

- By focusing on a particular case, they can provide a richer and more detailed picture than research based on large samples.
- This may result in new insights and fresh ideas.
- Case studies can provide useful information for a larger research project. For example, the experiences of one retired person could be used in a questionnaire in order to discover how far they apply to other retired people.
- There is a better chance of a questionnaire or interview being relevant and meaningful if it is based, at least in part, on a case study.
- Theories can be tested to see whether they apply in particular situations. Sociologists at Lancaster University tested the theory of secularisation (the idea that religion is becoming less important in modern societies) by conducting a case study of religion in a single town – Kendal in the Lake District.

Some of the advantages of case studies can be seen from Macbeath and Mortimore's (2001) study of school effectiveness. They used case studies of a small number of schools in addition to a large-scale social survey. The case studies helped them identify key themes to explore in their survey, allowed them to check that their survey findings held true in particular schools, and added depth to their quantitative data.

Case studies have sometimes been criticised as limited and unrepresentative. Since they are one-off instances, they cannot be used as a basis for generalisation. However, this is their strength. They are a valuable warning to rash and sweeping generalisations. A single case study can call into question the findings of a much larger study.

activity15 bullying – a case study

The only thing that prevented me from enjoying my first year at high school was one person in my class who started to bully me. This led to several other people following his example and my life became sheer misery. At first, I was upset but able to cope with it, then I became angry and distressed. I couldn't sleep for worrying about the next day. It would be name-calling, stone-throwing and threatening. It all got too much and I decided to tell my Mum and Dad. We all agreed that I had to tell the teacher. The next day, though worried, I did.

The teacher was very sympathetic and said it must stop. We had lunch meetings to discuss the problems. The bullies were very surprised that they were included instead of being punished. We discussed my feelings at being bullied and we would agree on some plan of action so that I would get support from my friends. Once the bullies realised that they were being included, the bullying ceased.

Source: Donnellan, 1994

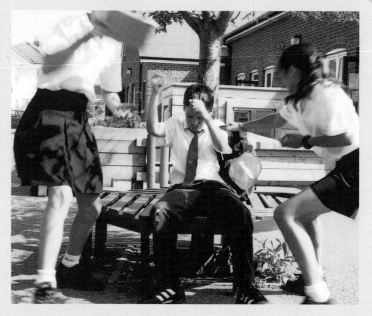

question

Using examples from this activity, suggest some advantages of the case study approach.

9.3 Longitudinal studies

How can you show what a person looks like? One way is to produce a photograph. This is similar to most sociological research which consists of a snapshot, a one-off investigation of an aspect of social life. Another way of showing what a person looks like is to produce a series of photographs taken at different points in their lifetime. This shows how their appearance changes and develops. The equivalent in sociology is the longitudinal study which examines the same group of people over a fairly long period of time.

As the following example shows, longitudinal studies can provide important insights. Each year from 1991 to 1995, 1125 young people in Merseyside and Greater Manchester filled in a confidential questionnaire about their attitudes to and use of illegal drugs. At the start of the research, members of the sample were aged 14, by the end, aged 18. The study was carried out by a team of sociologists led by Howard Parker (1998). Parker was interested in the extent of illegal drug use within this age group and whether sensational media reports about widespread drug abuse were accurate. The questionnaire was concerned with the types of drugs taken, reasons for the first use of drugs, how drug use changed over time and why some people refused to take drugs.

Parker's team found that cannabis was the most frequently used illegal drug. It was also the first drug that most of the sample experimented with. Working-class young people were more likely to experiment at an early age, though by 18 the middle class had caught up. There were few differences between boys and girls. By aged 18, 20-25% of the sample were regular users.

Advantages As these findings suggest, the strength of the longitudinal study is its ability to examine developments over time. By studying the same group, ie by keeping the same sample, the researcher can be sure that any changes in attitudes and behaviour are not simply due to changes in the makeup of the sample.

Disadvantages But keeping the same group is one of the main difficulties with longitudinal studies. The National Child Development Study has attempted to follow the lives of every child born in Britain between 3rd and 9th March 1958. Follow-up surveys were conducted in 1965, 1969, 1974, 1981, 1991 and 1999 to trace developments in health, education, family life, career and so on, and to try to establish links between these changes and factors such as class, gender and ethnicity. The survey began with 17,400 children but by 1999 researchers were able to contact only 11,400 members of the original sample.

Reasons for this *sample attrition* included death, emigration, refusal to participate and failure to trace. The result is not just a smaller sample but, in all probability, a less representative one.

Researchers are aware of this and attempt to minimise the problem of sample attrition. This can be seen from the lengths that some go in order to trace members of an original sample. Parker's team sent letters, follow-up letters, further reminders and even Christmas cards to their sample. If none of these worked they actually went from door to door tracking their 'lost' respondents. The National Child Development Study has adopted a similar approach, contacting relatives, visiting workplaces and searching telephone directories and electoral registers. As this suggests, longitudinal studies can cost a great deal of time and money. Few organisations have the resources to fund an investigation which continues for twenty years or more.

9.4 The comparative method

Comparative studies make comparisons between different societies, between different groups within the same society, and between societies and groups over time.

Durkheim's study of suicide is an example of a comparative study (see page 146). He compared suicide rates in different European societies, eg Italy, England, France and Denmark, at different time periods, eg 1866-70, 1871-75, 1874-78. He also compared suicide rates for different groups within society, eg rates for Protestants compared to Catholics, city dwellers compared to rural dwellers, and married compared to unmarried people.

The comparative method helps sociologists to investigate what causes what. For example, Durkheim's study suggested that religion may be a factor affecting the suicide rate. His figures indicated that the suicide rate for

*activity*16 *Britain and France*

Item A *Similarity – production technology*

Fawley oil refinery, Hampshire

Item B *Difference – nationality*

Britain and France

Duncan Gallie compared workers in oil refineries in Britain and France. Would the same kind of production technology – in this case the technology used in oil refineries – lead to the same kind of behaviour at work? Gallie found important differences between British and French workers, for example there were far more strikes in the French refineries.

Source: Gallie, 1978

question

How might the comparative method be useful for explaining behaviour at work?

Protestants *within* particular societies was higher than the rate for Catholics. The same applied to comparisons *between* societies – the suicide rate for Protestant countries was significantly higher than the rate for Catholic societies.

A natural laboratory The comparative method is the nearest most sociologists get to the laboratory method of the natural sciences. Unlike laboratory experiments, variables in the real world cannot be systematically manipulated and controlled. However, it is possible to find 'natural' laboratories which allow the influence of variables to be estimated.

Europe provided a natural laboratory for Durkheim. He found a statistical link between suicide rates and religion between European societies, within those societies, and over different time periods.

Cross-cultural studies Is social inequality universal – ie, is it found in every society? Is a division of labour based on gender natural – ie, is it natural to have male jobs and female jobs? These are important questions, particularly for those concerned about social inequality. Cross-cultural studies – studies based on a number of different cultures – help to answer this type of question. For instance, if cross-cultural evidence indicated that, in some societies, gender has little or no influence on job allocation, then this suggests that any influence of gender on the division of labour is based on culture rather than nature.

Evaluation The comparative method has some obvious strengths. It provides a natural laboratory for researchers to estimate the influence of variables. It allows researchers to look at the effect of culture on behaviour.

But cross-cultural research has inbuilt problems. How, for example, can a Western researcher understand non-Western cultures? When he or she compares marriage in various cultures, are they comparing like with like? Does marriage mean the same thing in different societies, does it involve the same rights and responsibilities? Despite these problems, the comparative method holds considerable promise (May, 2001).

9.5 Triangulation and methodological pluralism

The types of research outlined in this unit may draw data from various research methods and various sources. For example, a case study might be based on participant observation or interviews, on primary or secondary data, on quantitative or qualitative data. Sometimes, different kinds of data and research methods are combined within a single study.

Triangulation Some researchers combine different research methods and different types of data in order to check the validity and reliability of their findings. This is known as *triangulation*. For example, if participant observation and

activity 17 *methodological pluralism*

Our research on victims of crime was based on methodological pluralism. This approach favours neither qualitative or quantitative research methods. It is a position which recognises that different research techniques can uncover different layers of social reality and that the role of the researcher is to look for confirmations and contradictions between those different layers of information.

So, for example, for the first stage of our data-gathering process we walked round our two research areas with police officers, we frequented the public houses, and we engaged in in-depth interviews with a variety of people working in the localities.

Then, on the basis of this information, we produced a criminal victimisation survey questionnaire and conducted a survey in each area, and, on the basis of this experience, moved into focus group discussions with survey participants. So, as a research process, we were always moving between quantitative and qualitative data looking for ways of making sense of the different layers of social reality which were being revealed to us.

Source: Walklate, 2000

Victims of crime

question

According to this extract, what are the main advantages of methodological pluralism?

interviews produce conflicting findings, this raises questions about the validity of the data. This often leads to further research to re-examine the original findings.

Methodological pluralism Other researchers combine different research methods and different types of data in order to build up a fuller picture of social life. This approach is known as *methodological pluralism*.

It recognises that each method and type of data has its particular strengths and weaknesses. Combined they are seen to produce a more comprehensive and rounder picture of social reality. And their combination can also provide new insights and new directions for research.

Some of the strengths of methodological pluralism can be seen from Eileen Barker's (1984) study of the Moonies – the Unification Church. She conducted in-depth interviews, each lasting 6-8 hours, with a number of Moonies. The interviews dealt with their background, why they became a Moonie, their life in the church and the meaning of religion as they saw it. Barker also lived as a participant observer in several centres with the Moonies at various times during the six years of her research. This enabled her to gain the trust of many members of the church, resulting in information which would not have been given to an outsider. Two years after the start of her research, she constructed a large (41 page) questionnaire based on her findings from interviews and observation. This provided information from a larger sample and was intended to reveal 'social patterns, trends and tendencies and gain a more reliable understanding of regularities between variables – of "what goes with what"'.

Barker claims that combining different methods of investigation gave her a much fuller picture than any one method or data source could have provided.

key terms

Life history An account of an individual's life as told to a researcher.
Case study A study of one particular case or instance of something.
Longitudinal study A study of the same group of people at various times over a period of years.
Sample attrition The reduction in size of a sample during a longitudinal study.
Comparative studies Studies which make comparisons between different societies and different groups within the same society.
Cross-cultural studies Studies based on a number of different cultures. Studies which compare different cultures.
Triangulation Combining different research methods and different types of data in order to check the validity and reliability of findings.
Methodological pluralism Combining different research methods and different kinds of data in order to build up a fuller picture of social life.

summary

1. Life histories provide a first-hand account of people's life experience as they see it. This can result in valuable insights. However, life histories are dependent on people's memory which is often patchy and selective.

2. Case studies focus on a particular case. This can provide a rich and detailed picture. A single case study can call into question the findings of a much larger study.

3. The main strength of the longitudinal study is its ability to examine developments over time. The main problem is sample attrition – the steady loss of sample members.

4. The comparative method provides a 'natural laboratory' within which the influence of variables can be estimated. It allows researchers to examine the effect of culture on behaviour. The main difficulty for researchers is understanding different cultures.

5. Triangulation provides a check on the validity and reliability of research findings.

6. Methodological pluralism builds up a fuller picture of social life.

4 Education and methods

Introduction

Why do we spend the best years of our life in school? Until recently, most people managed quite well without a formal education. They learned what they needed from family, friends, and neighbours.

This type of informal education continues to be an important part of the socialisation process. What's new is a state system of formal education. It consists of specialised institutions – schools, colleges and universities – and selected knowledge and skills transmitted by professionals – teachers and lecturers.

Education is important. It takes up a significant proportion of people's lives – at least eleven years. And it affects them for the rest of their lives. It's very expensive – in 2006/07 government expenditure on education in the UK was £71.5 billion, 12.9% of all public expenditure. And the cost rises year by year (*HM Treasury*, 2007).

Starting out

chaptersummary

▶ **Unit 1** looks at the role of education in society.

▶ **Units 2, 3 and 4** outline explanations for the differences in educational attainment between different social classes, gender and ethnic groups.

▶ **Unit 5** focuses on the classroom. It examines the hidden curriculum, pupil subcultures, teacher-pupil relationships and the organisation of teaching and learning.

▶ **Unit 6** looks at how government policy has shaped the education system from 1870 to the present day.

Unit 1 The role of the education system

keyissues

1 What are the main views of the role of the education system?

2 What are their strengths and weaknesses?

This unit looks at the role of education in society. In simple terms, this means what does education do? Does it benefit society and if so, how? Is it harmful to society, or to certain groups within society? Is it doing its job well or badly?

1.1 Functionalist perspectives

Functionalism is a sociological theory which is based on the following ideas. Society has certain basic needs, the most important of which is the need for social order. Without order, society would tend to disintegrate, to fall apart. Social order is largely based on *social solidarity* – social unity. Social solidarity results from shared norms and values. Shared norms mean that social life is predictable and runs smoothly. Shared values usually result in people cooperating and pulling in the same direction.

When analysing a particular part of society, such as the family or the political system, functionalists often ask, 'What is its function?' By this they mean, 'How does it meet society's basic needs?'; 'How does it contribute to the maintenance and well-being of society?'

Functionalism is no longer fashionable. However, functionalist ideas about the role of education in society still influence some researchers. These ideas will now be examined.

Emile Durkheim

Social solidarity Writing over 100 years ago, the French sociologist Emile Durkheim argued that *social solidarity* –

activity1 social solidarity

Item A Oath of allegiance

American school children pledging loyalty to their flag and country.

Item B Teaching history

Davy Crockett's story has been retold on countless occasions in schools across the USA. Davy Crockett pulled himself up by his own bootstraps. He became a skilled hunter and marksman in the backwoods of Tennessee, before joining the US army as a scout. He was elected three times as a Congressman. Hearing of the Texans' fight for freedom against Mexico, he gathered a dozen volunteers to help them. He died fighting the Mexican army in 1836.

Source: Newark, 1980

Davy Crockett (right) at the Alamo

question

How can Items A and B be used to illustrate the view that education helps to unite members of society?

---

social unity – is essential for the survival of society. Social solidarity is based on 'essential similarities' between members of society. According to Durkheim, one of the main functions of education is to develop these similarities and so bind members of society together.

The USA provides a vivid illustration of Durkheim's views. Its population is drawn from all over the world. A common educational system has helped to weld this diverse mass of human beings into a nation. It has provided common norms and values, a shared sense of history and a feeling of belonging to a wider society.

History and social solidarity Durkheim sees a common history as vital for uniting members of society. American schoolchildren grow up with stories about their country's founders, eg George Washington cutting down his father's cherry tree, and their country's heroes, eg Davy Crockett who grew up in the backwoods of Tennessee, was elected to Congress, and died a hero, fighting for freedom against the overwhelming force of the Mexican army at the Battle of the Alamo in Texas in 1836.

With a shared history, people feel part of a wider social group – it is their country, made up of people like themselves. In this way, education contributes to the development of social solidarity.

Specialised skills Industrial society has a *specialised division of labour* – people have specialised jobs with specific skill and knowledge requirements. For example, the skills and knowledge required by plumbers, electricians, teachers and doctors are very different. In preindustrial societies there were fewer specialised occupations. Occupational skills were often passed from

parents to children. According to Durkheim, the specialised division of labour in industrial societies relies increasingly on the educational system to provide the skills and knowledge required by the workforce.

Talcott Parsons

Secondary socialisation Writing in the 1950s and 1960s, the American sociologist Talcott Parsons developed Durkheim's ideas. He saw the educational system as the main agency of *secondary socialisation*, acting as a bridge between the family and the wider society. Schools build on the primary socialisation provided by the family, developing *value consensus* – agreement about the values of society – and preparing young people for their adult roles (Parsons, 1951, 1961).

Individual achievement is a major value in modern industrial society. In schools, young people are encouraged to achieve as individuals. High achievement is rewarded with praise, high status, good grades and valuable qualifications. This prepares young people to achieve as individuals in the world of work.

Equality of opportunity – an equal chance for everybody – is another major value in modern society. Schools transmit this value by offering all their pupils an equal chance of success.

According to Parsons, schools are miniature versions of the wider society. They reflect the values of the wider society. Young people are required to act in terms of those values in the classroom. And, as a result, they are prepared for adult roles.

Role allocation Parsons sees *role allocation* as one of the main functions of the educational system. This involves sifting, sorting, assessing and evaluating young people in terms of their talents and abilities, then allocating them to appropriate roles in the wider society. For example, people with artistic talent are directed towards and trained for occupations such as photographer, graphic designer and fashion designer.

Role allocation involves testing students in order to discover their talents, developing those talents on appropriate courses, then matching those talents to the jobs for which they are best suited.

Functionalism and education – evaluation

The following criticisms have been made of functionalist views of education.

- Rather than transmitting society's values, the education system may be transmitting the values of a ruling class or ruling elite.

- History teaching in schools may reflect a white, middle-class view. This may discourage social solidarity. Many ethnic minority groups are demanding that history teaching reflect *their* historical experience and *their* viewpoint. For example, in the USA, African-American history is now a major part of the history curriculum.

- There is evidence that certain groups underachieve in schools – for example, the working class and certain ethnic minority groups. This suggests that a) pupils do not have an equal opportunity b) their talents have not been effectively developed and assessed and c) the system of role allocation is not very efficient.

- Is the educational system providing the knowledge and skills required in the workplace? It is difficult to see a direct link between many school subjects and the world of work.

1.2 Marxist perspectives

Marxism is a theory named after its founder, Karl Marx (1818-1883). It starts from the idea that the economic system largely shapes the rest of society. So, for example the political and educational systems are largely shaped by the economic system.

Marxists argue that there are two main classes in society – the *ruling class* and the *subject class*. The power of the ruling class comes from its ownership of the economic system. Thus in today's society, capitalists – those who own private industry – form the ruling class – and workers – those who sell their labour in return for wages – form the subject class. According to Marx, the ruling class exploit the subject class – they gain at the expense of the workers. Workers produce wealth in the form of goods and services yet a large part of that wealth is taken from them in the form of profits by the capitalist class.

In Marx's words the ruling class 'rule also as thinkers, as producers of ideas'. These ideas justify their position, conceal the true source of their power and disguise their exploitation of the subject class. In Marx's view this *ruling class ideology* is a far more effective means of domination than more obvious forms of control such as physical force. It presents a false picture of society which keeps the subject class in its place.

activity2 examinations

questions

How can the type of formal examinations pictured here:

a) encourage individual achievement

b) form part of the process of role allocation?

Education and ideology

Louis Althusser, a French Marxist philosopher, argues that no class can hold power for long simply by the use of force. Ideology provides a much more effective means of control – if people's hearts and minds are won over then force becomes unnecessary.

Althusser (1972) argues that in modern society the education system has largely replaced the church as the main agency for ideological control. In the past, people tended to accept their station in life because they saw it as God's will. Today, this acceptance comes in part from their experience of education.

First, schools transmit an ideology which states that capitalism is just and reasonable. Second, schools prepare pupils for their roles in the workforce. Most are trained as workers – they are taught to accept their future exploitation and provided with an education and qualifications to match their adult work roles. Some – the future managers, administrators and politicians – are trained to control the workforce. Their educational qualifications *legitimate* – justify and make right – their position of power. They become the 'agents of exploitation and repression'.

Althusser argues that ideology in capitalist society is fundamental to social control. He sees the main role of education as transmitting this ideology.

Correspondence theory

In *Schooling in Capitalist America* (1976) Samuel Bowles and Herbert Gintis claim that there is a close *correspondence* between the social relationships in the classroom and those in the workplace. This correspondence is essential for *social reproduction* – the reproduction of new generations of workers appropriately schooled to accept their roles in capitalist society.

School and workplace Schools, like the wider society, are based on hierarchies – layers of authority. Teachers give orders, pupils are expected to obey. Pupils have little control over their work, over the curriculum they follow. This corresponds to their later experience of lack of control in the workplace. Schools reward punctuality, obedience and hard work; they discourage creativity, independence and critical awareness. This is directly in line with the kind of worker required by employers in capitalist society.

Young people get little direct satisfaction from their education. They are motivated largely by external rewards

*activity*3 *social reproduction*

Item A *Role allocation and rewards*

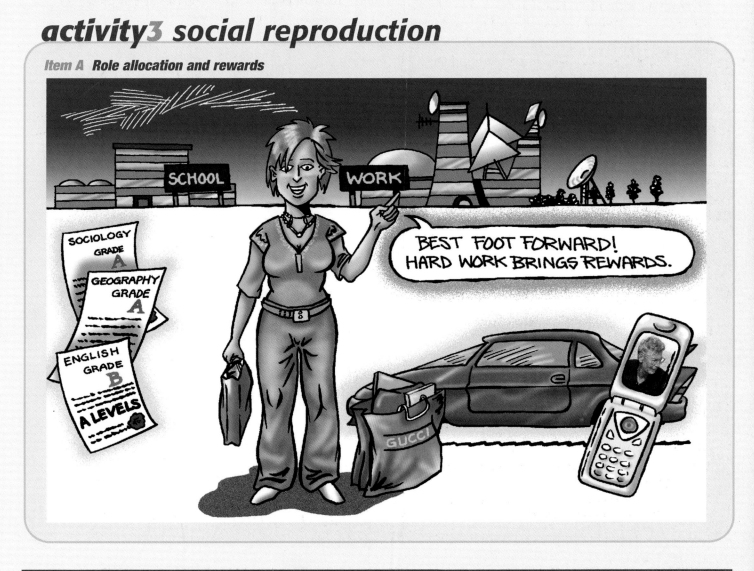

Item B Two views of role allocation

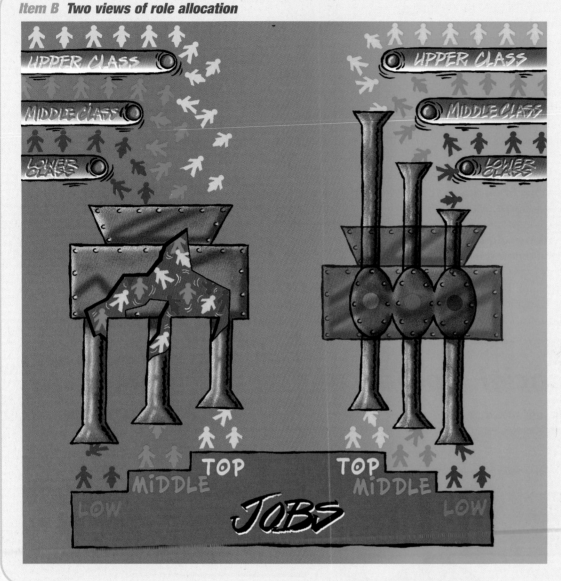

such as educational qualifications. This is reflected in the workplace – work itself provides little satisfaction, workers are motivated by external rewards such as pay. Bowles and Gintis argue that this correspondence between school and the workplace effectively reproduces workers from one generation to the next.

Social inequality Capitalist society is unequal. If this inequality were seriously questioned it might threaten social stability. One way of avoiding this is to promote the belief that inequality is justified. According to Bowles and Gintis, education legitimates social inequality by broadcasting the myth that it offers everybody an equal chance. It follows that those who achieve high qualifications deserve their success. And since high qualifications lead to top jobs, people who get those jobs have earned them. In this way social inequality appears just and legitimate.

However, Bowles and Gintis argue that rewards in education and occupation are based not on ability but on social background. The higher a person's class of origin – the class they began in – the more likely they are to attain high educational qualifications and a top job. The class system tends to reproduce itself from generation to generation and this process is legitimised by education. In Bowles and Gintis's words, 'Education reproduces inequality by justifying privilege and attributing poverty to personal failure'.

Role allocation Bowles and Gintis reject the functionalist view of role allocation. Those who get the highest qualifications and the top jobs do so because of their social background and because they work hard and do what they're told. Bowles and Gintis found that students with high grades tend to be hardworking, obedient, conforming and dependable rather than creative, original and independent. These characteristics are rewarded with high grades because they are the very qualities required for a subordinate, obedient and disciplined workforce.

Learning to labour

In a study entitled, *Learning to Labour: How working-class kids get working-class jobs* (1977), the British sociologist Paul Willis studied a group of 12 working-class boys (the 'lads') during their last year and a half at school and their first few months at work.

Counter-school culture Willis did not find a simple correspondence between school and work. Nor did he find that the lads were shaped by the educational system. Instead, the lads rejected school and created their own *counter-school culture*. But, it was this very rejection of school which prepared them for the low-skill, low-status jobs they were to end up in.

The lads rejected educational success as defined by the school. They saw the conformist behaviour of hardworking pupils – the 'ear 'oles' – as a matter for amusement and mockery. School was good for a laugh and not much else. Boredom was relieved by mucking around and breaking rules. The lads actively created a counter-school culture based on opposition to authority. In some respects this behaviour made sense. They were destined for low-skill jobs so why bother to work hard.

School and work Willis found a number of similarities between the attitudes and behaviour developed by the lads in school and those of the shopfloor at work. Having a laugh was important in both situations as a means of dealing with monotony, boredom and authority. And at work, as at school, a bunch of mates to mess around with and support you in an 'us and them' situation remained important.

So, like Bowles and Gintis, Willis argues for a correspondence between school and work. But this is not produced by the school – the lads are not the docile, obedient pupils of Bowles and Gintis's study. The lads themselves have produced the correspondence by their rejection of the school. And in doing so they have prepared themselves for their place in the workforce. They have learned to have a laugh, to put up with boredom and monotony, and to accept the drudgery of low-skill jobs.

methods 1 methodological pluralism

Paul Willis's study focused on 12 boys during their last 18 months at school and their first few months at work. He wanted to discover how the boys saw their experience of schooling and work. He used 'observation and participant observation in class, around the school and in leisure activities, regular recorded group discussions, informal interviews and diaries'.

Source: Willis, 1977

question

Willis's method is an example of methodological pluralism. Suggest possible advantages of this approach to his research.

activity 4 learning to labour

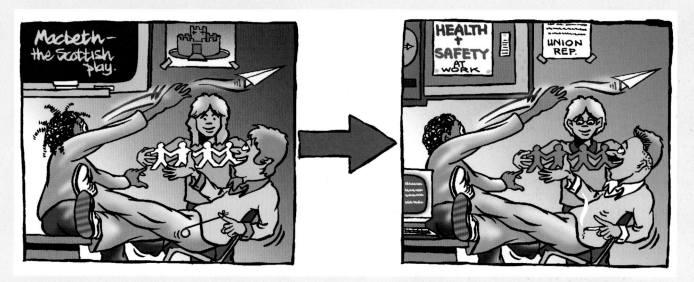

question

How does this cartoon illustrate Willis's view of how lads adapt to low-skill, boring jobs?

Twenty years on Willis's study was conducted in a secondary school in Birmingham in the 1970s. Twenty years later, a similar study was conducted in the West Midlands by Máirtín Mac an Ghaill (1994). Some of the working-class young men – the 'macho lads' – were similar to Willis's lads. They rejected the authority of the teachers and the values of the school. However, this was a time of high unemployment when many traditional low-skill working-class jobs were disappearing. Because of this, the macho lads' behaviour was 'outdated' – the jobs it prepared them for were fast becoming a thing of the past.

Business takeover of schools

Marxist views have become unfashionable in recent years. However, Glenn Rikowski (2002, 2005) argues that they are still relevant. He claims that education is becoming increasingly privatised as more and more aspects of education – for example, school dinners – are being subcontracted to private industry. Rikowski sees this as the beginning of a 'business takeover of schools'. He argues that education will become like any other private company – it will be run 'primarily for the benefit of shareholders' and its main concern will be to produce profit.

Marxism and education – evaluation

Marxists see education in a negative light. It transmits ruling class ideology and produces a passive and obedient workforce which fits the requirements of capitalism. And when young people actively reject schooling, this can prepare them for monotonous, low-skill jobs. This view of the role of education is based partly on the belief that capitalism is unjust and oppressive, and that it exploits the workforce.

However, it is possible to accept some of the findings of Marxist sociologists without accepting their view of capitalism. Both Bowles and Gintis and Willis provide evidence to support their claims. Schools *do* reward hard work, conformity and obedience. And some students who learn to live with what they see as the boredom of school are prepared for the monotony of low-skill jobs.

key terms

Ruling class ideology A false picture of society which justifies the position of the ruling and subject classes.
Legitimate Justify, make right.
Correspondence theory A theory which shows a correspondence or similarity between two things and suggests that they are causally related – for example, the experience of school and work is similar, and the requirements of the workplace shape what goes on in the classroom.
Social reproduction The reproduction of new generations of workers with the skills and attitudes required for their roles in capitalist society.
Counter-school culture A rejection of the norms and values of the school and their replacement with anti-school norms and values.

Critics argue that Rikowski has gone too far with his claim that education is heading for privatisation. While some services are being subcontracted to the private sector, there is little or no evidence that governments in the UK intend to privatise the educational system as a whole (Hatcher, 2005).

1.3 Feminist perspectives

Feminist perspectives focus on gender inequalities in society. Feminist research has revealed the extent of male domination and the ways in which male supremacy has been maintained. From a feminist viewpoint, one of the main roles of education has been to maintain gender inequality.

Gender and education

From the 1960s onwards, feminist sociologists highlighted the following gender inequalities in education.

Gendered language Reflecting the wider society, school textbooks (and teachers) tended to use *gendered language* – 'he', 'him', 'his', 'man' and 'men' when referring to a person or people. This tended to downgrade women and make them invisible.

Gendered roles School textbooks have tended to present males and females in traditional gender roles – for example, women as mothers and housewives. This is particularly evident in reading schemes from the 1960s and 1970s.

Gender stereotypes Reading schemes have also tended to present traditional gender *stereotypes*. For example, an analysis of six reading schemes from the 1960s and 70s found that:

- Boys are presented as more adventurous than girls
- As physically stronger
- As having more choices.
- Girls are presented as more caring than boys
- As more interested in domestic matters
- As followers rather than leaders (Lobban, 1974).

Women in the curriculum In terms of what's taught in schools – the *curriculum* – women tend to be missing, in the background, or in second place. Feminists often argue that women have been 'hidden from history' – history has been the history of men.

Subject choice Traditionally, female students have tended to avoid maths, science and technology. Certain subjects were seen as 'boys' subjects' and 'girls' subjects'. Often girls' subjects had lower status and lower market value.

Discrimination There is evidence of discrimination against girls in education simply because of their gender. For example, when the 11-plus exam was introduced in the 1940s, the pass mark for boys was set lower than the mark for girls in order to make sure there were roughly equal numbers of boys and girls in grammar schools. In other words girls were artificially 'failed' so boys could 'succeed'.

Further and higher education Traditionally, the number of female students going on to further and higher education has been lower than for boys. There is evidence that teachers often gave boys more encouragement than girls to go on to university (Stanworth, 1983).

Feminist perspectives – evaluation

Feminist perspectives have been valuable for exposing gender inequality in education. Partly as a result of sociological research, a lot has changed – for example, much of the *sexism* in reading schemes has now disappeared.

Today, women have overtaken men on practically every measure of educational attainment. Their grades at GCSE and A level are significantly higher than those of male students. And more women than men are going on to higher education. The concern now is the underachievement of boys rather than discrimination against girls.

methods2
content analysis

Content analysis was used to analyse the way gender roles were presented in six reading schemes used in primary schools in the 1960s and 1970s. The schemes included the Janet and John and Ladybird series. The results of the study are shown under the subheading 'gender stereotypes' in Section 1.3 (see also Activity 5, Item B).

The content analysis listed the toys played with and the activities performed by boys only, girls only, and both boys and girls. It noted who took the lead in the activities that both boys and girls took part in. And it listed the number of adult roles presented and the gender of the people who played those roles.

The author suggests that the distinctive gender activities and roles portrayed in the reading schemes may have an important influence on gender socialisation.

Source: Lobban, 1974

question

Assess the strengths and weaknesses of content analysis in studying the effect of reading schemes on gender socialisation.

key terms

Gendered language Language which uses one gender to refer to both genders.
Stereotype An exaggerated and distorted view of the characteristics of members of a social group.
Curriculum The subjects taught in school and their content.
Sexism Bias against a particular gender – usually females.

1.4 Social democratic perspectives

Social democratic perspectives on education developed in the 1960s. They have had an important influence on government educational policy.

Social democratic theorists start from the view that everybody should have an equal chance to succeed in the educational system. This is not only fair and just, it also brings practical benefits. A well-educated workforce will lead to economic growth.

Equal opportunity

The British sociologist A.H. Halsey is one of the leading social democratic theorists. He criticised functionalist views which claimed that the education system in Western industrial societies provided equality of opportunity. Halsey's work from the 1960s onwards showed clearly that social class has a significant effect on educational attainment. In general, the higher a person's social class of origin – the class into which they were born – the higher their educational qualifications. For example, middle-class students tend to achieve higher qualifications than working-class students. This suggests that schools are not providing equality of opportunity for all young people (Halsey et al., 1961; 1980).

According to social democratic theorists, this is both wrong and inefficient. It is wrong because in a democracy everybody has a right to equal opportunity. It is inefficient because it wastes talent. If people don't have the opportunity to develop their aptitudes and abilities, then their contribution to society as a whole will be reduced. Inequality of educational opportunity means that everybody suffers.

Education and the economy

According to social democratic theorists, there is a close link between education and economic growth. Modern economies require an increasingly specialised and highly-trained workforce. The educational system reflects this requirement (Halsey et al., 1961).

Over the past 50 years there has been more education, and more specialised education. The school leaving age has steadily risen and growing numbers of young people are continuing into further and higher education. There has also been a rapid growth in vocational education – education which aims to provide specific workplace skills.

Social democratic perspectives – evaluation

It is difficult to unravel the relationships between education and the economy. Some researchers argue that the growth in education greatly exceeds the needs of the economy. For example, Randall Collins (1972) points to studies which suggest that once mass literacy has been achieved, education makes little difference to economic growth. He claims that when companies do require specific skills, they

activity5 gender and education

Item A Learning to launder

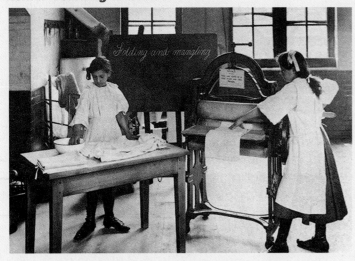

Girls at school learning to do the laundry, 1908. The girl on the right is using a mangle to get water out of the clothes.

Item B Peter and Jane

These pictures are taken from the Ladybird Key Words Reading Scheme published in 1964.

Item C In the classroom

Michelle Stanworth's research looked at gender relations in A level classes at a further education college.

Interviews with teachers and pupils revealed that both men and women teachers took more interest in their male pupils, asking them more questions in class and giving them more help. Asked which students they were most concerned about, women teachers named boys twice as often as girls. Male teachers named boys ten times as often as girls. When asked which pupils they were most 'attached' to, teachers named boys three times as often as girls.

Teachers underestimate girls' ambitions. Only one girl was mentioned as likely to get a management job and male teachers could not envisage any occupation other than marriage for two thirds of the girls. One girl, who was getting the top marks in her class in both her main A level subjects, and who wanted a career in the diplomatic service, was described by her woman teacher as likely to become 'the personal assistant to somebody rather important'.

Source: Stanworth, 1983

questions

1 How might a feminist sociologist analyse Items A and B?

2 Use Item C to support the view that there is discrimination against girls in the classroom.

---

usually provide their own training courses.

Other researchers claim that the growth in vocational education with its focus on workplace skills is vital for economic development. And still others argue that the increased pace of technological and economic change calls for a flexible workforce with a good general education rather than specific *vocational training* (Brown et al., 1997). These points will be returned to in Unit 4 of this chapter.

key term

Vocational education Education which aims to provide specific workplace skills.

1.5 Neoliberal / New Right perspectives

Neoliberal/New Right ideas developed in the early 1980s. They took a very different view of the route to educational and economic success.

The problem

According to neoliberal/New Right thinkers, advanced industrial economies such as the USA and Britain were declining. Much of this decline was due to social democratic policies. These policies resulted in:

- Too much state control – the 'nanny state' got too involved in people's lives.
- This crushed people's initiative and stifled their enterprise. They relied on the state rather than taking

activity6 a social democratic view

question

How does this cartoon illustrate the social democratic view of education?

responsibility for their own lives.

- This can be seen in welfare dependency – the poor had come to depend on state 'handouts' rather than pulling themselves up by their own bootstraps.
- State control and welfare benefits cost a lot of money which meant high taxation.
- Because of this there was less money to invest in private industry – the really productive sector of the economy.

The solution

Neoliberal/New Right perspectives offered the following solutions to the decline of advanced industrial societies.

- Restore enterprise and initiative.
- Roll back the state and make people responsible for their own destiny rather than relying on state institutions, state guidance and state handouts.
- Increase competition not only in the private sector but also the public sector – schools and hospitals should compete in much the same way as companies in the private sector.
- This will increase productivity and efficiency, and result in economic growth.

Education

Where does education fit into all this? The job of schools is to raise educational standards and instil enterprise, drive and competitive spirit.

The neoliberal/New Right programme for raising educational standards runs as follows.

- Competition between schools and colleges – the best will attract more students, the worst won't get any and go out of business. This means that teachers and administrators will have real incentives to improve standards. And parents and their children will have real choice.

- Allowing schools and colleges to become self-managing. This means giving teachers and administrators control over finance, staffing and school policy. This encourages grassroot initiative and enterprise rather than relying on direction from above. And this will motivate teachers to improve standards.
- The above measures will lead to better school management and higher quality teaching. This is what's needed to raise educational standards for all (Chubb & Moe, 1997).
- Higher standards will mean higher qualifications, particularly for those at the bottom. And this will give them a better chance of escaping from welfare dependency.

Education and globalisation

Neoliberal/New Right thinkers argue that education is essential for success in an increasingly competitive global market-place. A nation's position in the world market will depend on the quality of its education.

The way to achieve economic success is the *marketisation of schools*. This involves competition and choice – schools must compete in the market and offer a real choice. This will raise standards as parents and students will choose the most successful schools, which will expand to meet the demand for places, and reject the failing schools, which will contract or close (Lauder et al., 2006).

Neoliberal / New Right perspectives – evaluation

Neoliberal/New Right views leave a number of unanswered questions (Halsey et al., 1997).

First, does competition between schools raise standards? Measured in terms of GCSE and A level results, standards are improving. However, this may have little or nothing to do with competition between schools.

Second, is a choice of schools and colleges available? In some areas, there is no alternative to the local comprehensive. In other areas, where choice exists, middle-class parents are in a better position to get their children into the best schools. For example, where there are limited places, they tend to be more successful at negotiating with teachers.

Third, can schools make up for inequalities in the wider society? For example, with good management and high quality teaching, can schools provide equality of

opportunity for students from low-income backgrounds? Available evidence suggests that the answer is 'no' (Halsey et al., 1997).

key terms

Welfare dependency Depending on state benefits for support and accepting this as a way of life.
Marketisation of schools Competition between schools in the educational market-place.

summary

1. From a functionalist perspective, education performs the following functions:

    ● Developing and reinforcing social solidarity

    ● Providing the skills and knowledge required for a specialised division of labour

    ● Developing value consensus and preparing young people for adult roles

    ● Assessing young people in terms of their talents and abilities and allocating them to appropriate roles in the wider society.

2. From a Marxist perspective, education:

    ● Transmits ruling class ideology

    ● Prepares pupils for their role in the workplace

    ● Legitimises inequality and disguises exploitation

    ● Rewards conformity and obedience

    ● Reproduces new generations of workers, schooled to accept their place in capitalist society.

3. From a feminist perspective, education has promoted, and to some extent still does promote, male dominance by:

    ● The use of gendered language and gender stereotypes

    ● Omitting women from the curriculum

    ● Defining certain subjects as 'girls' subjects' and others as 'boys' subjects'

    ● Discriminating against female students in terms of grammar school, further and higher education places.

4. From a social democratic perspective, education:

    ● Should provide every young person with an equal chance to develop their talents and abilities

    ● This will benefit society as a whole by producing economic growth

    ● However, social class is a barrier to equality of educational opportunity.

5. According to neoliberal/New Right perspectives, the role of education is to instil drive, initiative and enterprise. This will come from:

    ● Competition between schools and colleges

    ● Motivating teachers to improve standards

    ● Providing parents and students with a choice of schools and colleges.

activity7 *the educational market-place*

question

How does this cartoon illustrate neoliberal/New Right views of education?

Unit 2 Social class and educational attainment

keyissues

1 What are the differences in educational attainment between social class groups?

2 What explanations are given for these differences?

Class, gender and ethnicity make a difference to *educational attainment* – the educational qualifications and grades students achieve. If you want the best possible start, you should be born at the top of the class system, as a female, and as a member of the Chinese ethnic group. Statistics indicate that *in general* the higher your social class, the higher your attainment, that Chinese are the most successful ethnic group, and that girls do better than boys.

How important are class, ethnicity and gender?

- **Class** is most important. Its effect on educational attainment is nearly three times greater than ethnicity.

- **Ethnicity** comes next. It has about twice the effect of gender.
- **Gender** Despite capturing public attention, gender is least important. Class has over five times the effect on educational attainment (Gillborn & Mirza, 2000).

This unit looks at class differences in educational attainment. The next two units look at ethnic and gender differences.

2.1 Measuring class and educational attainment

In general, the higher a person's social class of origin – the class they were born into – the higher their educational qualifications. This has been shown time and time again over the past 50 years by sociological research and government statistics.

methods3 official statistics

Most of the government statistics on social class and educational attainment are provided by the Youth Cohort Study – a series of longitudinal surveys based on large samples of young people aged 16–19 in England and Wales. As the statistics in Activity 8 show, data from the Youth Cohort Study provide a comparison over time of class differences in educational attainment.

The way things are defined and measured sometimes changes. This can be a major problem when comparing official statistics over time. Social class provides an example. In 2001, the government replaced the SEG (socio-economic group) classification of social class with the NS-SEC (National Statistics Socio-economic Classification). Although similar in many respects these two classifications are not the same.

question

What are the advantages and disadvantages of using official statistics to compare class differences in educational attainment over time?

methods4 longitudinal surveys and postal questionnaires

The Youth Cohort Study is a series of longitudinal studies. It usually contacts respondents at the end of compulsory schooling, then again at aged 17, 18 and 19. In 2000, the 10th Youth Cohort Study sent postal questionnaires to a random sample of 24,500 young people. 13,720 returned the completed questionnaire. They were then sent the second questionnaire a year later. The fourth and final questionnaire was completed and returned by only 5,572 people, 23% of the original sample.

question

What are the advantages and disadvantages of using longitudinal surveys and postal questionnaires to study social class and educational attainment?

The 10th Youth Cohort Study

Year	Number of questionnaires sent	Number completed and returned	Age
2000	24,500	13,720	16
2001	13,720	10,152	17
2002	10,152	7,208	18
2003	7,208	5,572	19

Source: *Youth Cohort Study*, 2004, Office for National Statistics

To what extent does social class affect educational attainment? How has the effect of class changed over time? This is where we run into problems. Is it possible to directly compare statistics over the years? The short answer is 'no'. Definitions of social class vary from study to study. The official definition of class used in government research changes – the last major change was in 2001. And

educational qualifications change – from O levels to GCSEs, from GNVQs to vocational A levels, and so on.

But whatever the level or type of educational qualification, and whatever the definition of social class, there is no doubt that class has a significant effect on educational attainment. To appreciate this effect, work carefully through Activity 8.

activity8 educational attainment and social class

Item A GCSE and social class, 2004

Pupils achieving five or more GCSE grades A* to C

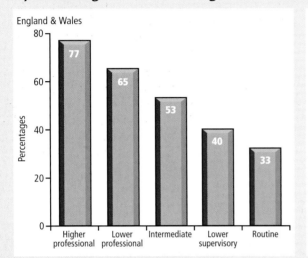

Source: *Youth Cohort Study*, 2004

Item B GCSE and social class, 1989 and 2000

Pupils achieving five or more GCSE grades A* to C

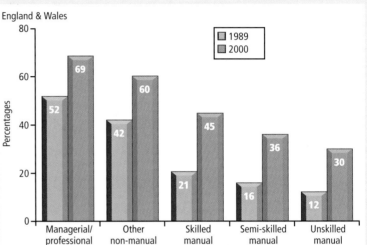

Youth Cohort Studies, *Social Trends*, 2001, Office for National Statistics

Item C Higher education and social class

Participation rates in higher education

Social class	1991	1992	1993	1994	1995	1996	1997	1998	1999	2000	2001	Gain 1991-2001
Professional	55	71	73	78	79	82	79	82	73	76	79	+24
Intermediate	36	39	42	45	45	47	48	45	45	48	50	+14
Skilled non-manual	22	27	29	31	31	32	31	29	30	33	33	+11
Skilled manual	11	15	17	18	18	18	19	18	18	19	21	+10
Partly skilled	12	14	16	17	17	17	18	17	17	19	18	+6
Unskilled	6	9	11	11	12	13	14	13	13	14	15	+9

Great Britain   Percentages

Adapted from *Age Participation Index*, Department of Education and Skills, 2003

The table shows the percentage of people under 21 from each social class who enter undergraduate courses in higher education. The figures on the right show the increase in percentage points for each class from 1991 to 2001.

questions

1 What does Item A suggest about the relationship between social class and educational attainment?

2 No matter what definition of social class is used, there are significant class differences in educational attainment. Comment on this statement using Items A and B which

use different definitions of class.

3 What changes does Item B indicate between 1989 and 2000?

4 Summarise the trends shown in Item C.

2.2 Explaining class differences in attainment

During the 1960s and 70s, class differences in attainment were the main focus of the sociology of education. During the 1980s and 90s, class went out of fashion. Sociologists turned to ethnic and gender differences in attainment. And some claimed that class was not nearly as important as it used to be.

Only in the last ten years have a few sociologists returned to class and attainment. Because of this, the research in this section is either recent or drawn from the 1960s and 70s. Despite the earlier research being dated, it remains important. Class is still the most significant social factor accounting for differences in educational attainment.

Class, intelligence and attainment

At every level of education – from nursery to university – upper and middle-class children tend to do better than working-class children. This remains the case even when they have the same intelligence quotient (IQ).

Most researchers believe that the same range of ability is present in every social class. This means that class differences in educational attainment are *not* due to class differences in intelligence.

Material deprivation

During the 1960s, sociologists claimed that the low attainment of many working-class pupils resulted from a lack of something. They were *deprived*. This deprivation was *material* – a lack of money and the things that money could buy – and *cultural* – an absence of the attitudes and skills that were needed for educational success.

In general, the higher a child's class of origin, the higher their family income. High income can provide many educational advantages – a comfortable well-heated home, spacious rooms with a desk to work at, a home computer with internet access, reference and revision books, extra home tuition and the option of private education.

At the other end of the scale, children in poverty often live in cramped, cold and draughty conditions. Shortage of money means they are more likely to have part-time jobs in the evenings and at weekends, and to leave school at the minimum leaving age. Poverty often leads to ill health. And this can result in absence from school, tiredness and irritability.

activity9 material deprivation

Item A *Growing up poor*

question

How might growing up in poverty disadvantage children at school?

Item B *Homelessness*

A report on the effects of homelessness on schoolchildren by Her Majesty's Inspectorate for Schools makes the following points.

Their chances of doing well are slim. 'Sustainable achievement is often beyond their reach.' Cramped sleeping conditions leave the children tired, listless and unable to concentrate. In one London school, a four-year-old boy spent a whole day sleeping outside the headteacher's office.

The inspectors found evidence of ill health caused by poor diet, and stress from permanent insecurity. For some, the crises which led to homelessness produce social and emotional difficulties.

Weak reading, writing and verbal skills among primary school children are combined with a poor self-image. 'I can't read,' a seven-year-old girl told her teacher. 'Don't you know I'm simple?'

The report notes that many hostel rooms lack such basics as chairs and table. As a result, children often find it hard to do homework. A fourth year GCSE pupil had to work on her bed and could only start when the sisters she shared the room with were asleep.

Source: *The Times*, 10.08.90

The costs of education Traditionally, many working-class students left school at the minimum leaving age because their parents could no longer afford to support them. However, since the introduction of the GCSE examination in 1988, a far higher proportion of 16-19 year olds have continued into further education.

More recently, the introduction of tuition fees and the abolition of student grants has meant that many young people with working-class backgrounds feel they cannot afford to go on to higher education. As Item C in Activity 8 shows, it is those at the top of the class system who have benefited most from the expansion of university places. Even though grants are available for students from low-income families, many are still put off by the costs of higher education (Machin, 2003).

Home and school

Many sociologists in the 1960s saw differences in primary socialisation as the main reason for class differences in attainment. In a large-scale study of British children entitled *The Home and the School*, J.W.B. Douglas (1964) claimed that middle-class children received more attention and encouragement from their parents during their early years. This provided a foundation for high attainment in their later years.

Based on questionnaires given to over 5000 parents, Douglas concluded that the degree of parents' interest in their children's education was the single, most important factor affecting attainment. His research suggested that, in general, middle-class parents showed more interest than working-class parents. They were more likely to visit the school and to encourage their children to stay on beyond the minimum school leaving age.

More recent research provides support for Douglas's conclusion. It is based on data from the National Child Development Study, an ongoing longitudinal study which follows the lives of every person born in Britain during one particular week in 1958. According to Leon Feinstein (2003), evidence from this study shows that class differences in parental interest and support is the most important factor accounting for class differences in educational attainment.

Class subcultures

Differences in *social class subcultures* – the norms, attitudes and values typical of each class – were often seen as part of the explanation for class differences in attainment.

The British sociologist Barry Sugarman (1970) described working-class subculture as:

- *Fatalistic* – accepting the situation rather than working to improve it
- *Present-time orientated* – living for the moment rather than planning for the future
- Concerned with *immediate gratification* – taking pleasures now rather than making sacrifices for the future.

By comparison, middle-class subculture was seen as non-fatalistic, future-time orientated and concerned with deferred gratification.

These differences in class subcultures were seen to place pupils from working-class backgrounds at a disadvantage. For example, fatalism will not encourage pupils to improve their grades. And present-time orientation and immediate gratification will discourage sustained effort for examination success.

Cultural deprivation theory

The views of sociologists such as Douglas and Sugarman have been used to provide support for what came to be known as *cultural deprivation theory*. This theory states that those at the bottom of the class system are deprived of important values, attitudes, experiences and skills which are essential for educational success. Their home life lacks the kind of stimulation needed for high attainment – for example, there is an absence of books and educational toys. They receive little encouragement from parents and, as a result, lack the motivation to succeed at school.

To make matters worse, what the 'culturally deprived child' does have tends to be seen as 'substandard' – well below the high quality norms and values of middle-class subculture. Deprived of what's needed for success and saddled with low standard norms and values, it's no wonder, so the argument goes, that culturally deprived children fail in droves.

Evaluation Cultural deprivation theory has been strongly criticised. There is evidence that if class differences in culture exist, then they are slight and of little significance. Much so-called culturally deprived behaviour may be due to lack of money rather than lack of the norms and values needed for high attainment. For example, working-class students may leave school earlier because of low income rather than lack of motivation and parental encouragement.

Cultural deprivation theory blames the failings of the child on his or her background. This diverts attention from the failings of the educational system which may contribute to, or account for, class differences in attainment. This view will be considered shortly.

---

key terms

Material deprivation A lack of money and the things that money can buy.

Cultural deprivation A lack of certain norms, values, attitudes and skills. In this case, those necessary for educational success.

Social class subcultures The distinctive norms and values shared by members of each social class.

Speech patterns and class

Cultural deprivation theory Extreme versions of cultural deprivation theory see the speech patterns of those at the bottom of the class system as inferior. For example, the American psychologist Carl Bereiter argues that the speech patterns of many low-income children are inadequate to meet the demands of the education system. As a result, they directly contribute to educational failure.

This view has been rejected by the American linguist William Labov (1973). He examined the speech patterns of low-income African-American children from Harlem in New York. He claimed that their speech patterns were not inferior to standard English, they were just different. Those who saw them as inferior simply failed to understand low-income black dialect.

Restricted and elaborated codes The British sociologist Basil Bernstein identified two forms of speech pattern, the *restricted code* and the *elaborated code*. The restricted code is a kind of shorthand speech, usually found in conversations between people who have a lot in common, eg friends and family members. It is often tied to a context, eg it cannot be fully understood outside the family circle, and its meanings tend to be particularistic, that is, specific to the speaker and listener. Sentences are often short, simple and unfinished, detail is omitted, explanations not given and information taken for granted. This is because a considerable amount of shared knowledge between speaker and listener is assumed.

By comparison, the elaborated code spells out what the restricted code takes for granted. Meanings are made explicit, explanations provided, details spelt out. As such, the elaborated code tends to be context-free (not tied to a context such as a particular friendship group) and its meanings are universalistic (they can be understood by everybody).

Class and speech codes According to Bernstein, most middle-class children have been socialised in both the restricted and elaborated codes and are fluent in each, whereas many working-class children are limited to the restricted code. Since teachers use the elaborated code, working-class pupils are placed at a distinct disadvantage. They are less likely to understand what teachers say and are more likely to be misunderstood and criticised for what they themselves say.

Bernstein insists that working-class speech patterns are not substandard or inadequate. However, they do place working-class pupils at a disadvantage since the elaborated code is the language of education.

activity 10 speech patterns

Bernstein showed four pictures to five-year-old boys and asked them to describe what was going on. Here are two examples, the first by a working-class boy using the restricted code, the second by a middle-class boy using the elaborated code.

Restricted code 'They're playing football and he kicks it, and it goes through there. It breaks the window and they're looking at it and he comes out and shouts at them because they've broken it. So they run away and then she looks out and she tells them off.'

Elaborated code 'Two boys are playing football and one boy kicks the ball and it goes through the window. The ball breaks the window and the boys are looking at it, and a man comes out and shouts at them because they've broken the window. So they run away and then that lady looks out of her window, and she tells the boys off.'

Source: Bernstein, 1973

question

How do the examples in Item A illustrate some of the features of the restricted and elaborated codes?

methods5 interviews

The boys in the following interviews are African-Americans from low-income working-class families in Harlem, New York.

Interview 1 An eight-year-old boy is interviewed by a 'friendly' White interviewer who presents him with a toy jet plane and asks him to describe it. The setting is formal. There are long silences followed by short two or three word answers, which hardly provide an adequate description of the plane.

Interview 2 Another Black boy from Harlem is interviewed. Again the setting is formal but this time the interviewer is Black and raised in Harlem. The boy responds in much the same way as the boy in the first interview.

Interview 3 The boy and the interviewer are the same as in the second interview. This time the interviewer sits on the floor, the boy is provided with a supply of potato crisps and his best friend is invited along. The change is dramatic. The boy's conversation is articulate and enthusiastic, and, in linguistic terms, rich and diverse. He provides a detailed description of the toy plane.

Source: Labov, 1973

question

What are the advantages and disadvantages of interviews in the study of class and young people's speech patterns?

Harlem, New York

Evaluation Bernstein's research shows how schools can contribute to class differences in educational attainment. Because schools demand the use of the elaborated code, middle-class pupils have a built-in advantage.

Some researchers have questioned Bernstein's view that members of the working-class are limited to the restricted code. He provides little hard evidence to support his view. And much of this evidence comes from interviews given by middle-class adults to five-year-old working-class boys. Such interviews may reveal little about the linguistic ability of young people – see Methods 5, interviews.

key terms

Restricted code Shorthand speech in which detail is omitted and information taken for granted.
Elaborated code A speech pattern in which details are spelt out, explanations provided and meanings made explicit.

Cultural capital

The French sociologist Pierre Bourdieu (1977) starts from the idea that there is a *dominant culture* in society. The higher people's position in the class system, the greater the amount of dominant culture they are likely to have. This culture is generally regarded as superior because those at the top have the power to define it as such. In reality, however, it is no better or worse than any other culture. But because it is highly valued and sought after, it forms the basis of the educational system.

Children born into the middle and upper classes have a built-in advantage. Their culture is closer to the culture of the school so they will be more likely to succeed. For example, their language is closer to that of teachers so they are more likely to understand what's being taught and to be rewarded for what they say and write.

According to Bourdieu, the dominant culture can be seen as *cultural capital* since it can be converted into material rewards – high qualifications, high status jobs, high salaries, high living standards.

Bourdieu concludes that the primary purpose of education is cultural and social reproduction. The education system reproduces the dominant culture and in doing so helps to reproduce the class system. And, by creating educational success and failure, it legitimates the positions of those at the top and those at the bottom.

Bourdieu's idea of cultural capital has been influential in the renewed interest in class and educational attainment in the 1990s and 2000s. This can be seen from the following three studies.

key terms

Dominant culture The culture of those in the higher levels of the class structure which is generally regarded as superior.
Cultural capital Culture that can be converted into material rewards such as high salaries and high living standards.

Class, mothers and cultural capital

In an important study entitled *Class Work: Mothers' involvement in their children's primary schooling*, Diane Reay (1998) states that, 'It is mothers who are making cultural capital work for their children'. Her research is based on interviews with the mothers of 33 children at two London primary schools.

All the mothers are actively involved in their children's education. The working-class mothers worked just as hard as the middle-class mothers. But it was not simply hard work that counted. In addition, it was the amount of cultural capital available. And the middle-class mothers had most.

Middle-class mothers had more educational qualifications and more information about how the educational system operated. They used this cultural capital to good effect – helping children with their homework, bolstering their confidence and sorting out problems with their teachers. Where the middle-class mothers had the confidence and self-assurance to make demands on teachers, the working-class mothers talked in terms of 'plucking up courage' and 'making myself go and see the teacher'. Where middle-class mothers knew what the school expected from their children and how to help them, working-class mothers felt they lacked the knowledge and ability to help their children.

Middle-class mothers not only have more cultural capital, they also have more material capital, ie, more money. Over half the middle-class mothers had cleaners, au pairs or both. This gave them more time to support their children. Working-class mothers could not afford help with domestic work. Nor could they afford private tuition which many middle-class mothers provided for their children.

According to Diane Reay, it is mothers who have the main influence on their children's education. Their effectiveness depends on the amount of cultural capital at their disposal. And this depends on their social class.

Education, class and choice

In recent years, government education policy has encouraged schools to compete, and offered parents and students choices between schools. Choosing the 'right' primary and secondary school is important. It can make a difference to students' examination results and their chances of climbing the educational ladder.

In *Class Strategies and the Education Market: The middle classes and social advantage*, Stephen J. Ball (2003) argues that government policies of choice and competition place the middle class at an advantage. They have the knowledge and skills to make the most of the opportunities on offer. Compared to the working class, they have more material capital, more cultural capital and more *social capital* – access to social networks and contacts which can provide information and support. In Ball's words, middle-class parents have 'enough capitals in the right currency to ensure a high probability of success for their children'.

Strategies The aim of parents is to give their children maximum advantage in the education system. The choice of school is vital. And this is where middle-class parents come into their own. Compared to working-class parents, they are more comfortable dealing with public institutions like schools. They are more used to extracting and assessing information. For example, they use their social networks to talk to parents whose children are attending the schools on offer. They collect and analyse information – for example, the GCSE results of the various schools. And they are more used to dealing with and negotiating with teachers and administrators. As a result, when entry into a popular school is limited, they are more likely to gain a place for their child.

The school/parent alliance Middle-class parents want middle-class schools. In general, schools with mainly middle-class pupils have the best results and the highest status. And these schools want middle-class pupils. They are seen as easy to teach and likely to perform well. They will maintain or increase the school's position in the exam league table and its status in the education market.

Conclusion Many middle-class parents work extremely hard to get their children into the most successful schools. But, what they gain for their children can be at the expense of working-class children.

Class and higher education

In *Degrees of Choice* (2005), Diane Reay, Miriam David and Stephen Ball looked at the influence of social class on university choice. They found that middle-class students from fee-paying schools were most likely to choose elite universities such as Oxford and Cambridge. This reflected the amount of cultural capital they possessed – they had the knowledge and confidence to select the top universities and to see themselves as suited for and entitled to 'the best'. Middle-class students from state schools tended to choose middle-ranking 'redbrick' universities such as Manchester and Liverpool. Working-class students were more likely to choose the lower-ranking, less prestigious 'new' universities. They had less cultural capital. They lacked confidence in their academic ability and social skills – they feared failure and felt they wouldn't fit in socially at higher-ranking universities. As a result, they did not apply to and so excluded themselves from the top universities.

As more and more people are going to university, the less valuable degrees become. Attending an elite university can raise the status of a degree. In general, the higher the class position of students, the more likely they are to choose a high status university. Again the middle class come out on top.

methods6 sampling

The sample of students for *Degrees of Choice* was drawn from six schools and colleges in and around London.

- An 11-18 mixed comprehensive with a large working class intake

- A comprehensive sixth-form consortium which served a socially mixed area

- A tertiary college with a large number of A level students

- A further education college which runs higher education access courses

- Two prestigious single-sex private schools – one boys and one girls.

The educational institutions selected for the sample varied considerably in terms of the social class background of their students.

Source: Reay, David and Ball, 2005

questions

1. Judging from the institutions from which the sample was drawn, would you say it was representative? Give reasons for your answer.

2. Why did the authors aim to produce a representative sample?

key term

Social capital The support and information provided by contacts and social networks which can be converted into material rewards.

2.3 Social class in schools

This section looks at social class in the classroom. In particular, it looks at evidence which suggests that schools sometimes discriminate against working-class pupils and in favour of middle-class pupils.

Labelling theory

Pupils are constantly being assessed and classified. They are defined as able or less able, placed in particular sets or streams, entered for particular examinations and given or denied access to certain parts of the school curriculum. Research indicates that teachers are more likely to define middle rather than working-class pupils as 'able', 'good students' and 'well behaved'. This may well disadvantage working-class pupils.

A *label* is a major identifying characteristic. If, for example, a pupil is labelled as 'bright', others will tend to respond to them and interpret their actions in terms of this label. There is a tendency for a *self-fulfilling prophecy* to result. The pupil will act in terms of the label and see themselves as bright (so fulfilling the prophecy others have made).

Setting and streaming

Most secondary schools have some system for placing pupils in teaching groups in terms of their perceived ability – ie, the way teachers see their ability. These groups include *sets* in which pupils are placed in subject groups (they may be in set 1 for maths, set 3 for art) or *streams* in which they are placed into class groups (class 1, 2, 3) and taught at that level for all subjects.

A number of studies (eg Hargreaves, 1967; Lacey, 1970; Ball, 1981) have looked at the effects of ability grouping in secondary schools. In general, they have found a tendency for middle-class pupils to be placed in the higher groups and for working-class pupils to be placed in the lower groups.

Most teachers prefer to teach higher ability groups. The conduct of pupils in higher groups is likely to be better than of those in lower groups. Those in lower groups tend to develop an *anti-school subculture* in which breaking school rules is highly regarded by some pupils. Teachers spend more time controlling behaviour in these groups at the expense of teaching. They expect less from these pupils, deny them access to higher level knowledge and skills, and place them in lower level examination tiers.

Evaluation To what extent does setting and streaming advantage the largely middle-class higher groups and disadvantage the largely working-class lower groups? The evidence is inconclusive – it is not possible to reach a firm conclusion. In general, more recent research indicates that setting and streaming have little or no effect on pupils' achievement. However, there is some evidence that ability grouping may raise attainment in the top groups and lower it in the bottom groups (Ireson & Hallam, 2001). Where ability groups do have a major effect is in setting for examination entry.

Examination sets

GCSE examinations are tiered. Most are split into higher and foundation tiers. Pupils entered for the foundation tier cannot obtain Grades A* to B. In other words, the highest grade they can achieve is Grade C. Until recently, mathematics was divided into three tiers – higher, intermediate and foundation. Grades A* to B were only available to students entered for the higher level. Grade C was the highest grade possible in the intermediate exam, Grade D was the highest grade possible in the foundation exam.

Students are usually placed in sets for exam entry – for example, in the higher or lower history set for entry to the higher or foundation tier history exam. Middle-class students tend to be placed in the higher sets, working-class

activity11 cultural and social capital

Item A Supporting your child

Liz, a middle-class mother, spells out how she supports her son at primary school.

> 'One is the support I give him at home, hearing him read, making him read every night, doing homework with him, trying to get the books he needs for his project. I see that as a support role. The other side, in the particular case of Martin, is where he has had difficulties and finds reading very, very difficult. So a lot of my time has been spent fighting for extra support for him and I mean fighting.'

Later in the interview, she discusses the tuition Martin receives.

> 'Well he just wasn't making enough progress in school so we decided we'd have to get him a tutor.'

Josie, a working-class mother talks about her son's reading difficulties.

> 'I have tried, I really have. I knew I should be playing a role in getting Leigh to read but I wasn't qualified. Therefore it put extra pressure on me because I was no good at reading myself, it was too important for me to handle and I'd get very upset and angry at Leigh.'

> 'I always found if I went to the class teacher, she'd take it very personal and think I was attacking her. I wasn't. I was just bringing it to her attention in case she didn't know, you know, that in my opinion he's not progressing.'

Source: Reay, 1998

Item B Choosing a school

Here are some comments from middle-class mothers about choosing schools for their children.

> 'You talk to other people who've got children there who come from Riverway, how are they coping. You spend a lot of time talking outside the school gates to people you know in the same situation, that's how you discover things really.'
>
> (Mrs Grafton)

> 'We spoke to teachers in the schools, spoke to other parents, and spoke to my friends who are scattered across the borough and where their children went and what they thought about it.'
>
> (Mrs Gosling)

> 'There was definitely a feeling that this step into secondary education would have a very, very big influence on what they do in the rest of their life. So you had to put a lot of your attention into each school and approach each school as if your child was definitely going to go there, and size it up, assess your own reactions to it and all the rest of it.'
>
> (Mrs Cornwell)

Source: Ball, 2003

Item C The school/parent alliance

questions

1 Using Item A, suggest how cultural capital might give middle-class children an advantage.

2 Using Item B, suggest how social capital might give middle-class children an advantage.

3 How does the cartoon in Item C illustrate the school/parent alliance?

students in the lower sets. Set placement is based on teachers' assessment of students' ability. According to research by David Gillborn and Deborah Youdell (2001), teachers are more likely to see middle-class students as having the ability to enter higher level exams. And this has more to do with teachers' perceptions of what counts as ability than students' actual ability. The result is discrimination against many working-class students. They are denied the opportunity of even attempting to obtain the higher grades.

methods7 participant observation

David Hargreaves (1967) examined the effects of streaming on the behaviour of students and teachers in a boys' secondary school. He used participant observation as his main research method. He sat at the back of the classroom observing students and teachers.

Some of the teachers changed their behaviour when observed. Mr H made the boys work quietly from their textbooks. Mr O usually set written work and joined Hargreaves at the back of the classroom for a chat. Mr L sent boys to the back of the room with their books to show Hargreaves their work. For the most part, however, the teachers 'appeared to behave quite naturally and act as if I was not in the room at all'.

The boys noted some changes in their teachers' behaviour.

- 'When you're in he tries to act calmly.'
- 'They put on a show for you.'
- 'If you weren't there he'd get real mad.'

At first Hargreaves' presence 'also caused changes in the boys' behaviour though I am convinced that once the boys became accustomed to me, they behaved normally'.

Source: Hargreaves, 1967

question

What are the strengths and weaknesses of participant observation for conducting research in the classroom?

Conclusion

This section has looked at social class and educational attainment in terms of what happens within the school. Some researchers argue that class differences in attainment result from the sifting, sorting and assessment of pupils in terms of teachers' perceptions of social class, ability and conduct.

Others argue that class differences in attainment are primarily due to what happens outside the school – to the social inequalities generated by the class structure. Schools from this point of view do little more than reflect and rubber stamp existing inequalities.

Other researchers see class differences in attainment resulting from a combination of what happens inside and outside the school. From this viewpoint the inequalities of the class system are reinforced in the classroom.

key terms

Label A major identifying characteristic placed on a person by others. It identifies them as a certain kind of person.
Self-fulfilling prophecy A person sees themselves in terms of the label placed upon them and acts accordingly. In this way, the prophecy others have made comes to pass.
Anti-school subculture Another term for counter-school culture. A rejection of the norms and values of the school and their replacement with anti-school norms and values.
Setting The placement of pupils into subject groups in terms of their perceived ability.
Streaming The placement of pupils into class groups in terms of their perceived ability. They are taught at that level for all subjects.

summary

1. Class, ethnicity and gender make a difference to educational attainment. Class makes the greatest difference.

2. The following explanations have been given to explain why pupils with working-class backgrounds are less successful.

   - Material deprivation – a lack of money and the things that money can buy.

   - A lack of encouragement, stimulation and interest from parents.

   - Working-class subculture with its emphasis on fatalism, present-time orientation and immediate gratification.

   - Cultural deprivation – an absence of the norms, values and skills needed for high attainment. This view has been strongly criticised.

   - The use of the elaborated code in schools which disadvantages many working-class pupils.

   - A lack of cultural capital. According to Diane Reay, it is mothers who have the main influence on their child's

   education. Their effectiveness largely depends on the amount of cultural capital at their disposal. Middle-class mothers have most.

   - A lack of social capital. Stephen Ball's research argues that social capital is vital when choosing schools. Middle-class mothers, with their wide social networks, have most.

   - In general, students with larger amounts of cultural and social capital will choose to attend the more prestigious universities.

   - Middle-class pupils are more likely to be placed in higher streams, working-class pupils in lower streams. In general, research indicates that streaming and setting have little or no effect on pupils' achievement. However, they may raise attainment in the top groups and lower it in the bottom groups.

   - What does have an effect is the tendency to enter more working-class pupils for lower level exams, so denying them the opportunity to obtain the top grades.

Unit 3 *Gender and educational attainment*

keyissues

1 What are the gender differences in educational attainment?

2 What explanations are given for these differences?

In the 1960s and 70s, sociologists were concerned about the apparent underachievement of girls. Why weren't they more ambitious? Why did fewer girls than boys take high status subjects such as maths, physics and chemistry? Why were girls less likely to go to university?

By the 1990s, the concern had shifted to underachieving boys. The so-called *gender gap* in education now meant failing boys and successful girls. For the late Professor of Education, Ted Wragg, 'the underachievement of boys has become one of the biggest challenges facing society today'. For the former Chief Inspector of Schools, Chris

activity12 *gender and educational attainment*

Item A GCSEs

Percentage of pupils attaining five or more GCSE grades A*-C (England)

	Boys %	Girls %	Gender difference %
2007	59.7	66.8	7.1
2006	52.6	62.2	9.6
2004	48.4	58.4	10.0
2002	46.4	57.0	10.6
2000	44.0	54.6	10.6
1998	41.3	51.5	10.2
1996	39.9	49.4	9.5
1994	39.1	47.8	8.7
1992	34.1	42.7	8.6
1990	30.8	38.4	7.6

Source: Department for Education and Skills

Item B A levels

Attainment of two or more GCE A levels or equivalent qualifications (United Kingdom)

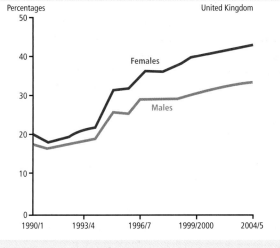

Source: National Statistics Online

Item C Higher education

Students in higher education

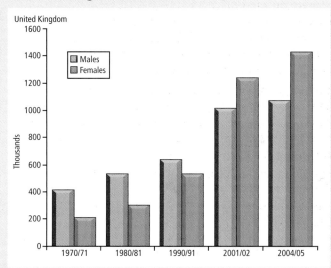

Source: Various issues of *Social Trends*, Office for National Statistics

question

Briefly summarise the trends shown in Items A, B and C.

Woodhead, underachieving boys are 'one of the most disturbing problems facing the education system'.

The impression sometimes given by the media is of boys failing in droves and of girls racing ahead. But is there really a gender crisis in education? Work carefully through Activity 12. It contains the kind of statistics on which claims of a gender crisis are often based. Then we'll look at various ways of interpreting this evidence.

3.1 Interpreting the statistics

The picture of failing boys and achieving girls is based on the kind of statistics presented in Activity 12. What's wrong with this picture?

Boys are doing better Over the past 50 years, the educational performance of boys and young men has steadily improved. Overall, the performance of girls has risen at a faster rate. However, this hardly justifies blanketing all boys as underachievers. Many boys are doing extremely well (Coffey, 2001).

Only some boys are failing Only certain groups of boys are underachieving. There is a close link between male underachievement and social class – compared to other groups, a high proportion of working-class boys are failing (Epstein et al., 1998).

What's new? In some respects, there's nothing new about girls outperforming boys. When the 11-plus exam was introduced in the 1940s, more girls passed than boys. The results were fiddled so that roughly equal numbers of boys and girls went to grammar schools. If the results hadn't been 'adjusted', then two-thirds of grammar school places would have gone to girls (Chitty, 2002).

Hiding girls' failure The preoccupation with so-called 'failing boys' diverts attention from underachieving girls. A high proportion of working-class girls are failing in the school system (Plummer, 2000).

What has changed? In general, the educational performance of girls has improved significantly since the 1980s. And, in general, their improvement has been greater than that of boys. But this does not mean that boys as a group are failing. As noted earlier, the educational performance of most boys is improving.

Gender, class and ethnicity Although the gender gap is significant, it is important to note that class has over five times the effect on educational attainment than gender, and ethnicity twice the effect (Gilborn & Mirza, 2000).

3.2 Explaining girls' improvement

Why are girls doing so well? Here are some of the explanations suggested by researchers.

Changes in attitudes

Judging from a number of studies, girls and young women's attitudes towards education, work and marriage have changed in recent years. Sue Sharpe compared the attitudes of working-class girls in London schools in the early 1970s and 1990s (Sharpe, 1976 & 1994). She found that the 1990s girls were:

- more confident
- more assertive
- more ambitious
- more committed to gender equality.

The main priorities of the 1970s girls were 'love, marriage, husbands and children'. By the 1990s, this had changed to 'job, career and being able to support themselves'. And education was seen as the main route to a good job and financial independence.

Changes in the labour market and attitude to work

There has been a steady rise in the number of women in the labour market. Between 1971 and 2006, the UK employment rate for working age women rose from 56% to 70% (*Social Trends*, 2007). This has been accompanied by a rise in women's occupational ambitions – increasing numbers are looking forward to careers rather than simply jobs. This has led to a higher value being placed on education as a means to a good job. Studies of primary and secondary pupils indicate that girls are increasingly aiming for occupations which require degree level qualifications (Francis & Skelton, 2005).

In the past, women tended to see employment as a stopgap before marriage. Increasingly, they see their occupation as reflecting their identity and as a means for self-fulfilment (Francis & Skelton, 2005).

According to Sue Sharpe (1994), girls are increasingly wary of marriage. They have seen adult relationships breaking up all around them. And they have seen women coping alone in what was once a 'man's world'. Girls were now concerned with standing on their own two feet rather than being dependent on a man. As a result, they were more likely to see education as a means to financial independence.

Changes in marriage and marital breakup

Over the past 30 years, there have been fewer marriages, more divorces and more lone-parent families, most of which are headed by women (*Social Trends*, 2007).

Changes in schools

The abolition of the 11-plus exam and the introduction of comprehensive schools by most local education authorities has removed some of the barriers to girls' achievement. No longer are girls artificially 'failed' in order to get equal numbers of boys and girls into grammar schools.

There has been a growing awareness of gender bias in schools and attempts to remove it. For example, there was a recognition that girls were put off by what were traditionally seen as 'boys' subjects' such as maths, technology, physics and chemistry. This led to the introduction of equal opportunity initiatives such as Girls into Science and Technology.

In 1988, the National Curriculum provided a compulsory core curriculum for all students up to the age of 16 – no matter what their gender. Although the compulsory core has now been slimmed down, all students still have to take maths and science.

Changes in society – risk and individualisation

A number of sociologists claim that today's society is characterised by risk, uncertainty and *individualisation*. For example, with the rising divorce rate, the future of marriage is increasingly uncertain. And the same applies to the future of work. 'Jobs for life' have largely disappeared and a person's working life is becoming more unpredictable.

At the same time, a process of individualisation is occurring. People are increasingly seeing themselves as individuals rather than as members of social groups. In an insecure, risk-filled society, they look to themselves, becoming more self-reliant and self-sufficient. Financial independence is one way of guarding against risk and becoming self-sufficient. And education is one of the main routes to well-paid jobs which can provide this independence.

Ulrich Beck (1992) argues that women are leading the move towards the individualised self. They are 'setting the pace for change'. As a result, it is women who are in the forefront of the improvement in educational attainment.

> **key term**
>
> **Individualisation** The process whereby people see themselves as individuals rather than members of social groups.

activity 13 *changing girls*

Item A Girl power

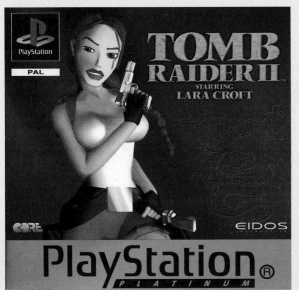

Item B Changing drinks and changing times

Early 1970s

Early 1990s

2007

question

How might Items A and B help to explain girls' rising educational attainment?

3.3 Why are some boys failing?

As noted earlier, most boys and young men are improving their performance in primary, secondary, further and higher education. However, their levels of attainment are rising more slowly than those of girls. And some boys are doing badly – in particular some working-class boys.

Working-class boys have always had problems with the educational system for the reasons outlined in Unit 2. Some researchers believe that these problems have grown in recent years for the following reasons.

Changes in the job market

Manual jobs With the decline in manufacturing and the increasing automation of production, there has been a rapid reduction in semi-skilled and unskilled jobs. The shrinking of this section of the job market has hit working-class males hard. In 2002, the highest unemployment rate – at 10% – was for men in semi-skilled and unskilled occupations which do not usually require formal qualifications (*Social Trends*, 2003).

Manual 'macho' jobs fitted traditional working-class masculine identities. The collapse of this sector of the job market has left these identities uncertain, threatened and confused (Jackson, 1998).

Service sector jobs The new jobs in the service sector tend to be desk jobs in offices and call centres, or jobs involving care for others which require sensitivity and interpersonal skills. These jobs do not sit happily with traditional working-class masculine identities. And even the more 'macho' jobs in the public services – eg, police, fire service and paramedics – now require higher levels of sensitivity and social skills (Mahony, 1998).

Changes in male roles

Traditionally the working man was a father, husband and breadwinner. With increasing numbers of lone-parent families, over 90% of which are headed by women, these roles are closed to many men (see pages 95-98). And boys growing up in these families lack the role models of father, husband and breadwinner.

Lone-parent, mother-headed families are concentrated in the lower working class. Growing up in such families can threaten traditional working-class masculine identities (Jackson, 1998).

Work, home and school

In recent years, working-class boys have become increasingly vulnerable and insecure. They have seen jobless men in the neighbourhood, dependent on welfare with little hope for the future. They have seen traditional working-class jobs drying up. They have seen more and more men fail as breadwinners and fathers.

This has been seen as a 'crisis' in working-class masculinity. How do boys deal with this crisis at school?

School and working-class identity Some working-class boys attempt to deal with the identity problem by adopting an aggressive, macho 'laddishness'. They reject what they see as the middle-class values of the school. Schoolwork is defined as 'sissy' work. As one boy put it, 'The work you do here is girls' work. It's not real work' (Mac an Ghaill, 1994). In other words, it's not the kind of work that 'real' men do. Those who work hard are put down as 'swots' and 'keenos'.

As a result, the anti-school subculture described by Paul Willis in his study of working-class 'lads', develops and directs the boys' behaviour (see page 165). Rejecting the values of the school, some boys look for acceptance, recognition and respect by acting out the norms and values of the anti-school subculture. Reinforced by their peers, they make a considerable contribution to their own educational failure.

Laddish behaviour

The anti-school subculture of a section of working-class 'lads' has a long history. It has been described by sociologists over the past 50 years. What appears to have changed in recent years is that aspects of this subculture have spread to a far larger part of the school population.

In *Lads and Ladettes in School*, Carol Jackson (2006) examined what she calls 'laddish behaviour' among 13-14 year old boys and girls. This behaviour was based on the idea that it is uncool to work hard at school. And, if you're seen as uncool, you won't be popular. This view was held

methods8 semi-structured interviews

In *Lads and Ladettes in School*, Carol Jackson (2006) gave semi-structured interviews to 203 Year 9 pupils in eight schools. She conducted some of the interviews herself – Jackson was a white British woman in her mid-30s. The other interviews were conducted by her colleague a White British woman in her 40s.

While Jackson found the interviews provided 'rich information', she found it difficult to get students to spell out the motives for their behaviour. Why did they behave in laddish ways? She was worried about asking leading questions and directing them to give the answers she expected and believed were correct.

Source: Jackson, 2006

question

What are the advantages and disadvantages of using semi-structured interviews in a study of laddish behaviour?

activity 14 a changing world

Item A The decline of manufacturing

Derelict engineering works, Willenhall, West Midlands

Item C New opportunities

Working in a call centre

If the sort of work available to young working-class people is largely in the service industries, they will need qualities such as warmth, empathy, sensitivity to unspoken needs, and high levels of interpersonal skills to build an effective relationship with customers.

Source: Mahoney, 1998

Item B Aggressive masculinity

For many working-class boys, the traditional route to status, pride and security is closed. What some boys are left with is a bitter sense that trying to get work is pointless, and an aggressive culture of masculinity to fill in the despairing gaps.

Source: Jackson, 1998

question

Use Items A to C to provide an explanation for the educational failure of some working-class boys.

---

by nearly all the boys and girls in Jackson's study, whatever their social class background.

The boys based their laddish behaviour on the dominant view of masculinity – they acted tough, messed around, had a laugh, disrupted lessons and rejected school work as 'feminine'. Most wanted to do well at school but feared losing popularity if they were seen to work hard. The solution was to work secretly, usually at home. However, particularly for the working-class boys who often lacked appropriate facilities at home (eg, a computer with internet access), this was at best a partial solution. For many, laddish behaviour at school reduced their chances of success.

Why has laddish behaviour developed in recent years? First, as noted earlier, the decline of manual jobs has threatened traditional working-class masculinity. Laddish behaviour may be seen as an attempt to rebuild a masculine identity. Second, there is increasing pressure to succeed. Schools are striving to raise standards and improve their standing in league tables. This places growing pressure on pupils to attain high grades. Laddish behaviour can help to deal with the fear of possible failure and with the shame of actual failure that this pressure produces. This is summarised in the following quote: 'I'm not stupid, I just didn't do any work' (Jackson, 2006).

key term

Laddish behaviour In terms of behaviour in school, messing around, having a laugh, disrupting lessons, acting tough, public rejection of hard work.

summary

1. The educational performance of females has improved significantly since the 1980s. They have overtaken males at every level from primary to higher education.

2. Overall, the performance of males has also improved, but at a slower rate.

3. The following reasons have been suggested for the improvement in female performance:
   - Changes in attitudes – eg, increasing concern with financial independence
   - Changes in the labour market – more women in the workforce
   - Changes in marriage – rising divorce rate and growth of lone-parent families
   - Changes within schools – eg, reduction in gender bias
   - Changes in society – risk, uncertainty, individualisation.

4. The following reasons have been suggested for the relatively low attainment of boys, particularly some working-class boys.
   - The threat to working-class masculinity resulting from the reduction in traditional working-class jobs and the growth in female-headed families
   - The development of an anti-school culture which rejects the values of the school and helps rebuild a masculine identity
   - The spread of laddish behaviour as a response to the fear of failure and the shame of failure.

Unit 4 *Ethnicity and educational attainment*

keyissues

1 How does ethnicity affect educational attainment?
2 What explanations have been given for ethnic differences in attainment?

As noted earlier (see page 171) class has the most important effect on educational attainment – three times greater than ethnicity. Ethnicity comes next. It has around twice the effect of gender (Gillborn & Mirza, 2000). The evidence indicates that:

● All ethnic groups have improved their educational attainment.

● There are significant differences in the attainment of ethnic groups (Gillborn & Mirza, 2000).

The following section looks at some of the evidence on which these statements are based.

4.1 Ethnicity and attainment – evidence

Activity 15 looks at ethnicity and educational attainment at GCSE level.

Ethnicity Activity 15 shows that all groups have improved their performance at GCSE level since 1992. Bangladeshi students have made the most significant improvement. And Indian students have the highest percentage of A*-C grades. White students have made the smallest improvement. And Black students have the lowest percentage of A*-C grades. Despite overall improvement, there are still significant differences in attainment between ethnic groups.

Ethnicity and gender Just how much are the differences in attainment at GCSE due to ethnicity? We already know that social class and gender affect attainment. Before going further, it is important to look at their influence in order to assess the effect of ethnicity.

Work through Activity 16 now in order to assess the effect of gender.

The bar chart in Activity 16 shows that in each of the ethnic groups, girls do better than boys. Clearly, there is a gender gap in attainment. But, even taking this into account, there are still important ethnic differences. For example, Chinese girls do better than Chinese boys, but they also do better than girls from other ethnic groups.

The effect of gender varies in different ethnic groups. For example, the highest gender gap is between Black Caribbean girls and boys – over 16 percentage points. And the lowest gender gap is between Chinese girls and boys – just over 9 percentage points. These figures suggest that gender does not operate in isolation. In this case, it appears to be affected by ethnicity.

Ethnicity and class Recent figures on the relationship between ethnicity, social class and educational attainment at GCSE are not available. However, figures are available for a comparison of attainment at GCSE of pupils eligible for free school meals (FSM) – those from low income groups – and those not eligible for free school meals (non-FSM) – those from higher income groups. The comparison gives some indication of the effects of class, since class involves income inequality. Look at the bar chart in Activity 17 to see the effect of income differences on attainment at GCSE.

activity15 *ethnicity and attainment*

Attainment of 5 or more GCSEs A*- C by ethnicity

England and Wales   percentages

Ethnic group	1992	1996	2000	2004	2006	Gain 1992-2006
White	37	45	50	55	58	+21
Black	23	23	39	34	48	+25
Indian	38	48	60	72	72	+34
Pakistani	26	23	29	37	51	+25
Bangladeshi	14	25	29	45	57	+43

Note: Black includes people of African-Caribbean and Black African origin.

Source: Various Youth Cohort Studies, Office for National Statistics

question

Summarise the relationship between ethnicity and educational attainment indicated by the table.

*activity*16 *ethnicity, gender and attainment at GCSE*

Attainment of 5 or more GCSE grades A*-C, by ethnicity and gender, England (percentages), 2006

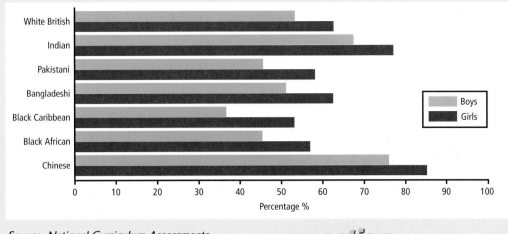

Source: *National Curriculum Assessments,*
SFR 04/2007, DfES, London

question

What relationships between ethnicity, gender and educational attainment are indicated by the bar chart?

*activity*17 *ethnicity, income inequality and attainment at GCSE*

Pupils achieving 5 or more GCSE grades A*-C, by ethnic group and FSM (free school meals) status, 2003 (percentages)

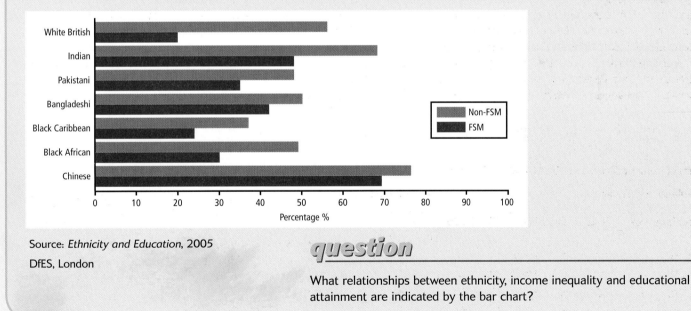

Source: *Ethnicity and Education, 2005*
DfES, London

question

What relationships between ethnicity, income inequality and educational attainment are indicated by the bar chart?

The bar chart in Activity 17 shows that income inequality affects all ethnic groups. However, its influence varies from group to group. Coming from a low-income background appears to affect White British more than minority ethnic pupils. For example, in 2003, 56% of non-FSM and 20% of FSM White British pupils attained A*-C grades at GCSE – a difference of 36 percentage points. By comparison, 50% of non-FSM and 43% of FSM Bangladeshi pupils attained

these grades – a difference of only 7 percentage points (DfES, 2005).

Post-16 education

Young people from minority ethnic groups are more likely to continue their education after 16 than the majority White group. Table 1 shows full-time and part-time initial participation rates for higher education, that is rates for *starting* higher education courses. Whites have the lowest rate at 38%, Black Africans the highest at 73% (Connor et al., 2004). Members of minority ethnic groups make up 16% of home undergraduates in England, nearly double their share of the population (Modood, 2006).

However, apart from the Chinese and Indian students, minority ethnic group students are less likely to attend prestigious universities, more likely to drop out and less likely to obtain a high-grade degree (Modood, 2006).

Table 1 *Higher education initial participation rates England, 2001/2 (percentages)*

Ethnic group	Male	Female	All
White	34	41	38
All minority ethnic groups	55	58	56
Black Carribbean	36	52	45
Black African	71	75	73
Black other	56	72	64
Indian	70	72	71
Pakistani	54	44	49
Bangladeshi	43	33	39
Chinese	47	50	49

Source: Connor, H., Tyers, C., Modood, T. and Hillage, J. (2004)

4.2 Explaining ethnic differences in attainment

This section looks at factors in 1) the wider society and 2) within schools that may affect the attainment levels of ethnic groups.

Ethnicity, society and attainment

Explaining ethnic differences in attainment is difficult because of:

- Changes over time – for example, at GCSE Bangladeshi students have made major improvements from 1992 to 2006, significantly greater than other ethnic groups.

- Changes at different levels of the educational system. For example, the attainment of many African-Caribbean boys declines during secondary education. However, it improves significantly after compulsory schooling as a high proportion participate in further and higher education.

Social class As outlined in Unit 2, class has a significant effect on educational attainment. Ethnic groups who tend to be less successful in secondary school have a higher proportion of pupils from working-class backgrounds. Part of their level of educational attainment can therefore be explained in terms of class rather than ethnicity.

However, the influence of class on ethnic performance appears to vary from group to group. In particular, class appears to affect Whites to a greater extent than minority ethnic groups. For example, Bangladeshi pupils are most likely to come from working-class backgrounds, yet their performance at GCSE in 2006 was little different from Whites. In general working-class Bangladeshi pupils do better than working-class White pupils at age 16. The same applies to higher education. Compared to working-class Whites, a higher proportion of working-class minority ethnic group members attend higher education (Modood, 2004).

Cultural factors To some degree, ethnic groups have their own subcultures – norms, values and beliefs which are distinctive to each particular group. Does this have any effect on educational attainment?

Language differences have been seen as a reason for differences in educational attainment. As the most recent immigrant group, Bangladeshis are likely to be less familiar with the English language. However, the experience of other groups suggests that this will be a temporary disadvantage. The high attainment of Indian pupils indicates that a second language is not a barrier to achievement (Modood et al., 1997). And, as the GCSE results in Activity 15 suggest, Bangladeshi pupils appear to be rapidly overcoming any language barriers which might have slowed their progress.

The value placed on education can affect the levels of parental encouragement and pupil motivation, which, in turn, influence educational attainment. Research evidence indicates that minority ethnic parents may place a higher value on education, give their children greater encouragement and expect more from them than many White parents (Connor et al., 2004). This may explain why class appears to have less effect on minority ethnic attainment and on minority ethnic entry into higher education.

A large body of research has focused on the low attainment of African-Caribbean boys in secondary schools. Tony Sewell (1997), an African-Caribbean writer, argues that cultural factors provide part of the explanation. A high proportion of African-Caribbean boys are raised in lone-parent families, usually headed by women. Lacking the male role model of a father figure, some are drawn into gangs which emphasise an aggressive masculinity and reject authority. In schools, this version of Black masculinity can result in opposition to the authority of teachers and a rejection of academic achievement.

Sewell claims that only a minority of African-Caribbean boys adopt this approach (see pages 197-198 for further details of his research). And, as Table 1 indicates, many may well grow out of this form of masculinity – 36% go on to higher education compared to 34% for White males.

Sewell's research has been criticised for what some see as blaming the boys rather than the schools. Critics argue that the way African-Caribbean boys are treated in schools is the main reason for their relatively low attainment at GCSE.

The influence of culture can be seen from the attainment of Chinese students. Compared to other ethnic groups, their attainment is higher, the gender gap is smaller and the effect of class is less. A study based on semi-structured interviews with 80 14-16 year-old Chinese students, 30 Chinese parents and 30 teachers from London schools reported the following findings (Archer, 2006). Both students and parents placed a very high value on education – it was seen as a 'way of life'. For both middle and working-class families, university was 'a must'. Parents invested considerable time, energy and money in their children's education – 'education is very much a family project'. A family's standing in the community is partly due to the educational performance of the children. And children appreciated their parents' high expectations, encouragement and support.

Ethnicity, schools and attainment

The focus now moves from the wider society to what goes on in the classroom.

School effectiveness

Some schools are better than others when it comes to exam results. In *The School Effect,* David Smith and Sally Tomlinson (1989) followed the progress of over 2,400 pupils from the age of 11 to 16 in 18 multi-ethnic comprehensives. They found that different schools achieved very different results with children of similar background and ability. According to the authors, 'what school a child goes to makes far more difference than which ethnic group he or she belongs to'.

Evaluation Reviewing *The School Effect*, David Gillborn and David Drew (1992) state that, 'Crucially the work reminds us that individual schools possess the power to influence the educational experiences, achievements and future life chances of their pupils'.

But they see two major problems. The first concerns methodology – in particular, the size and nature of the sample. For example, there were only 146 African-Caribbean pupils at age 16, too small a number on which to base conclusions. A second concern is Smith and Tomlinson's view that racism was not a significant factor in the education of ethnic minorities. The results of their questionnaire given to parents and teachers suggested that racism was not a problem in school. But there is a growing body of research which suggests that racism is widespread in many schools. And it may well have a significant effect on educational attainment.

Racism in schools

Racism refers to *prejudice* and *discrimination* against groups seen as racially different. Prejudice means members of those groups are prejudged in terms of negative stereotypes – sweeping generalisations are made about all members of the group – for example, they are aggressive, lazy and so on. Discrimination means acting against

people simply because they are seen to be members of a particular group – for example, not giving them a job because of their group membership.

People may be completely unaware that they are discriminating against others. And they are often shocked when this is revealed to them.

methods**9** questionnaires

In *The School Effect* Smith and Tomlinson (1989) gave questionnaires to parents and teachers.

questions

1 Why might a questionnaire fail to reveal racism in schools?

2 Why might parents and teachers be the wrong people to ask about racism in schools?

Discrimination and setting Jayleigh – not its real name – is a comprehensive school. In 1988, 41% of its pupils were of Asian origin.

At Jayleigh a greater proportion of White pupils (77%) were entered for GCSEs than Asian pupils (70%). In addition, White pupils were entered for more GCSEs (an average of 6.2) than Asian pupils (5.8). Whether or not pupils could take GCSEs depended largely on teachers' assessment of their attainment and potential.

Pupils at Jayleigh were set in terms of ability. Asian pupils were more likely to be placed in lower sets even when they had the same assessment from the same primary school as White pupils. And to get in the top sets, Asians generally needed higher marks than Whites. Pupils tended to remain in the same sets throughout secondary school. And set placement largely determined GCSE entry. As a result, fewer Asians were entered for GCSEs, and those that were entered took fewer GCSEs.

This study by the Commission for Racial Equality (1992) concluded that, 'Here was a school which, however unintentionally, was using a setting system that appears to have set up barriers to a significant number of Asian pupils, and, in some instances, might have discriminated against them unlawfully'.

It is impossible to estimate the extent of the 'Jayleigh situation'. However, similar examples of systematic discrimination on ethnic grounds have been found in other schools. This can be seen from Activity 18 which looks at setting in a Midlands comprehensive school. It refers to CSEs and O levels which were replaced by GCSEs. CSE is a lower level examination. A CSE grade 1 is equivalent to an O level grade C.

activity18 ethnicity and setting

Item A Allocation to exam sets

Ethnicity	Pupil	Third year exam results (marks out of 100)				Set placement (O = GCE O level)			
		English	Maths	French	Physics	English	Maths	French	Physics
African-	A	73	44	58	---	CSE	CSE	CSE	---
Caribbean	B	62	63	60	59	CSE	CSE	CSE	CSE
	C	64	45	56	72	CSE	CSE	---	CSE
	D	68	37	82	---	CSE	CSE	CSE	---
Asian	E	51	77	---	55	O	O	---	O
	F	60	56	58	---	O	O	O	---
	G	61	62	55.5	---	O	O	O	---
	H	54	55	---	40	O	O	---	O
White	I	61	62	---	62	O	O	---	O
	J	52	57	55	---	O	O	O	---
	K	75	82	77.5	72	O	O	O	O
	L	54	75	64	72	O	O	O	O

A CSE grade 1 is equivalent to an O level grade C.   Source: Education for Save by John Egglestone © Trentham Books Ltd. 1986

Item B Setting and perceived behaviour

The deputy head admitted that setting was not based solely on exam results – 'It is the case that the school tends to put the dutiful children in O level groups'. Some teachers saw African-Caribbean students as 'less cooperative'. One English teacher described all her African-Caribbean students as 'a disruptive influence'. It appeared that at least some students were placed in lower sets on the basis of teachers' views of their behaviour rather than ability.

Source: Wright, 1986

In view of Items A and B, do you think that racial discrimination played a part in the setting of students? Explain your answer.

Classroom interaction

Primary schools The evidence examined so far suggests that ethnic minority students experience discrimination during their school careers. Studies of classroom interaction support this. Cecile Wright's research, conducted in 1988/89, was based on classroom observation in four inner-city primary schools (Wright, 1992). It found that teachers perceived and treated ethnic minority children differently from White children.

Asian children, especially the younger ones, were often seen as a problem, but as a problem that could be largely ignored. They received least attention, were often excluded from classroom discussions and rarely asked to answer questions. Teachers tended to assume that their command of English was insufficient for full classroom participation. Yet they also saw Asian pupils as well disciplined and highly motivated.

African-Caribbean children – especially boys – were expected to behave badly. They received considerable attention – nearly all of it negative. Their behaviour was usually seen as aggressive, disobedient and disruptive. They were often singled out for criticism, even for actions which were ignored in other pupils. As a result, they often felt picked on and treated unfairly.

Secondary schools Research by David Gillborn (1990) largely reflects Wright's findings. He spent two years studying an inner-city comprehensive school gathering data from classroom observation and interviews with teachers and students. He found that the vast majority of teachers tried to treat all students fairly. However, they perceived students differently and on this basis treated them differently. In particular, they often saw the actions of African-Caribbean students as a threat where no threat was intended. And they reacted accordingly by disciplining them.

African-Caribbean students were more likely to be criticised and punished, even when members of other ethnic groups committed the same offence. As a result, there was considerable tension and conflict between White teachers and African-Caribbean students.

activity 19 different treatment

The following is taken from observation of a nursery class of four-year-olds.

Teacher:	Let's do one song before home time.
Peter:	(*White boy*) Humpty Dumpty.
Teacher:	No, I'm choosing today. Let's do something we have not done for a while. I know, we'll do the Autumn song. What about the Autumn song we sing. Don't shout out, put your hand up nicely.
Mandy:	(*shouting out*) Two little leaves on a tree.
Teacher:	She's nearly right.
Marcus:	(*African-Caribbean boy with his hand up*) I know.
Teacher:	(*talking to the group*) Is she right when she says 'two little leaves on a tree'?
Whole group:	No.
Teacher:	What is it Peter?
Peter:	Four.
Teacher:	Nearly right.
Marcus:	(*waving his hand for attention*) Five.
Teacher:	Don't shout out Marcus, do you know Susan?
Susan:	(*White girl*) Five.
Teacher:	(*holding up one hand*) Good because we have got how many fingers on this hand?
Whole group:	Five.
Teacher:	OK, let's only have one hand because we've only got five leaves. How many would we have if we had too many. Don't shout out, hands up.
Mandy:	(*shouting out*) One, two, three, four, five, six, seven, eight, nine, ten.
Teacher:	Good, OK how many fingers have we got?
Marcus:	Five.
Teacher:	Don't shout out Marcus, put your hand up. Deane, how many?
Deane:	Five.
Teacher:	That's right, we're going to use five today. What makes them dance about, these leaves?
Peter:	(*shouting out*) The wind.
Teacher:	That's right.

Source: Wright, 1992

question

Make out a case that the teacher's treatment of Marcus is

a) racist

b) non-racist.

methods 10 ethnography

Supporters of ethnography argue that we should study people in their normal, everyday settings.

question

What are the advantages and disadvantages of using the ethnographic method for studying racism in schools.

Máirtín Mac an Ghaill (1988) studied a boys' comprehensive in the early 1980s. The school was streamed with boys being demoted to lower streams for what was seen as bad behaviour. In the words of one teacher 'There are boys of relatively higher ability in the lower sets, especially among the West Indians. I've told you before Johnson and Brian were marvellous at Maths, especially problem-solving. But it's their, it's the West Indians' attitude and that must decide it in the end. You can't promote a boy who is known to be a troublemaker, who's a dodger. It will look like a reward for bad behaviour.'

Many African-Caribbean pupils responded with resistance. They formed an anti-school peer group, the Rasta Heads, which rejected many of the school's norms and values.

Racism in schools – evaluation

Methodology Wright, Gillborn and Mac an Ghaill's studies use a research method known as *ethnography*. This involves direct observation of relatively small groups, often over fairly long periods of time. Because the samples are small, it is not possible to make generalisations – ie, to say that the findings apply to all multi-ethnic schools.

However, the insights ethnography provides are unlikely to come from research methods such as questionnaires. For example, in *The School Effect*, Smith and Tomlinson's questionnaire to parents and teachers revealed little evidence of racism in schools. Ethnographic methods often give a very different picture. But not always.

An alternative view Peter Foster (1990) conducted an ethnographic study of a multi-ethnic comprehensive between 1985 and 1987. He found no evidence of racism. Students from ethnic minorities were not treated differently from White students. In fact, minority students, especially African-Caribbean girls – achieved better results than White pupils.

Foster admitted that the school he studied was distinctive. It was situated in a community with a long history of ethnic cooperation. And, at the time of his study, the staff were involved in an anti-racist programme. Whatever the differences between this school and others, Foster's study warns against the dangers of generalising from a few examples.

Despite this warning, there is evidence of racism in schools. Ethnic minority pupils tend to be over-represented in the lower sets and in the lower tiers for GCSE exam entry. And African-Caribbean boys in particular tend to be regarded as badly behaved and troublesome by many teachers, even when their behaviour is similar to that of White boys. This can only disadvantage ethnic minority pupils (Pilkington, 2003).

key terms

Prejudice Prejudging members of groups in terms of stereotypes – sweeping generalisations which are applied to all members of the group. Prejudice can be positive or negative.

Discrimination Acting in a certain way towards people because they are seen to be members of a particular group. Discrimination can be positive or negative.

Racism Prejudice and discrimination against groups seen as racially different.

Ethnography A research method based on direct observation of relatively small groups, often over fairly long periods of time.

summary

1. There are significant differences in the educational attainment of ethnic groups. However, these differences change over time – eg, over the past 20 years – and vary from one level of the educational system to another – eg, from secondary to higher.

2. The following factors outside the school have been seen to affect ethnic differences in attainment.

   - Social class – affects the attainment of all ethnic groups, but its influence varies from one group to the next. White students appear most affected by class.

   - Cultural factors – there is evidence that cultural factors, such as the value parents place on education and peer group subcultures, may partly account for ethnic differences in attainment.

3. The following factors within schools have been seen to affect ethnic differences in attainment.

   - Racism – particularly directed against African Caribbeans

   - Discrimination in setting

   - Discrimination in everyday classroom interaction.

Unit 5 **Relationships and processes within schools**

keyissues

1 What is the hidden curriculum and how does it operate?

2 What are pupil subcultures and how do they develop?

3 What factors shape teacher-pupil relationships?

4 How are teaching and learning organised?

5.1 The hidden curriculum

Look back to Activity 19 on page 191, which shows how Marcus, a four-year-old African-Caribbean boy, is given a hard time by his teacher. Let's assume that Marcus has a tendency to over-enthusiasm, but apart from this is a well-behaved and likeable boy. What message is the teacher sending to Marcus and the other children?

If she consistently puts all African-Caribbean children down, then her unspoken message states that African-Caribbean children are different, that they should not be shown the same kindness and consideration as other children, and that they are troublesome and need keeping in check. If other teachers treat African-Caribbean pupils in the same way, then they are all transmitting similar messages. And these messages will form part of the *hidden curriculum* of the school.

Defining the hidden curriculum

The *formal school curriculum* consists of the knowledge and skills which pupils are expected to acquire. In state schools, part of this curriculum – the National Curriculum – is laid down by the government. It is spelt out in detail in official publications.

The hidden curriculum is the messages schools transmit to pupils without directly teaching them or spelling them out. It consists of ideas, beliefs, norms and values which are often taken for granted and transmitted as part of the normal routines and procedures of school life. It includes the unwritten and often unstated rules and regulations which guide and direct everyday school behaviour (Ballantine & Spade, 2001).

How is the hidden curriculum transmitted?

The hidden curriculum is transmitted in many different ways. Think about the following.

activity20 *hidden messages*

Item A *Power and gender*

In Britain's secondary schools, women tend to remain in the lower teaching ranks and in particular subject areas. Those who are promoted often end up as head of year, responsible for pastoral care – dealing with students' problems.

Source: Langham, 2000

Item C *School assembly*

Assembly started when teachers marched their tutorial groups to the hall, where they were expected to stand in straight lines. Here, senior house staff were much in evidence as they were concerned that pupils should stand up straight and stand quietly until the headmaster arrived. Meanwhile, other teachers stood around the edge of the hall, talking to each other, making jokes, and exchanging stories until the headmaster entered.

Source: Burgess, 1983

question

What messages are being transmitted by Items A, B and C?

Item B *Social control and ethnicity*

Exclusion is one of the methods of social control which schools can use to deal with students they regard as troublesome. Black pupils are more likely to be excluded than White pupils. In 2004/05, 39 in every 10,000 African-Caribbean pupils were permanently excluded compared to 13 in every 10,000 White pupils.

Source: *Social Trends*, 2007, Office for National Statistics

School organisation

- Is there a hierarchy of power, status and authority?
- Who holds the top posts (eg, headteacher, senior staff), who occupies the lowest (eg, cleaners)? What is their class, gender, ethnicity and age group?
- Are there mixed-ability classes, or are pupils divided into streams or sets? Are certain groups – eg, working-class boys – usually found in certain sets?
- Are lots of pupils excluded? If so, which pupils?

The behaviour and attitudes of those in authority

- How do the head, senior staff, other teachers and support staff (eg cooks and caretakers) relate to each other and to pupils?
- Are pupils allowed to have a say in school life?
- How do those in authority relate to pupils in general and to the class, gender and ethnicity of pupils?

Transmitting messages Messages are transmitted in all these areas. For example, if the top posts are filled by males, this says something about gender relationships. If pupils have little or no say in the running of the school, this says something about power in organisations. If disproportionate numbers of working-class boys are found in the lower sets, this says something about inequality in the wider society.

The hidden curriculum – functionalist and Marxist views

Functionalist and Marxist perspectives on education were outlined in Unit 1. Each contains a particular view of the hidden curriculum – what it is, how it is transmitted and how it relates to the wider society.

Functionalist views As outlined earlier, functionalists see the transmission of society's core values as one of the main functions of the education system. This can be seen as part of the hidden curriculum. It is hidden in the sense that teachers and pupils are often unaware of the process. It is part of the curriculum because it's found in every school.

Talcott Parsons (1951, 1961) provides an example using the value of individual achievement, one of the major values in Western industrial society. In schools young people are required to achieve as individuals. They take exams on their own, not as a member of a team. Their individual achievements are carefully graded and assessed. High achievement is rewarded with praise, high status, good grades and valuable qualifications. In this way, young people are encouraged to value individual achievement. And this prepares them to achieve as individuals in the wider society.

Marxist views As outlined earlier, Marxists argue that the main job of schools is social reproduction – producing the next generation of workers *schooled* to accept their roles in capitalist society.

For Bowles and Gintis (1976), this is done primarily through the hidden curriculum. They claim that schools produce subordinate, well-disciplined workers who will submit to control from above and take orders rather than question them. Schools do this by rewarding conformity, obedience, hard work and punctuality, and by penalising creativity, originality and independence.

Schools are seen to transmit ruling class ideology – a false picture of society which justifies social inequality and the capitalist system.

activity21 views of the hidden curriculum

Item A *Prize day*

Awards for academic excellence in an American school

Item B *Learning to submit*

In a study of 237 students in their final year at a New York high school, the researchers claimed that high grades were linked with perseverance, obedience, consistency, dependability and punctuality. Students with high grades were often below average when measured in terms of creativity, originality and independence of judgement.

Source: Bowles & Gintis, 1976

questions

1 How can Item A be used to support a functionalist view of the hidden curriculum?

2 How can Item B be used to support a Marxist view of the hidden curriculum?

Conclusion

The idea of a hidden curriculum is useful. Clearly, there's a lot more being taught and learned in schools than the formal curriculum of English, maths, science, and so on. And clearly much of this is 'hidden' – teachers and learners are often unaware of what's going on.

The content of the hidden curriculum is open to interpretation. Have the functionalists got it right? Have the Marxists got it right? This partly depends on how you see capitalist society.

5.2 Pupil subcultures

Pupil subcultures are the distinctive norms and values developed by groups of young people in schools. The anti-school subculture identified by Paul Willis in his study of working-class boys in a secondary school is an example of a pupil subculture (see page 165).

This section asks what subcultures exist in schools and where do they come from. Are they a reflection of life outside the school – do pupils bring their subculture from the neighbourhood into the school? Or, do subcultures develop in response to pupils' experiences within schools – for example, their placement in particular sets? Or, do they develop from young people's experiences both inside and outside the school?

A white, male, middle-class subculture

One of the earliest studies of pupil subcultures was conducted in the late 1950s/early 60s by Colin Lacey (1970). The pupils were mainly middle class and attended Hightown Grammar School (not its real name). Many had been high achievers at their local primary school – they were the 'top scholars, team leaders, head boys and teachers' favourites'.

In their first year, all new boys showed high levels of commitment to the school, proudly wearing their school caps and jackets, and enthusiastically attending school functions and clubs. In class, they were eager, straining to answer questions, cooperating with their teachers and competing among themselves. Six months into the second year, one class was seen by their teachers as difficult to teach. In the words of one teacher, 'They're unacademic, they can't cope with the work'. What had happened to transform a group of high-achieving, academically-able first year pupils into 'unacademic' second year pupils? To help explain this, Lacey introduced two concepts – *differentiation* and *polarisation*.

Differentiation This is the process by which teachers judge and rank pupils in terms of their academic ability (as perceived by the teacher) and their behaviour. On this basis, they are differentiated into streams. As time goes on, pupils get a sense of how both teachers and fellow pupils rate and rank them.

Polarisation Gradually, a gap opened up – and kept growing – between the pupils who were defined as successful and those defined as unsuccessful – the two groups became polarised.

The subculture of success Pupils in the top stream accepted the value system of the school – they worked hard and were well-behaved. The system rewarded them with prestige – they were praised and respected by teachers. And the boys reinforced each other's behaviour – they were members of a successful peer group sharing the same values.

The subculture of failure Pupils in the bottom stream developed an anti-school subculture which became more extreme as the years went by. The school's values were turned upside down – boys gained prestige for giving cheek to a teacher, truanting, refusing to do homework, and for smoking and drinking.

This was a group thing – boys gained respect from other members of the group for anti-school behaviour. In this way, they reinforced each other's behaviour. And in the process, their school work steadily deteriorated.

Conclusion Lacey's study suggests that pupil subcultures develop within the school. They are a response to the way pupils are perceived by teachers, by other pupils, and by themselves. And they are a reaction to the way school classes are organised – in this case, streamed – and all that this 'says' about pupils in different streams.

> ## key terms
>
> *Pupil subcultures* The distinctive norms and values developed by groups of young people in schools.
>
> *Differentiation* Separating pupils into groups on the basis of their perceived ability and behaviour.
>
> *Polarisation* The widening gap in terms of measured ability and behaviour between top and bottom classes.

White, male, working-class subcultures

The lads As outlined earlier, Paul Willis studied a small group of working-class boys – the 'lads' – during their last year and a half at school (see page 165). In many ways the anti-school subculture developed by the lads was similar to the behaviour of the boys in the bottom stream in Lacey's study of Hightown Grammar. However, Willis's explanation of the subculture's development is very different.

According to Willis, the lads' behaviour reflected a) their expectations of future employment and b) the working-class subculture they brought to school with them. The lads were keen to leave school as soon as possible and looked forward to 'real' work – adult, male, manual jobs. School was a waste of time.

- The lads didn't need academic qualifications for the jobs they wanted.
- They despised those who conformed to the school's values – who they called the 'ear 'oles' – seeing them as cissies.

- They wanted a context – manual work – where they could be real men.

The lads' anti-school subculture reflected the working-class culture they'd learned from their fathers, elder brothers and other men in the neighbourhood. Having a 'laff', a lack of respect for authority and messing around are aspects of manual working-class male subculture. The lads are attracted to this kind of behaviour and reproduce it in the classroom.

For Willis, the lads' anti-school subculture is shaped mainly by their expectations about the jobs they hope to get and by the working-class subculture they bring with them to school.

Working-class peer groups Willis has been criticised for basing his conclusion on a very small sample – 12 boys – and for ignoring other pupil subcultures in the school. Máirtín Mac an Ghaill (1994) studied Year 11 students in the early 1990s, in Parnell School (not its real name), a comprehensive in the West Midlands. He identified three working-class male peer groups, each with a distinctive subculture.

Mac an Ghaill argues that to some extent these subcultures are shaped by:

- the way students are organised into sets
- the type of curriculum they follow
- the teacher-student social relations which result from the above.

Macho Lads The Macho Lads were relegated to the bottom two sets for all their subjects. They were academic failures and treated as such by their teachers. Like Willis's lads, they rejected the school's values and the teachers' authority. Their concerns were acting tough, having a laugh, looking after their mates and looking smart. The teachers viewed them with suspicion and policed their behaviour, banning certain clothes and hairstyles, and making constant demands – 'Sit up straight', 'Look at me when I'm talking to you' and 'Walk properly down the corridor'.

Academic Achievers Apart from the Macho Lads, Mac an Ghaill identified two other working-class pupil subcultures. The Academic Achievers saw hard work and educational qualifications as the route to success. They were in the top sets, and received preferential treatment in terms of timetabling, books and experienced teachers. The Academic Achievers tended to come from the upper levels of the working class.

New Enterprisers The New Enterprisers saw a different route to success. They focused on vocational subjects such as business studies and technology and looked forward to a future in high-skilled areas of the labour market.

White, female subcultures

Most of the research has focused on male subcultures. However, the following studies suggest some interesting

activity22 the Macho Lads

Darren:	It's the teachers that make the rules. It's them that decide that it's either them or us. So you are often put into a situation with teachers where you have to defend yourself. Sometimes it's direct in the classroom. But it's mainly the headcases that would hit a teacher. Most of the time it's all the little things.
Interviewer:	Like what?
Gilroy:	Acting tough by truanting, coming late to lessons, not doing homework, acting cool by not answering teachers, pretending you didn't hear them; that gets them mad. Lots of different things.
Noel:	Teachers are always suspicious of us (the Macho Lads). Just like the cops, trying to set you up.

Source: Mac an Ghaill, 1994

Messing around

question

Provide a brief explanation for the attitudes expressed above.

methods11 involving participants

Mac an Ghaill's research at Parnell School was based mainly on participant observation. He also used informal group discussions, semi-structured interviews, questionnaires, and diaries kept by the students. He aimed to break down the barriers between himself and the research participants. There was give and take as they shared their life histories. And the students directly contributed to the research process by helping Mac an Ghaill construct the questionnaire that they later completed. Involving the research participants seemed to

work. As one student said to Mac an Ghaill, 'I've talked to you in a way that I've never talked to anyone and still don't, can't'.

Source: Mac an Ghaill, 1994

question

How effective do you think Mac an Ghaill's research methods were? Give reasons for your answer.

contrasts between male and female pupil subcultures.

Exaggerated femininity Research by Scott Davies (1995) in Canada indicates that girls' resistance to schooling is less aggressive and confrontational than male anti-school behaviour. Where the 'lads' display an 'exaggerated masculinity', the Canadian girls adopt an 'exaggerated femininity'.

They expressed their opposition to school by focusing on traditional gender roles. In Davies's words, 'Girls accentuate their femininity in exaggerated displays of physical maturity and hyper-concerns with "romance" on the one hand, and prioritise domestic roles such as marriage, child-rearing and household duties over schooling on the other hand'. So they wrote school off and invested their hopes in romance and future domestic roles.

You're wasting my time John Abraham's study of an English comprehensive indicates a different strategy of resistance. The girls pushed the school rules to the limit and responded to discipline by suggesting that it prevented them from getting on with their work. Teachers' objections to their behaviour were rejected as a waste of their valuable time (Abraham, 1995).

African-Caribbean male subcultures

Anti-school subcultures A number of studies have identified African-Caribbean anti-school subcultures. These subcultures are seen to develop from factors both inside and outside the school (Gaine & George, 1999).

Within schools, teachers tend to see African-Caribbean males as aggressive, challenging and disruptive. Often this is a misreading of African-Caribbean youth subculture – ways of walking, talking and dressing are sometimes interpreted by teachers as a challenge to their authority when none is intended. As a result of these misconceptions, African-Caribbean students tend to be singled out for punishment when White and Asian students are just as guilty. This leads some pupils to suspect teachers of racism. And this can lead to anti-school subcultures (Connolly, 1998).

As a result of both their class and ethnicity, a disproportionate number of African-Caribbean students are

labelled as less able and placed in lower sets. Again, this can lead to anti-school subcultures.

As noted earlier, African-Caribbean students sometimes bring Black street culture into the classroom. And this can be seen by some teachers as disruptive with its emphasis on aggressive masculinity.

A variety of subcultures Sociologists tend to focus on anti-school subcultures. In some ways, they are more interesting and colourful than conformist subcultures. Particularly in the case of African-Caribbeans, this tends to overlook the variety of responses to schooling.

In a study of African-Caribbean students in a boys-only, 11-16 comprehensive school, Tony Sewell (1997) identifies four main responses.

- **Conformists** These pupils (41%) accepted the value of education and the means to achieve educational success – behaving well and working hard. Conformists felt they couldn't succeed educationally *and* embrace the values and norms of their own Black peer group. This is a gamble, because if they don't succeed, they may lose the security which comes from being seen as a part of the Black community.
- **Innovators** These students (35%) accepted the value of education and wanted academic success but rejected the schooling process. Although anti-school, they tried to keep out of trouble. They attempted to distance themselves from the conformists and from teachers.
- **Retreatists** A small group (6%) of loners who made themselves as inconspicuous as possible. Many had special educational needs.
- **Rebels** These students (18%) rejected the school and projected an image of aggressive masculinity. Some modelled themselves on the Jamaican Yard Man, noted for his supposed physical and sexual prowess. They treated the Conformists with contempt, they were challenging and confrontational, and sometimes violent. Many saw academic qualifications as worthless – White racism would prevent them from achieving high status occupations.

Conclusion The above study is important because it shows the variety of African-Caribbean pupil subcultures rather

activity23 African-Caribbean students

Item A Working for himself

Calvin has set up in business as a 'mobile barber'. Although still at school, he says he can make up to £300 a week.

Interviewer:	How important is it for you to own your own business?
Calvin:	It is important for Black people to make money because White people don't take us seriously because we're poor.
Interviewer:	Is education important to you?
Calvin:	Not really. I know what I need to know from the street. I'll give it three years and I bet no-one will bother with school. There ain't no jobs for no-one and they don't want to give jobs to Black people.

Source: Sewell, 1997

Item B Setting a good example

Interviewer:	Do you belong to a gang?
Kelvin:	No, because my mum says I shouldn't hang around students who get into trouble. I must take my opportunity while I can.
Interviewer:	What students in this school do you avoid?
Kelvin:	They are fourth years, you can easily spot the way they walk around in groups, they are mostly Black with one or two Whites. They're wearing baseball hats and bopping (*Black stylised walk*).
Interviewer:	Don't you ever bop?
Kelvin:	Sometimes for a laugh, but it's really a kind of walk for bad people. I wouldn't walk like this in school in front of the teachers. It sets a bad example.

Source: Sewell, 1997

Item C Celebrating

Celebrating successful GCSE results

questions

1 It is important not to see the anti-school subculture as the typical response of African-Caribbean young men. Discuss with some reference to Items A and B.

2 Briefly explain why African-Caribbean girls often do well at school and college.

---

than simply focusing on anti-school subcultures.

This study also shows how pupil subcultures are influenced by what goes on inside and outside the school. For example, the Rebels drew on Black street culture, arriving at school with patterns in their hair. This was banned, despite White boys being allowed to wear ponytails. This is seen as a lack of respect and pupils responded aggressively. Teachers punished them and so an anti-school subculture developed, shaped by factors from both inside and outside the school (Sewell, 1997).

African-Caribbean female subcultures

A number of studies of African-Caribbean female pupil subcultures have produced the following picture (Mac an Ghaill, 1988, 1992; Gillborn, 1990; Mirza, 1992). These findings apply to many, though by no means all, students.

Generally, African-Caribbean girls are pro-education – they are ambitious, determined to succeed, and are aiming for high-status, well-paid occupations. However, they tend not to identify with their teachers and school. This is partly

in response to the open racism of a small number of teachers and the clumsy, well-meaning but often unhelpful 'help' offered by many teachers in response to the girls' ethnicity (Mirza, 1992) – see page 200.

African-Caribbean girls usually keep a low profile, keep their distance and avoid confrontation. In this way, they maintain their self-respect and don't have to compromise.

5.3 Teacher-pupil relationships

This section looks at the relationships between teachers and pupils. It focuses on the way teachers define, classify and evaluate pupils and how these processes affect pupils' behaviour.

Teacher expectations

A famous study conducted in 1964 by Robert Rosenthal and Leonora Jacobson, looked at the effects of teachers' expectations on pupils' behaviour. The researchers told teachers in a primary school in California that they had identified a number of pupils – the 'spurters' – as likely to make rapid progress. Unknown to the teachers, these pupils were selected at random. Yet, judging from the results of intelligence tests, the spurters made greater progress than their classmates over the next year.

Rosenthal and Jacobson concluded that their progress was due to the way they were defined. Their teachers expected more from them, conveyed this expectation to them, and the pupils acted accordingly. Yet, in Rosenthal and Jacobson's (1968) words, the only difference between the 'spurters' and their classmates was 'entirely in the minds of teachers'.

Rosenthal and Jacobson used the idea of a *self-fulfilling prophecy* to explain their results. If people are defined in a certain way, this definition includes a prediction or prophecy of their future behaviour. If others act as if the prophecy is true, then there is a tendency for it to come to pass – to fulfil itself.

The definition acts as a *label.* According to *labelling theory,* if someone is labelled as a certain kind of person, others will respond to them in terms of the label. And there is a tendency for the person to adopt that identity and act in terms of it.

Evaluation Rosenthal and Jacobson's research has been extremely influential. However, attempts to replicate (repeat) their study have produced mixed results with some suggesting that labelling was of little or no significance. However, many researchers argue that labelling is important, that the self-fulfilling prophecy is real, and that it can help to explain differences in educational attainment.

methods **12** replication

question

Using Rosenthal and Jacobson's study as an example, suggest why it is important to replicate studies.

Teachers' perceptions and social class

How do teachers assess pupils' ability? To some extent by their exam results and the reports of other teachers on pupils' progress and potential. But, as Units 2, 3 and 4 indicate, teachers' assessments can be affected by pupils' social class, ethnicity and gender. And this in turn, can affect teachers' relationships with pupils.

Class and the 'ideal pupil' An early study looking at the influence of pupils' class on teachers' perceptions was conducted in the early 1950s by the American sociologist Howard Becker. He interviewed 60 teachers from Chicago high schools and found they tended to share an image of the 'ideal pupil'.

Teachers perceived middle-class pupils as closest to this ideal, and pupils from the lower working class as furthest

from it. Those in the lowest class grouping were seen as less able, lacking motivation and difficult to control. As a result, teachers felt the best they could do was 'just try to get some basic things over to them' (Becker, 1971).

Teachers were unaware that the social class background of pupils influenced their assessments. Nor did they realise that perceptions of class also influenced the level of work they felt appropriate for pupils.

Class in a nursery school An American study of children starting nursery school shows how early and how quickly the link between class and ability can be made. By the eighth day, children had been allocated to one of three tables depending on the teacher's perception of their ability. And this perception, unknown to the teacher, was

activity **24** an ideal pupil

questions

How does this cartoon illustrate:

a) the ideas of labelling and the self-fulfilling prophecy

b) teachers' expectations of and relationships with pupils?

based on the child's class background, with working-class children being placed on the 'lower-ability' table (Rist, 1970).

Class and 'ability' Research in Britain presents a similar picture. David Gillborn and Deborah Youdell (2001) conducted research in two London secondary schools from 1995 to 1997. They discovered that teachers had a 'common sense understanding of ability'. Using this as a yardstick, they allocated pupils to different examination sets.

Working-class pupils were more likely to be seen as disruptive, as lacking in motivation and lacking in parental support. As a result, they 'face a particular problem in convincing teachers that they have "ability"'. And because of this, they are more likely to be placed in lower level sets and entered for foundation tier examinations.

As a result of making a link between so-called 'ability' and social class, teachers systematically discriminated against working-class pupils (Gillborn & Youdell, 2001).

Class and teacher-pupil relationships As the section on pupil subcultures indicated, teachers' perceptions of students can have an important effect on day-to-day relationships. Generally, teachers prefer to teach pupils they see as able and highly motivated. They place these students in higher sets and respond more favourably towards them. As a result, teacher-pupil relationships tend to be positive.

Conversely, teachers' views of students who have been defined as less able and placed in lower sets tend to be less favourable. These students may respond with resentment and hostility. And this can result in discipline problems and negative relationships between teachers and pupils.

Teachers' perceptions and ethnicity

African-Caribbeans Gillborn and Youdell's (2001) findings about working-class pupils outlined above apply equally to African-Caribbean pupils, no matter what their social class. Thus, there was a tendency to see African-Caribbean pupils as less able and more disruptive. This reflects the findings of a number of studies, particularly of African-Caribbean boys (see pages 197-198).

Primary schools As noted earlier, Cecile Wright's research in inner-city primary schools indicated that teachers tended to see African-Caribbean children, especially boys, as aggressive and disobedient. They were singled out for criticism and punishment, for which they felt picked on and unfairly treated. As a result, teacher-pupil relationships tended to be negative – abrasive and sometimes hostile (Wright, 1992).

Secondary schools Wright's findings from primary schools are mirrored in studies of secondary schools. For example, Tony Sewell's (1997) study of a boys' 11-16 comprehensive school suggested that African-Caribbean boys' were singled out for punishment. For example, they made up 32% of the student population but comprised 85% of those excluded.

Relationships with teachers were often strained and difficult. According to Sewell, teachers were sometimes frightened by the physical size and aggression of some of the more assertive pupils. There was a tendency to lump all African-Caribbean boys together. Those who conformed to the school's values and those who rebelled against them were often judged and treated in terms of the same negative stereotypes.

Sewell divided the teachers into three groups in terms of their relationships with African-Caribbean pupils.

1 **Supportive teachers** About 10% of staff. They did their best to support and guide pupils and usually established good relationships.

2 **Irritated teachers** About 60% of staff. Although they could be supportive, they felt firmer discipline was needed. They blamed the boys' street culture for many of the school's problems.

3 **Antagonistic teachers** Around 30% who were either openly racist or objected to African-Caribbean street culture – for example, hairstyles and 'bopping' (a stylised walk). As the term 'antagonistic teachers' suggests, their relationships with African-Caribbean pupils were strained and sometimes hostile.

African-Caribbean girls A study by Heidi Mirza (1992) of two south London comprehensives focused on 62 young Black women, aged 15-19. Mirza identifies five types of teacher in terms of their relationships with and attitudes towards Black students.

1 **Overt racists** A small minority who the girls avoided where possible.

2 **The Christians** Tried to be 'colour blind', claiming to see no difference between ethnic groups and the White majority, and refusing to see racism as a problem. They sometimes expected too little of the girls and gave them glowing reports for average achievement.

3 **The crusaders** Anti-racists who tried to make their lessons relevant to Black students. Because they knew little about their students, lessons tended to be confusing and irrelevant.

4 **Liberal chauvinists** Like the crusaders, they were well-meaning, but tended to underestimate their students' ability.

5 **Black teachers** A small group who showed no favouritism and were liked and respected. The girls found their help and advice extremely valuable.

In general, the young women in Mirza's research were ambitious, hard-working and determined to succeed. They rejected the negative views of their blackness, the low expectations of their potential, and the patronising and unhelpful 'help'. They tended to keep their distance and maintain a cool relationship with their teachers.

South Asian pupils Cecile Wright's study of four inner-city primary schools gives the following picture of the relationship between teachers and Asian children in the nursery units.

Asian children, especially the younger ones, were often seen as a problem, but as a problem that could be largely ignored. They received least attention, were often excluded from classroom discussions and rarely asked to answer questions. Teachers tended to assume that their command of English was insufficient for full classroom participation. Yet they also saw Asian pupils as well disciplined and highly motivated (Wright, 1992).

Paul Connolly's (1998) study of a multi-ethnic, inner-city primary school gives the following picture of the relationship between South Asian five and six-year-olds and their teachers. The children were seen as obedient, hard working and conformist. Teachers expected them to produce high quality work.

Girls were seen as models of good behaviour. When the boys did misbehave, this was seen as 'silly' rather than a challenge to the teacher's authority. As a result, they were not punished as much as African-Caribbean boys. Boys were often praised for good work, while girls tended to be left alone – teachers felt they didn't need the same help and encouragement (Connolly, 1998).

Teachers' perceptions and gender

'Girls get much less attention than boys 'cos boys make a fuss and make themselves noticed – they wanna be noticed so they make a racket' (quoted in Lees, 1986). This complaint finds support from a number of studies.

Typical boys and girls In his study of a comprehensive school, conducted in 1986, John Abraham (1995) asked teachers to describe a typical boy and a typical girl. The typical boy is not particularly bright, likes a laugh, sometimes deliberately misbehaves and always wants to be noticed. The typical girl is bright, well-behaved and hardworking, doesn't say much, can be timid, silly and gigglish.

Boys tend to be seen as behaviour problems. They were told off for misbehaviour much more often than girls. However, not all this attention was negative. Boys were asked many more questions than girls in maths and in some English classes. Maybe as a result of this imbalance, girls asked teachers far more questions than boys.

Attending to boys In *Invisible Women: The schooling scandal*, Dale Spender (1983) tape-recorded lessons given by herself and other teachers. Boys received over 60% of teachers' time – 62% in her case even though she tried to divide her time equally between boys and girls. Compared to boys, girls were 'invisible'. They tended to blend into the background, a strategy encouraged by the fact that boys often poked fun at their contributions to lessons. And teachers usually allowed boys to get away with insulting and abusive comments to girls.

Michelle Stanworth's (1983) study of A-level students and teachers in a college of further education reflects this focus on boys. Stanworth found that teachers gave more time and attention to boys, were more likely to know boys' names, and expressed more concern and interest in them.

Gender and society Some studies suggest that if only teachers got rid of their sexist attitudes then everything would be alright. Boys and girls would then be treated equally. But classroom interaction is a two-way process. It is not simply teacher led.

Jane French (1986) argues that pupils bring their own behaviour patterns to the classroom, patterns which differ for boys and girls. Basing her research on video recordings of children in infant schools, French found that boys were more mobile and active, they were more disruptive and demanded more attention. Although girls were eager and interested, they were more likely to obey rules, for example, raising their hands and waiting for permission to speak. Simply because their behaviour was more problematic, boys got more attention.

Gender behaviour is shaped by the wider society and brought into the classroom. In French's view, 'the most determined action taken within the school cannot effectively counter the influence of peer group, magazines, television and family'.

5.4 The organisation of teaching and learning

This section looks at how pupils are allocated to teaching groups, and how this shapes what they are taught and the examinations they take. It draws together and develops material from various parts of the chapter.

There are two main types of teaching groups – *ability groups* and *mixed-ability groups*.

Ability groups These are groups of pupils who are seen to have similar abilities. *Setting* and *streaming* are two ways of dividing students into ability groups. Setting allocates pupils to subject groups – a pupil could be in set 1 for English and set 3 for maths. Streaming places pupils in the same ability group for all subjects – for example, a pupil is placed in class 3 and taught at that level for all subjects.

Mixed-ability groups In these groups, pupils are randomly or intentionally mixed in terms of their perceived ability.

Setting is the most common form of ability grouping in schools in England and Wales. It becomes increasingly common as pupils approach GCSE. Streaming was typical of primary schools in the 1940s and 50s. It began to die out with the decline of the 11-plus exam. Mixed-ability teaching throughout pupils' school careers is found in only a small number of schools.

Ability groups

Supporters of ability groups make the following points.

Different abilities – different teaching Young people have different abilities. This means they need to be taught:

- At different speeds
- In different ways
- At different levels.

The most efficient way of doing this is to create teaching groups of pupils with similar abilities.

Different abilities – different tasks There's no point in giving the same tasks to pupils of different ability. For example, only some can cope with higher level maths.

Different abilities – different exams Because pupils have different abilities, they need different exams at different levels – for example, GCSE at higher and foundation levels.

Mixed-ability groups

Supporters of mixed-ability groups make the following points.

Social benefits Mixed-ability groups encourage cooperation and friendly relationships between students. For the wider society, they reduce class differences and class conflict.

Ability is not fixed In practice, most pupils remain in the same set or stream. This assumes that their ability is fixed – that it won't change. However, there is a lot of evidence which suggests that ability – as measured by tests – is not fixed.

Setting affects attainment The set or stream in which a pupil is placed can affect their attainment. For example, it can raise attainment in the top set and lower attainment in the bottom set. This is unfair – all pupils should have an equal chance.

activity25 *teachers and pupils*

Item A Social class

Teacher A: Some of the class have written to Oldham Town Council for material for the New Town project.

Teacher B: They're really bright, are they?

Teacher A: Mostly from middle-class families, well motivated.

Source: Keddie, 1973

A Head of Faculty in a secondary school explains the school's poor showing in the 'league tables'. 'We are weighted down the lower end, unfortunately, because we are a working-class school.'

Source: Gillborn & Youdell, 2001

Item C Gender

Alison: All the teachers I didn't like, they always favoured the boys and never taught us – the girls.

Researcher: How did they favour the boys in their teaching?

Alison: It was usually the boys who were noisy in the class and if a girl put her hand up they always keep her waiting and just never get round to it. And if a boy and a girl put up their hand at the same time they'd always talk to the boy. They'd never have time for the girls.

Source: Abraham, 1995

Item B Ethnicity

Samuel, a seven-year-old African-Caribbean pupil, talks to a researcher.

Samuel: I always get done and always get picked on. I want to go to a Black school with all Black teachers, it's better. I want to go to a school with just Black people.

Researcher: Why?

Samuel: Because when you go to a school with White people they give you horrible food and you're always picked on when you don't do nothing. When it's White people, they just say stop that and stop doing this.

Researcher: How does this make you feel?

Samuel: (*Long thoughtful pause*) Sad.

Source: Wright, 1992

YES, JANET, WE'LL COME TO YOU LATER ...NOW, JOHN...

questions

1 What does Item A suggest about teachers' perceptions of middle and working-class pupils?

2 Read Item B. Samuel may deserve everything he gets *or* he may not. Briefly discuss.

3 In what ways do Alison's comments in Item C reflect the findings of research?

Setting discriminates Those allocated to lower sets or streams tend to be from working-class or minority ethnic backgrounds. This can prevent them from obtaining the knowledge required for a high grade in examinations – for example, at GCSE level. In contrast, a disproportionate number of White, middle-class pupils are placed in the upper sets/streams. Ability groups discriminate in favour of the White middle-classes and against those from working-class and minority ethnic backgrounds.

Behaviour rather than ability This can be used as a basis for allocating pupils to ability groups. For example, there is evidence that African-Caribbean pupils have been placed in examination sets which were below their measured ability because their behaviour was seen as unsuitable for higher sets (see pages 189-190).

What are the effects of ability grouping?

A large number of studies have been carried out on the effects of ability grouping on pupils' attainment. Here are the conclusions of two surveys of these studies.

- 'In general, the research findings indicate that streaming and setting compared with mixed-ability teaching have no effect, either positive or negative, on average pupil achievement (across the ability range) at either primary or secondary level' (Sukhnandan & Lee, 1998).

- 'The weight of evidence from research on ability groupings within schools indicates that they have rather little impact on overall attainment' (Ireson & Hallam, 2001).

So, what's all the fuss about? It appears that allocating pupils to ability groups makes little or no difference. There

is *some* research, however, which indicates that it does make a difference. This research suggests that although the *overall* attainment level may remain the same, this is because those in the top sets do better and those in the bottom sets do worse. Possible reasons for this have already been outlined – labelling, the self-fulfilling prophecy, teacher expectations, and pupil subcultures.

Where does this leave us? The short answer is we don't really know. Research evidence on the effects of ability grouping is inconclusive – it is not clearcut.

Setting and tiered exams

League tables and setting From 1992 onwards, the test and examination results of every secondary school in the country were published. Results from primary schools were published from 1997. This led to local and national 'league tables' as schools were ranked in terms of their results. In the words of one Head of Year in a London

key terms

Ability groups Groups of pupils who are seen to have similar abilities.
Setting Allocating pupils to ability groups in terms of subjects – for example, set 1 or 2 for English.
Streaming Placing pupils in the same ability group for all subjects – for example, class 1 or 2.
Mixed-ability groups Groups in which pupils are randomly or intentionally mixed in terms of their ability.
Tiered exams Exams with two levels. The maximum possible grade varies with each tier.

summary

1. The hidden curriculum transmits messages to pupils which are not spelled out. It consists of ideas, beliefs, norms and values which are embedded in the normal routines and procedures of school life.

2. From a functionalist view, the transmission of society's core values can be seen as part of the hidden curriculum.

3. From a Marxist view, social reproduction and the transmission of ruling class ideology are part of the hidden curriculum.

4. Pupil subcultures can reflect:
   - Neighbourhood subcultures
   - Ability groupings within the school
   - A combination of both.

5. Pupil subcultures are influenced by:
   - Social class
   - Gender
   - Ethnicity.

6. The way teachers define, classify and evaluate pupils can affect pupils' behaviour and teacher-pupil relationships.

7. Teachers' evaluation of and relationship with pupils is affected by their perception of pupils' ability.

8. Teachers' views of ability are affected by pupils':
   - Social class
   - Gender
   - Ethnicity.

9. There are two main types of teaching groups – ability groups and mixed-ability groups.

10. Research indicates that in general ability groups, eg sets or streams, compared with mixed-ability groups have no significant effect on overall attainment.

11. However, there is some evidence that higher ability groups increase attainment levels and lower ability groups decrease attainment levels.

12. The pressure in schools to improve exam results has led to an increase in setting.

13. Setting for exams can have a real effect on attainment – for example, placing students in sets for GCSE foundation tiers denies them any opportunity of achieving the higher grades.

comprehensive, 'A school now lives or dies on its results' (quoted in Gillborn and Youdell, 2001).

The pressure to improve results led to an increase in setting in the belief that this would lead to improved examination performance. This belief was reinforced by government policy. The Labour Party's election manifesto of 1997 stated that:

'Children are not all of the same ability, nor do they learn at the same speed. That means "setting" children in classes to maximise progress, for the benefit of high fliers and slower learners alike.'

Tiered exams and setting GCSE exams are tiered. Pupils are allocated to sets for examination entry. For example,

they may be allocated to the higher or foundation set for English. And this is where ability grouping in terms of sets has a major effect. It actually prevents those in lower sets from having *any* chance of attaining higher grades.

GCSEs have two levels – higher and foundation. The highest grade that pupils entered for foundation level can attain is grade C. There is no way they can get an A*, A or B.

According to David Gillborn and Deborah Youdell (2001), this system discriminates against pupils in lower sets. And it discriminates against working-class and African-Caribbean pupils who are disproportionately allocated to lower sets.

activity26 setting

Item A Tony Blair

Tony Blair visits the Ridings School in Halifax

'Different children move at different speeds and have differing abilities. The modernisation of the comprehensive principle requires that all pupils are encouraged to progress as far and as fast as they are able. Grouping children according to ability is an important way of making that happen.'

Source: *The Guardian*, 08.06.96

Item B Tiered exams

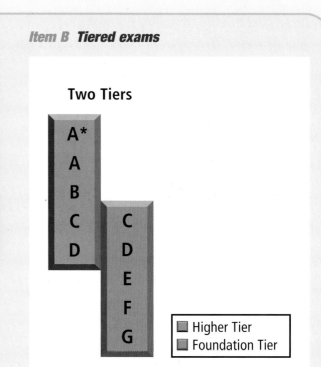

Two Tiers

A* A B C D

C D E F G

■ Higher Tier
■ Foundation Tier

Source: Gillborn & Youdell, 2001

Item C Teachers' comments

Teacher A: You don't find any behaviour problems with the top set – they've got the intelligence.

Teacher B: When you get your next year's timetable and you see that it is a top or bottom set then you get certain images. If you get a top set you tend to think that their behaviour will be better. You tend to think with a bottom set you will get more discipline problems. I look forward to teaching my top-set third year but dread my bottom-set third year. With the bottom group I go in with a stony face but I know that with the top set if I say fun's over they will stop. But if I give a bottom set rope they'll take advantage of you.

Source: Abraham, 1995

questions

1 Write a letter of no more than 100 words to Tony Blair about his views in Item A.

2 Using the information in Item B, state why setting for examinations can make a real difference to pupils' attainment.

3 How might the teachers' views in Item C affect pupils' attainment?

Unit 6 Social policy and education

keyissues

1 What have been the main policies on education from 1870 onwards?

2 What effect have they had on the role of education and students' experience of education?

6.1 The 1870 Education Act

Before 1870, public schools educated the children of upper classes, and grammar schools taught the children of the middle classes. Both types of school were fee-paying. Working-class children were limited to elementary schools run by churches and charities. Standards were often appallingly low and around one third of children received no schooling at all (Royle, 1997).

The 1870 Education Act aimed to 'fill the gaps' left by church and charity schools. It provided state-run elementary schools for five to eleven-year-olds. They charged a maximum fee of nine pence a week.

In 1880, elementary education was made compulsory up to the age of 10. It aimed to teach basic literacy and numeracy, 'morality' and Biblical knowledge. In 1891, elementary education was made free. The school leaving age was raised to 12 in 1889 and to 14 in 1918.

The 1902 Education Act This Act made local authorities responsible for secondary education. It encouraged the building of fee-paying grammar schools, many of which offered free places to children from low-income backgrounds who passed a scholarship exam.

In broad terms, up to the Second World War (1939-1945), there were three types of school for children from different class backgrounds:

- elementary schools for the working classes
- grammar schools for the middle classes
- public schools for the upper classes.

6.2 The 1944 Education Act

During and after the Second World War, there was widespread debate over the kind of society that should follow the war. Education was a central issue in this debate. It was felt that the nation was not making full use of the talents of its people, particularly those in the lower classes. Changes in the education system were seen as a way to remedy this.

The 1944 Education Act aimed to give every pupil an equal chance to develop their abilities to the full within a free system of state education. The Act reorganised the structure of education in England and Wales into three stages.

- Primary for 5 to 11-year-olds
- Secondary for 11 to 15-year-olds
- Further/higher education.

The tripartite system

The major changes were in the secondary sector. The question was, what sort of secondary education would provide equality of educational opportunity for all children from the age of 11?

Types of pupil The response owed much to the theories of psychologists and educationalists of the 1920s and 1930s. These theories were based on the idea that there were different types of pupils, with differing aptitudes and abilities, and that a child's type could be identified by intelligence testing. On the basis of this, the 1944 Act

activity27 intelligence tests

- Underline the odd one out:

    House   Igloo   Bungalow   Office   Hut

- Underline which of these is not a famous composer:

    ZOTRAM   SATSURS   REVID   MALESO

- Insert the word missing from the brackets:

    Fee (Tip) End
    Dance (....) Sphere

- Underline the odd one out:

- Draw the next one in the sequence:

questions

1 Answer the test questions.

2 What are the problems of forecasting children's academic ability on the basis of intelligence tests?

introduced a national test for 11-year-olds – the 11-plus test – as a means of allocating children to one of three types of secondary school.

Types of school The three types of secondary school were grammar schools, technical schools and secondary modern schools. This became known as the *tripartite system* of secondary education.

Grammar schools were intended for pupils defined as bright and academic – those whose abilities lay in reasoning and solving logical problems. They were to study classics, mathematics, science and other 'difficult' subjects in preparation for GCE O and A-level exams. Around 20% of the school population went to grammar schools. Technical schools were intended for children with an aptitude for technical subjects. These schools emphasised vocational training and technical skills and were attended by around 5% of the school population. Most children went to secondary modern schools. These children were seen as less academic and more practical. They were given a basic education with little opportunity to take external examinations until CSEs – a lower level exam – were introduced in the 1960s.

The tripartite system was intended to provide separate but equal types of schooling geared to the particular talents of the child. The Act stated that each type of school should have equal status, or 'parity of esteem', with buildings, equipment and staffing being of similar quality. However, these ideals did not work in practice.

Criticisms of the tripartite system

The 11-plus was unreliable It became increasingly clear that a young person's educational future could not be predicted by an IQ test at 11. When secondary modern pupils were finally allowed to take GCE O levels, some were getting better results than many grammar school pupils.

The selection process was unfair and wasteful Selecting pupils at 11 was unfair – it denied many the opportunity of continuing their education beyond 15. It was also a waste of ability, both for the student and for the nation.

No parity of esteem Secondary modern schools were seen as second-rate by parents, pupils and employers. Grammar schools always had higher status because they specialised in academic subjects which led to well-paid, high-status occupations. As a result, there was no parity of esteem – no equality of status – between the schools in the tripartite system.

Three-quarters of students 'failed' For most pupils, the alternatives at age 11 were a grammar or secondary modern school. There were relatively few technical schools. The 11-plus was intended as a selection device for allocating pupils to appropriate schools. It was soon seen as a pass/fail exam. Three-quarters of the school population 'failed' and went to secondary modern schools. And with this 'failure' came the danger of labelling and the self-fulfilling prophecy.

Social class divisions One of the main aims of the 1944 Act was to widen educational opportunities for working-class pupils. But the class divide in education remained. Research indicates that two-thirds of boys from middle-class backgrounds went to grammar schools compared to only a quarter of boys from working-class backgrounds (Halsey et al., 1980).

6.3 The comprehensive system

Educational policy in the 1960s was directed by social democratic ideas (see pages 167-168). From a social democratic perspective, everybody should have an equal chance to succeed. Clearly, the tripartite system was not providing equality of educational opportunity.

This was seen as both wrong and inefficient. A well-educated workforce leads to economic growth. The tripartite system wasted talent. This reduced people's contribution to the economy, which meant that everybody suffers.

Three into one The tripartite system had provided three schools of unequal quality and unequal status. Why not replace them with a single school for everyone? This simple solution would end inequality between schools. It promised equal opportunities for all young people to develop their talents and abilities in schools of equal status – in *comprehensive schools*.

In a comprehensive system, young people of all abilities and from all social backgrounds attend the same type of school (except for those in private education). They are provided with the same opportunities to obtain qualifications and training. There is no entrance exam, no selection at age 11.

The development of comprehensives

In 1965, the newly elected Labour government sent a circular to local authorities requesting them to submit plans to reorganise secondary education along comprehensive lines. In 1970, when the Labour government was defeated, around one-third of young people in secondary education were attending comprehensive schools.

The Labour Party returned to power in 1974 and passed legislation requiring local authorities to go comprehensive. By the end of its period in office (May, 1979), over 80% of secondary school pupils attended comprehensives.

The limitations of comprehensives

There was a lot of hope riding on comprehensives. To some extent, this hope was justified. But it was too much to expect comprehensives to compensate for the inequalities in the wider society and provide equal opportunities for all.

Examination results Critics of the comprehensive system claimed it would lower educational standards. They believed that the 'high academic standards' of the grammar schools would be diluted in the comprehensives. Table 2

activity28 *successes and failures*

Item A **Failing**

As a youngster, I was a product of the 11-plus examination. In 1955, I failed the exam and still today remember the trauma, grief and unhappiness it caused. I can remember how, as 11-year-olds, we were called into the school hall and a list was read out of who had passed the exam. When my name was not read out, I was devastated. I can remember running out of the school gates, home. Because I had failed the 11-plus, my mother was distraught and I can recall the feeling of failure. It took many years to get over the trauma. I was fortunate to go to a secondary modern school that took GCEs and it was not until I had successfully passed those exams that the feeling of failure partially disappeared.

Source: *The Guardian*, 22.01.96

Item B **Pigeon-holed**

questions

1 Why did Gerald Steinberg feel a failure?

2 What does the cartoon suggest about the tripartite system?

---

suggests that they were wrong. Educational standards were higher in 1983, when less than 4% of secondary school pupils went to grammar schools, than in 1969, when 21% went to grammar schools.

Social class divisions Supporters of comprehensive education hoped that class differences in educational attainment would be reduced by the comprehensive

Table 2 **Highest qualifications of school leavers**

	1969 (%)	1983 (%)
One or more A levels	12	14
5 or more O levels (A-C grades)	7	10
1 to 4 O levels (A-C grades)	18	28
1 or more O levels (D-E grades)	37	52
No qualifications	50	10

Source: *Social Trends*, 1972 and 1986, Office for National Statistics

system. In particular, they hoped that the examination results of working-class pupils would improve compared to those of middle-class pupils. Although the educational qualifications of *all* school leavers improved, class differences remained largely unchanged. In other words, examination results in general got better but the gap between top and bottom stayed more or less the same (Ferri et al., 2003).

Breaking down class barriers Many of those who supported the comprehensive system looked forward to schools attended by pupils from across the entire social class spectrum. They hoped that this social mix would help to break down class barriers. However, most comprehensives recruit from a local catchment area. Often, these areas are largely middle class or working class. As a result, many comprehensives are primarily 'single class', so tending to reinforce rather than break down existing class divisions.

Streaming and setting Many comprehensives divide pupils into ability groups. A disproportionate number of middle-class pupils are placed in the top streams and sets and a disproportionate number of working-class pupils in the bottom streams and sets. Some see this as another form of selection, not unlike the tripartite system.

6.4 Conservative educational policy, 1979-1997

In May 1979, the Conservative Party, led by former Education Minister Margaret Thatcher, were elected. Their aims were to:

- Develop an educational system which met the needs of industry
- Raise standards throughout Britain's schools and colleges.

The new vocationalism

Until the 1970s, vocational training – training for work – was seen as the responsibility of employers. They would teach new recruits the skills needed in the workplace. This view began to change with the rise in youth unemployment in the 1970s. Schools, it was argued, were producing young people who lacked the skills required by industry. And industry in turn was suffering from a skills shortage. This line of argument led to the *new vocationalism* – direct government involvement in youth training.

Training schemes Conservative governments introduced a number of training schemes for young people. For example, the Youth Training Scheme (YTS), started in 1983, was a one-year, work-based training scheme for school leavers. It was replaced by Youth Training (YT) in 1990. In addition to workplace training, YT offered young people the chance to take vocational qualifications.

Vocational qualifications The development of training schemes was accompanied by new vocational qualifications. The National Council for Vocational Qualifications, set up in 1986, established National Vocational Qualifications (NVQs) for a range of specific occupations.

More general vocational qualifications were also introduced. General National Vocational Qualifications (GNVQs) allowed young people to keep their options open rather than specialise in a particular occupation. GNVQs assessed skills, knowledge and understanding in broad occupational areas such as Art and Design, Business, Health and Social Care, Manufacturing, and Leisure and Tourism. They have now been replaced by Vocational GCSEs and Vocational A levels.

activity29 class in the comprehensive

question

What problems of comprehensive schools are illustrated by this cartoon?

The new vocationalism – evaluation

Jobs not training are needed A number of critics argued that youth unemployment was due to a lack of jobs, not to a lack of skills. In other words, the problem was with the economy, not with young people and their education (Finn, 1987).

Quality and relevance of training According to Phil Cohen (1984), many trainees spent most of their time 'running errands' and 'being useful'. Few received any real occupational training, most were a source of cheap labour.

Not all youth training fitted this description. The better schemes and employers offered effective training in skills that were in demand in the labour market.

A second-best option Middle-class students usually avoided Youth Training, seeing it as a second-best option to staying on at school or college. In practice, YT students tended to be young people from working-class backgrounds who couldn't get a job. It has been argued that YT was training for the less able which channelled them into low status, low paid occupations (Lee et al., 1990).

Status of vocational qualifications Traditionally, vocational qualifications have been seen as inferior to GCSEs and A levels. The introduction of NVQs and GNVQs may have improved their status. Vocational GCSEs and Vocational A levels may continue this improvement.

Raising standards

The first major aim of Margaret Thatcher's Conservative government was to make education more responsive to the needs of industry. The second major aim was to raise standards throughout Britain's schools and colleges.

Where Labour had been influenced by social democratic ideas, Conservative governments were influenced by neoliberal/New Right perspectives (see pages 168-170). In line with neoliberal/New Right ideas, the aim was to create an education market-place in which the providers – schools and colleges – competed, and the consumers – parents and students – made choices. This would drive up standards since the consumers would choose successful schools and colleges, leaving unsuccessful institutions to go out of business.

To put these ideas into practice, the Conservatives gave schools more freedom and self-government in some areas and increased government control in other areas. This can be seen clearly from the Education Reform Act.

activity30 youth training

Item A Training at the bank

Each year about 20 young people, many with no qualifications, are recruited from the inner-city area to train under the Bank of England's clerical youth training scheme.

18-year-old Elton Thomas is in his second year, and came in without any qualifications. However, he's working towards achieving an NVQ this summer.

'I use computers a lot at the moment. I spend a lot of time on the phone chasing statements and invoices. I've worked in four different offices and gained a variety of experience. It's great working here. I really like wearing a suit to work and looking sharp. I'm in the bank's football team. We play other banks and companies and win a few and lose a few!'

Source: Employment Department Group and BBC Radio One, 1991

Trainees at the Bank of England

Item B Cheap labour

Well, the thing is, my son's education was all right until he left school and he'd got no job to go to. So he went to these job creation schemes, which is the biggest con there ever was. All it was was cheap labour, I mean, I saw all this because the firm I worked for actually got kids in and they were working as hard, if not harder, than the men that earned the money, but they never got paid for it. He was a damn good worker, keen to learn, but as soon as the training period was over, they got rid of him and started a new one, because it was cheap labour.

Source: McKenzie, 2001

The quality of youth training depends on who's providing the training. Briefly discuss with reference to Items A and B.

The Education Reform Act

The 1988 Education Reform Act is the most important and far reaching educational legislation since the 1944 Education Act. It established a national curriculum for all state schools in England and Wales and a national system of testing and assessment. It reduced the role of local education authorities by giving greater control to individual schools and their governing bodies. It established city technology colleges and grant maintained schools, both independent of local authority control.

Competition and choice Part of the thinking behind the Education Reform Act can be seen from a government circular entitled Our Children's Education: The Updated Parent's Charter (Department of Education, 1994). It tells parents that, 'Your choice of school directly affects that school's budget; every extra pupil means extra money for the school'. And 'the right to choose will encourage schools to aim for the highest possible standards'. From this point of view, parental choice means that schools will compete in order to attract pupils (and money) and in the process standards of education will rise.

Diversity and choice Will parents have a real choice? Aren't all comprehensives much of a muchness? In an attempt to offer real choice, the Education Reform Act encouraged diversity. It introduced two new types of school.

- **Grant maintained schools** are created when sufficient parents vote to withdraw the school from local authority control. They are financed directly by central government. They are self-governing with governors and headteachers taking decisions about the employment of staff, the curriculum, the provision of goods and services and the way pupils are selected for entry. The idea was to free schools to specialise – for example, in particular subjects or particular types of pupils such as the 'more academically able'. In this way, the choice for parents was seen to be widened.

- **City technology colleges** for 11 to 18-year-olds are financed by central government and private sector sponsorship. Located mainly in inner-city areas, they teach the National Curriculum while concentrating on maths, science and technology.

In the 1990s, the Conservatives introduced two further types of schools – schools specialising in either languages or technology. They were called colleges to indicate their prestige and importance.

By 1996, there were 1,100 grant maintained schools, including 660 secondary schools, accounting for one in five of all secondary students. There were 15 city technology colleges, 30 language colleges and 151 new technology colleges (Chitty, 2002).

The National Curriculum The Education Reform Act introduced the National Curriculum. For the first time in the history of state education, the government told teachers in England and Wales exactly what to teach. From the age of 5 to 16, all pupils in state schools must study three *core subjects* – English, maths and science – and seven foundation subjects. Pupils were tested in the core subjects by Standard Assessment Tasks (SATs – now renamed National Tests) at the ages of 7, 11 and 14. SATs results provided parents with information on which to judge the performance of schools.

League tables In 1992, all state secondary schools were required to publish the results of their SATs, GCSEs and A levels. In 1997, primary schools had to publish their SATs results. Local and national 'league tables' of schools were based on these results. They provided parents with information on which to base their choice of school. They were also intended to encourage competition between schools by spurring headteachers and staff to improve their position in the league.

Evaluation of Conservative policy

Choice Do parents have a real choice of schools? Popular schools are likely to be full, or to have only limited places. Where places are available, it is the articulate middle-class parents with their social and cultural capital who tend to obtain them. And in this situation, schools have more choice than parents – they are likely to choose middle-class pupils to maintain their position in the league tables. As a result, what choice exists is not equal – it operates on class lines and favours the middle class (Ball, 2003; Smith & Noble, 1995).

League tables Parents often look closely at examination results when assessing and choosing schools. But a simple league table which ranks schools in terms of results can be very misleading. There is evidence that some of the best schools in Britain do poorly on this kind of league table. These schools, often in run-down inner-city areas, are achieving extremely good results given the social background of their pupils. They may be doing a far better job than schools well above them in the league table (see Activity 32).

Selection There is some evidence of selection on academic and/or social grounds in popular schools. They may be reluctant to accept pupils with special needs, low academic ability or so-called behaviour problems, seeing them as a threat to their standing in the league tables. In the early 1990s, around one-third of grant maintained schools selected pupils on the basis of interviews with parents and/or pupils and reports from previous schools (Bush et al., 1993).

Critics have seen this as a means of 'back door selection'. They see a return of the grammar school in the guise of the grant maintained secondary school. And there will be no need for a selection process like the 11-plus. The government will have provided the evidence with SATs at age 11.

Marketing schools Increased competition has led to schools using a variety of marketing strategies to present

activity31 the education market-place

question

How does this cartoon illustrate the aims of the Education Reform Act?

themselves in an attractive and positive light. These include glossy brochures, mission statements, open evenings and adverts in the local press. The resources devoted to marketing mean that less money is available to spend on things which directly benefit pupils – for example, teachers and textbooks (Gewirtz et al., 1995).

However, this emphasis on marketing has its benefits. Schools now give more attention to academic standards, to pastoral care, to discipline, and the state of their buildings. In the words of one researcher, schools have had to 'address their academic weaknesses and capitalise on their strengths' (Coffey, 2001).

6.5 Labour educational policy, 1997-2008

During the election campaign of 1997, Tony Blair proclaimed that Labour's top three priorities were 'education, education, education'. Labour was elected in May 1997 with surprisingly little in the way of new policies for education. Some of their policies were influenced by neoliberal/New Right perspectives, others by social democratic ideas.

Diversity and choice

In many ways the Labour government continued the Conservatives' policies of diversity and choice which were based on neoliberal/New Right thinking.

Modernisation and comprehensives Tony Blair rejected what he called the 'one-size-fits-all' idea of comprehensive education. He saw the existing comprehensive system as providing the same type of school for everyone. Past Labour governments had seen this uniformity and standardisation as a way of providing equal opportunities for all. Labour now rejected this view, arguing that schools should reflect the diversity of young people – their particular aptitudes and talents, and their varying abilities.

Comprehensives should be 'modernised'. And part of this process involved more specialist schools.

Specialist schools In May 1997, Labour inherited 196 specialist schools from the Conservatives. By late 2002, they had almost 1000 in place. By 2003, sports, arts, business and enterprise, engineering, maths and computing, music, and humanities colleges had been added to the Conservatives' specialist schools. By 2007, there were over 2,500 specialist schools – over 75% of all secondary schools in England (www.standards.dfes.gov.uk /specialistschools, 2007).

The idea of specialist schools is to provide centres of excellence and expertise in particular subject areas. They are intended to raise standards of teaching and learning in these subjects. They can select up to 10% of their pupils, choosing those who have an aptitude for their specialist subject.

Diversity within schools The diversity of aptitude and ability must also be reflected *within* schools. Tony Blair rejected mixed-ability groups, arguing that ability grouping is the best way of making sure that *all* pupils progress as far and fast as they can. In his view, this was essential for the modernisation of comprehensive schools.

Evaluation Many of the criticisms of Conservative policy also apply to Labour's policy of diversity and choice – see pages 209 and 210-211. Choice usually means limited places and selection at the more popular schools. In this situation, the middle class with their cultural and social capital have the advantage.

Standards have risen in many specialist schools. This may be due to specialisation, but standards have often risen in subjects outside the school's specialist area. Rising standards may be due to the additional government funding given to specialist schools and/or to a growing middle-class intake (Select Committee on Education and Skills, 2005).

Competition and league tables

Labour accepted the neoliberal/New Right view that competition between schools would raise standards. And they accepted school league tables as a means for parents to assess a school's performance. In 2006, an additional table based on social factors was introduced. This measure indicates what pupils might be expected to achieve given their social background. It means that schools in low-income areas with average exam results might score highly because their results are better than expected in view of the background of their students (Crace, 2006).

Evaluation Despite alternative league tables, parents tend to accept the original measure – exam results. This encourages schools to prioritise results and 'teach to the test' rather than improving understanding and developing a wide range of talents (Thrupp & Hursh, 2006).

Equality of opportunity

Part of Labour's education policy was based on social democratic views, with an emphasis on equality of opportunity.

Within three months of their election, in 1997 the new Labour government published a policy document entitled *Excellence in Schools* (DfEE, 1997). It stated that they intended 'to overcome economic and social disadvantage and to make equality of opportunity a reality'. This involved finding new ways of motivating young people in deprived inner-city areas and doing something about 'underachieving schools'. New types of schools and new programmes were developed for this purpose.

Sure Start This programme is aimed mainly at pre-school children and their families in disadvantaged areas of England. It assumes that the early years are vital to a child's future and looks to improve their health, education and job prospects. It provides home visits, play centres and financial help for childcare. The first Sure Start local programmes were set up in 1999. By 2003, there were over 500 programmes involving around 300,000 children.

Evaluation Sure Start is difficult to evaluate because each local programme is different and only short-term results are available. Its effects may only become apparent in early adulthood. The National Evaluation of Sure Start (2005) examined 150 local programmes and found that, after three years, they had little impact on parents and children. However, it is too early to assess their effect on children's education in the school system (Anning, 2006).

activity 32 an alternative league table

This league table refers to the top 20 local education authorities in England. The figures in brackets are taken from the 'official' league table based on exam results from secondary schools. The 'unofficial' placings from 1 to 20 are based on 'value-added scores'. These scores look at pupils' attainment levels when they first arrive at secondary school then see how much schools improve on these levels – that is, how much value is added.

The results show that schools can – and do – make an enormous difference. There are local authorities with a high proportion of very poor children who do badly in both tables. But the most significant finding is the number of inner-city authorities, languishing in the lower regions of the Department for Education table, who do exceedingly well in the new table.

Source: *The Observer*, 20.3.1994

1	Wirral	(31)	11	Bolton	(42)
2	Camden	(57)	12	Hackney	(102)
3	Barnet	(3)	13	W. Sussex	(2)
4	Kingston	(1)	14	E. Sussex	(17)
5	Sutton	(9)	15	Dorset	(12)
6	Bromley	(4)	16	Wigan	(30)
7	Liverpool	(98)	17	Harrow	(7)
8	Tower Hamlets	(105)	18	Cheshire	(18)
9	Lambeth	(100)	19	Redbridge	(23)
10	Bucks	(5)	20	Herts	(10)

question

Why is a league table based on value-added scores important?

activity33 diversity and choice

Item A Specialist schools

'Specialist schools and colleges will have a key contribution to make in raising standards and delivering excellence in schools. They will help thousands of young people to learn new skills and progress into employment, further training and higher education, according to their individual abilities, aptitudes and ambitions.'

Former Education Minister Estelle Morris quoted in Chitty, 2002

Item B Diversity and inequality

In a class-divided and competitive society, specialisms are not equal: they rapidly become ranked in a hierarchy of status.

A divided secondary system, with its hierarchy of schools firmly established, will continue to work to the advantage of the powerful, the influential and the articulate; while large numbers of children find themselves in less favoured institutions which attract the sort of criticisms once levelled at the secondary modern schools.

Source: Chitty, 1997

questions

1 How does the cartoon illustrate Labour's policy of diversity and choice?

2 With some reference to Item B, discuss how diversity can lead to inequality of educational opportunity.

Education Action Zones (EAZs) These zones were located in deprived urban areas with low levels of educational attainment. By April 2003 there were 72 EAZs, each run by an Action Forum made up of parents, representatives from local schools and businesses and from local and national government. Each zone was given £1 million to spend. Teachers and schools were encouraged to be flexible and innovative – for example, running Saturday classes and a variety of work-related courses.

Evaluation Education Action Zones ploughed money and energy into disadvantaged areas, they encouraged innovation, and brought together expertise from local and national government. An Ofsted report found some improvement at Key Stage 1 in EAZ areas, but no change at Key Stage 3 or GCSE (McKnight et al., 2005). Like similar experiments in the 1960s, such as Educational Priority

Areas, EAZs may fail to make up for the economic and social disadvantages of pupils from low-income, inner-city areas (Kirton, 1998).

Excellence in Cities (EiC) This programme steadily replaced Education Action Zones. It aimed to raise standards in low-income inner-city areas by providing:

- Resources to stretch the most able pupils
- Learning mentors to support and work with pupils
- City learning centres with high quality ICT facilities
- Encouragement for schools to specialise and network with neighbouring schools
- Learning support units within schools for pupils at risk of exclusion.

Evaluation An Ofsted report (2005) praised Excellence in Cities for raising standards at Key Stage 3 and 4. In EiC areas, the percentage of pupils achieving five or more A*-C grades at GCSE increased by around 11 percentage points from 39.8% in 2001 to 50.6% in 2005. This compares to around 5 percentage points in non-EiC schools – from 52.2% in 2001 to 57.5% in 2005 (www.standards.dfes.gov.uk/sie/eic). The EiC programme ended in April 2006. All EiC funding is now paid to schools as part of their overall School Development Grant.

Academies The aim of academies is to raise achievement in deprived areas by replacing poorly performing secondary schools or by providing new school places where they are needed. They are sponsored by individuals, businesses, faiths, charities and city education authorities. Sponsors contribute around £2 million and central government around £25 million for each new academy. The first three academies were opened in 2002, by 2006 there were 46, with a total of 200 planned for 2010 (National Audit Office, 2007).

Evaluation In terms of GCSE results, academies are doing well. In most cases, they have achieved better results than the schools they replaced, they have improved at a faster rate than other secondary schools, and in terms of value added measures they are doing better than the average for all secondary schools. However, their performance in 16-19 educations is well below the national average (National Audit Office, 2007).

Critics claim that the improvement at GCSE is largely due to extra money pumped in by central government and to academies taking fewer pupils with special needs or behavioural problems (Tomlinson, 2005).

methods 13
measurement

question

Why is it difficult to measure the effects of education policy? Refer to Sure Start and academies in your answer.

key terms

Sure Start Programmes designed to give pre-school children in low-income areas a head start in the school system.

Education Action Zones (EAZs) Programmes designed to raise teaching standards and attainment levels in schools in deprived inner-city areas

Excellence in Cities (EiC) Replaced EAZs. Same aims, but more targeted programmes.

Academies A new type of school designed to raise standards in low-income urban areas by replacing poorly performing secondary schools. Academies are financed by central government and sponsors – individuals, businesses, faiths, charities and city education authorities.

Further and higher education (FE and HE) Labour has attempted to reduce inequality of educational opportunity by increasing 1) the number of students and 2) the proportion of working-class students in FE and HE. It has succeeded in increasing numbers. For example, the number of full-time students in higher education in the UK increased from 748,000 in 1990/91 to 1,456,000 in 2004/05 (*Social Trends*, 2007).

However, Labour has failed to increase the *proportion* of working-class students in FE and HE. In fact, the opposite has happened. It is the middle classes who have gained most from the expansion of places. For example, in Britain in 2001, 72% of young people from professional backgrounds were in HE compared with 55% in 1991 – a gain of 24 percentage points. At the other end of the scale, 15% of young people from unskilled manual backgrounds were in HE in 2001, compared with 6% in 1991 – a gain of only 9 percentage points (Galindo – Rueda et al., 2004). This trend has since continued.

Loans and tuition fees The widening class gap in higher education may have something to do with the replacement of grants by student loans and the introduction of tuition fees in 1998. A survey of nearly 2000 prospective higher education students found that fear of debt was greatest among students from low-income backgrounds. And students who were afraid of debt were four times less likely to go on to higher education (Callender & Jackson, 2004).

Vocational education and training

Aims Labour's policies for vocational education have focused on two main areas.

- First, to provide the training needed for a high wage/high skill economy, so that the UK can compete successfully in world markets.
- Second, to reduce unemployment, particularly for young people (Strathdee, 2003).

New qualifications GNVQs were replaced by Vocational GCSEs and Vocational A levels. Part of the reason for this change was to raise the status of vocational qualifications

activity34 grants not fees

National Union of Students demonstrate against tuition fees and the student loans scheme.

question

Would you support this demonstration? Refer to the conclusion on page 216 in your answer.

to the level of academic qualifications.

National Vocational Qualifications (NVQs) were extended. They now ranged from an Initial Award – gained after a 26 week introductory training period – to a Level 5 award which is equivalent to a degree. The aim of NVQs is to raise skill levels in a wide range of jobs.

Evaluation NVQs have yet to prove themselves. Surveys suggest that about two-thirds of employers see little value in these qualifications. The government may have overestimated the demand for highly-skilled workers. In the 1990s, the fastest growing job was care assistant in hospitals and nursing homes, not a particularly high-skilled job (Strathdee, 2003).

The New Deal Labour introduced the New Deal in 1998. It offered education and training for young people between the ages of 18 and 24 who had been out of work for more than six months. It was later extended to older people.

The New Deal provided personal advisors who offered direction and support to the unemployed, guiding them through the various options – academic courses, vocational training, self-employment, or voluntary work.

Evaluation The New Deal got off to a good start. Two years into the scheme, Tony Blair claimed that it had helped more than 250,000 young people find jobs. And it helped others move into higher education. Critics question this optimistic view. Some argue that youth unemployment was falling steadily when the New Deal was introduced and further reductions were simply a continuation of this trend. Others see the New Deal as moderately successful, resulting in a fall in youth unemployment of around 17,000 a year (Van Reenen, 2004).

Globalisation and equal opportunity

Prime Minister Gordon Brown sees the various aspects of Labour's education policy working together (Brown, 2008). In his words, 'The challenge this century is the global skills race and that is why we need to push ahead faster with our reforms to extend education opportunities for all'. It is crucial for Britain to be able to compete successfully in the global economy. This means developing the talents of and teaching high level skills to *all* young people.

According to Gordon Brown, 'A precondition for unleashing talent is to eradicate failure across our education system'. Academies have a major part to play as 'a means of advancing opportunity for all' and as 'engines in disadvantaged areas for social mobility and social justice'.

Universities will be encouraged to sponsor academies and to become directly involved with secondary education. This is the next step in widening access to higher education for working-class students. These policies will contribute to the twin goals of social justice and success in the global skills race (Brown, 2008).

Conclusion

Government policies come and go, but one thing stays the same – the middle class gains! Whether it's the tripartite system, the comprehensive system or specialist schools, the attainment gap between the middle and working classes shows little change. And in higher education, the gap has widened. A longitudinal study has followed the lives of two groups of British children, one born in 1958 and the other in 1970 (Ferri et al., 2003). It shows that the chances of a young middle-class person gaining a degree have grown at a higher rate than those of a young working-class person. And this is despite the rapid expansion in university places from the 1980s onwards.

Many sociologists believe that changes in the educational system are unlikely to reduce the attainment gap between the middle and working classes. They argue that a reduction in inequality in the wider society is necessary to reduce inequality of educational opportunity and close the class attainment gap.

methods 14
longitudinal studies

question

Why are longitudinal studies important for studying the effects of government education policy?

summary

1. The 1870 Education Act provided the first state-run schools.

2. The 1944 Education Act set up the tripartite system of secondary education – grammar, technical and secondary modern schools.

3. The tripartite system provided schools of unequal status and unequal quality. Middle-class pupils tended to go to high-status grammar schools, working-class pupils to low-status secondary modern schools.

4. The comprehensive system was designed to provide equality of opportunity by replacing the tripartite system with a single type of school for all young people.

5. Class differences in attainment remained, partly because pupils were placed in streams or sets with a disproportionate number of middle-class pupils in higher ability groups and working-class pupils in lower ability groups.

6. Conservative governments from 1979 to 1997 introduced work-related training schemes and vocational qualifications.

7. The Education Reform Act of 1988 aimed to provide competition between schools, a variety of schools, and choice for parents. In theory, standards would rise as parents chose successful schools, while failing schools would go out of business.

8. Choice usually meant limited places and selection at the more popular schools. In this situation, the middle class with their cultural and social capital have the advantage.

9. The National Curriculum, introduced in 1988, was assessed by SATs in its core subjects. The results of these tests provided parents with information to judge the performance of schools.

10. Labour's education policy was influenced by both neoliberal/New Right and social democratic perspectives.

11. Labour continued the Conservatives' policy of diversity and choice in a competitive educational market-place. Standard comprehensives were steadily replaced by specialist schools.

12. Labour introduced a range of measures designed to raise standards in low-income, inner-city areas. These included Sure Start, Education Action Zones, Excellence in Cities and academies.

13. The number of places in higher education was rapidly expanded by Labour. The middle class gained most from this expansion.

14. The New Deal offered education and training for young people who had been out of work for over six months.

15. It is difficult to measure the effects of Labour's education policy. In some cases, it is too early to make a judgement. In other cases, the evidence can be interpreted in different ways. One thing is clear – class differences in educational attainment have remained largely unchanged.

References

Abbott, D. (2000). Identity and new masculinities. *Sociology Review, 10,* 1.

Abraham, J. (1995). *Divide and school: Gender and class dynamics in comprehensive education.* London: Falmer.

Acheson, D. (1998). *Inequalities in Health Report.* London: HMSO

Adler, P. & Adler, P. (1998). *Peer Power.* New Jersey: Rutgers University Press.

Allan, G. & Crow, G. (2001). *Families, households and society.* Basingstoke: Palgrave.

Allan, G. (1985). *Family life.* Oxford: Blackwell.

Allen, I. & Dowling, S.B. (1999). Teenage mothers: Decisions and outcomes. In S. McRae (Ed.), *Changing Britain: Families and households in the 1990s.* Oxford: Oxford University Press.

Alexander, C. (1996). *The art of being Black.* Oxford: Clarendon Press.

Alexander, C. (2002). Beyond Black. *Ethnic and Racial Studies.* July

Alibhai-Brown, Y. (1997) Bring England in from the cold. *New Statesman,* 11 July

Althusser, L. (1972). Ideology and ideological state apparatus: Notes towards an investigation. In B.R. Cosin (Ed.), *Education, structure and society.* Harmondsworth: Penguin.

Anderson, M. (1971). Family, household and the industrial revolution. In M. Anderson (Ed.), *Sociology of the family.* Harmondsworth: Penguin.

Anning, A. (2006). Early Years Education: Mixed Messages and Conflicts in D. Kassom, H. Mufti & J. Robinson (Ed.) *Educational Studies: Issues and Cultural Perspectives.* Maidenhead: Open University Press.

Appleyard, D. (2002). *Out of love.* London: Black Swan.

Arber, S. (1993). Designing samples. In N. Gilbert (Ed.), *Researching social life.* London: Sage.

Archer, J. & Lloyd, B. (1985) *Sex and Gender.* Cambridge: Cambridge University Press.

Archer, L. (2006). Why are British-Chinese students so successful in British schools? *Social Science Teacher, 36,* 1, 16-19.

Ariès, P. (1962). *Centuries of childhood.* London: Jonathan Cape.

Atkinson, J.M. (1978). *Discovering suicide.* London: Macmillan.

Atkinson, R. (2006). I hoped our baby would be deaf. *Society Guardian,* 21 March.

Back, L. (1996). *New Ethnicities and Urban Culture.* London: UCL Press.

Ball, S.J. (1981). *Beachside Comprehensive.* Cambridge: Cambridge University Press.

Ball, S.J. (2003). *Class strategies and the education market: The middle classes and social advantage.* London: RoutledgeFalmer.

Ballantine, J. & Spade, J. (2001). *Schools and society.* Belmont: Wadsworth.

Ballard, R. (Ed.) (1994). *Desh pradesh.* London: Hurst & Co.

Bandura, A. (1973). *Aggression: A social learning analysis.* Englewood Cliffs, NJ: Prentice Hall.

Barker, E. (1984). *The making of a Moonie.* Oxford: Blackwell.

Bartholomew, J.(1998). Has shopping become the new religion? *Daily Mail ,* 15 September.

Bauman, Z.(2001). *Community.* Cambridge: Polity Press.

Baxter, J. & Western, M. (1998). Satisfaction with housework: Examining the paradox. *Sociology, 32,* 101-120.

Beattie, J. (1964). *Other cultures: Aims, methods and achievements in social anthropology.* London: Routledge & Kegan Paul.

Beck, U. (1992). *Risk society: Towards a new modernity.* London: Sage.

Beck, U. (1998). The cosmopolitan manifesto. *New Statesman,* 20 March

Beck, U. & Beck-Gernsheim, E. (1995). *The normal chaos of love.* Cambridge: Polity Press.

Beck, U. & Beck-Gernsheim, E. (2001). *Individualisation.* London: Sage.

Becker, H.S. (1971). Social-class variations in teacher-pupil relationship. In B.R. Cosin, I.R. Dale, G.M. Esland & D.F. Swift (Eds.), *School and society.* London: Routledge.

Beck-Gernsheim, E. (2002). *Reinventing the family.* Cambridge: Polity.

Bedell, G. (2002). One step beyond. *OM,* October 6.

Bennett, A. (2001). *Cultures of popular music.* Buckingham: Open University Press.

Benston, M. (1972). The political economy of women's liberation. In N. Glazer-Malbin & H. Y. Waehrer (Eds.), *Woman in a man-made world.* Chicago: Rand McNally.

Beresford, P., Green, D., Lister, R. & Woodard, K. (1999). *Poverty first hand: Poor people speak for themselves.* London: CPAG.

Berger, P. (1971). *Looking for America.* New Jersey: Prentice Hall.

Bernades, J. (1997). *Family studies: An introduction.* London: Routledge.

Bernstein, B. (1973). *Class, codes and control.* London: Paladin.

Berthoud, R. & Beishon, S. (1997). People, families and households, In Modood, T. et al. (Eds.), *Ethnic minorities in Britain: Diversity and disadvantage.* London: Policy Studies Institute.

Berthoud, R., McKay, S. & Rowlingson, K. (1999). Becoming a single mother. In S. McRae (Ed.), *Changing Britain: Families and households in the 1990s.* Oxford: Oxford University Press.

Billig, M. (1995). *Banal nationalism.* London: Sage.

Blackmore, S. (1999). *The meme machine.* Oxford: Oxford University Press.

Bourdieu, P. & Passeron, J. (1977). *Reproduction in education, society and culture.* London: Sage.

Bourdieu, P. (1984). *Distinction.* London: Routledge Kegan Paul.

Bowie, F. (1993). Wales from Within. In S.MacDonald (Ed.), *Inside European Identities.* Oxford: Berg.

Bowles, S. & Gintis, H. (1976). *Schooling in capitalist America.* London: Routledge & Kegan Paul.

Boyle, R. (2007). The 'now' media generation. *Sociology Review, 17,* 1.

Brazier, C. (1995). African village. *New Internationalist,* June.

British Psychological Society. (1998). *Code of conduct, ethical principles and guidelines.* Leicester: British Psychological Society.

British Sociological Association. (1996). *Statement of ethical practice.* Durham: British Sociological Association.

Brown, G. (2008). We'll use our schools to break down class barriers. *The Observer,* 8 February.

Brown, P., Halsey, A. H., Lauder, H. & Wells, A. (1997). The transformation of education and society: An introduction. In A. H. Halsey et al. (Eds.), *Education: Culture, economy, society.* Oxford: Oxford University Press.

Bruce, S. (1995). Religion and the sociology of religion. In M. Haralambos (Ed.), *Developments in Sociology,* Volume 11. Ormskirk: Causeway Press.

Buckingham, D. (2000). *After the death of childhood: Growing up in the age of electronic media.* Cambridge: Polity.

Bukatko, D. & Daehler, M.W. (2001). *Child development: A thematic approach* (4th Ed.). Boston: Houghton Mifflin Company.

Burgess, R. (1983). *Experiencing comprehensive education.* London: Methuen.

Bush, T., Coleman, M. & Glover, D. (1993). *Managing autonomous schools: The grant-maintained experience.* London: Paul Chapman.

Butler, C.(1995). Religion and Gender. *Sociology Review,* February

Callender, C. & Jackson, J. (2004). *Fear of debt and higher education participation,* Families & Social Capital ESRC Research Group, London: London South Bank University.

Cameron, D. & Asthana, A. (2006). The flag is everywhere, *Observer,* 28 May

Cantle, T. (2005). *Community cohesion.* London: Macmillan

Cartland, B. (1997). Back to basics and the search for love. In G. Dench (Ed.), *Rewriting the Sexual Contract.* London: Institute of Community Studies.

Cecil, R.(1993). The Marching Season in Northern Ireland. In S.MacDonald (Ed.), *Inside European identities.* Oxford: Berg.

Chagnon, N. (1968). *Yanomamo.* New York: Holt, Rinehart & Winston.

Charles, N. (1990). Food and family ideology. In C.C. Harris (Ed.), *Family, economy and community.* Cardiff: University of Wales Press.

Charles, N. & Kerr, M. (1988). *Women, food and families.* Manchester: Manchester University Press.

Cheal, D. (1999). The one and the many: Modernity and postmodernity. In G. Allan (Ed.), *The sociology of the family: A reader.* Oxford: Blackwell.

Chester, R. (1984). Divorce. In E. Butterworth & D. Weir (Eds.), *The new sociology of modern Britain.* Glasgow: Fontana.

Chitty, C. (1997). Choose...education? *Sociology Review,* April.

Chitty, C. (2002). *Understanding schools and schooling.* London: RoutledgeFalmer.

Chubb, J. & Moe, T. (1997). *Politics, markets and the organisation of schools.* In A.H. Halsey et al. (Eds.), Education: Culture, economy, society. Oxford: Oxford University Press.

Clarke, J. & Saunders, C. (1991). Who are you and so what? *Sociology Review, 1,* 1.

Cockburn, A. (1993). Class of 93. *Observer Life,* December 12.

Cockett, M. & Tripp, J. (1994). *The Exeter family study: Family breakdown and its impact on children.* Exeter: Exeter University Press.

Coffey, A. (2001). *Education and social change.* Buckingham: Open University Press.

Cohen, P. (1984). Against the new vocationalism. In I. Bates et al. (Eds.), *Schooling for the dole?* London: Macmillan.

Cohen, S. (1987). *Folk devils and moral panics.* Oxford: Blackwell.

Collins, R. (1972). Functional and conflict theories of educational stratification. In B.R. Cosin (Ed.), *Education, structure and society.* Harmondsworth: Penguin.

Commission for Racial Equality (1992). *Set to fail? Setting and banding in secondary schools.* London: Commission for Racial Equality.

Connell, R.W. (1995). *Masculinities.* Cambridge: Polity Press.

Connolly, P. (1998). *Racism, gender identities and young children.* London: Routledge.

Connor, H., Tyers, C., Modood, T., & Hillage, J. (2004). *Why the difference? A closer look at higher education minority ethnic students and graduates.* DfES research report RB552 www.dfes.gov.uk/research/data/uploadfiles/R B552.pdf.

Coontz, S. (2006). *Marriage, a history: How love conquered marriage.* New York: Penguin.

Crace, J. (2006). Hidden triumphs. *The Guardian.* November 7.

Crossman, R.H.S. (1975). *The diaries of a cabinet minister.* London: Jonathan Cape.

Crow, G. & Hardy, M. (1992). Diversity and ambiguity among lone-parent households in modern Britain. In C. Marsh & S. Arber (Eds.), *Families and households.* London: Macmillan.

Cumberbatch, G. & Negrine, R. (1992). *Images of disability on television.* London: Routledge.

Curtice, J. & Norris, P. (2007). Isolates or socialites? In A.Park et al. (Eds.), *British social attitudes 23rd report.* London: Sage.

Davies, N. (1997). *Dark heart.* London: Chatto & Windus.

Davies, S. (1995). Reproduction and resistance in Canadian high schools: An empirical examination of the Willis thesis. *British Journal of Sociology, 46,* 4.

Day, G. (2006). *Community and everyday life.* London: Routledge.

Dean, H. & Taylor-Gooby, P. (1992). *Dependency culture.* Hemel Hempstead: Harvester Wheatsheaf.

Delphy, C. & Leonard, D. (1992). *Familiar exploitation.* Cambridge: Polity.

Dennis, N. & Erdos, G. (2000). *Families without fatherhood* (3rd ed.). London: Institute for the Study of Civil Society.

Dennis, N., Henriques, F. & Slaughter, C. (1956). *Coal is our life.* London: Eyre & Spottiswoode.

Denscombe, M. (1994). *Sociology update 1994.* Leicester: Olympus Books.

Devine, F. (1992). *Affluent workers revisited: Privatisation and the working class.* Edinburgh: Edinburgh University Press.

Devine, F. (1997). *Social Class in America and Britain.* Edinburgh: Edinburgh University Press.

DfEE (1997). *Excellence in schools.* London: HMSO.

Diamond, J. (1998). *C: Because cowards get cancer.* London: Vermillion.

Ditton, J. (1977). *Part-time crime.* London: Macmillan.

Donnellan, C. (Ed.) (1994). *The rights of the child.* Cambridge: Independence.

Douglas, J.W.B. (1964). *The home and the school.* London: MacGibbon & Kee.

Douglas, M. (Ed.), (1964). *Man in society: Patterns of human organisation.* London: Macdonald & Co.

Doward, J. (2004). Yo, Blingland! *The Observer,* 22 February.

Dowds, L. & Young, K. (1996). National Identity. In R. Jowell, J. Curtice, A. Park, L. Brook & K. Thomson (Eds.), *British social attitudes 13th report.* Aldershot: Dartmouth Publishing Company.

Duncombe, J. & Marsden, D. (1993). Love and intimacy. *Sociology, 27,* 221-241.

Duncombe, J. & Marsden, D. (1995). Workaholics and whingeing women: Theorising intimacy. *Sociological Review, 43,* 150-169.

Dunham, C. (1992). Brotherly love. *Observer Magazine,* 18 October.

Dunne, G. (1997). *Lesbian lifestyles: Women's work and the politics of sexuality.* London: Macmillan.

Durkheim, E. (1970). *Suicide: A study in sociology.* London: Routledge.

Edgell, S. (1980). *Middle-class couples.* London: George Allen & Unwin.

Edholm, F. (1982). The unnatural family. In E. Whitelegg et al. (Eds.), *The changing experience of women.* London: Martin Robertson/Open University.

Elias, N. (1978). *The civilising process, vol 1.* Oxford: Basil Blackwell.

Employment Department Group & Radio One (1991). *Action special 91.* London: HMSO.

Engels, F. (1972). *The origin of the family, private property and the state.* London: Lawrence & Wishart.

Epstein, D., Elwood, J., Hey, V. & Maw, J. (Eds.) (1998). *Failing boys? Issues in gender and achievement.* Buckingham: Open University Press.

Featherstone, M. & Hepworth, M. (1989). Ageing and Old Age. In B.Blytheway et al. (Eds.), *Becoming and being old.* London: Sage.

Feinstein, L. (2003). Inequality in the early cognitive development of British children in the 1970 cohort. *Economica, 70, 277,* 73-98.

Ferri, E., Bynner, J. & Wadsworth, W. (2003). *Changing Britain, changing lives.* London: Institute of Education.

Festinger, L. et al. (1964). *When prophecy fails.* New York: Harper Torchbooks.

Fielding, N. (1981). *The National Front.* London: Routledge & Kegan Paul.

Fielding, N. (1993). Qualitative interviewing. In N. Gilbert (Ed.), *Researching social life.* London: Sage.

Finch, J. & Mason, J. (1993). *Negotiating family responsibilities.* London: Routledge.

Finn, D. (1987). *Training without jobs.* London: Macmillan.

Firth, R. (1963). *We the Tikopia: A sociological study of kinship in primitive Polynesia.* Palo Alto: Stanford University Press.

Fitzgerald, B. (1999). Children of lesbian and gay parents: A review of the literature. *Marriage & Family Reviews, 29,* 57-75.

Fletcher, R. (1966). *The family and marriage in Britain.* Harmondsworth: Penguin.

Fortes, M. (1950). Kinship and marriage among the Ashanti. In A.R. Radcliffe Brown & D. Forde (Eds.), *African systems of kinship and marriage*. London: Oxford University Press.

Foster, P. (1990). *Policy and practice in multicultural and antiracist education*. London: Routledge.

Fox, K. (2005). *Watching the English*. London: Hodder & Stoughton.

Francis, B. & Skelton, C. (2005). *Reassessing gender and achievement: questioning contemporary key debates*. Abingdon: Routledge.

Frankenberg, R. (1966). *Communities in Britain*. Harmondsworth: Penguin.

French, J. (1986). Gender and the classroom. *New Society*, 7 March.

Furedi, F. (2001). *Paranoid parenting*. London: Penguin.

Gaine, C. & George, R. (1999). *Gender, 'race' and class in schooling: A new introduction*. London: Falmer.

Gallie, D. (1978). *In search of the new working class*. Cambridge: Cambridge University Press.

Gewirtz, S., Ball, S.J. & Bowe, R. (1995). *Markets, choice and equity in education*. Milton Keynes: Open University Press.

Giddens, A. (1991). *Modernity and self-identity*. Cambridge: Polity Press.

Giddens, A. (1992). *The transformation of intimacy: Sexuality, love and eroticism in modern societies*. Cambridge: Polity Press.

Giddens, A. (2001). *Sociology* 4th ed. Cambridge: Polity Press.

Gillborn, D. (1990). *'Race', ethnicity and education: Teaching and learning in multi-ethnic schools*. London: Unwin Hyman.

Gillborn, D. & Drew, D. (1992). 'Race', class and school effects. *New Community, 18*, 4.

Gillborn, D. & Mirza, H.S. (2000). *Educational inequality: Mapping race, class and gender*. London: OFSTED.

Gillborn, D. & Youdell, D. (2001). The new IQism: Intelligence, 'ability' and the rationing of education. In J. Demaine (Ed.), *Sociology of education today*. Basingstoke: Palgrave.

Gillespie, M.(1993). Technology and Tradition. In A.Gray & J.McGuigan (Eds.), *Studying culture*. London: Edward Arnold.

Gilroy, P. (1987). *There ain't no black in the Union Jack*. London: Hutchinson

Gittins, D. (1993). *The family in question* (2nd ed.). Basingstoke: Macmillan.

Giulianotti, R. & Robertson, R. (2006). Glocalisation, globalisation and migration., *International Sociology, 21*, 2.

Goffman, E. (1968). *Asylums*. Harmondsworth: Penguin.

Goffman, E. (1968). *Stigma*. Harmondsworth: Penguin.

Goffman, E. (1969). *The presentation of self in everyday life*. Harmondsworth: Penguin.

Goldberg, S. (1977). *Male dominance*. London: Abacus

Goldthorpe, J.H., Lockwood, D., Bechofer, F. & Platt, J. (1969). *The affluent worker in the class structure*. Cambridge: Cambridge University Press.

Goulborne, H. (1999). The transnational character of Caribbean kinship in Britain. In S. McRae (Ed.), *Changing Britain*: Families and households in the 1990s. Oxford: Oxford University Press.

Graham, H. (1987). Being poor: Perceptions and coping strategies of lone mothers. In J. Brannen & G. Wilson (Eds.), *Give and take in families*. London: Allen & Unwin.

Griffin, J.H. (1960). *Black like me*. New York: Signet.

Halfpenny, P. (1984). *Principles of method*. York: Longman.

Hall, E.T. (1973). *The silent language*. New York: Doubleday.

Hall, S. (1992). The question of cultural identity. In S. Hall, D. Held & T. McGrew (Eds.), *Modernity and its futures*. Cambridge: Polity Press.

Hall, S. (Ed.) (1997). *Representation*. London: Sage.

Hall, R., Ogden, P.E. & Hill, C. (1999). Living alone: Evidence from England and Wales and France for the last two decades. In S. McRae (Ed.), *Changing Britain: Families and households in the 1990s*. Oxford: Oxford University Press.

Halsey, A.H., Floud, J. & Anderson, C.A. (1961). *Education, economy and society*. New York: Free Press.

Halsey, A.H., Heath, A. & Ridge, J.M. (1980). *Origins and destinations: Family, class and education in modern Britain*. Oxford: Clarendon.

Halsey, A.H., Lauder, H., Brown, P. & Wells, A. (1997). *Education: Culture, economy, society*. Oxford: Oxford University Press.

Haralambos, M. (1994). *Right on: From blues to soul in Black America*. Ormskirk: Causeway Press.

Hargreaves, D.H. (1967). *Social relations in a secondary school*. London: Routledge & Kegan Paul.

Harris, M. (1984). The strange saga of the Video Bill. *New Society*, 26 April, 140-142.

Hart, N. (1985). The sociology of health and medicine. In M. Haralambos (Ed.), *Sociology: New directions*. Ormskirk: Causeway Press.

Haskey, J. (1994). Stepfamilies and stepchildren in Great Britain. *Population Trends, 76*, 17-28.

Haskey, J. (2001). Cohabitation in Great Britain: Past, present and future trends – and attitudes. *Population Trends, 103*, 4-19.

Haskey, J. (2002). One-parent families – and the dependent children living in them – in Great Britain. *Population Trends, 109*, 46-57.

Hatcher, R. (2005). Business sponsorship of schools: For-profit takeover or agents of neoliberal change? http://journals.aol.co.uk/rikowskigr/Volumizer/entires/2005/11/07.

Hetherington, E.M. (2002). *For better or for worse: Divorce reconsidered*. New York: Harper & Brothers.

Hewitt, R. (1996). *Routes of Racism*. Stoke-on-Trent: Trentham Books.

Hey, V. (1997). *The company she keeps*. Milton Keynes: Open University Press.

Hill, A. (2007). There's no shame in going solo, says mum. *The Observer,* 4 November.

Hill, G. (1995). The American dream. *The Guardian,* 15 February.

HM Treasury (2007). *Public expenditure statistical analyses 2007*. London: The Stationery Office.

Hobbs, D. (1988). *Doing the business*. Oxford: Oxford University Press.

Hobsbawm, E. (1996). Identity politics and the Left. *New Left Review,* June.

Hoebel, E.A. (1960). *The Cheyennes*. New York: Holt, Rinehart & Winston.

Hoggart, R. (1957). *Uses of literacy*. London: Chatto and Windus.

Homan, R. (1991). *The ethics of social research*. Harlow: Longman.

Hopkins, N. (2000). Tide of violence in the home: Domestic attacks occur every six seconds. *The Guardian,* 26 October.

Hornsby-Smith, M. (1993). Gaining access. In N. Gilbert (Ed.), *Researching social life*. London: Sage.

Humphreys, L. (1970). *Tearoom trade: Impersonal sex in public places*. Chicago: Aldine.

Iannucci, A. (1995). Play your card right. *The Guardian,* 2 May.

Inglis, D. (2005). *Culture and everyday life*. Abingdon: Routledge.

Ireson, J. & Hallam, S. (2001). *Ability grouping in education*. London: Sage.

Jackson, C. (2006). *Lads and ladettes in school: Gender and a fear of failure*. Maidenhead: Open University Press.

Jackson, D. (1998). Breaking out of the binary trap: Boys' underachievement, schooling and gender relations. In D. Epstein et al. (Eds.), *Failing boys? Issues in gender and achievement*. Buckingham: Open University Press.

Jefferson, T. (Ed.). (1975). *Resistance through rituals*. Birmingham: Centre for Contemporary Cultural Studies.

Kassam, N. (Ed.). (1997). *Telling it like it is*. London: Women's Press.

Keddie, N. (1973). Classroom knowledge. In N. Keddie (Ed.), *Tinker, tailor...the myth of cultural deprivation*. Harmondsworth: Penguin.

Kellner, P. (1994). The figures are Shere Nonsense. *The Sunday Times,* 27 February.

Kerr, M. (1958). *The people of Ship Street*.

London: Routledge & Kegan Paul.

Kiernan, K. & Mueller, G. (1999). Who divorces? In S. McRae (Ed.), *Changing Britain: Families and households in the 1990s*. Oxford: Oxford University Press.

Kirton, A. (1998). Labour and education: The story so far. *S magazine*, September.

Kitzinger, J. (1993). Understanding AIDS. In J. Eldridge (Ed.), *Getting the message: News, truth and power*. London: Routledge.

Kluckhohn, C. (1951). The study of culture. In D.Lerner & H.Lasswell (Eds.), *The policy sciences*. Stanford: Stanford University Press.

Kulick, D. (1998). *Travesti – Sex, gender and culture among Brazilian transgendered prostitutes*. Chicago: University of Chicago Press.

Kurz, D. (1995). *For richer, for poorer: Mothers confront divorce*. London: Routledge.

Labov, W. (1973). The logic of nonstandard English. In N. Keddie (Ed.), *Tinker, tailor...the myth of cultural deprivation*. Harmondsworth: Penguin.

Lacey, C. (1970). *Hightown Grammar*. Manchester: Manchester University Press.

Lader, D., Short, S., & Gershuny, J. (2006). *The time use survey, 2005*. London: Office for National Statistics.

Langham, S. (2000). Feminism and the classroom. *Sociology Review*, November.

LaPiere, R.T. (1934). Attitudes vs. actions. *Social Forces, 13*, 230-237.

Laslett, P.K. (1965). *The world we have lost*. London: Methuen.

Laslett, P.K. (1977). *Family life and illicit love in earlier generations*. London: Methuen.

Lauder, H., Brown, P., Dillabough, J. & Halsey, A.H., (Ed.) (2006). *Education globalization and social change*. Oxford: Oxford University Press.

Lawson, A. (1988). *Adultery: an analysis of love and betrayal*. Oxford: Blackwell.

Leach, E.R. (1967). *A runaway world?* London: BBC publications.

Lee, D., Marsden, D., Rickman, P. & Dunscombe, J. (1990). *Scheming for youth: A study of YTS in the enterprise culture*. Milton Keynes: Open University Press.

Lee, N. (2001). *Childhood and society: Growing up in an age of uncertainty*. Buckingham: Open University Press.

Lees, S. (1986). *Losing out: Sexuality and adolescent girls*. London: Hutchinson.

Lees, S. (1993). *Sugar and spice*. Harmondsworth: Penguin.

Leonard, M. (2000). Back to the future: The domestic division of labour. *Sociology Review*, November, 26-28.

Lèvi-Strauss, C. (1956). The family. In H. L. Shapiro (Ed.), *Man, culture and society*. London: Oxford.

Levy, A. (2007). Kissing gates and stiles are under threat from political correctness. *Daily Mail*, 30 November.

Lewis, J. (2001). Women, men and the family. In A. Sheldon (Ed.), *The Blair effect: The Blair government 1997-2001*. London: Little, Brown and Company.

Lewis, O. (1951). *Life in a Mexican village: Tepoztlan restudied*. Urbana IL: University of Illinois Press.

Liebow, E. (1967). *Tally's Corner*. Boston: Little Brown.

Lister, R. (1996). Back to the family: Family policies and politics under the Major government. In H. Jones & J. Millar (Eds.), *The politics of the family*. Aldershot: Avebury.

Livi-Bacci, M. (2007). *A concise history of world population* (4th Ed.). Oxford: Blackwell.

Lobban, G. (1974). Data report on British reading schemes. *The Times Educational Supplement*, 1 March.

Long Lance, Chief Buffalo Child (1956). *Long Lance*. London: Corgi Books.

Mac an Ghaill, M. (1988). *Young, gifted and Black: Student-teacher relations in the schooling of Black youth*. Milton Keynes: Open University Press.

Mac an Ghaill, M. (1992). Coming of age in 1980s England: Reconceptualising Black students' schooling experience. In D. Gill, B. Mayor & M. Blair (Eds.). *Racism and education: Structures and strategies*. London: Sage.

Mac an Ghaill, M. (1994). *The making of men: Masculinities, sexualities and schooling*. Buckingham: Open University Press.

Macbeath, J. & Mortimore, P. (2001). *Improving school effectiveness*. Buckingham: Open University Press.

Macdonald, K. & Tipton, D. (1993). Using documents. In N. Gilbert (Ed.), *Researching social life*. London: Sage.

Machin, S. (2003). Unto them that hath... *Centrepiece, 8*, 4-9.

MacInnes, J. (1998). Manly virtues and masculine vices. *Living Marxism*, November.

Mahony, P. (1998). Girls will be girls and boys will be first. In D. Epstein et al. (Eds.), *Failing boys? Issues in gender and achievement*. Buckingham: Open University Press.

Mair, L. (1971). *Marriage*. Harmondsworth: Penguin.

Malinowski, B. (1927). *Sex and repression in savage society*. London: Routledge.

Mann, M. (1986). *The sources of social power*. Cambridge: Cambridge University Press.

Mansfield, P. & Collard, J. (1988). *The beginning of the rest of your life?* Basingstoke: Macmillan.

Mars, G. (1982). *Cheats at work: An anthropology of workplace crime*. London: Allen & Unwin.

Marshall, G., Rose, D., Newby, H. & Vogler, C. (1989). *Social Class in modern Britain*.

London: Unwin Hyman.

May, T. (2001). *Social research: Issues, methods and process* (3rd Ed.). Buckingham: Open University Press.

McCrone, D. & Surridge, P. (1998). National identity and national pride. In R.Jowell et al. (Eds.), *British and European social attitudes*. Aldershot: Ashgate.

McDonough, F. (1997). *Class and politics*. In Storry, M. and Childs, P. (Eds.), *British cultural identities*. London. Routledge.

McGlone, F., Park, A. & Roberts, C. (1999). Kinship and friendship: Attitudes and behaviour in Britain, 1986-1995. In S. McRae (Ed.), *Changing Britain: Families and households in the 1990s*. Oxford: Oxford University Press.

McGrew, A. (1992). A global society. In S.Hall et al. (Eds.), *Modernity and its futures*. Cambridge: Polity.

McKenzie, J. (2001). *Changing education: A sociology of education since 1944*. Harlow: Pearson Education.

McKnight, A., Glennerster, H., & Lupton, R. (2005). Education, education, education: An assessment of Labour's success in tackling education inequalities in Hillis, J., & Stewart, K. (Ed.) *A more equal society: New Labour, poverty, inequality and exclusion*. Bristol: Policy Press.

McMahon, A. (1999). *Taking care of men: Sexual politics in the public mind*. Cambridge: Cambridge University Press.

McRae, S. (1999). Introduction: Family and household change in Britain. In S. McRae (Ed.), *Changing Britain: Families and households in the 1990s*. Oxford: Oxford University Press.

Mead, M. (1935). *Sex and temperament in three primitive societies*. New York: Morrow.

Mirza, H. (1992). *Young, female and Black*. London: Routledge.

Mirza, M., Senthilkumaran, A. & Ja'far, Z. (2007). *Living apart together*. London: Policy Exchange.

Modood, T., Berthoud, R., Lakey, J., Nazroo, P., et al. (1997). *Ethnic minorities in Britain: Diversity and disadvantage*. London: Policy Studies Institute.

Modood, T. (2004). Capitals, ethnic identity and educational qualifications. *Cultural Trends, 13(2)*, 50, 87-105.

Modood, T. (2006). Ethnicity, Muslims and higher education entry in Britain. *Teaching in Higher Education 11*, 2, 247-250.

Morgan, P. (1999). *Farewell to the family: Public policy and family breakdown in Britain and the USA*. London: The IEA Health and Welfare Unit.

Moser, C.A. & Kalton, G. (1971). *Survey methods in social investigation* (2nd ed.). London: Heinemann.

Murdock, G.P. (1949). *Social structure*. New York: Macmillan.

Murray, C. (1990). *The emerging British underclass*. London: Institute of Economic Affairs.

Murray, C. (1994). The New Victorians and the New Rabble. *Sunday Times,* 29 May.

Murray, C. (2001). *Underclass + 10: Charles Murray and the British underclass, 1990-2000*. London: Civitas.

National Audit Office. (2007). *The academics programme*. London: National Audit Office.

National Evaluation of Sure Start. (2005). *Variation in Sure Start local programmes' effectiveness: Early preliminary findings*. DfES Research Report NESS/2005/FR/014. London: HMSO

Neale, B. & Smart, C. (1997). Experiments with parenthood? *Sociology, 31,* 201-219.

Newark, P. (1980). *The illustrated encyclopedia of the old West*. London: Andrè Deutsch.

Newby, H. (1977). In the field: Reflections on a study of Suffolk farm workers. In C. Bell & H. Newby (Eds.), *Doing sociological research*. London: Allen & Unwin.

Newell, R. (1993). Questionnaires. In N. Gilbert (Ed.), *Researching social life*. London: Sage.

Nissel, M. (1995). Vital statistics. *New Statesman,* 27 January.

O'Brien, M. (2000). Family life. In M. Haralambos (Ed.), *Developments in Sociology, Volume 16*. Ormskirk: Causeway Press.

O'Connell Davidson, J. & Layder, D. (1994). *Methods, sex and madness*. London: Routledge.

O'Hagan, A. (1995). *The missing*. London: Picador.

O'Hara, M. (2007). 'Living with a label', *Guardian Society* 24 January.

Oakley, A. (1974). *The sociology of housework*. London: Martin Robertson.

Okely, J. (1983). *The traveller-gypsies*. Cambridge: Cambridge University Press.

Page, R. (2002). New Labour and the welfare state. In M. Holborn (Ed.), *Developments in Sociology, Volume 18*. Ormskirk: Causeway Press.

Pahl, J. (1989). *Money and marriage*. Basingstoke: Macmillan.

Pakulski, J. & Waters, M. (1996). *The death of class*. London: Sage.

Parker, H., Aldridge, J. & Measham, F. (1998). *Illegal leisure: The normalisation of adolescent recreational drug use*. London: Routledge.

Parker, S. (1976). *Sociology of leisure*. London: Allen & Unwin.

Parsons, T. (1951). *The social system*. New York: Free Press.

Parsons, T. (1961). The school class as a social system. In A. H. Halsey et al. (Eds.), *Education, economy and society*. New York: Free Press.

Parsons, T. & Bales, R.F. (1955). *Family, socialisation and interaction process*. New York: The Free Press.

Pawson, R. (1995). Methodology. In M. Haralambos (Ed.), *Developments in Sociology, Volume 5*. Ormskirk: Causeway Press.

Pearson, G. (1983). *Hooligan: A history of respectable fears*. London: Macmillan.

Philo, G. & Miller, D. (2002). Circuits of communication and power: Recent developments in media sociology. In M. Holborn (Ed.), *Developments in Sociology, Volume 18*. Ormskirk: Causeway Press.

Pilkington, A. (2003). *Racial disadvantage and ethnic diversity in Britain*. London: Palgrave.

Platt, J. (1976). *Realities of social research*. London: Chatto & Windus.

Pleck, J. (1985). *Working wives, working husbands*. London: Sage.

Plummer, G. (2000). *Failing working-class girls*. Stoke on Trent: Trentham Books.

Polhemus, T. (1997). In the supermarket of style. In S. Redhead (Ed.), *The clubcultures reader*. Oxford: Blackwell.

Postman, N. (1983). *The disappearance of childhood*. London: W.H. Allen.

Prison Reform Trust (2006). *Bromley briefings prison factfile*. London: Prison Reform Trust.

Punch, M. (1979). Observation and the police. In M. Hammersley (Ed.), *Social research: Philosophy, politics and practice*. London: Sage.

Reay, D. (1998). *Class work: Mothers' involvement in their children's primary schooling*. London: UCL Press.

Reay, D. David, M.E., & Ball, S. (2005). *Degrees of choice: Class, race, gender and higher education*. Stoke on Trent: Trentham Books.

Redfield, R. (1930). *Tepoztlan: A Mexican village*. Chicago: University of Chicago Press.

Renold, E. (2001). Learning the 'hard' way. *British Journal of Sociology of Education,* 22, 3.

Rikowski, G. (2002) *Globalization and Education: A paper prepared for the House of Lords Select Committee on Economic Affairs. Inquiry into the global economy.*

Rikowski, G. (2005) *In the dentist's chair: A response to Richard Hatcher's Critique of Habituation of the Nation – Part One*. www.flowideas.co.uk/print.php?page=147.

Rist, R. (1970). Student social class and teacher expectations: The self-fulfilling prophecy in ghetto education. Harvard *Educational Review,* 40.

Ritzer, G. (2002). *McDonaldization: The reader*. Thousand Oaks: Pine Forge Press.

Roberts, K. (1978). *Contemporary society and the growth of leisure*. New York: Longman.

Roberts, K. (1995). Great Britain: socioeconomic polarisation and the implications for leisure. In C.Critcher, P.Bramham & A. Tomlinson (Eds.), *Sociology of leisure: A reader*. London: E. & F.N. Spon.

Roberts, K. (2001). *Class in modern Britain*. Basingstoke: Palgrave.

Rodgers, B. & Pryor, J. (1998). *Divorce and separation: The outcomes for children*. York: Joseph Rowntree Foundation.

Rojek, C. (2000). Leisure and the rich today. *Leisure Studies, 19,* 1.

Rosenthal, R. & Jacobson, L. (1968). *Pygmalion in the classroom*. New York: Holt, Rinehart & Winston.

Royle, E. (1997). *Modern Britain: A social history 1750-1997*. London: Hodder Headline.

Saunders, P. (1990). *Social class and stratification*. London: Routledge.

Saunders, P. (2000). Afterward: Family research and family policy since 1992. In N. Dennis & G. Erdos *Families without fatherhood* (3rd ed.). London: Institute for the Study of Civil Society.

Savage, M., Barlow, J., Dickens, P. & Fielding, T. (1992). *Property, bureaucracy and culture*. London: Routledge.

Savage, M. Bagnall, G. & Longhurst, B. 2001, Ordinary, ambivalent and defensive. *Sociology, 35,* 2.

Scanzoni, J., Polonko, K., Teachman, J. & Thompson, L. (1989). *The sexual bond*. Newbury Park: Sage.

Scase, R. (2000). *Britain in 2010*. Oxford: Capstone Publishing.

Scott, J. (1990). *A matter of record*. Cambridge: Polity Press.

Scout Association (2007). *Typical young people*. London: nfpSynergy.

Select Committee on Education and Skills (2005). *Fifth Report, Summary*. www.publications.parliament.uk/pa/cm2004 05/cmselect/cmeduski/86/8603.htm.

Sewell, T. (1997). *Black masculinities and schooling*. Stoke on Trent: Trentham Books.

Sharpe, S. (1976). *Just like a girl: How girls learn to be women*. Harmondsworth: Penguin.

Sharpe, S. (1984). *Double identity*. Harmondsworth: Penguin.

Sharpe, S. (1994). *Just like a girl: How girls learn to be women: The 70s to the 90s*. Harmondsworth: Penguin.

Shaw, C. (1930). *The Jack Roller*. Chicago: University of Chicago Press.

Sissons, M. (1970). *The psychology of social class*. Milton Keynes: Open University Press.

Skelton, C. (2001). *Schooling the Boys*. Buckingham: Open University Press.

Smith, D. & Tomlinson, S. (1989). *The school effect: A study of multi-racial comprehensives*. London: Policy Studies Institute.

Smith, J., Gilford, S. & O'Sullivan, A. (1998).

The family background of homeless young people. London: Family Policy Studies Centre (now available through the Joseph Rowntree Foundation).

Smith, T. & Noble, M. (1995). *Poverty and schooling in the 1990s*. London: CPAG.

Spender, D. (1983). *Invisible women: The school scandal*. London: Women's Press.

Stacey, J. (1996). *In the name of the family: Rethinking family values in the postmodern age*. Boston MA: Beacon Press.

Stainton Rogers, W. (2001). Constructing childhood, constructing child concern. In P. Foley, J. Roche & S. Turner (Eds.), *Children in society: Contemporary theory, policy and practice*. Basingstoke: Palgrave.

Stands In Timber, J. & Liberty, M. (1967). *Cheyenne memories*. New Haven, Yale University Press.

Stanworth, M. (1983). *Gender and schooling*. London: Hutchinson.

Strathdee, R. (2003). Labour market change, vocational education and training, and social class. In M. Holborn (Ed.), *Developments in Sociology, Volume 19*. Ormskirk: Causeway Press.

Sugarman, B. (1970). Social class, values and behaviour in schools. In M. Craft (Ed.), *Family, class and education*. London: Longman.

Sukhnandan, L. & Lee, B. (1998). *Streaming, setting and grouping by ability*. Slough: NFER.

Taylor, L. & Cohen, S. (1992). *Escape attempts* (2nd Ed.). London: Routledge.

Tebbit, N. (1990). Fanfare on Being British. *The Field*, May.

Thomas, W.I. & Znaniecki, F. (1958). *The Polish peasant in Europe and America*. New York: Dover.

Thrupp, M., & Hursh, D. (2006). The limits of managerialist school reform: The case of target-setting in England and the USA. In H. Lauder, et al (Eds.), *Education, globalization and social change*. Oxford: Oxford University Press.

Tomlinson, S. (2005). *Education in a post-welfare society* (2nd Ed.). Maidenhead: Open University Press.

Turnbull, C. (1961). *The forest people*. London: Jonathan Cape.

Van Reenen, J. (2004). Active labour market policies and the British New Deal for unemployed youth in context. In R. Blundell, D. Card & R. Freeman (Eds.), *Seeking a premier league economy*. Chicago, IL: University of Chicago Press.

Veblen, T. (1899). *The theory of the leisure class*. New York: Dover.

Vogler, C. & Pahl, J. (1994). Money, power and inequality within marriage. *Sociological Review, 42*, 263-288.

Waddington, P.A.J. (1999). Police (canteen) sub-culture. *British Journal of Criminology, 39*, 2.

Walford, G. (1993). Researching the City Technology College Kingshurst. In R. Burgess (Ed.), *Research Methods*. London: Nelson.

Walklate, S. (2000). Researching victims. In R.D. King & E. Wincup (Eds.), *Doing research on crime and justice*. Oxford: Oxford University Press.

Walvin, J. (1978). *Leisure and society 1830-1950*. London: Longman.

Warde, A. (2006). Cultural capital and the place of sport. *Cultural Trends, 15*, 2/3.

Weber, M. (1958). *The Protestant ethic and the spirit of capitalism*. New York: Charles Scribner's Sons.

Weeks, J., Heaphy, B. & Donovan, C. (1999a). Partners by choice: Equality, power and commitment in non-heterosexual relationships. In G. Allan (Ed.), *The sociology of the family: A reader*. Oxford: Blackwell.

Weeks, J., Heaphy, B. & Donovan, C. (1999b). Families of choice: Autonomy and mutuality in non-heterosexual relationships. In S. McRae (Ed.), *Changing Britain: Families and households in the 1990s*. Oxford: Oxford University Press.

Westwood S. & Bhachu, P. (1988). Images and realities. *New Society*, 6 May.

Whyte, W.F. (1955). *Street corner society* (2nd ed.). Chicago: University of Chicago Press.

Wilkinson, H. (1997). The androgynous generation. In G. Dench (Ed.), *Rewriting the sexual contract*. London: Institute of Community Studies.

Williams, B. (1981). *Obscenity and film censorship*. Cambridge: Cambridge University Press.

Williams, J.A. Jr. (1971). Interviewer-respondent interaction. In B.J. Franklin & H.W. Osborne (Eds.), *Research methods*. Belmont: Wadsworth.

Willis, P. (1977). *Learning to labour: How working-class kids get working-class jobs*. Farnborough: Saxon House.

Willmott, P. (1986). *Social networks, informal care and public policy*. London: Policy Studies Institute.

Womack, S. (2006). Family size shrinking due to cost of children. *The Telegraph*, 10 April.

Wright, C. (1986). School processes – An ethnographic study. In S.J. Eggleston, D. Dunn & M. Angali (Eds.), *Education for some*. Stoke on Trent: Trentham Books.

Wright, C. (1992). Early education: Multiracial primary school classrooms. In D. Gill, B. Mayor & M. Blair (Eds.), *Racism and education*. London: Sage.

Young, M. & Willmott, P. (1957). *Family and kinship in East London* Harmondsworth: Penguin.

Young, M. & Willmott, P. (1973). *The symmetrical family*. London: Routledge & Kegan Paul.

Text acknowledgements

Sociology in Focus for AQA AS Level by Mike Haralambos, John Richardson, Peter Langley, Paul Taylor & Alan Yeo
(ISBN: 978-1405-896719). Acknowledgements prepared on 27th March 2008. Amended 9th April 2008.

We are grateful to the following for permission to reproduce copyright material:

Cengage Learning Services Limited for a table from *Image of Disability on Television* by Guy Cumberbatch & Ralph Negrine copyright © Routledge 1992, reproduced by permission of CEngage Learning Services Limited; DfES for the table "Higher education initial participation rates England, 2001/2 (percentages)" adapted from *Why the difference: A closer look at higher education minority ethnic students and graduates* DfES research report RB552 by H. Connor, C. Tyers, T. Modood and J. Hillage, 2004 www.dfes.gov.uk; Guardian News & Media Ltd for extracts adapted from "Tables are turned on top schools" by Barry Hugill published in *The Observer* 20 March 1994, "American dreams and nightmares" by Graham Hill published in *The Guardian* 15 February 1995, "Have mortgages fight to keep out have-nots" by Angella Johnson published in *The Guardian* 22 September 1995, "Comprehensive cant" by Gerald Steinberg published in *The Guardian* 22 January 1996, "Trail of cyber-sex, lies and floppy disks ends in divorce suit" by Ian Katz published in *The Guardian* 3 February 1996, "The new voice of opera" by Dan Glaister published in *The Guardian* 16 January 1998, "Hoedown showdown as Norman changes to Norma" by Jamie Wilson published in *The Guardian* 17 April 1998 and "Motherhood was just what girls did" by Amelia Hill published in *The Observer* 18 March 2007 © Guardian 1994, 1995, 1996, 2007; Hodder Education for the graph 'Deaths from Tuberculosis 1840-1970 England & Wales' from *The Modern Rise of Population* by T McKeown, 1976 reproduced by permission of Edward Arnold (Publishers) Ltd; National Centre for Social Research for 2 questions from *British Social Attitudes: the 17th Report,* 2000 and the *British Social Attitudes Survey,* 1998, reproduced by permission; News International Syndication for an extract from "Sans home, sans school, sans everything" by Nicholas Pyke published in *The Times Educational Supplement* 10 August 1990 copyright © NI Syndication Ltd 1990; Office for National Statistics for the tables "Highest qualifications of school leavers" published in *Social Trends* 1972, 1986 by Census, Labour Force Survey and Office for National Statistics; "Percentage of pupils attaining five or more GCSE grades A* to C (England) 1990-2007" by Department for Education and Skills; "Attendance at selected events: by socio-economic group, 2000-1" published in *Social Trends* 2002 by Target Group Index and BMRB International; "Participation rates in higher education" Great Britain published in *Age Participation Index* 2003, by Department for Education and Skills; "Marketable wealth, United Kingdom, 2003" published in *Social Trends* 2007 by Office for National Statistics, General Register Office for Scotland and Northern Ireland Statistics and Research Agency; "The 10th Youth Cohort Study" and "Attainment of 5 or more GCSEs A* - C by ethnicity" England and Wales both from *Youth Cohort Study* 2004 by Department for Education and Skills; the graphs "Life expectancy at birth, UK 1901, 1951, 1991, 2003-05" published in *Social Trends and Annual Abstract of Statistics by* Office for National Statistics and Government Actuary's Department; "Live births, deaths and natural change 1901-2005, United Kingdom"; "Students in higher education 1970–2005" published in *Social Trends* by Census, Labour Force Survey and Office for National Statistics; "Attainment of two or more GCE A Levels or equivalent qualifications (United Kingdom) 1990-2005" published on National Statistics online; "Pupils achieving 5 or more GCSE grades A*-C, by ethnic group and FSM status, 2003 published in *Ethnicity and Education* by Department for Education and Skills; "Percentage of women who reported that they had pre-martially cohabited with their future husband for (a) all first marriages and (b) all second marriages by year of marriage, Great Britain" published in *Population Trends, 103* 2001 by General Household Survey and the tables "Divorce: decrees absolute" (England and Wales) and "Divorce rates" (England and Wales) from *Population Trends*; 'Lone-parent families', "Household income" and "Stepfamilies" all from *General Household Survey* 2005; "Households: by type of household and family" published in *Social Trends* 2002, 2007 by Census, Labour Force Survey and Office for National Statistics; "People in households: by type of household and family" published in *Social Trends* 2002, 2007 by Census, Labour Force Survey and Office for National Statistics; "Time spent on housework and childcare as main and secondary activities with rates of participation by sex, 2000 and 2005", and "Time spent on housework for full time workers by sex, 2005" both published in *The Time Use Survey* 2005, July 2006; "Attainment of 5 or more GCSE grades A*-C, by ethnicity and gender, England, 2006" published by *National Curriculum Assessments* by Department for Children, Schools and Families; "Marriages and divorces" published in *Social Trends* 37 2007 by Office for National Statistics, General Register Office for Scotland and Northern Ireland Statistics and Research Agency; "Live births" United Kingdom published in *Social Trends* 2007 by Office for National Statistics, Government Actuary's Department, General Register Office for Scotland and Northern Ireland Statistics and Research Agency; "Total Fertility Rate" United Kingdom published in *Social Trends* 2007 by Office for National Statistics, General Register Office for Scotland and Northern Ireland Statistics and Research Agency; and graphs and data from "Pupils achieving five or more GCSE grades A* to C" 2004 England and Wales and "Pupils achieving five or more GCSE grades A* to C" 1989 and 2000 England and Wales from *Youth Cohort Study 2004* by Department for Education and Skills and *Social Trends* by Census, Labour Force Survey and Office for National Statistics; data adapted from British Social Attitudes Survey (BSA) Series 1984 & 1994; details from "Average weekly pay" Great Briton, 2002 published in the *Labour Market New Earnings Survey 2002;* "Why the difference: A closer look at higher education minority ethnic students and graduates" by H Connor, C Tyers, T Modood and J Hillage, 2004 report by Department for Education and Skills; and details from the Social Class Scheme © Crown copyright 2007; Palgrave Macmillan for the figure 'Diversity and ambiguity among lone-parent households in modern Britain' by G Crow & M Hardy from *Families & Households: Divisions and Change* edited by Catherine Marsh & Sara Arber copyright © Palgrave Macmillan, reproduced with permission of Palgrave Macmillan; Sage Publications for the tables 'Designing Samples' by S. Arber and 'Questionnaires' by R. Newell published in *Researching Social Life* edited by N Gilbert, 1993 © copyright SAGE Publications, London, Los Angeles, New Delhi and Singapore 1993, reproduced by permission; The Scout Association for an extract about The Scout Association, 2007 reproduced with permission; Solo Syndication for extracts adapted from "Boy who was raised by monkeys" by Chris Brooke published in *The Daily Mail* 23 September 1999, "Girls of 12 put cosmetic surgery on their wish list" by Jenny Hope published in *The Daily Mail* 11 November 2000, "The Feral Gangs who rule our streets" by Michael Seamark published in *The Daily Mail* 18 May 2005, "Now schools are told to let Muslim girls wear head-to-toe 'birkinis' for swimming lessons" by Daniel Boffey published in *The Mail on Sunday* 24 June 2007 and "Must we kiss goodbye to the country gate?" by Andrew Levy published in *The Daily Mail* 30 November 2007 copyright © Daily Mail & The Mail on Sunday 1999, 2000, 2005, 2007; Jo Tatchell for an extract adapted from "Meet the Islamic Barbie" published in *The Guardian* on 30 September 2004 copyright © Jo Tatchell, reproduced with permission; and Trentham Books Limited for the table 'School processes -an ethnographic study' by C. Wright from *Education for Some: The Educational and Vocational Experiences of 15-18 Year-old Members of Minority Ethnic Groups* by John Eggleston et al, 1986 copyright © Trentham Books Limited.

In some instances we have been unable to trace the owners of copyright material and we would appreciate any information that would enable us to do so.

Author index

A

Abbott, D. 43
Abraham, J. 197, 201, 202, 204
Acheson, D. 53
Adler, P. 15
Alexander, C. 30
Alibhai-Brown, Y. 31
Allan, G. 88-90, 96, 98-100, 102, 105, 107, 110
Allen, I. 102
Althusser, L. 163
Anderson, M. 79, 85
Anning, A. 212
Appleyard, D. 91
Arber, S. 134
Archer, J. 39
Archer, L. 189
Ariès, P. 113-115
Atkinson, J.M. 125
Atkinson, R. 26, 27

B

Back, L. 32
Bales, R.F. 67
Ball, S.J. 177-180, 210
Ballantine, J. 193
Ballard, R. 32
Bandura, A. 129
Barker, E. 144, 159
Bartholomew, J. 58
Bauman, Z. 20
Baxter, J. 109
Beattie, J. 65
Beck, U. 20, 90, 102, 118, 183
Becker, H.S. 141, 199
Beck-Gernsheim, E. 20, 90, 102, 118,
Bedell, G. 100
Beishon, S. 101
Bennett, A. 31
Benston, M. 71
Bereiter, C. 175
Beresford, P. 97
Berger, P. 26
Bernades, J. 73, 97
Bernstein, B. 175, 176
Berthoud, R. 97, 101, 102
Bhachu, P. 101
Billig, M. 36, 37
Blackmore, S. 18
Bourdieu, P. 47, 59, 176
Bowie, F. 35
Bowles, S. 163-166, 194
Boyle, R. 57
Brazier, C. 63
Brown, G. 216
Brown, P. 168
Bruce, S. 137
Buckingham, D. 115
Bukatko, D. 114
Burgess, R. 193
Bush, T. 210
Butler, C. 16
Callender, C. 214
Cantle, T. 34
Cecil, R. 18
Chagnon, N. 143
Charles, N. 110
Charles, N. 107
Cheal, D. 65
Chester, R. 89

Chitty, C. 182, 210, 213
Chubb, J. 169
Clarke, J. 52
Cockburn, A. 52
Cockett, M. 90
Coffey, A. 182, 211
Cohen, P. 209
Cohen, S. 56
Collard, J. 110
Collins, R. 167
Connell, R.W. 41
Connolly, P. 197, 201
Connor, H. 188
Cooley, C. 19
Coontz, S. 90
Crace, J. 212
Crossman, R.H.S. 154
Crow, G. 88-90, 95, 96, 98-100, 102, 105, 110
Cumberbatch, G. 152
Curtice, J. 57

D

Daehler, M.W. 114
Davies, S. 197
Day, G. 58
Dean, H. 51
Delphy, C. 71
Dennis, N. 69, 81
Denscombe, M. 148
Devine, F. 53, 83, 105
Diamond, J. 19
Ditton, J. 127, 144
Donnellan, C. 156
Douglas, J.W.B. 174
Douglas, M. 76
Doward, J. 33
Dowds, L. 37
Dowling, S. B. 102
Drew, D. 189
Duncombe, J. 107, 108
Dunham, C. 63
Dunne, G. 110, 111
Durkheim, E. 125, 157, 158, 160, 161

E

Edgell, S. 108, 109
Edholm, F. 64
Elias, N. 5, 6
Engels, F. 70
Epstein, D. 182
Erdos, G. 69

F

Featherstone, M. 26, 58
Feinstein, L. 174
Ferri, E. 207
Festinger, L. 143, 144
Fielding, N. 127, 128, 140, 141, 145
Finch, J. 83
Finn, D. 209
Firth, R. 112
Fitzgerald, B.100
Fletcher, R. 84, 89
Fortes, M. 65
Foster, P. 192
Fox, K. 35
Francis, B. 182
Frankenberg, R. 78
French, J. 201
Furedi, F. 13

Gaine, C. 197
Gallie, D. 157
George, R. 197
Gewirtz, S. 211
Giddens, A. 20, 89-91, 102, 104
Gillborn, D. 171, 179, 182, 186, 189, 190, 192, 200, 202, 204
Gillespie, M.16
Gilroy, P. 29
Gintis, H. 163?166, 194
Gittins, D. 90, 93
Giulianotti, R. 37
Goffman, E. 19, 27, 28, 142
Goldberg, S. 40
Goldthorpe, J.H. 81, 83
Goulborne, H. 102
Graham, H. 98
Griffin, J.H. 142

H

Halfpenny, P. 124
Hall, E.T. 8
Hall, R. 87
Hall, S. 7, 34
Hallam, S. 178, 203
Halsey, A.H. 167, 169, 170, 206
Haralambos, M. 144
Hardy, M. 95
Hargreaves, D.H. 147, 178, 180
Harris, M. 138
Hart, N. 117
Haskey, J. 88, 95, 97, 99
Hatcher, R. 166
Hepworth, M. 26
Hetherington, E.M. 92
Hewitt, R. 31
Hey, V. 127
Hill, A. 97, 98
Hill, G. 38
Hobbs, D. 143, 147
Hobsbawm, E. 20
Hoebel, E.A. 7
Hoggart, R. 50
Homan, R. 126
Hopkins, N. 71
Hornsby-Smith, M. 145
Humphreys, L. 124, 126, 143, 145
Hursh, D. 212

I

Iannucci, A. 21
Inglis, D. 59
Ireson, J.178, 203

J

Jackson, C. 184, 185
Jackson, D. 184, 185
Jackson, J. 214
Jacobson, L. 198, 199
Jefferson, T. 23

K

Kalton, G. 132
Kassam, N. 33
Keddie, N. 202
Kellner, P. 134
Kerr, M. 81, 107
Kiernan, K. 92, 101
Kirton, A. 214
Kitzinger, J. 151, 152

Kluckhohn, C. 8
Kulick, D. 124
Kurz, D. 90

L
Labov, W. 142, 175, 176
Lacey, C. 178, 195
Langham, S. 193
LaPiere, R.T. 138
Laslett, P.K. 79, 85
Lauder, H. 169
Lawson, A. 133
Layder, D. 105, 138, 140, 145, 152
Leach, E.R. 93
Lee, B. 203
Lee, D. 209
Lee, N. 144, 155
Lees, S. 39, 42, 201
Leonard, D. 71
Leonard, M. 106
Lévi-Strauss, C. 75
Levy, A. 27
Lewis, J. 73
Lewis, O. 145
Liberty, M. 155
Liebow, E. 143
Lister, R. 73
Livi-Bacci, M. 117
Lloyd, B. 39
Lobban, G. 167
Long Lance, Chief Buffalo Child. 112

M
Mac an Ghaill, M. 43, 184, 166, 192, 196-98
Macbeath, J. 155
Macdonald, K. 152
Machin, S. 174
MacInnes, J. 5
Mahony, P. 184, 185
Mair, L. 63
Malinowski, B. 142
Mann, M. 34
Mansfield, P. 110
Mars, G. 143
Marsden, D. 107, 108
Marshall, G. 53
Mason, J. 83
May, T. 139, 158
McCrone, D. 34
McDonough, F. 49, 50
McGlone, F. 83, 84
McGrew, A. 34
McKenzie, J. 209
McKnight, A. 213
McMahon, A. 83, 107
McRae, S. 87, 88, 93
Mead, G. H. 19
Mead, M. 40
Miller, D. 151
Mirza, H. 198, 200
Mirza, H.S. 171, 182, 186
Modood, T. 32, 188
Moe, T. 169
Morgan, P. 72, 92
Mortimore, P. 155
Moser, C.A. 132
Mueller, G. 92, 101
Murdock, G.P. 61-63, 65-67
Murray, C. 52, 69
Neale, B. 95

Negrine, R. 152
Newark, P. 161
Newby, H. 132
Newell, R. 136
Nissel, M. 148
Noble, M. 210
Norris, P. 57

O
O'Brien, M. 95
O'Connell Davidson, J. 138, 140, 145, 152
O'Hara, M. 26
Oakley, A. 40, 80, 105, 110, 112, 133
Okely, J. 143

P
Page, R. 73
Pahl, J. 108
Pakulski, J. 52
Parker, H. 128, 156
Parker, S. 55
Parsons, T. 67, 77, 78, 85, 89, 161, 162, 194
Passeron, J. 176
Pawson, R. 150, 151
Pearson, G. 23, 151, 152
Pheonix, A. 15
Philo, G. 151
Pilkington, A. 192
Platt, J. 141
Pleck, J. 106
Plummer, G. 182
Polhemus, T. 24
Postman, N. 115
Pryor, J. 92
Punch, M. 147

R
Reay, D. 13, 177, 179, 180
Redfield, R. 145
Renold, E. 41
Rikowski, G. 166
Rist, R. 200
Ritzer, G. 17
Roberts, K. 47?49, 55
Robertson, R. 37
Rodgers, B. 92
Rojek, C. 47
Rosenthal, R. 198, 199
Royle, E. 205

S
Saunders, C. 52
Saunders, P. 51, 52, 72
Savage, M. 49, 53
Scanzoni, J. 65
Scase, R. 87
Scott, J. 47, 152
Sewell, T. 188, 197, 198, 200
Sharpe, S. 118, 182
Shaw, C. 155
Sissons, M. 130
Skelton, C. 14, 41, 182
Smart, C. 95
Smith, D. 189
Smith, J. 140
Smith, T. 210
Spade, J. 193
Spender, D. 201
Stacey, J. 103, 104
Stainton Rogers, W. 114, 115

Stands In Timber, J. 155
Stanworth, M. 167, 168, 201
Strathdee, R. 215
Sugarman, B. 174
Sukhnandan, L. 203
Surridge, P. 34

T
Taylor, L. 56
Taylor-Gooby, P. 51
Tebbit, N. 36
Thomas, W.I. 155
Thrupp, M. 212
Tipton, D. 152
Tizard, B. 15
Tomlinson, S. 189, 214
Tripp, J. 90
Turnbull, C. 143

V
Van Reenen, J. 216
Veblen, T. 59
Vogler, C. 108
Waddington, P.A.J. 17
Walford, G. 143
Walklate, S. 139
Walvin, J. 54
Warde, A. 55
Waters, M. 52
Weber, M. 151
Weeks, J. 100, 110
Western, M. 109
Westwood S. 101
Whyte, W.F. 143, 144, 146
Wilkinson, H. 44
Williams, B. 129
Williams, J.A. 140
Willis, P. 165, 166, 195, 196
Willmott, P. 50, 81?83, 85, 105, 132
Womack, S. 118
Wright, C. 190?192, 200?202

Y
Youdell, D.179, 200, 202, 204
Young, K. 37
Young, M. 50, 81?83, 85, 105, 132

Z
Znaniecki, F. 155

Subject index

A

ability 201-204
    teachers' perceptions of 198-200
ability groups 178-179, 189-190, 195-196, 198-200, 201-204
academies 214, 216
adoption 64
African Caribbeans
    educational attainment and 186-192
    family and 102
    identity and 29-30, 32
    pupil subcultures and 196-198
    teachers' perceptions of 200-201
age 23-27
    identity and 23-27
    old 25-26
    youth 23-24
ageing population 117
anticipatory socialisation 11, 16
anti-school subculture 165-166, 178, 184-185, 195-198
Asians (see South Asians)
audience research 151

B

Bangladeshis
    educational attainment and 186-192
behaviour schedule 145
birth rate 116, 117
Britishness 34-35

C

capitalism 70-71
case studies 155-156
childhood 112-115
    control view of 114
    end of 115
    history of 113-114
    images of 114
    in an age of uncertainty 114
    social construction of 112-113
    welfare view of 114
Chinese
    educational attainment and 186, 187, 189
city technology colleges 210
civil partnerships 85
class, social
    anti-school subculture and 165-166, 178, 184-185, 195-196
    classlessness 52-53
    divorce and 92
    educational attainment and 171-180, 184-185, 188, 195-196, 206, 207-208, 210
    family and 79, 81-83, 100-101
    identities 45-54, 184
    inequalities 53
    middle 49-50
    ruling class 9, 162-163
    subject class 9, 162-163
    teachers' views of pupils and 199-200
    upper 47-48
    underclass 51, 52
    working 50-51
classlessness 52-53
closed questions 135-136
coding

interviews and 141
    questionnaires and 135
cohabitation 87-88, 97
comparative method 157-158
comprehensive system 206-208, 211
confluent love 102
Conservative Party
    education policy 208-211
    family policy 73-74
consumer culture 58-60
consumer society 58
consumption 52, 58-60
    class and 53
    identity and 58-60
content analysis 150, 167
contraception 88
correlation 128
correspondence theory 163-164
counter-school culture 165 (see also anti-school subculture)
creative singlehood 86-87
crime statistics 149-150
crisis of masculinity 43
cross-cultural studies 158
culture 5, 6, 7-11
    class 47
    global 9, 37-38
    high 8-9
    low 8-9
    mass 9
    national 35-36, 37
    popular 9
cultural capital 176-177, 179
cultural deprivation theory 174

D

data
    primary 120, 128-147
    qualitative 120-121
    quantitative 120-121
    secondary 120, 147-154
death rate 116, 117
decision making
    in domestic division of labour 108-111
demographic trends (in UK) 116-119
disability 26-28
    impairment and 27
    rights 27
    spoiled identities and 27-28
divorce 86, 88-93
    consequences of 92-93
    explanations for 89-91
    extent of 88-89
    social distribution of 91-92
documents 150-154
    audience research and 151
    formal content analysis of 150
    historical 151-154
    textual analysis of 150-151
    thematic analysis of 150
domestic labour 71, 105-111

E

education
    academies and 214, 216
    anti-school subculture and 165-166, 178, 184-185, 195-198
    attainment (see educational attainment)

city technology colleges and 210
    comprehensive system and 206-208, 211
    correspondence theory and 163-164
    economy and 167-168
    equality of opportunity and 161, 162, 167, 206, 212-214, 216
    ethnicity and 171, 186-192, 197-198, 200-201
    feminist perspectives on 166-167
    functionalist theories of 160-162
    functions of 160-162
    gender and 166-167, 171, 181-185, 194-198, 201
    globalisation and 169, 216
    grant maintained schools and 210
    hidden curriculum and 193-195
    Marxist theories of 162-166
    National Curriculum and 210
    New Right perspectives on 168-170
    pupil subcultures and 194-198
    social class and 171-180, 184-185, 188, 195-196, 206, 207-208, 210
    social democratic perspectives on 167-168, 206
    socialisation and 14-15
    specialist schools and 210, 211-212, 213
    social policy and 205-216
    teacher-pupil relationships and 198-201
    tripartite system and 205-206
    vocational 208-209, 214-216
Education Action Zones (EAZs) 213-214
educational attainment
    class and 171-180, 184, 188
    class subcultures and 174
    cultural capital and 176, 179
    cultural deprivation theory and 174
    ethnicity and 171, 186-192
    gender and 171, 181-185
    labelling theory and 178-179, 198-199
    material deprivation and 173-174, 212-214
    racism and 189-192
    school effectiveness and 189
    setting and 178-179, 195, 201-204
    social capital and 177-179
    speech patterns and 175-176
    streaming and 178-179, 195, 201-202
    teachers' expectations and 198-199
Education Reform Act 210
    elaborated code 175, 176
    emotion labour/work 71, 107
Englishness 35
equality of opportunity
education and 161, 162, 167, 206, 212-214, 216
ethics
    experiments and 130
    participant observation and 145
    research and 125-128
ethnicity
    educational attainment and 171, 186-192
    family and 101-102
    identity and 28-33
    population in UK
ethnography 143, 192

experimental effect 151
experimenter bias 151
experiments 128-130
    field 130
    laboratory 128-129
extended family 63-64, 79, 81-82
    modified 83

F
family
    African Caribbean 102
    as a production unit 74-78
    as a unit of consumption 83
    Conservative policy and 73-74
    cottage industry and 74-76
    decision making within 108-111
    definitions of 61-66
    diversity 64-65, 84, 93-104
    divorce and 88-93
    domestic labour and 71, 105-111
    emotion labour/work and 71, 107-108
    ethnicity and 101-102
    extended 63-64, 79, 81-82, 83
    feminist theories of 71
    finances 108
    functionalist theories of 66-68, 77-78, 83-84
    functions of 66-68, 77-78, 83-84
    gay 100, 101, 110-111
    in kinship-based societies 74-75
    in late modern society 102
    in postmodern society 102-104
    industrialisation and 76-85
    isolated nuclear 77-78
    Labour policy and 73-74
    lesbian 100, 101, 104, 110-111
    lone-parent 95-98
    Marxist theories of 70-71
    modified extended 83
    multicultural 102
    New Right perspectives on 68-70, 72-73
    nuclear 62, 70, 77-78, 81-84, 93, 94-95
    of choice 100, 101
    pre-industrial 74-79, 81
    reconstituted 64, 99-100, 104
    size 117, 118
    social change and 74-85
    social class and 79, 81-84, 100-101
    social policy and 72-74
    socialisation and 11-14, 66-68
    South Asian 101-102
    symmetrical 81, 82
    urbanisation and 76-79
    working-class extended 79, 81-84
farming families 75, 78
feminist perspectives
    education and 166-167
    family and 71
feral children 5, 6
fertility 116, 117-118, 119
field experiments 130
formal content analysis 150
functionalism
    education and 160-162
    family and 66-68, 77-78, 83-84
    hidden curriculum and 194

G
gay families 100,101
    domestic division of labour and 110-111
gender
    domestic labour and 105-111
    education and 166-167
    educational attainment and 171, 181-185
    emotion work and 107-108
    family finances and 108
    identities 39-45
    leisure and 55
    sex and 39-40
    socialisation 40-43
    stereotypes 39
generalisation
    participant observation and 145
    sampling and 131
genes 4, 5
global culture 9
global identities 37-38
globalisation 90, 37-38
    education and 169, 216
glocalisation 37, 38
grammar schools 205-206
grant maintained schools 210
group interviews 139

H
Hawthorne effect 130
high culture 8-9
hidden curriculum 16, 193-195
    functionalist views of 194
    Marxist views of 194
historical documents 151-154
household 61, 79, 94-95
housewives 80
hypothesis 128, 130

I
identity 19-60
    African-Caribbean 29-30, 32
    age and 23-26
    Asian 30-31, 32
    British 34
    class 45-54
    constructing 18-19
    consumption and 59-60
    defining 18
    disability and 26-28
    ethnicity and 28-33
    gender 39-45
    global 37-38
    hybrid 32-33
    in late modern society 20-21
    in modern society 20
    in postmodern society 20
    leisure and 54-57
    national 35-37
    older 25-26
    politics 20-22
    personal 18
    social 18-19
    spoiled 27-28
    symbolic interactionism and 19
    virtual 57
    White 31
    youth and 22-24
ideology

education and 162-163
    of nuclear family 93-94
    ruling class 9, 162-163
impression management 25, 158
Indians
    educational attainment and 186-193
individualisation 20, 118, 183
industrialisation
    family and 76-85
infant mortality rate 116, 117
inner self 18
instinct 4
internet 57
interpretivism 124-125, 137, 145, 149
interview questionnaire 134, 139
interviewer bias 140
interviews 139-142, 176, 184
    active 141
    focus groups 139
    group 139
    interviewer bias and 140
    non-directive 141
    rapport and 141
    semi-structured 139, 184
    sensitive groups and 139-140
    social desirability and 140
    structured 139
    unstructured 139-141
isolated nuclear family 77-78

K
key informant 143

L
labelling theory 178, 199
laboratory experiments 128-129
Labour Party
    education policy 211-216
    family policy 73-74
late modernity
    family in 102
    identity in 20
leisure 54-56
    as a central life interest 55-56
    group differences in 55
    mass 54
    patterns of 55
lesbian families 100, 101, 104
    domestic division of labour and 110-111
life expectancy 116
life history 155
lone-parent families 95-98
    definition 95
    explanations for 96-97
    trends in 95-96
    types of 96
    views of 97-98
longitudinal studies 156-157, 171, 216
looking glass self 19
low culture 8-9

M
marriage 63, 64, 85-86
    cohabitation and 87-88
    domestic division of labour and 105-111
Marxist theory 10
    culture and 10
    education and 162-166

family and 70-71
hidden curriculum and 194
official statistics and 149
mass culture 9
mass media
in postmodern society 20
socialisation and 15-16
meanings 7
methodological pluralism 158-159, 165
middle class 49-50
culture 49
identity 49-50
values 49-50
mixed ability groups 201-202
modified extended family 83
multicultural family 102

N
nation states 34
National Curriculum 210
national cultures 35-36, 37
national identity 34-37
nationalism 36-37
neoliberal perspectives
on education 168-170, 209
New Deal
lone parents and 73
young people and 215-216
New Right perspectives
on education 168-170, 209
on family 68-70, 72-73
on lone-parent families 97-98
new vocationalism 208-209
non-decision making
in domestic division of labour 108-110
non-participant observation 145
norms 7
nuclear family 62, 70, 77-78, 81-84, 93, 94-95
ideology of 93
isolated 77-78

O
observation 142-147
covert 143, 145
non-participant 145
overt 143
participant 142-145, 146-147
official statistics 148-150
crime and 149-150
educational attainment and 171
interpretivist views 149
Marxist views 149
positivist views 149
validity and 148
older people 25-26
open questions 136
operationalising 135

P
Pakistanis
educational attainment and 186-189
participant observation 142-145, 146-147, 180
ethics and 145
ethnography and 143
generalisation and 145
replication and 145
peer group
socialisation and 15
personal identity 18
pilot study 136

polyandry 63
polygamy 63
polygyny 63
popular culture 9
population 116-119
positivism 124-125, 137, 145, 149
postal questionnaires 136, 171
postmodern society/postmodernity
family in 102-104
identity in 20
pre-industrial family 74-79, 81
primary relationships 65
primary socialisation 11-12, 66-67
primary sources 120, 128-147

Q
qualitative data 120-121
quantitative data 120-121
experiments and 128
questionnaires and 135
questionnaires 134-138, 171, 189
closed questions and 135-136
coding and 135
interview 134
open questions and 136
postal 136, 171
self-completion 134, 136
structured interview and 134
quota samples 132

R
racism
in schools 189-192
random samples 132
reconstituted families 64, 99-100
diversity within 99
extent of 99
tensions within 99-100
reliability 121
experiments and 128
religion
socialisation and 16
remarriage 85, 86
replication 128, 130, 145, 199
research methods
case studies 155-156
choosing 123-125
comparative method 157-158
cross-cultural studies 158
experiments 128-130
interviews 139-142, 176, 184
life history 155
longitudinal studies 156-157, 171, 216
methodological pluralism 158-159, 165
non-participant observation 145
observation 142-147
participant observation 142-145,
146-147, 180
questionnaires 134-138, 171, 189
social surveys 131-134, 148
triangulation 158-159
re-socialisation 11
restricted code 175-176
risk 118, 183
roles 8
role allocation 162, 164
role conflict 11
ruling class 9, 162
ideology 9, 162

S
samples 131-133, 134
quota 132
random 132
snowball 132-133
stratified 132, 134
systematic 132
volunteer 132-133, 134
sampling 131-133, 134, 178
frame 132
unit 131-132
school effectiveness 189
school meals 117, 119
secondary socialisation 11, 161
secondary sources 147-159
self 18-19
self-completion questionnaire 134, 136
self-fulfilling prophecy 178, 198-199
semi-structured interviews 139, 184
setting 178-179, 195, 201-203
singlehood 86-87
snowball samples 132-133
social capital 176, 177
social change 26-30
family and 74-85
social class (see class, social)
social democratic perspectives
on education 167-168, 206
social desirability
interviews and 140
social identity 18-19 (see also identity)
social policy
education and 205-216
family and 72-74
social reflexivity 20
social roles 8
social solidarity 160-161
social surveys 131-133
government 148
responding to surveys 133
socialisation 11-18
agents of 11-18
anticipatory 11, 16
education/schools and 14, 160-162
family/parents and 11-14, 66-68
formal 16-17
gender 40-43
informal 17
mass media and 15-16
peer group and 15
primary 11, 66, 67
religion and 16
re-socialisation 11, 16
secondary 11, 161
work and 17-18
South Asians
educational attainment and 186-192
family and 101-102
identity and 30-31, 32
teachers' perceptions of ability 200-201
specialised division of labour 161
specialist schools 210, 211-213
speech patterns 175-176
stabilisation of adult personalities 67-68
status symbols 59
step families (see reconstituted families)
stratified diffusion 82
stratified samples 132, 134
streaming 178-179, 195, 201-202
structured interview 134, 139

subcultures 8
    anti-school 165-166, 178, 184-185, 195-198
    pupil 195-198
    social class 174
subject class 9, 162
suicide 126, 157-158
symbolic interactionism
    identity and 19
symmetrical family 81, 82
systematic samples 132

T
textual analysis 150-151
thematic analysis 150
total fertility rate 116
triangulation 158-159
tripartite system 205-206

U
underclass 51
upper class 47-48

unstructured interviews 139-141
urbanisation
    family and 76-79

V
validity 121
    interviews and 140
    official statistics and 148
    participant observation and 144
value consensus 16
values 7
    middle class 49-50
    research and 122
    upper class 47-48
    underclass 51
    working 50-51
virtual communities 57
virtual identities 57
vocational education 208-209, 214-216
volunteer samples 132-133

W
welfare dependency
    education and 168-169
    family and 68, 69
Whites
    identity and 30-31
work
    leisure and 54
    socialisation and 17-18
working class
    identity 50-51
    'new' 50-51
    traditional 50

Y
youth 23-24